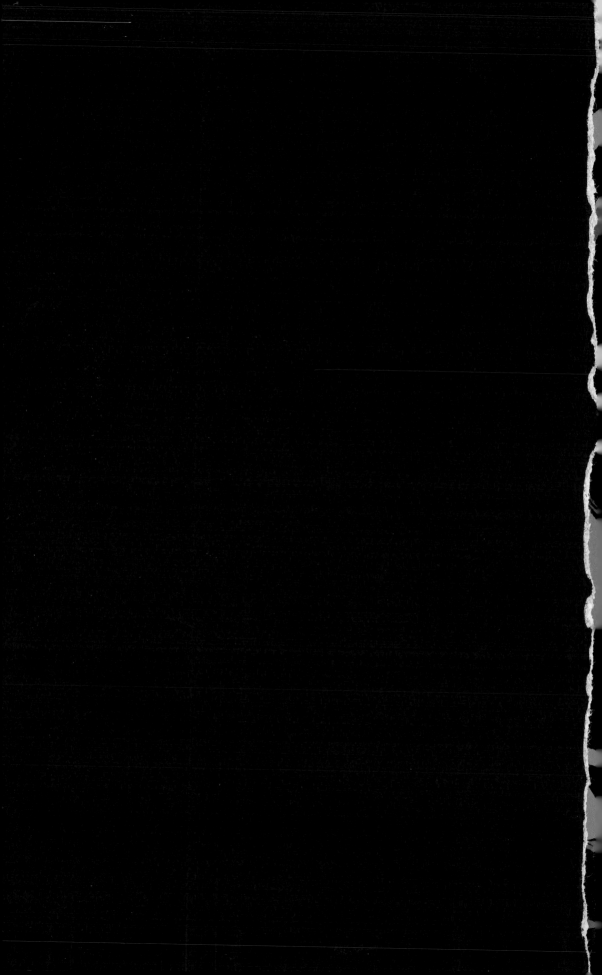

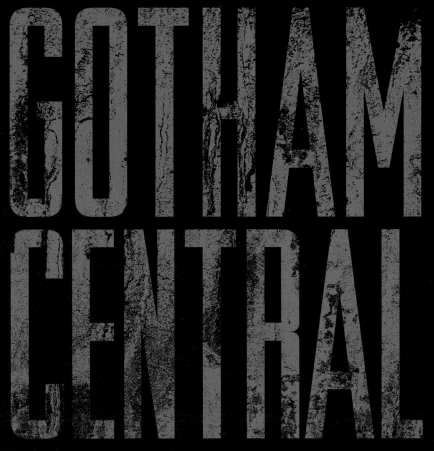

GOTHAM CENTRAL

BOOK FOUR: CORRIGAN

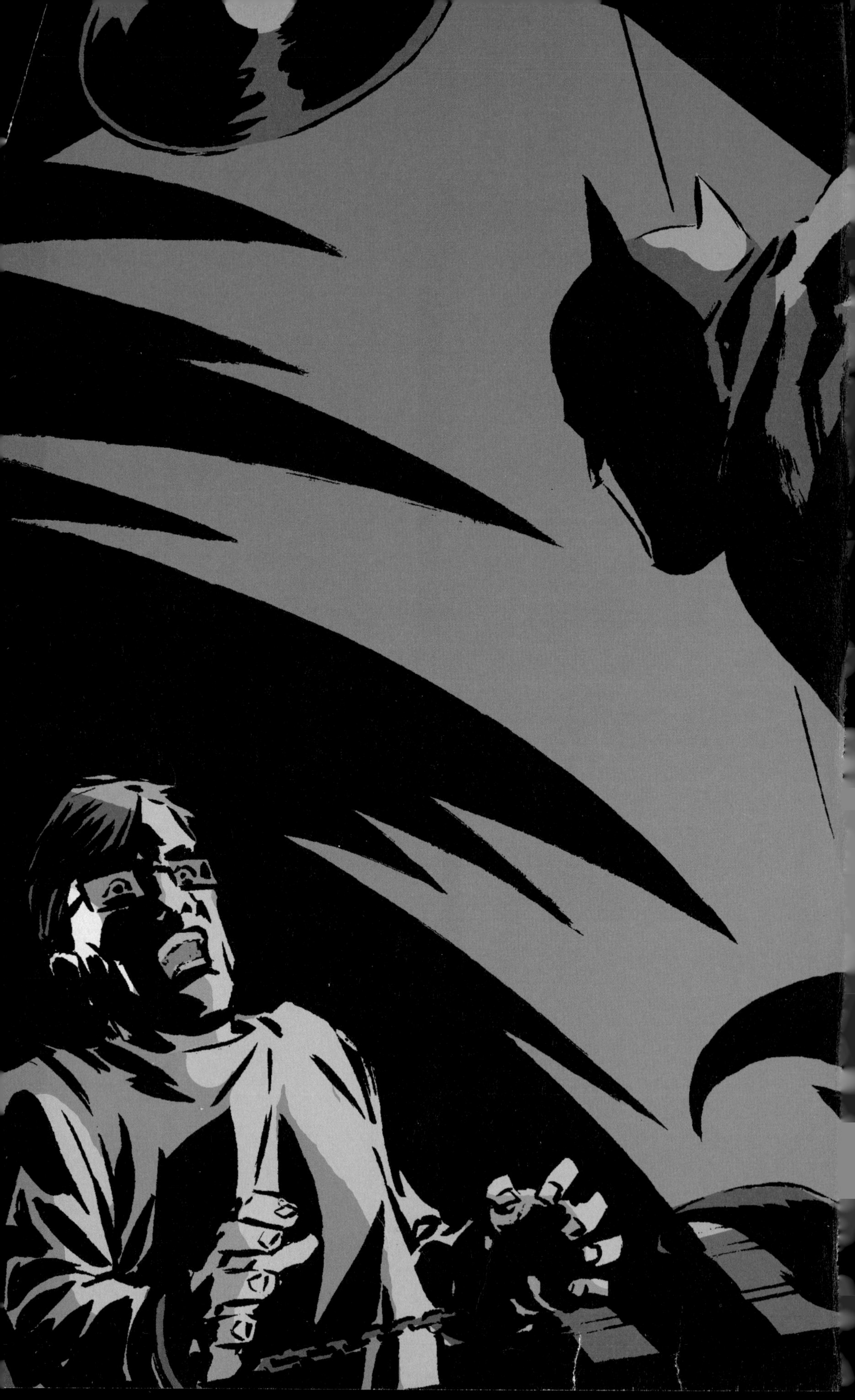

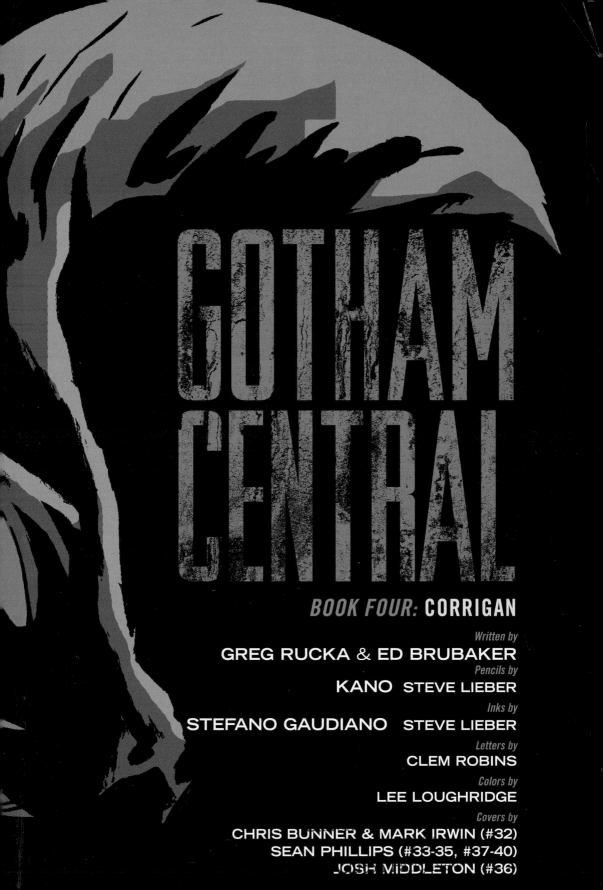

GOTHAM CENTRAL

BOOK FOUR: CORRIGAN

Written by
GREG RUCKA & ED BRUBAKER

Pencils by
KANO STEVE LIEBER

Inks by
STEFANO GAUDIANO STEVE LIEBER

Letters by
CLEM ROBINS

Colors by
LEE LOUGHRIDGE

Covers by
CHRIS BUNNER & MARK IRWIN (#32)
SEAN PHILLIPS (#33-35, #37-40)
JOSH MIDDLETON (#36)

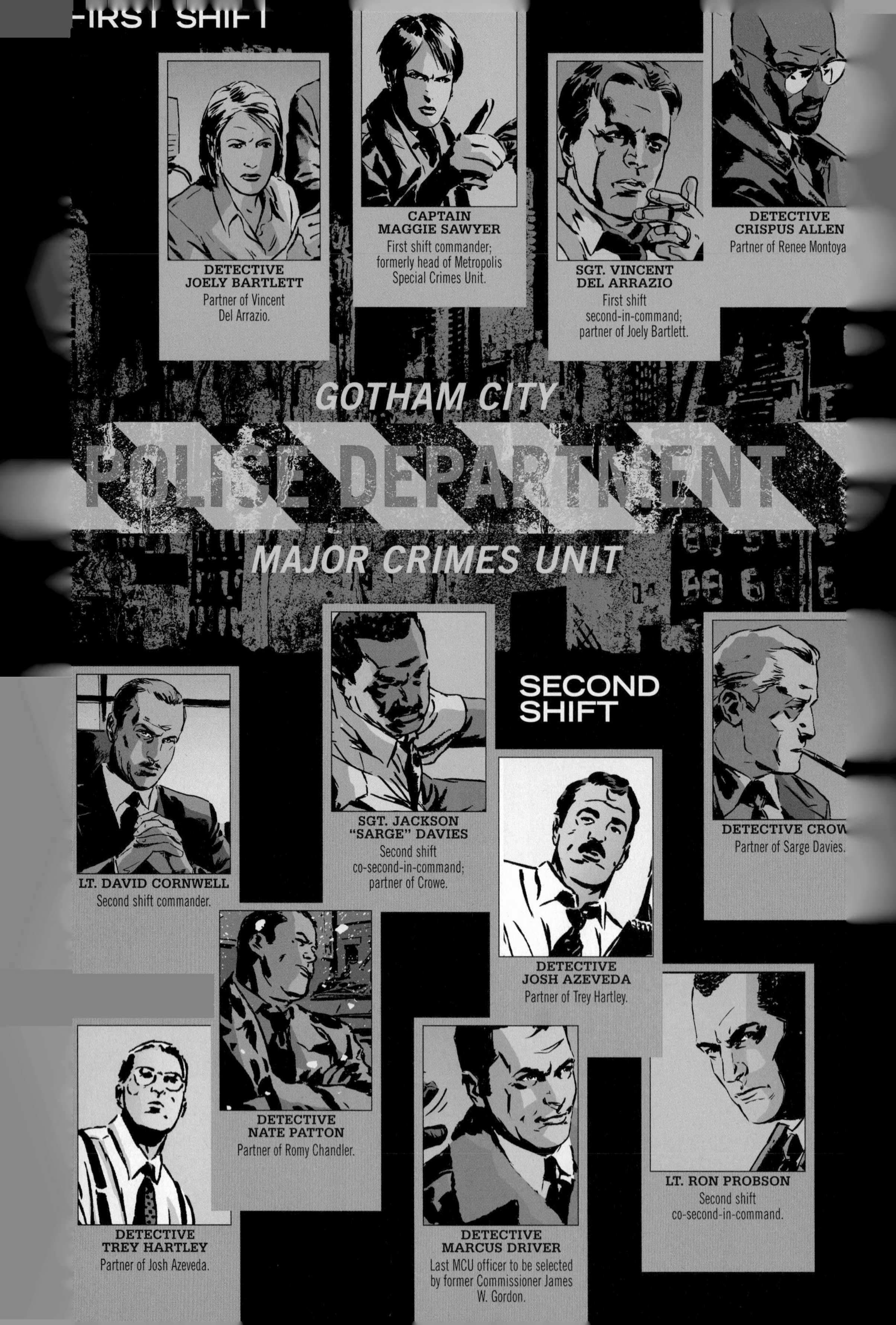
FIRST SHIFT
DETECTIVE JOELY BARTLETT
Partner of Vincent Del Arrazio.
CAPTAIN MAGGIE SAWYER
First shift commander; formerly head of Metropolis Special Crimes Unit.
SGT. VINCENT DEL ARRAZIO
First shift second-in-command; partner of Joely Bartlett.
DETECTIVE CRISPUS ALLEN
Partner of Renee Montoya
GOTHAM CITY
POLICE DEPARTMENT
MAJOR CRIMES UNIT
SECOND SHIFT
LT. DAVID CORNWELL
Second shift commander.
SGT. JACKSON "SARGE" DAVIES
Second shift co-second-in-command; partner of Crowe.
DETECTIVE CROW
Partner of Sarge Davies.
DETECTIVE JOSH AZEVEDA
Partner of Trey Hartley.
DETECTIVE NATE PATTON
Partner of Romy Chandler.
DETECTIVE TREY HARTLEY
Partner of Josh Azeveda.
DETECTIVE MARCUS DRIVER
Last MCU officer to be selected by former Commissioner James W. Gordon.
LT. RON PROBSON
Second shift co-second-in-command.

**DETECTIVE
ERIC COHEN**
Partner of Andi Kasinsky.

**DETECTIVE
ANDI KASINSKY**
Partner of Eric Cohen.

**DETECTIVE 2ND GRADE
RENEE MONTOYA**
Partner of Crispus Allen.

**DETECTIVE
TOMMY BURKE**
Partner of
Dagmar Procjnow.

**DETECTIVE
JOSEPHINE "JOSIE
MAC" MACDONALD**
Has the distinction of being
the first MCU officer selected after
Jim Gordon's retirement.

**DETECTIVE
DAGMAR
PROCJNOW**
Partner of Tommy Burke.

**DETECTIVE
ROMY CHANDLER**
Partner of Nate Patton.

POLICE SUPPORT

NORA FIELDS
City coroner.

STACY
Receptionist;
only person permitted to
operate the Bat-Signal.

**COMMISSIONER
MICHAEL AKINS**
Former commissioner
for Gateway City,
replaced James W. Gordon.

JIM CORRIGAN
GCPD crime scene
investigator.

JAMES W. GORDON
Former Gotham City police
commissioner, and 20-year
veteran of the force. Currently
teaches criminology at
Gotham University.

MATT IDELSON EDITOR-ORIGINAL SERIES
NACHIE CASTRO ASSISTANT EDITOR-ORIGINAL SERIES
BOB HARRAS GROUP EDITOR-COLLECTED EDITIONS
ANTON KAWASAKI EDITOR
ROBBIN BROSTERMAN DESIGN DIRECTOR-BOOKS

DC COMICS
DIANE NELSON PRESIDENT
DAN DIDIO AND JIM LEE CO-PUBLISHERS
GEOFF JOHNS CHIEF CREATIVE OFFICER
PATRICK CALDON EVP-FINANCE AND ADMINISTRATION
JOHN ROOD EVP-SALES, MARKETING AND BUSINESS DEVELOPMENT
AMY GENKINS SVP-BUSINESS AND LEGAL AFFAIRS
STEVE ROTTERDAM SVP-SALES AND MARKETING
JOHN CUNNINGHAM VP-MARKETING
TERRI CUNNINGHAM VP-MANAGING EDITOR
ALISON GILL VP-MANUFACTURING
DAVID HYDE VP-PUBLICITY
SUE POHJA VP-BOOK TRADE SALES
ALYSSE SOLL VP-ADVERTISING AND CUSTOM PUBLISHING
BOB WAYNE VP-SALES
MARK CHIARELLO ART DIRECTOR

Cover by Josh Middleton.

GOTHAM CENTRAL BOOK FOUR: CORRIGAN

Published by DC Comics. Cover and compilation Copyright © 2011 DC Comics. All Rights Reserved.

Originally published in single magazine form in GOTHAM CENTRAL #32-40. Copyright © 2006, 2007 DC Comics.
All Rights Reserved. All characters, their distinctive likenesses and related elements featured in this publication
are trademarks of DC Comics. The stories, characters and incidents featured in this publication are entirely fictional.
DC Comics does not read or accept unsolicited submissions of ideas, stories or artwork.

DC Comics, 1700 Broadway, New York, NY 10019
A Warner Bros. Entertainment Company
Printed by RR Donnelley, Salem, VA, USA. 2/4/11. First Printing.
HC ISBN: 978-1-4012-3003-6 SC ISBN: 978-1-4012-3194-1

SUSTAINABLE
FORESTRY
INITIATIVE

Certified Chain of Custody
Promoting Sustainable
Forest Management
www.sfiprogram.org

Fiber used in this product line meets the
sourcing requirements of the SFI program.
www.sfiprogram.org SGS-SFI/COC-US10/81072

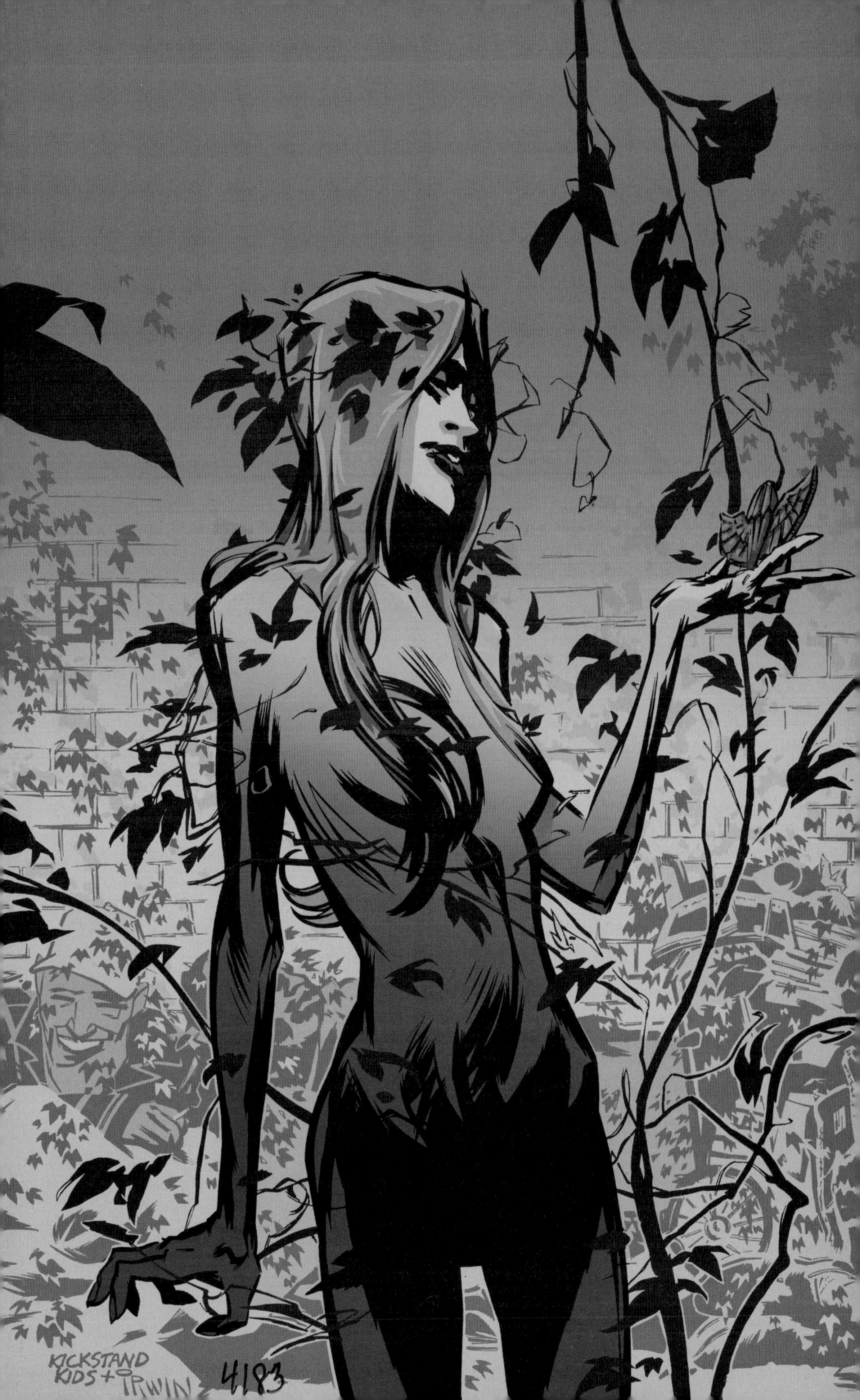
KICKSTAND KIDS + IRWIN
4183

NATURE

Written by
GREG RUCKA

Art by
STEVE LIEBER

Colors by
LEE LOUGHRIDGE

Letters by
CLEM ROBINS

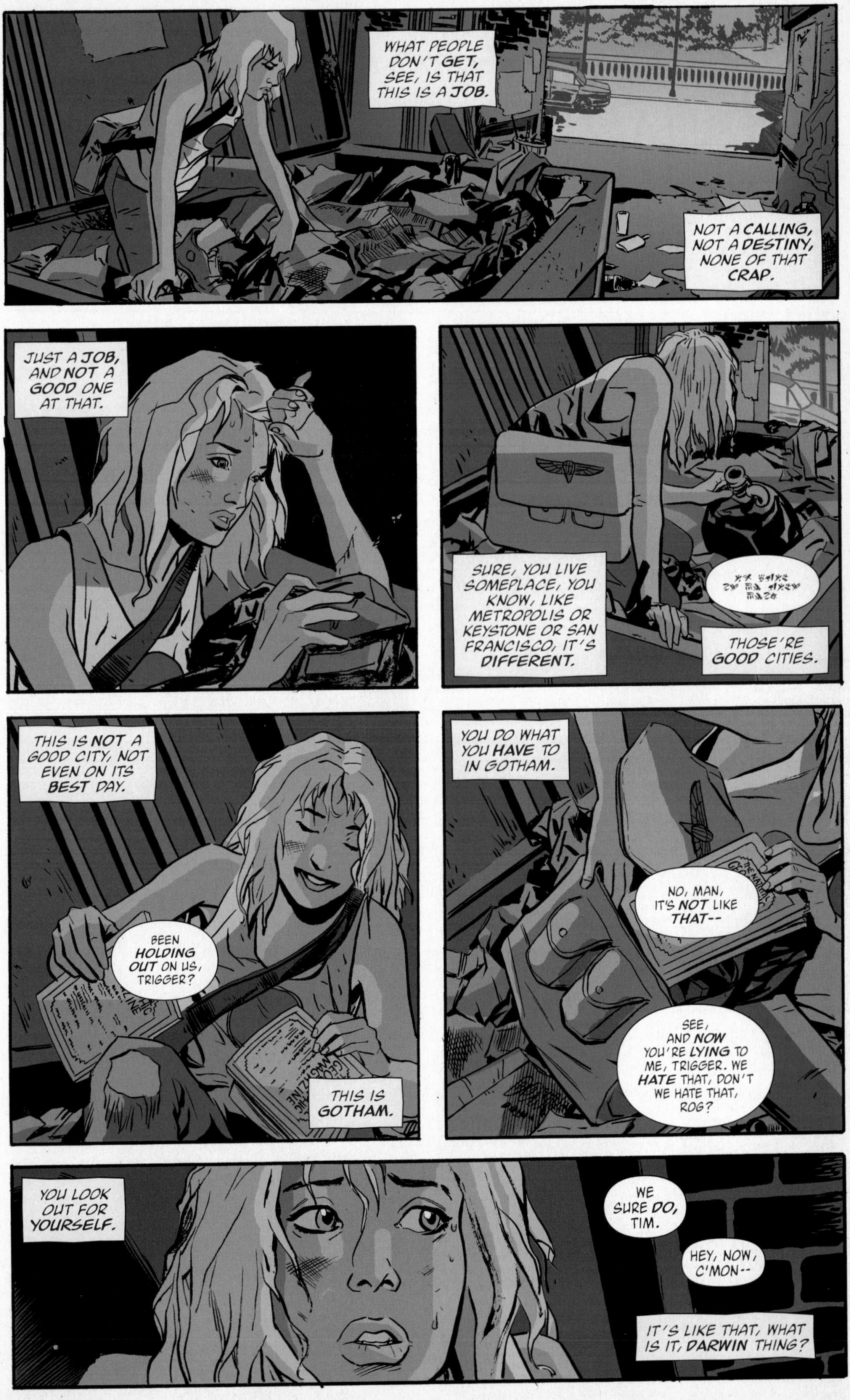
WHAT PEOPLE DON'T GET, SEE, IS THAT THIS IS A JOB.
NOT A CALLING, NOT A DESTINY, NONE OF THAT CRAP.
JUST A JOB, AND NOT A GOOD ONE AT THAT.
SURE, YOU LIVE SOMEPLACE, YOU KNOW, LIKE METROPOLIS OR KEYSTONE OR SAN FRANCISCO, IT'S DIFFERENT.
THOSE'RE GOOD CITIES.
THIS IS NOT A GOOD CITY, NOT EVEN ON ITS BEST DAY.
BEEN HOLDING OUT ON US, TRIGGER?
THIS IS GOTHAM.
YOU DO WHAT YOU HAVE TO IN GOTHAM.
NO, MAN, IT'S NOT LIKE THAT--
SEE, AND NOW YOU'RE LYING TO ME, TRIGGER. WE HATE THAT, DON'T WE HATE THAT, ROG?
YOU LOOK OUT FOR YOURSELF.
WE SURE DO, TIM.
HEY, NOW, C'MON--
IT'S LIKE THAT, WHAT IS IT, DARWIN THING?

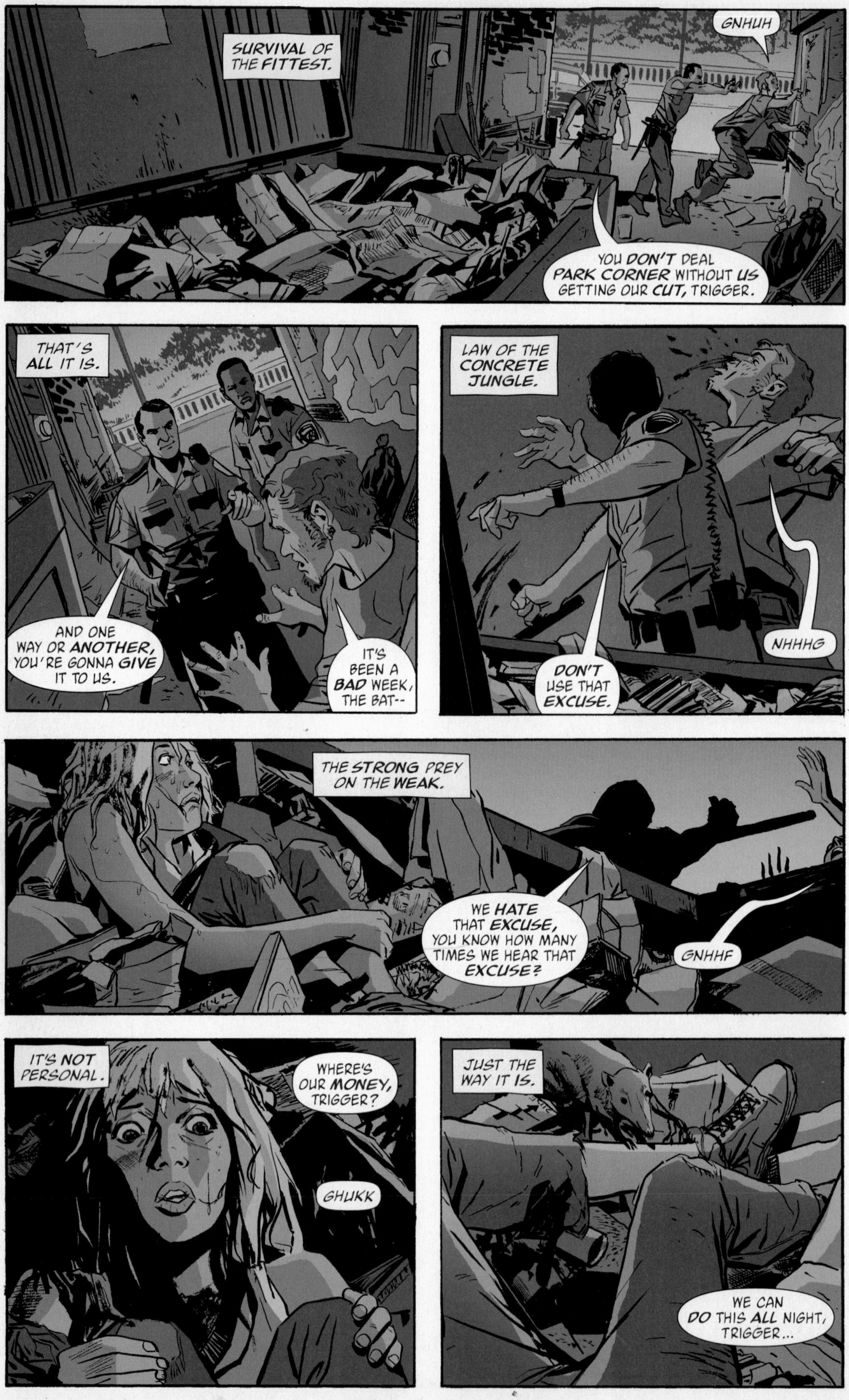
SURVIVAL OF THE FITTEST.
GNHUH
YOU DON'T DEAL PARK CORNER WITHOUT US GETTING OUR CUT, TRIGGER.
THAT'S ALL IT IS.
AND ONE WAY OR ANOTHER, YOU'RE GONNA GIVE IT TO US.
IT'S BEEN A BAD WEEK, THE BAT--
LAW OF THE CONCRETE JUNGLE.
DON'T USE THAT EXCUSE.
NHHHG
THE STRONG PREY ON THE WEAK.
WE HATE THAT EXCUSE, YOU KNOW HOW MANY TIMES WE HEAR THAT EXCUSE?
GNHHF
IT'S NOT PERSONAL.
WHERE'S OUR MONEY, TRIGGER?
GHUKK
JUST THE WAY IT IS.
WE CAN DO THIS ALL NIGHT, TRIGGER...

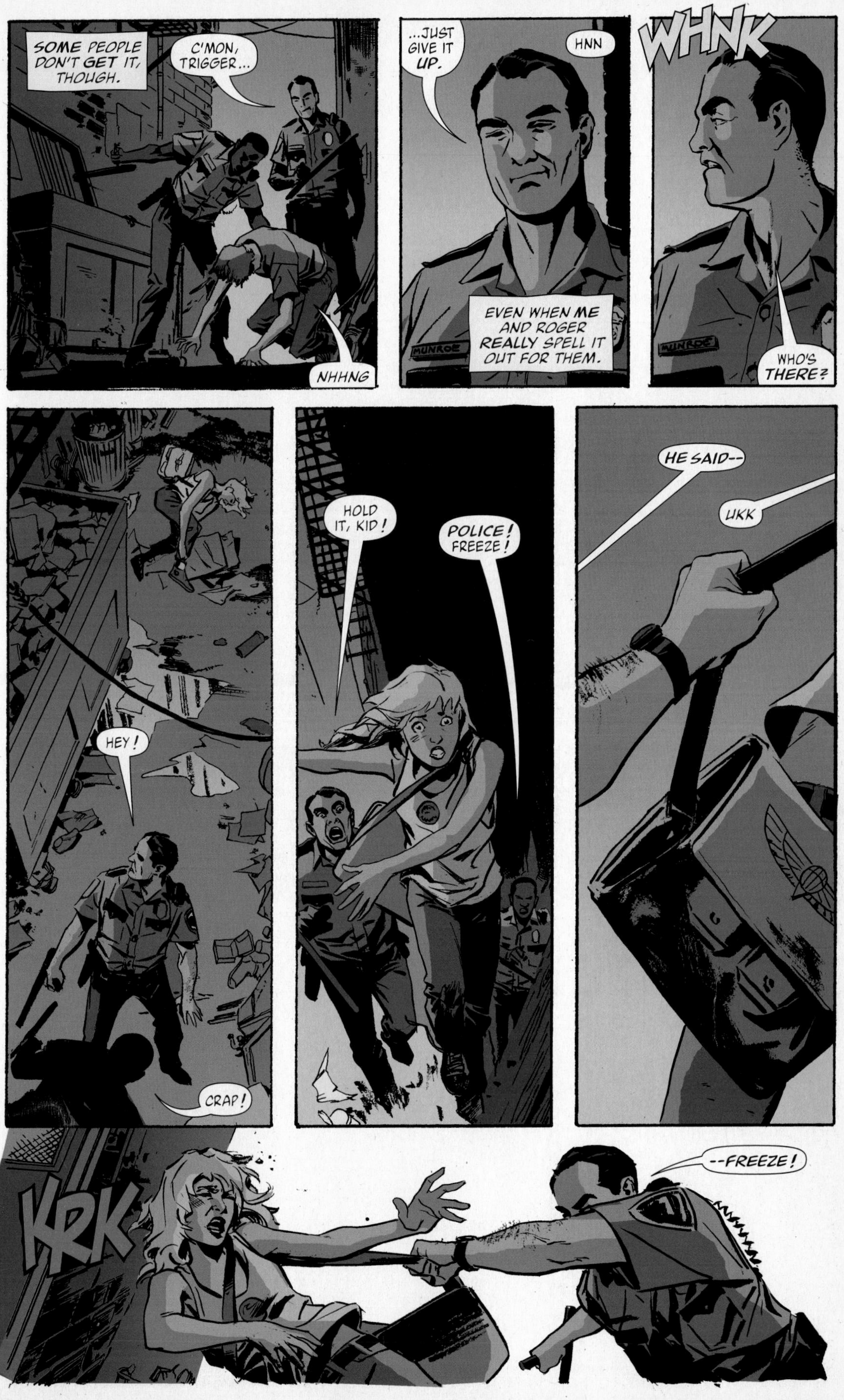
SOME PEOPLE DON'T GET IT, THOUGH.
C'MON, TRIGGER...
NHHNG
...JUST GIVE IT UP.
HNN
EVEN WHEN ME AND ROGER REALLY SPELL IT OUT FOR THEM.
MUNROE
WHNK
MUNROE
WHO'S THERE?
HEY!
CRAP!
HOLD IT, KID!
POLICE! FREEZE!
HE SAID--
UKK
KRK
--FREEZE!

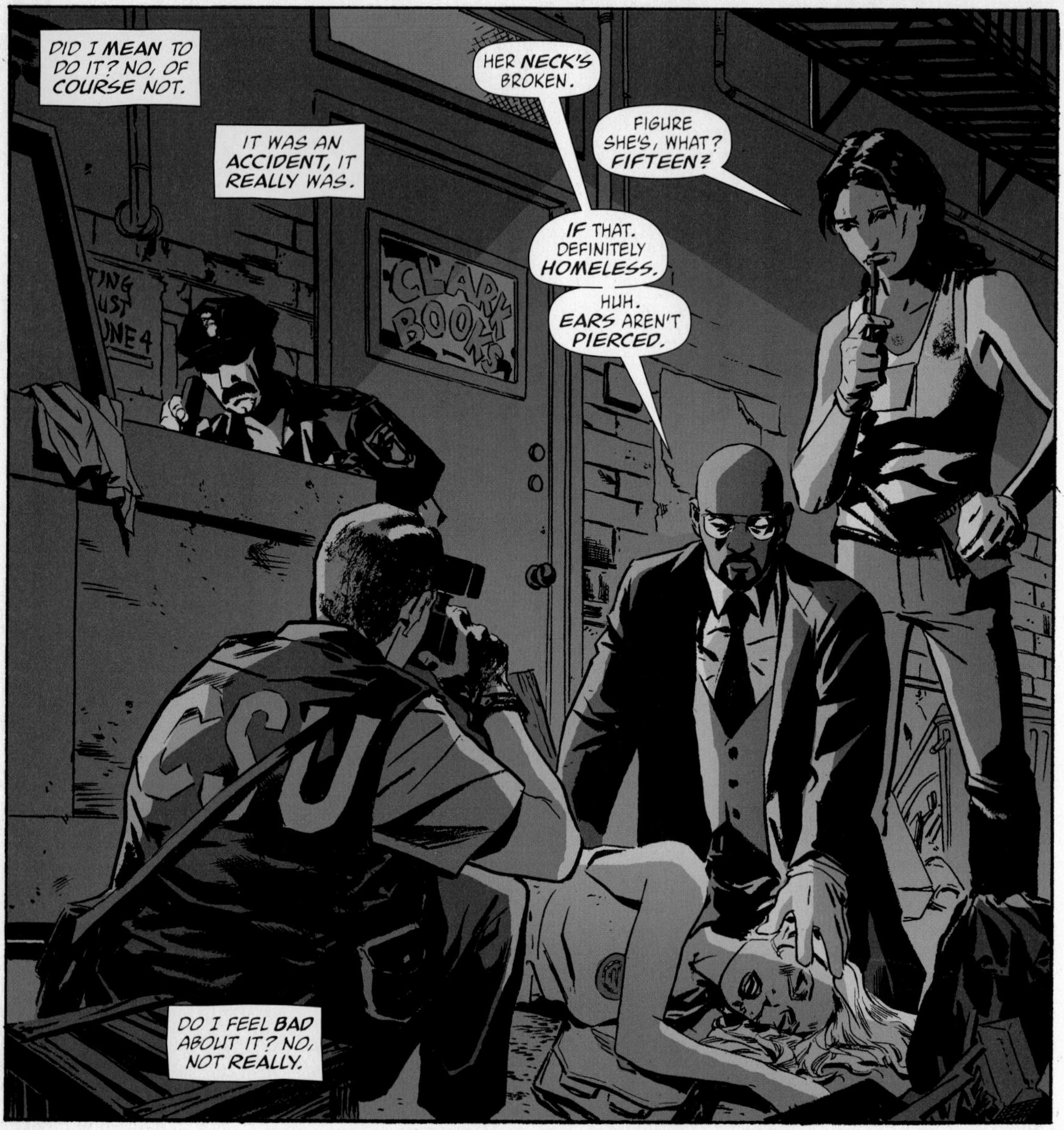
DID I MEAN TO DO IT? NO, OF COURSE NOT.
IT WAS AN ACCIDENT, IT REALLY WAS.
HER NECK'S BROKEN.
FIGURE SHE'S, WHAT? FIFTEEN?
IF THAT. DEFINITELY HOMELESS.
HUH. EARS AREN'T PIERCED.
CLARK BOOKS
CSU
DO I FEEL BAD ABOUT IT? NO, NOT REALLY.

NATURE

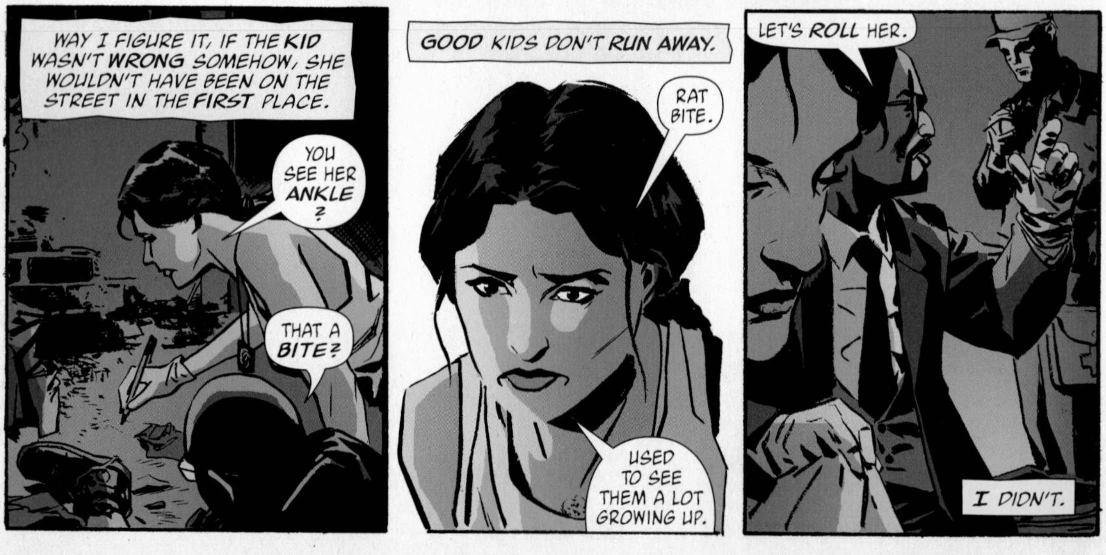
WAY I FIGURE IT, IF THE KID WASN'T WRONG SOMEHOW, SHE WOULDN'T HAVE BEEN ON THE STREET IN THE FIRST PLACE.
YOU SEE HER ANKLE?
THAT A BITE?
GOOD KIDS DON'T RUN AWAY.
RAT BITE.
USED TO SEE THEM A LOT GROWING UP.
LET'S ROLL HER.
I DIDN'T.

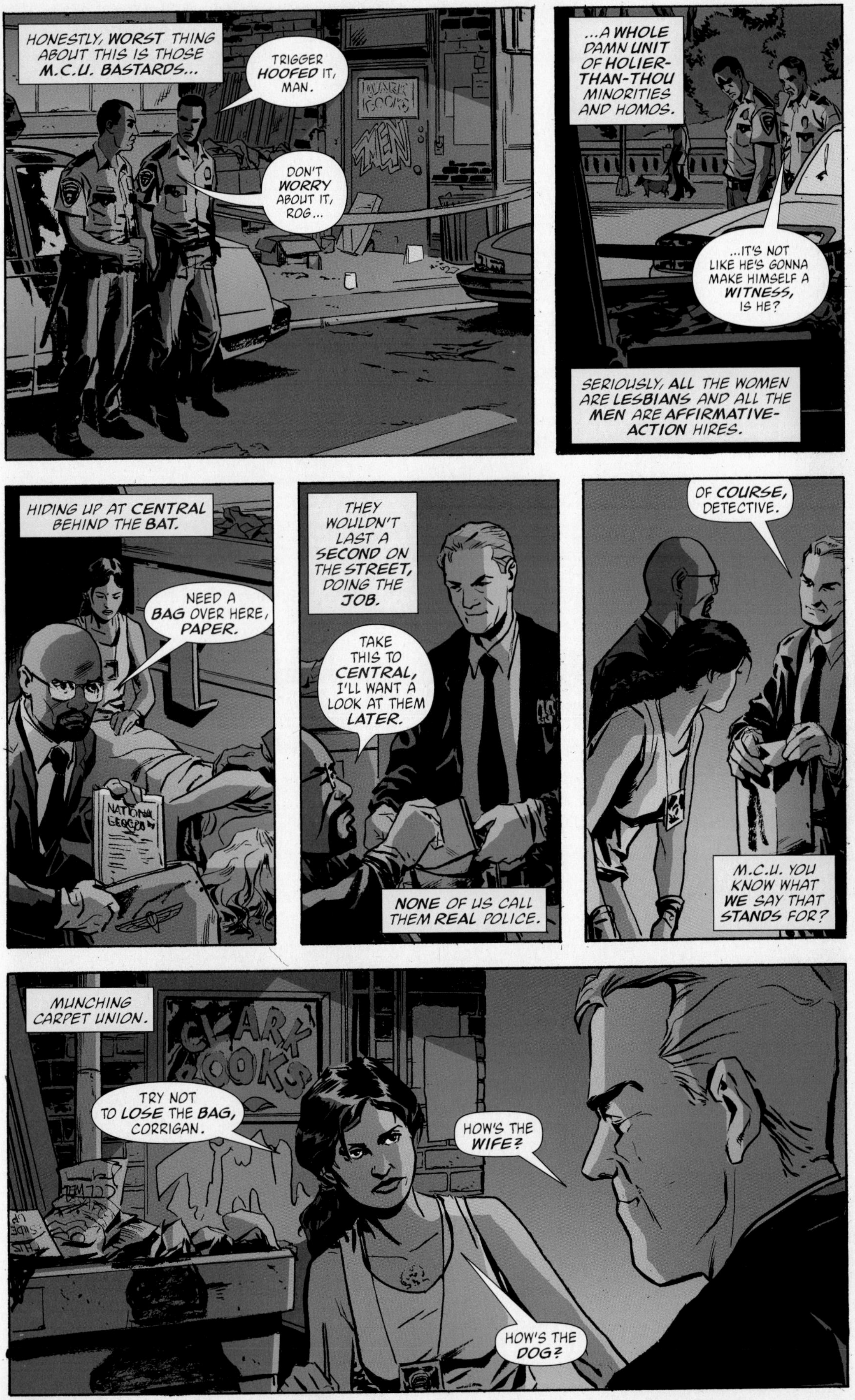
HONESTLY, WORST THING ABOUT THIS IS THOSE M.C.U. BASTARDS...
TRIGGER HOOFED IT, MAN.
DON'T WORRY ABOUT IT, ROG...
...A WHOLE DAMN UNIT OF HOLIER-THAN-THOU MINORITIES AND HOMOS.
...IT'S NOT LIKE HE'S GONNA MAKE HIMSELF A WITNESS, IS HE?
SERIOUSLY, ALL THE WOMEN ARE LESBIANS AND ALL THE MEN ARE AFFIRMATIVE-ACTION HIRES.
HIDING UP AT CENTRAL BEHIND THE BAT.
NEED A BAG OVER HERE, PAPER.
THEY WOULDN'T LAST A SECOND ON THE STREET, DOING THE JOB.
TAKE THIS TO CENTRAL, I'LL WANT A LOOK AT THEM LATER.
NONE OF US CALL THEM REAL POLICE.
OF COURSE, DETECTIVE.
M.C.U. YOU KNOW WHAT WE SAY THAT STANDS FOR?
MUNCHING CARPET UNION.
CLARK BOOKS
TRY NOT TO LOSE THE BAG, CORRIGAN.
HOW'S THE WIFE?
HOW'S THE DOG?

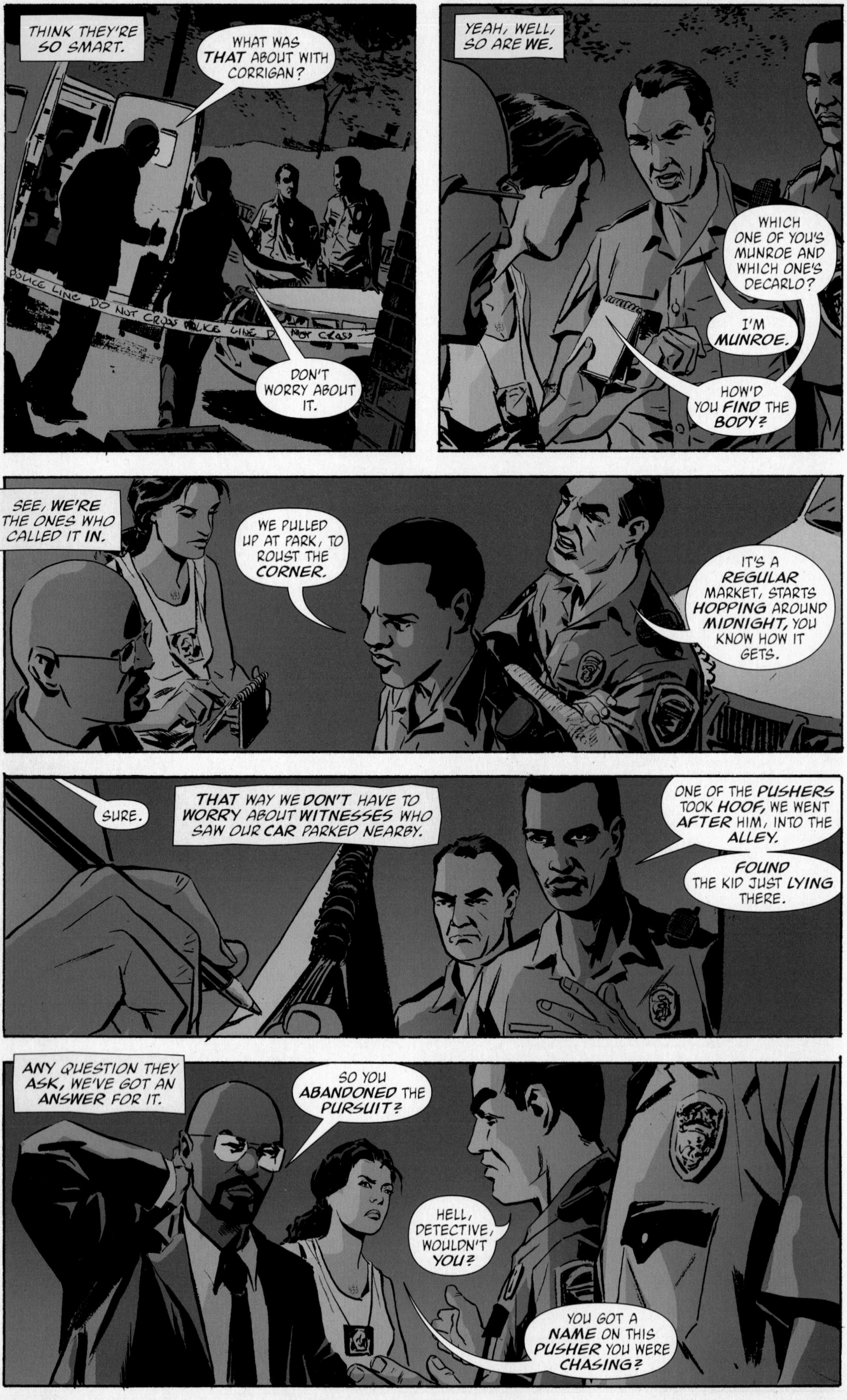
THINK THEY'RE SO SMART.
WHAT WAS THAT ABOUT WITH CORRIGAN?
POLICE LINE DO NOT CROSS POLICE LINE DO NOT CROSS
DON'T WORRY ABOUT IT.
YEAH, WELL, SO ARE WE.
WHICH ONE OF YOU'S MUNROE AND WHICH ONE'S DECARLO?
I'M MUNROE.
HOW'D YOU FIND THE BODY?
SEE, WE'RE THE ONES WHO CALLED IT IN.
WE PULLED UP AT PARK, TO ROUST THE CORNER.
IT'S A REGULAR MARKET, STARTS HOPPING AROUND MIDNIGHT, YOU KNOW HOW IT GETS.
SURE.
THAT WAY WE DON'T HAVE TO WORRY ABOUT WITNESSES WHO SAW OUR CAR PARKED NEARBY.
ONE OF THE PUSHERS TOOK HOOF, WE WENT AFTER HIM, INTO THE ALLEY.
FOUND THE KID JUST LYING THERE.
ANY QUESTION THEY ASK, WE'VE GOT AN ANSWER FOR IT.
SO YOU ABANDONED THE PURSUIT?
HELL, DETECTIVE, WOULDN'T YOU?
YOU GOT A NAME ON THIS PUSHER YOU WERE CHASING?

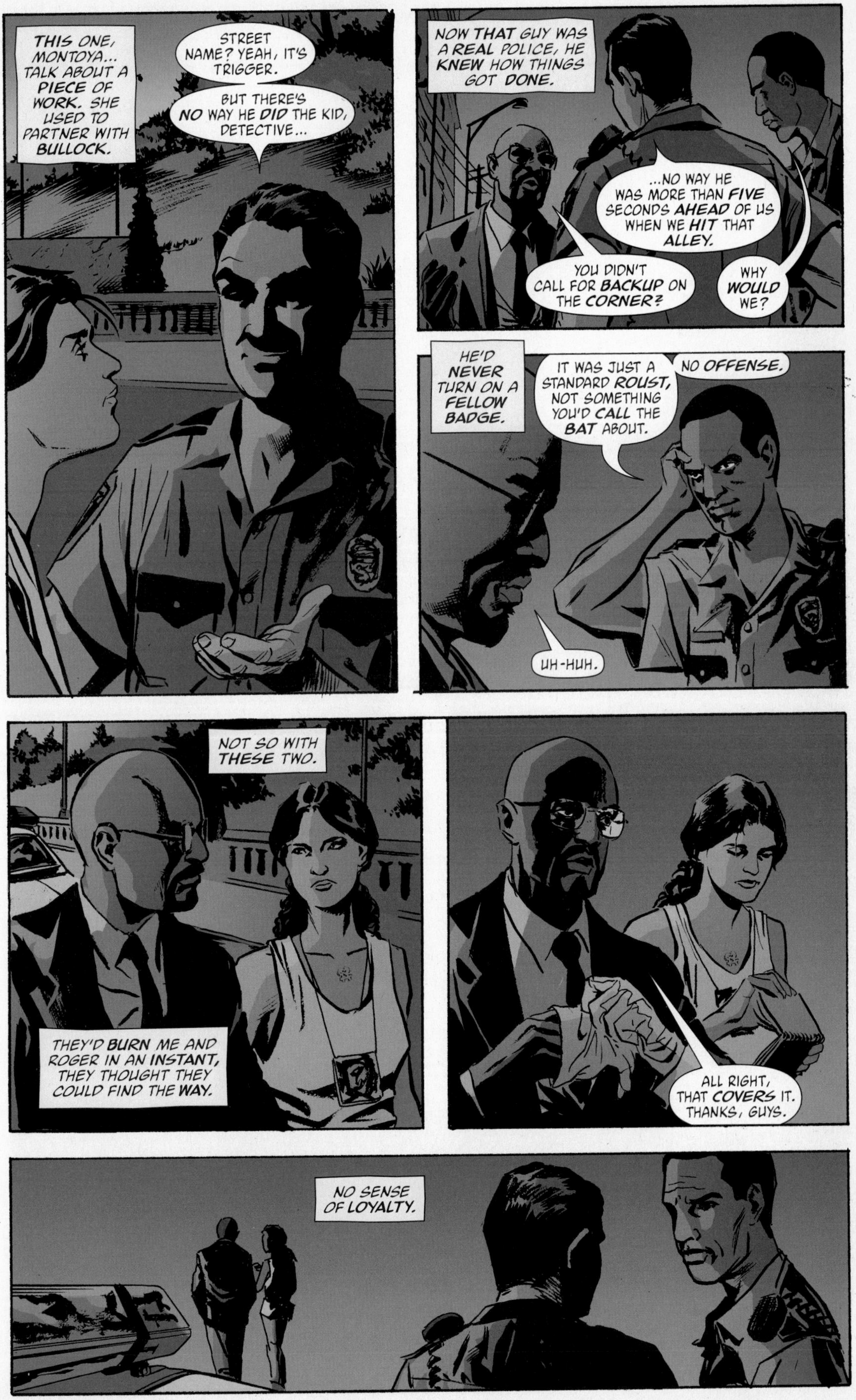
THIS ONE, MONTOYA... TALK ABOUT A PIECE OF WORK. SHE USED TO PARTNER WITH BULLOCK.
STREET NAME? YEAH, IT'S TRIGGER.
BUT THERE'S NO WAY HE DID THE KID, DETECTIVE...
NOW THAT GUY WAS A REAL POLICE, HE KNEW HOW THINGS GOT DONE.
...NO WAY HE WAS MORE THAN FIVE SECONDS AHEAD OF US WHEN WE HIT THAT ALLEY.
YOU DIDN'T CALL FOR BACKUP ON THE CORNER?
WHY WOULD WE?
HE'D NEVER TURN ON A FELLOW BADGE.
IT WAS JUST A STANDARD ROUST, NOT SOMETHING YOU'D CALL THE BAT ABOUT.
NO OFFENSE.
UH-HUH.
NOT SO WITH THESE TWO.
THEY'D BURN ME AND ROGER IN AN INSTANT, THEY THOUGHT THEY COULD FIND THE WAY.
ALL RIGHT, THAT COVERS IT. THANKS, GUYS.
NO SENSE OF LOYALTY.

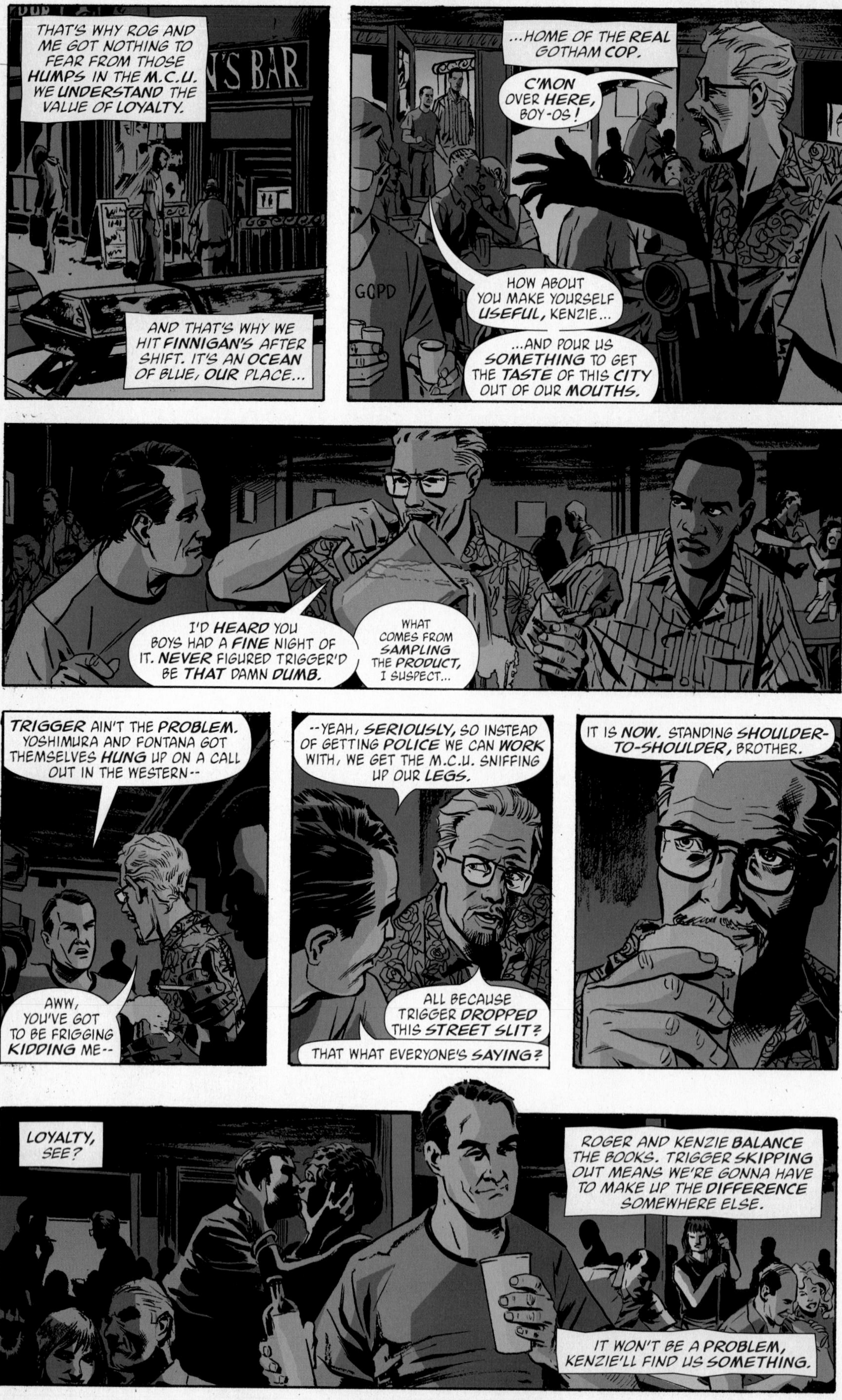
THAT'S WHY ROG AND ME GOT NOTHING TO FEAR FROM THOSE HUMPS IN THE M.C.U. WE UNDERSTAND THE VALUE OF LOYALTY.
N'S BAR
AND THAT'S WHY WE HIT FINNIGAN'S AFTER SHIFT. IT'S AN OCEAN OF BLUE, OUR PLACE...
...HOME OF THE REAL GOTHAM COP.
C'MON OVER HERE, BOY-OS!
GCPD
HOW ABOUT YOU MAKE YOURSELF USEFUL, KENZIE...
...AND POUR US SOMETHING TO GET THE TASTE OF THIS CITY OUT OF OUR MOUTHS.
I'D HEARD YOU BOYS HAD A FINE NIGHT OF IT. NEVER FIGURED TRIGGER'D BE THAT DAMN DUMB.
WHAT COMES FROM SAMPLING THE PRODUCT, I SUSPECT...
TRIGGER AIN'T THE PROBLEM. YOSHIMURA AND FONTANA GOT THEMSELVES HUNG UP ON A CALL OUT IN THE WESTERN--
AWW, YOU'VE GOT TO BE FRIGGING KIDDING ME--
--YEAH, SERIOUSLY, SO INSTEAD OF GETTING POLICE WE CAN WORK WITH, WE GET THE M.C.U. SNIFFING UP OUR LEGS.
ALL BECAUSE TRIGGER DROPPED THIS STREET SLIT?
THAT WHAT EVERYONE'S SAYING?
IT IS NOW. STANDING SHOULDER-TO-SHOULDER, BROTHER.
LOYALTY, SEE?
ROGER AND KENZIE BALANCE THE BOOKS. TRIGGER SKIPPING OUT MEANS WE'RE GONNA HAVE TO MAKE UP THE DIFFERENCE SOMEWHERE ELSE.
IT WON'T BE A PROBLEM, KENZIE'LL FIND US SOMETHING.

I GO LOOKING FOR **CORRIGAN.**

USED TO BE, HE WAS THE **LIFE** OF THE **PARTY.** SPEND **ALL** DAY SEARCHING **PUDDLES** OF **BLOOD,** GUY NEEDS TO **UNWIND,** RIGHT?

BUT A COUPLE MONTHS BACK, **MONTOYA** BEAT HIM **DOWN** IN THE **ALLEY** OUT BACK.

NOW HE JUST **SITS** AND **DRINKS,** PLOTTING HIS **REVENGE** OR SOMETHING **ELSE,** I DON'T KNOW.

I DON'T MUCH **CARE,** HONESTLY.

I'M **NOT** WORRIED THAT **ALLEN** AND **MONTOYA** ARE GONNA GET **ANYONE** IN **UNIFORM** TO **RAT** US OUT.

BUT THERE ARE **OTHER** WAYS FOR THEM TO MAKE A **CASE.** PHYSICAL **EVIDENCE,** FOR ONE.

GOING TO **CORRIGAN** IS LIKE TAKING OUT **INSURANCE.**

WONDERED WHEN YOU'D BE **BY.**

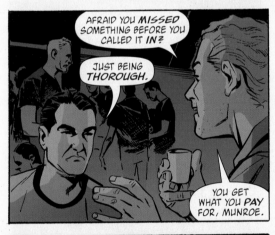

AFRAID YOU **MISSED** SOMETHING BEFORE YOU CALLED IT **IN?**

JUST BEING **THOROUGH.**

YOU GET WHAT YOU **PAY** FOR, MUNROE.

TWO LARGE.

FIVE.

THREE.

AND **NOTHING** COMES BACK ON US.

HEY, IT WAS JUST SOME **STREET BRAT.** WHO'S GONNA COME **LOOKING?**

THAT'S WHAT I'M **PAYING** YOU FOR, JIMMY.

YOU CAN **KEEP** THE **BOTTLE.**

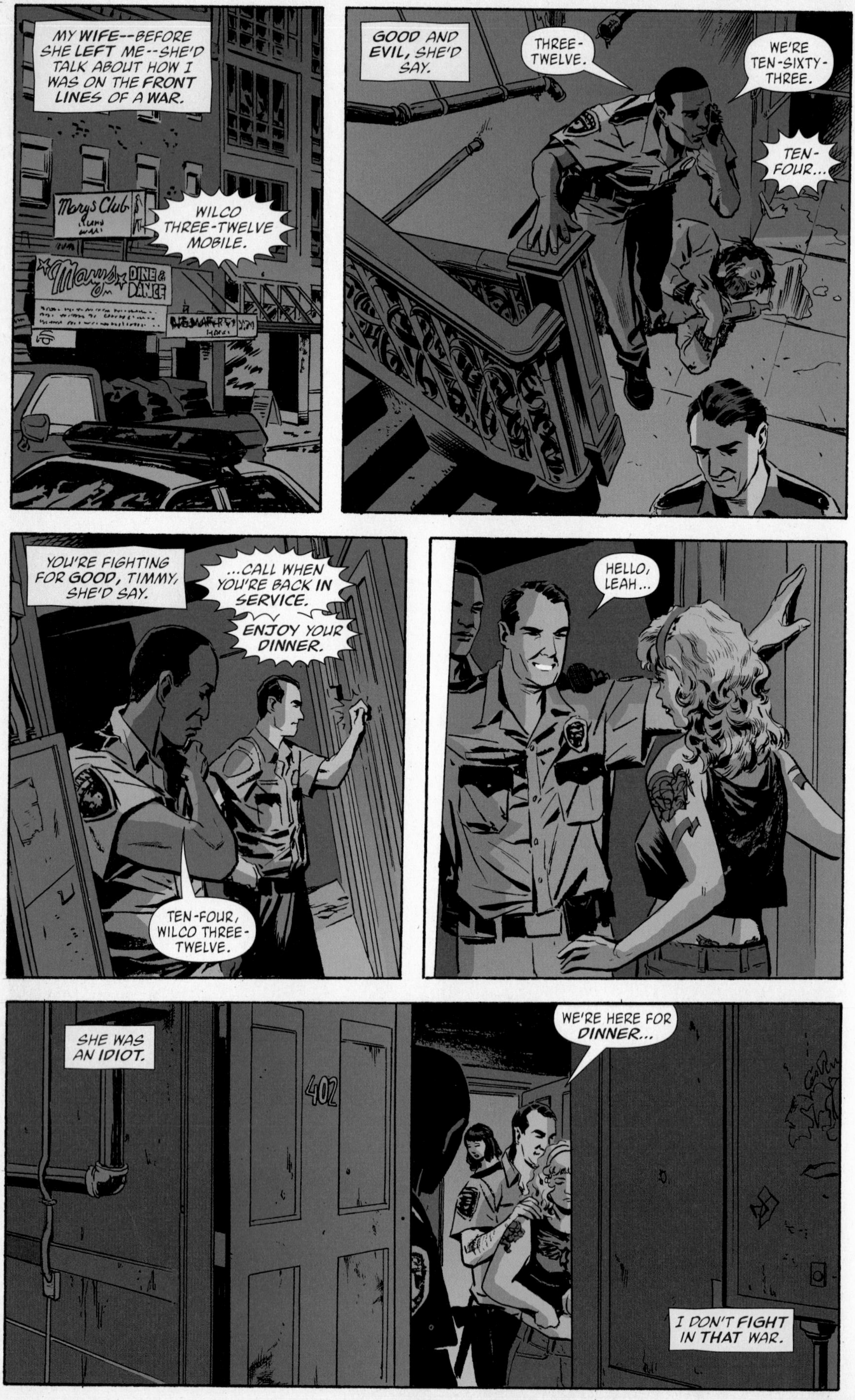
MY WIFE--BEFORE SHE LEFT ME--SHE'D TALK ABOUT HOW I WAS ON THE FRONT LINES OF A WAR.
Mary's Club
Mary's DINE & DANCE
WILCO THREE-TWELVE MOBILE.
GOOD AND EVIL, SHE'D SAY.
THREE-TWELVE.
WE'RE TEN-SIXTY-THREE.
TEN-FOUR...
YOU'RE FIGHTING FOR GOOD, TIMMY, SHE'D SAY.
...CALL WHEN YOU'RE BACK IN SERVICE.
ENJOY YOUR DINNER.
TEN-FOUR, WILCO THREE-TWELVE.
HELLO, LEAH...
SHE WAS AN IDIOT.
402
WE'RE HERE FOR DINNER...
I DON'T FIGHT IN THAT WAR.

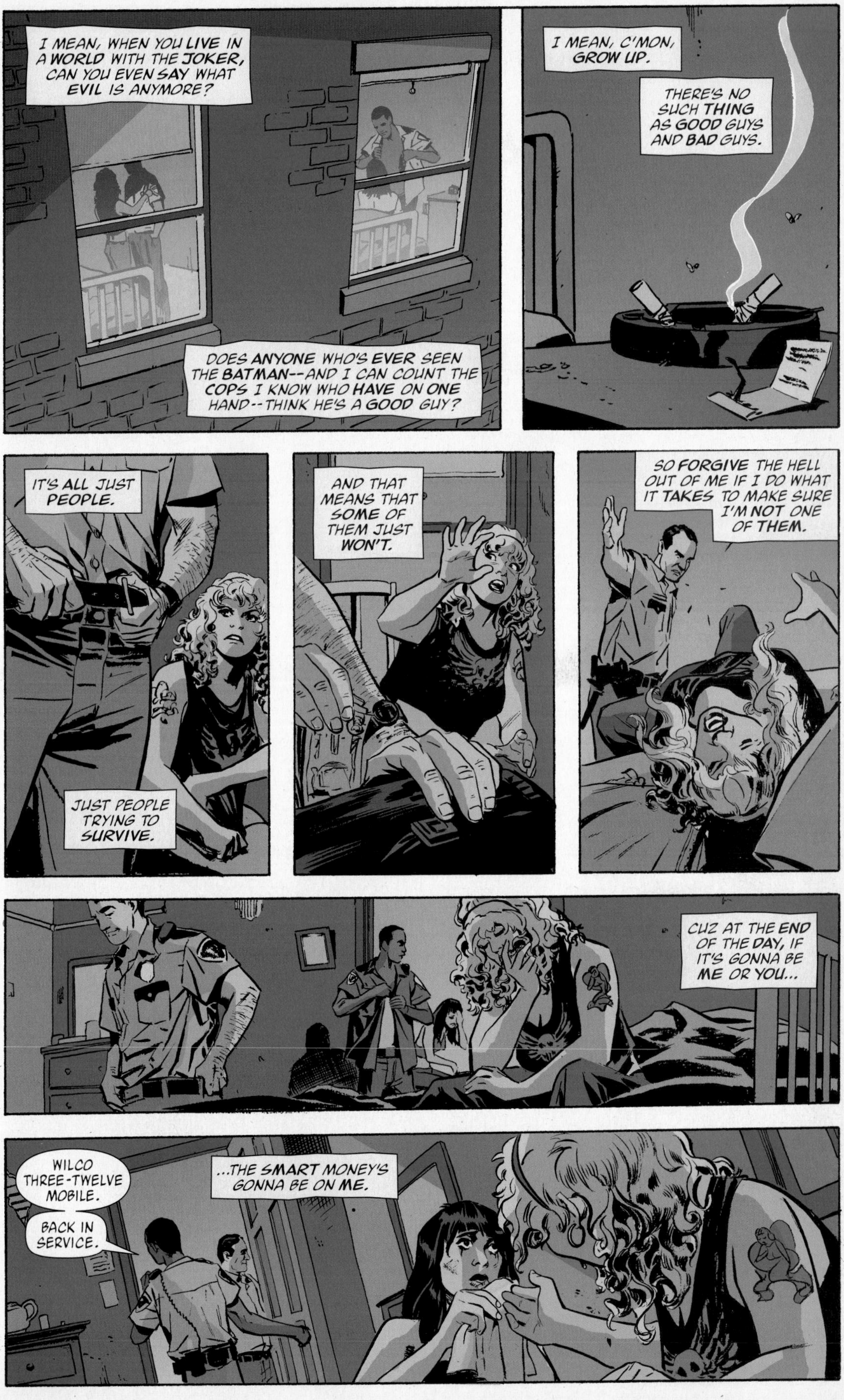
I MEAN, WHEN YOU LIVE IN A WORLD WITH THE JOKER, CAN YOU EVEN SAY WHAT EVIL IS ANYMORE?
DOES ANYONE WHO'S EVER SEEN THE BATMAN--AND I CAN COUNT THE COPS I KNOW WHO HAVE ON ONE HAND--THINK HE'S A GOOD GUY?
I MEAN, C'MON, GROW UP.
THERE'S NO SUCH THING AS GOOD GUYS AND BAD GUYS.
IT'S ALL JUST PEOPLE.
JUST PEOPLE TRYING TO SURVIVE.
AND THAT MEANS THAT SOME OF THEM JUST WON'T.
SO FORGIVE THE HELL OUT OF ME IF I DO WHAT IT TAKES TO MAKE SURE I'M NOT ONE OF THEM.
CUZ AT THE END OF THE DAY, IF IT'S GONNA BE ME OR YOU...
WILCO THREE-TWELVE MOBILE.
BACK IN SERVICE.
...THE SMART MONEY'S GONNA BE ON ME.

SON OF A BITCH.

IF CORRIGAN SCREWED US, I'LL KILL HIM.

WHAT THE HELL?

KEEP IT COOL.

...SAID YOU'D KNOW WHERE TO FIND THIS GUY?

I CAN KEEP AN EYE OPEN, THAT'S THE BEST I CAN PROMISE, DETECTIVE.

OFFICERS.

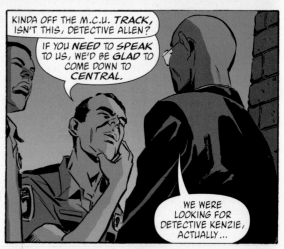

KINDA OFF THE M.C.U. TRACK, ISN'T THIS, DETECTIVE ALLEN?

IF YOU NEED TO SPEAK TO US, WE'D BE GLAD TO COME DOWN TO CENTRAL.

WE WERE LOOKING FOR DETECTIVE KENZIE, ACTUALLY...

...HOPING HE MIGHT HAVE A LINE ON YOUR MAN, TRIGGER.

HAVEN'T SEEN HIM AROUND, HAVE YOU?

CAN'T SAY WE HAVE.

WELL, LET US KNOW IF YOU DO.

STAY SAFE.

YEAH... YOU, TOO.

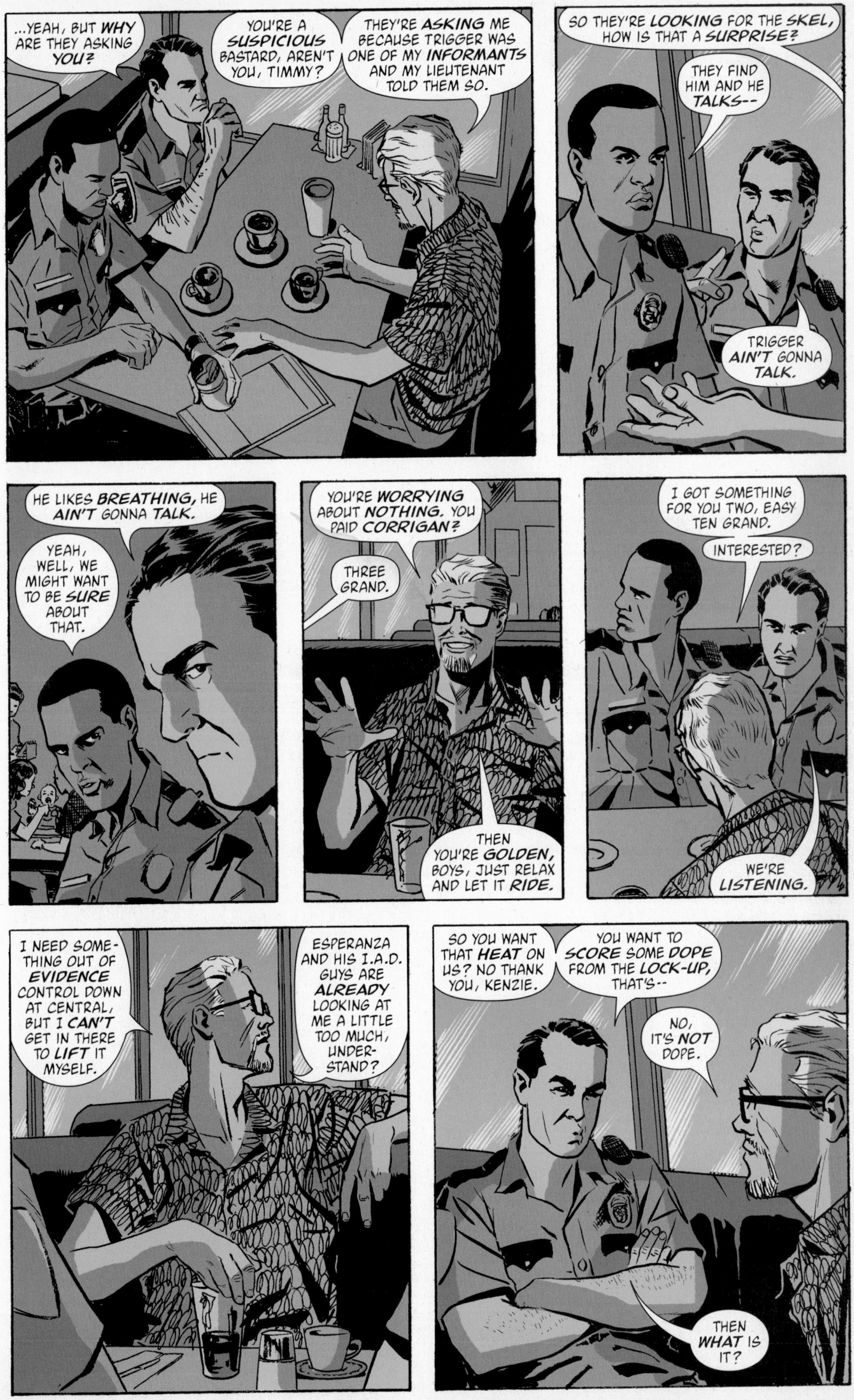
...YEAH, BUT WHY ARE THEY ASKING YOU?
YOU'RE A SUSPICIOUS BASTARD, AREN'T YOU, TIMMY?
THEY'RE ASKING ME BECAUSE TRIGGER WAS ONE OF MY INFORMANTS AND MY LIEUTENANT TOLD THEM SO.
SO THEY'RE LOOKING FOR THE SKEL, HOW IS THAT A SURPRISE?
THEY FIND HIM AND HE TALKS--
TRIGGER AIN'T GONNA TALK.
HE LIKES BREATHING, HE AIN'T GONNA TALK.
YEAH, WELL, WE MIGHT WANT TO BE SURE ABOUT THAT.
YOU'RE WORRYING ABOUT NOTHING. YOU PAID CORRIGAN?
THREE GRAND.
THEN YOU'RE GOLDEN, BOYS, JUST RELAX AND LET IT RIDE.
I GOT SOMETHING FOR YOU TWO, EASY TEN GRAND.
INTERESTED?
WE'RE LISTENING.
I NEED SOME-THING OUT OF EVIDENCE CONTROL DOWN AT CENTRAL, BUT I CAN'T GET IN THERE TO LIFT IT MYSELF.
ESPERANZA AND HIS I.A.D. GUYS ARE ALREADY LOOKING AT ME A LITTLE TOO MUCH, UNDER-STAND?
SO YOU WANT THAT HEAT ON US? NO THANK YOU, KENZIE.
YOU WANT TO SCORE SOME DOPE FROM THE LOCK-UP, THAT'S--
NO, IT'S NOT DOPE.
THEN WHAT IS IT?

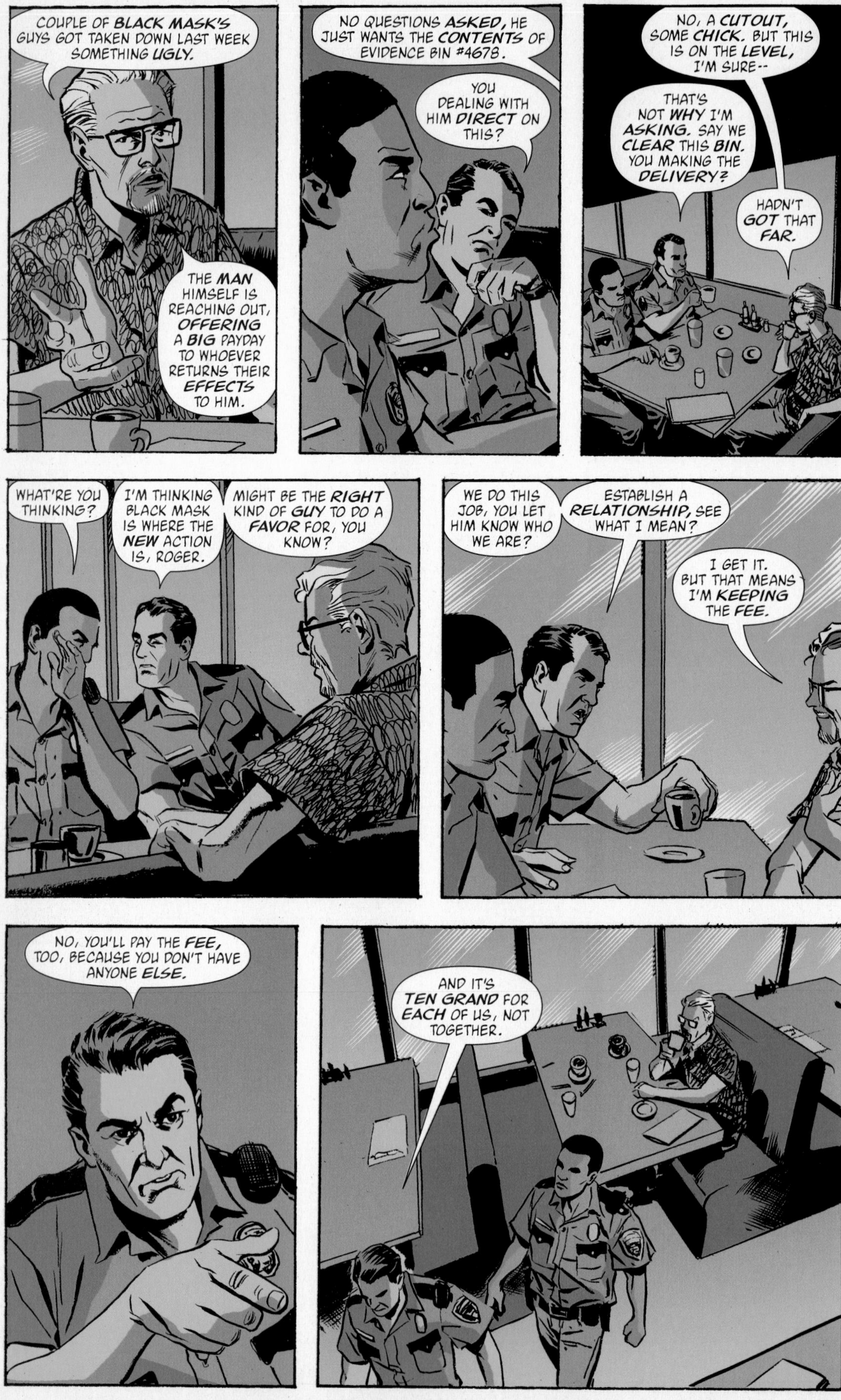
COUPLE OF BLACK MASK'S GUYS GOT TAKEN DOWN LAST WEEK SOMETHING UGLY.
THE MAN HIMSELF IS REACHING OUT, OFFERING A BIG PAYDAY TO WHOEVER RETURNS THEIR EFFECTS TO HIM.
NO QUESTIONS ASKED, HE JUST WANTS THE CONTENTS OF EVIDENCE BIN #4678.
YOU DEALING WITH HIM DIRECT ON THIS?
NO, A CUTOUT, SOME CHICK. BUT THIS IS ON THE LEVEL, I'M SURE--
THAT'S NOT WHY I'M ASKING. SAY WE CLEAR THIS BIN. YOU MAKING THE DELIVERY?
HADN'T GOT THAT FAR.
WHAT'RE YOU THINKING?
I'M THINKING BLACK MASK IS WHERE THE NEW ACTION IS, ROGER.
MIGHT BE THE RIGHT KIND OF GUY TO DO A FAVOR FOR, YOU KNOW?
WE DO THIS JOB, YOU LET HIM KNOW WHO WE ARE?
ESTABLISH A RELATIONSHIP, SEE WHAT I MEAN?
I GET IT. BUT THAT MEANS I'M KEEPING THE FEE.
NO, YOU'LL PAY THE FEE, TOO, BECAUSE YOU DON'T HAVE ANYONE ELSE.
AND IT'S TEN GRAND FOR EACH OF US, NOT TOGETHER.

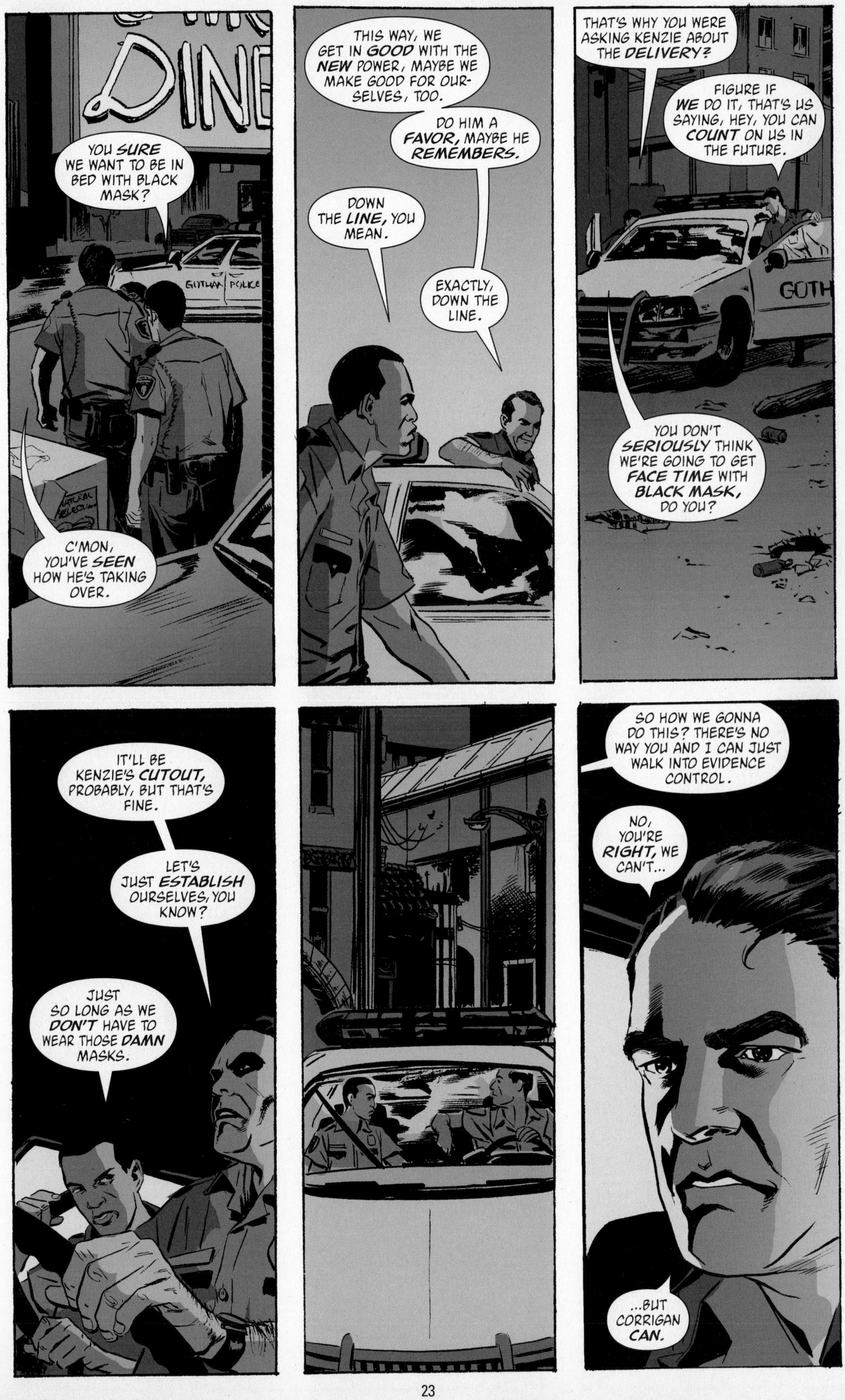
YOU SURE WE WANT TO BE IN BED WITH BLACK MASK?
C'MON, YOU'VE SEEN HOW HE'S TAKING OVER.
THIS WAY, WE GET IN GOOD WITH THE NEW POWER, MAYBE WE MAKE GOOD FOR OURSELVES, TOO.
DO HIM A FAVOR, MAYBE HE REMEMBERS.
DOWN THE LINE, YOU MEAN.
EXACTLY, DOWN THE LINE.
THAT'S WHY YOU WERE ASKING KENZIE ABOUT THE DELIVERY?
FIGURE IF WE DO IT, THAT'S US SAYING, HEY, YOU CAN COUNT ON US IN THE FUTURE.
YOU DON'T SERIOUSLY THINK WE'RE GOING TO GET FACE TIME WITH BLACK MASK, DO YOU?
IT'LL BE KENZIE'S CUTOUT, PROBABLY, BUT THAT'S FINE.
LET'S JUST ESTABLISH OURSELVES, YOU KNOW?
JUST SO LONG AS WE DON'T HAVE TO WEAR THOSE DAMN MASKS.
SO HOW WE GONNA DO THIS? THERE'S NO WAY YOU AND I CAN JUST WALK INTO EVIDENCE CONTROL.
NO, YOU'RE RIGHT, WE CAN'T...
...BUT CORRIGAN CAN.

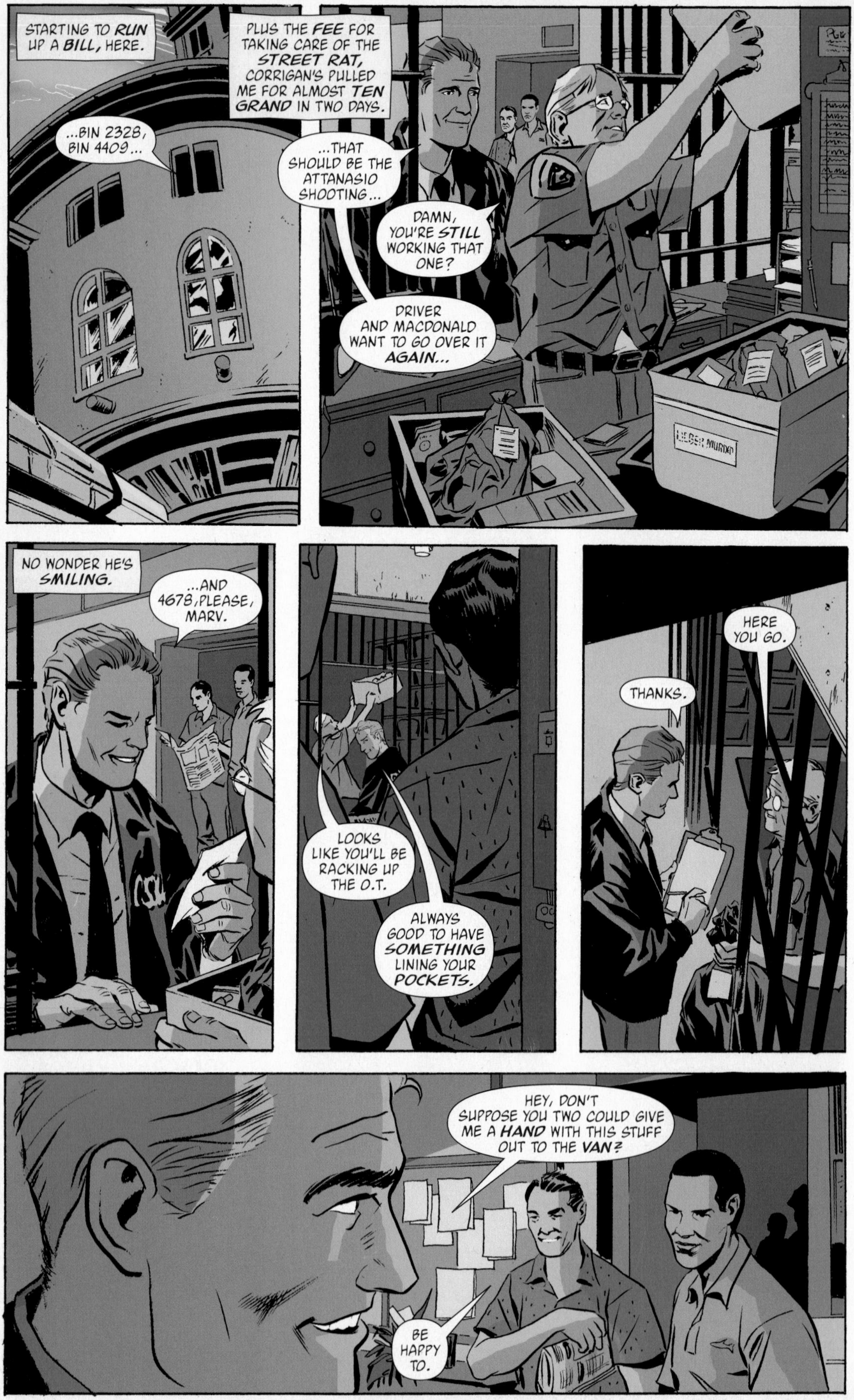
STARTING TO RUN UP A BILL, HERE.
...BIN 2328, BIN 4409...
PLUS THE FEE FOR TAKING CARE OF THE STREET RAT, CORRIGAN'S PULLED ME FOR ALMOST TEN GRAND IN TWO DAYS.
...THAT SHOULD BE THE ATTANASIO SHOOTING...
DAMN, YOU'RE STILL WORKING THAT ONE?
DRIVER AND MACDONALD WANT TO GO OVER IT AGAIN...
NO WONDER HE'S SMILING.
...AND 4678, PLEASE, MARV.
LOOKS LIKE YOU'LL BE RACKING UP THE O.T.
ALWAYS GOOD TO HAVE SOMETHING LINING YOUR POCKETS.
HERE YOU GO.
THANKS.
HEY, DON'T SUPPOSE YOU TWO COULD GIVE ME A HAND WITH THIS STUFF OUT TO THE VAN?
BE HAPPY TO.

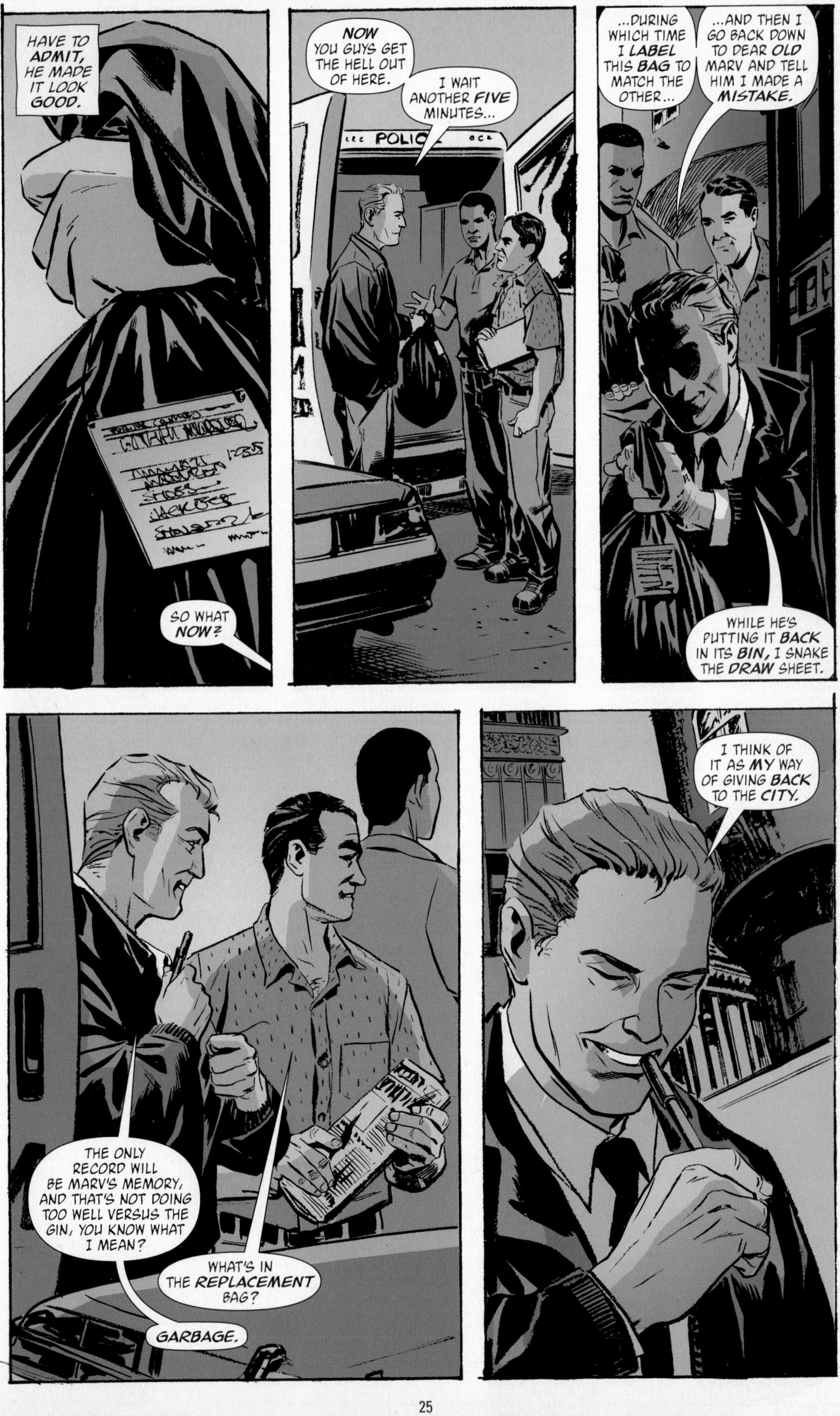
HAVE TO ADMIT, HE MADE IT LOOK GOOD.
SO WHAT NOW?
NOW YOU GUYS GET THE HELL OUT OF HERE.
I WAIT ANOTHER FIVE MINUTES...
...DURING WHICH TIME I LABEL THIS BAG TO MATCH THE OTHER...
...AND THEN I GO BACK DOWN TO DEAR OLD MARV AND TELL HIM I MADE A MISTAKE.
WHILE HE'S PUTTING IT BACK IN ITS BIN, I SNAKE THE DRAW SHEET.
THE ONLY RECORD WILL BE MARV'S MEMORY, AND THAT'S NOT DOING TOO WELL VERSUS THE GIN, YOU KNOW WHAT I MEAN?
WHAT'S IN THE REPLACEMENT BAG?
GARBAGE.
I THINK OF IT AS MY WAY OF GIVING BACK TO THE CITY.

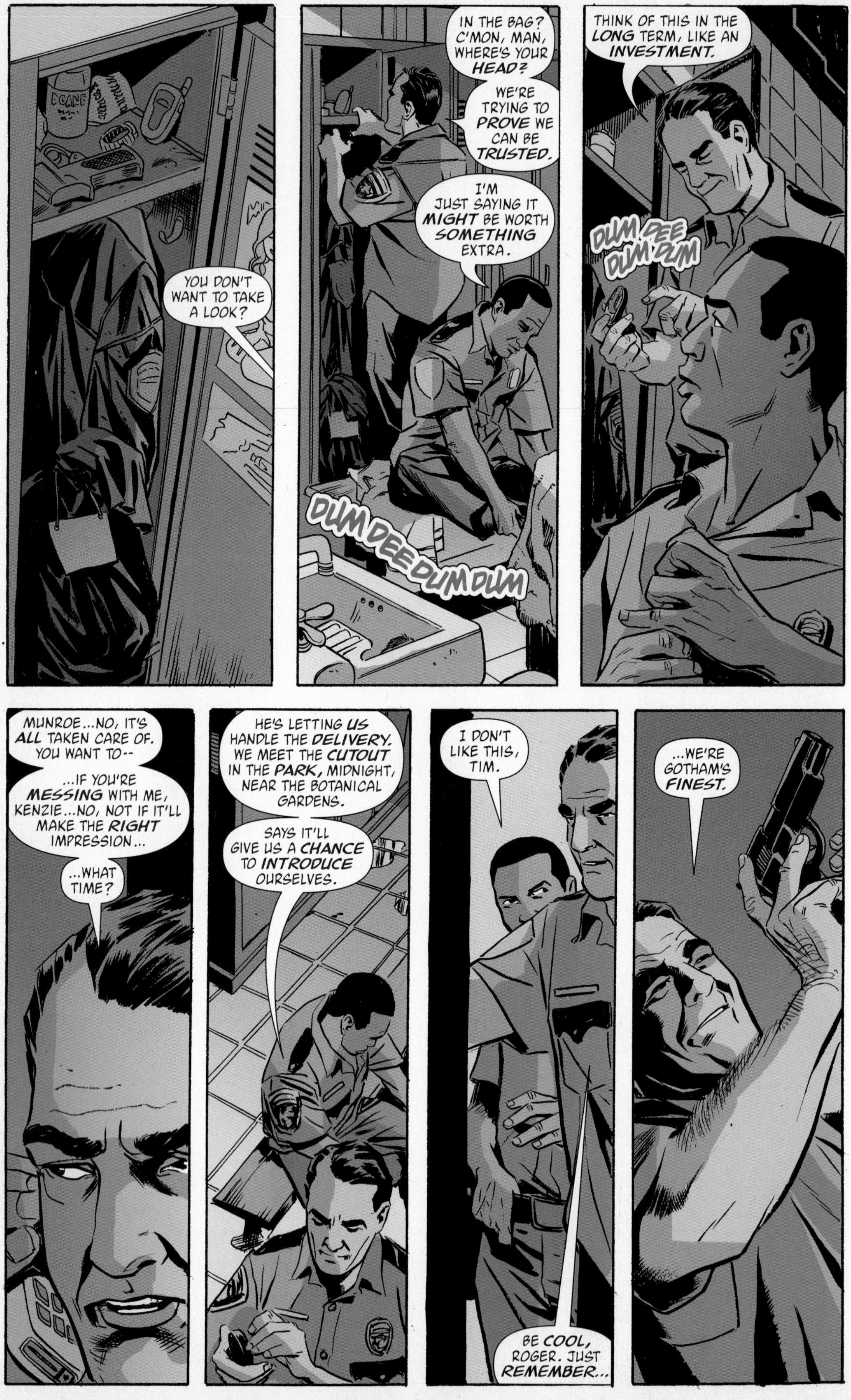
YOU DON'T WANT TO TAKE A LOOK?
IN THE BAG? C'MON, MAN, WHERE'S YOUR HEAD?
WE'RE TRYING TO PROVE WE CAN BE TRUSTED.
I'M JUST SAYING IT MIGHT BE WORTH SOMETHING EXTRA.
DUM DEE DUM DUM
THINK OF THIS IN THE LONG TERM, LIKE AN INVESTMENT.
DUM DEE DUM DUM
MUNROE...NO, IT'S ALL TAKEN CARE OF. YOU WANT TO--
...IF YOU'RE MESSING WITH ME, KENZIE...NO, NOT IF IT'LL MAKE THE RIGHT IMPRESSION...
...WHAT TIME?
HE'S LETTING US HANDLE THE DELIVERY. WE MEET THE CUTOUT IN THE PARK, MIDNIGHT, NEAR THE BOTANICAL GARDENS.
SAYS IT'LL GIVE US A CHANCE TO INTRODUCE OURSELVES.
I DON'T LIKE THIS, TIM.
BE COOL, ROGER. JUST REMEMBER...
...WE'RE GOTHAM'S FINEST.

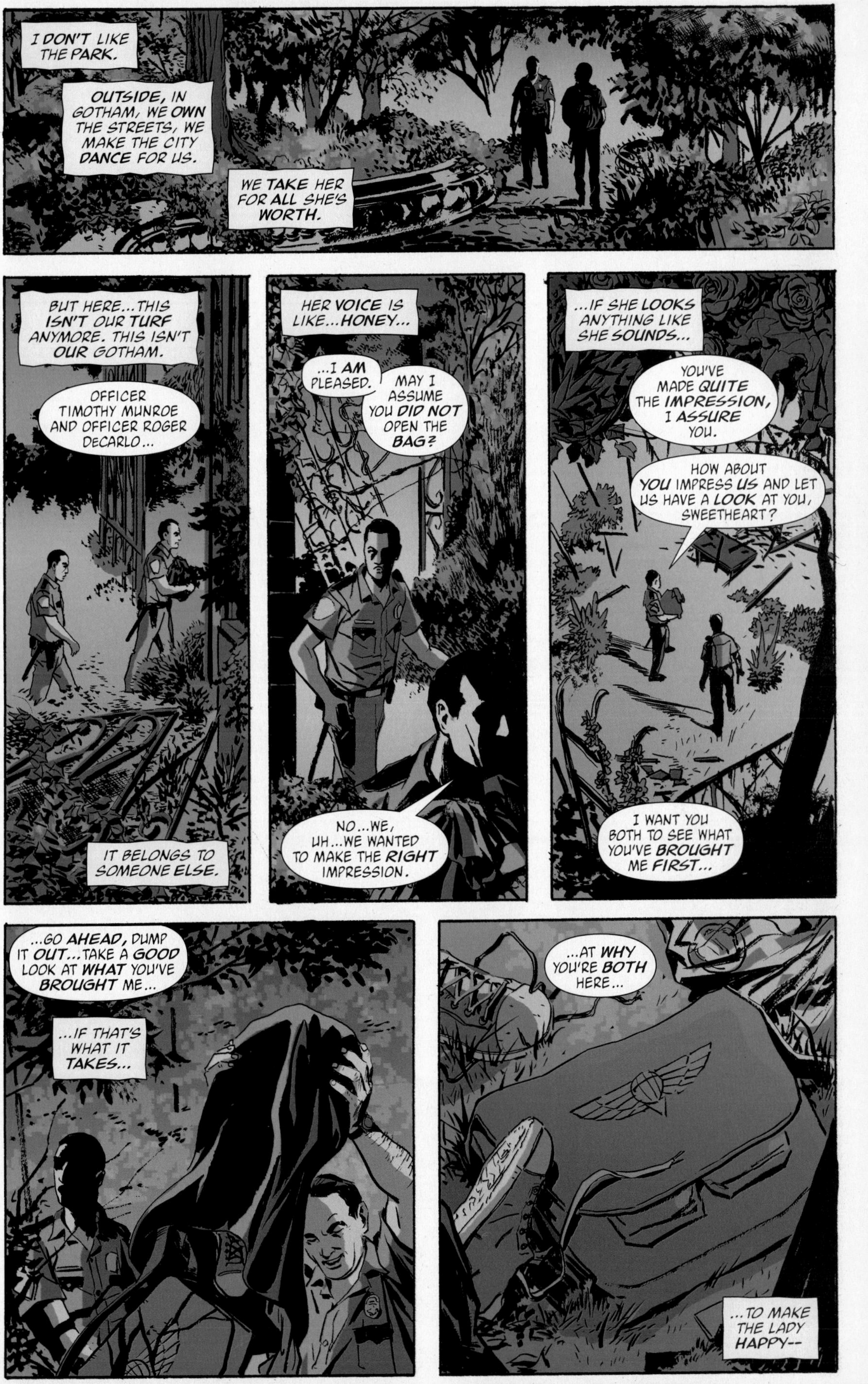
I DON'T LIKE THE PARK.
OUTSIDE, IN GOTHAM, WE OWN THE STREETS, WE MAKE THE CITY DANCE FOR US.
WE TAKE HER FOR ALL SHE'S WORTH.
BUT HERE...THIS ISN'T OUR TURF ANYMORE. THIS ISN'T OUR GOTHAM.
OFFICER TIMOTHY MUNROE AND OFFICER ROGER DECARLO...
IT BELONGS TO SOMEONE ELSE.
HER VOICE IS LIKE...HONEY...
...I AM PLEASED.
MAY I ASSUME YOU DID NOT OPEN THE BAG?
NO...WE, UH...WE WANTED TO MAKE THE RIGHT IMPRESSION.
...IF SHE LOOKS ANYTHING LIKE SHE SOUNDS...
YOU'VE MADE QUITE THE IMPRESSION, I ASSURE YOU.
HOW ABOUT YOU IMPRESS US AND LET US HAVE A LOOK AT YOU, SWEETHEART?
I WANT YOU BOTH TO SEE WHAT YOU'VE BROUGHT ME FIRST...
...GO AHEAD, DUMP IT OUT...TAKE A GOOD LOOK AT WHAT YOU'VE BROUGHT ME...
...IF THAT'S WHAT IT TAKES...
...AT WHY YOU'RE BOTH HERE...
...TO MAKE THE LADY HAPPY--

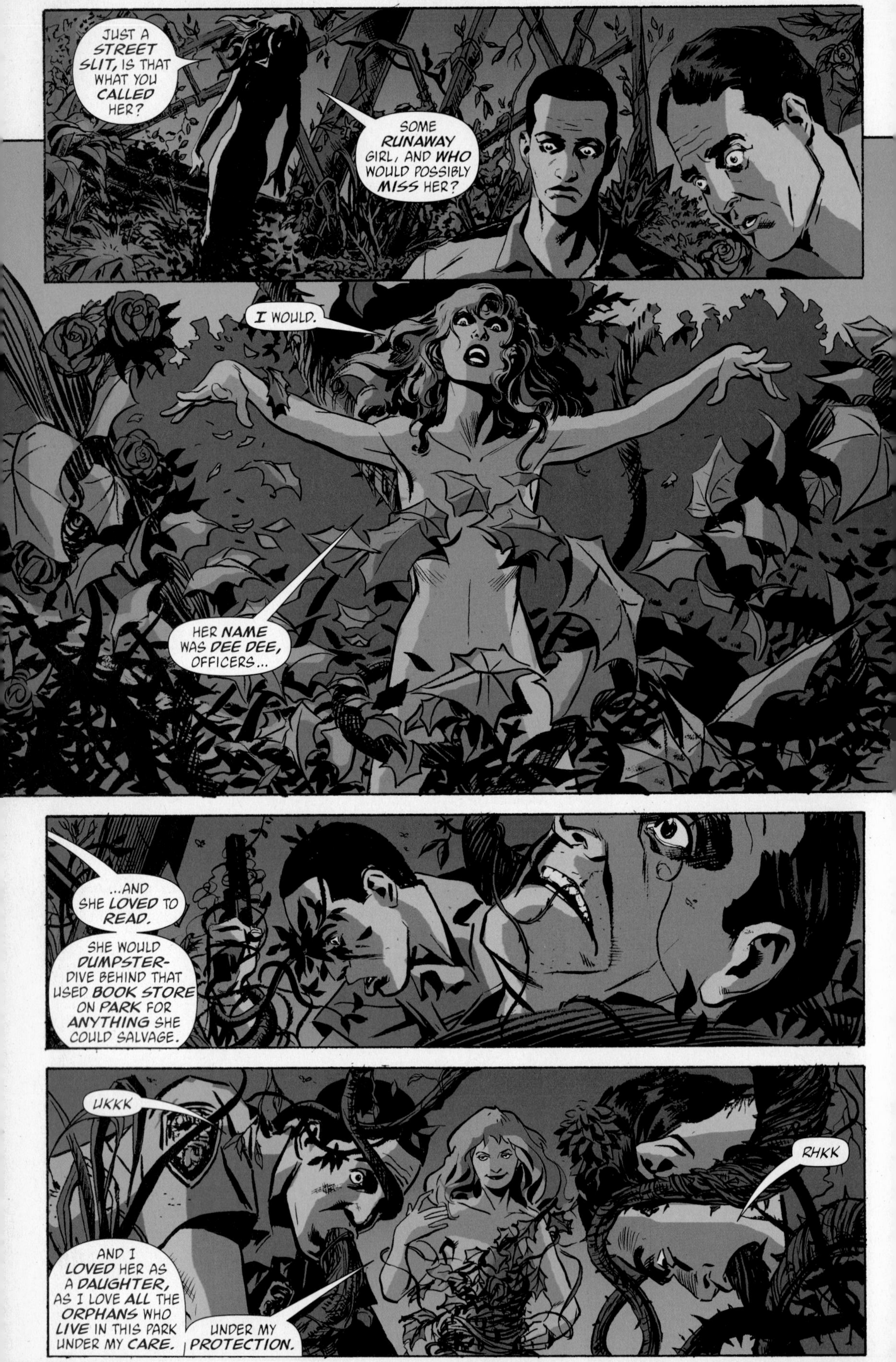
JUST A STREET SLIT, IS THAT WHAT YOU CALLED HER?
SOME RUNAWAY GIRL, AND WHO WOULD POSSIBLY MISS HER?
I WOULD.
HER NAME WAS DEE DEE, OFFICERS...
...AND SHE LOVED TO READ.
SHE WOULD DUMPSTER-DIVE BEHIND THAT USED BOOK STORE ON PARK FOR ANYTHING SHE COULD SALVAGE.
UKKK
RHKK
AND I LOVED HER AS A DAUGHTER, AS I LOVE ALL THE ORPHANS WHO LIVE IN THIS PARK UNDER MY CARE.
UNDER MY PROTECTION.

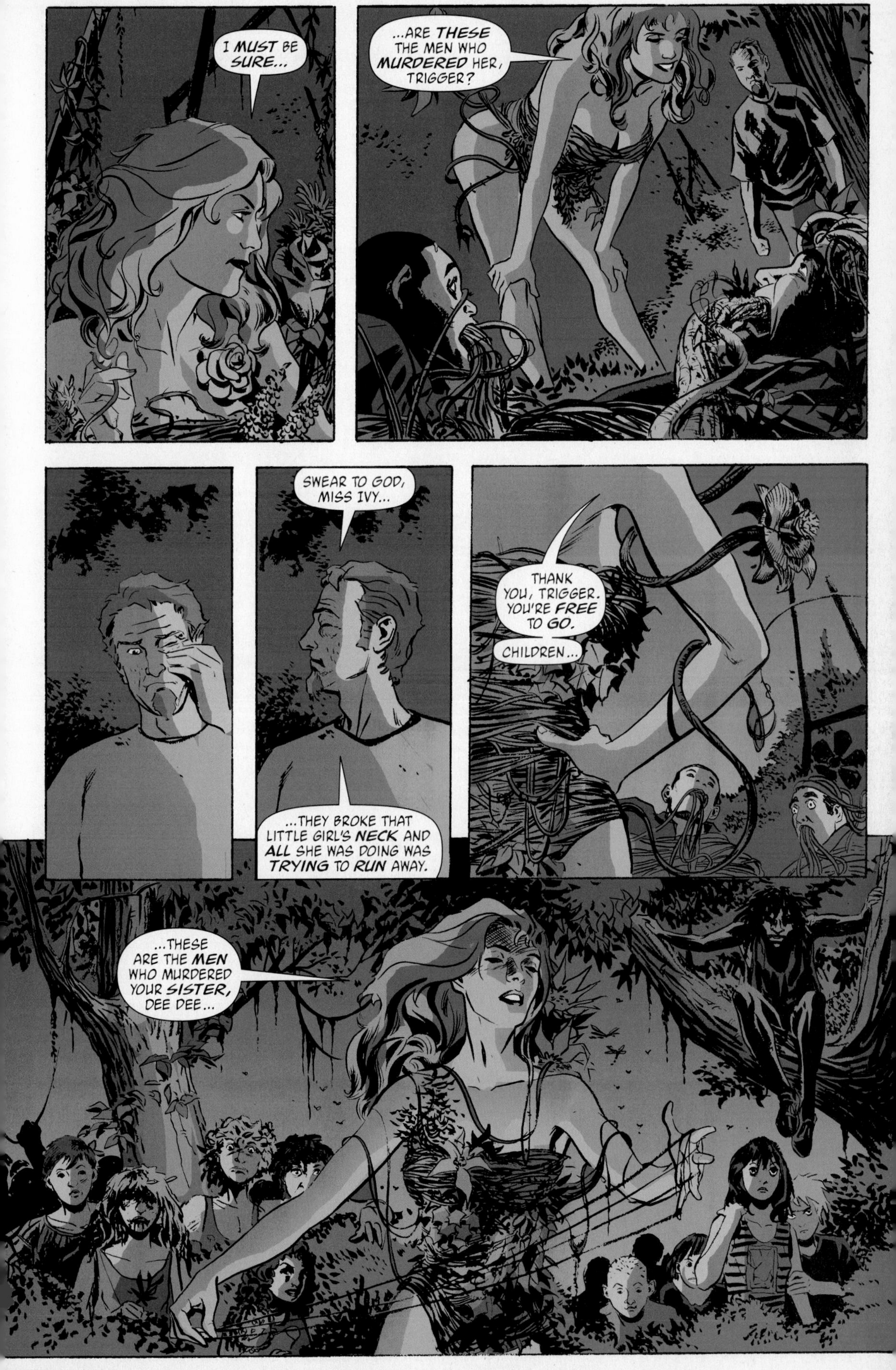
I MUST BE SURE...
...ARE THESE THE MEN WHO MURDERED HER, TRIGGER?
SWEAR TO GOD, MISS IVY...
...THEY BROKE THAT LITTLE GIRL'S NECK AND ALL SHE WAS DOING WAS TRYING TO RUN AWAY.
THANK YOU, TRIGGER. YOU'RE FREE TO GO.
CHILDREN...
...THESE ARE THE MEN WHO MURDERED YOUR SISTER, DEE DEE...

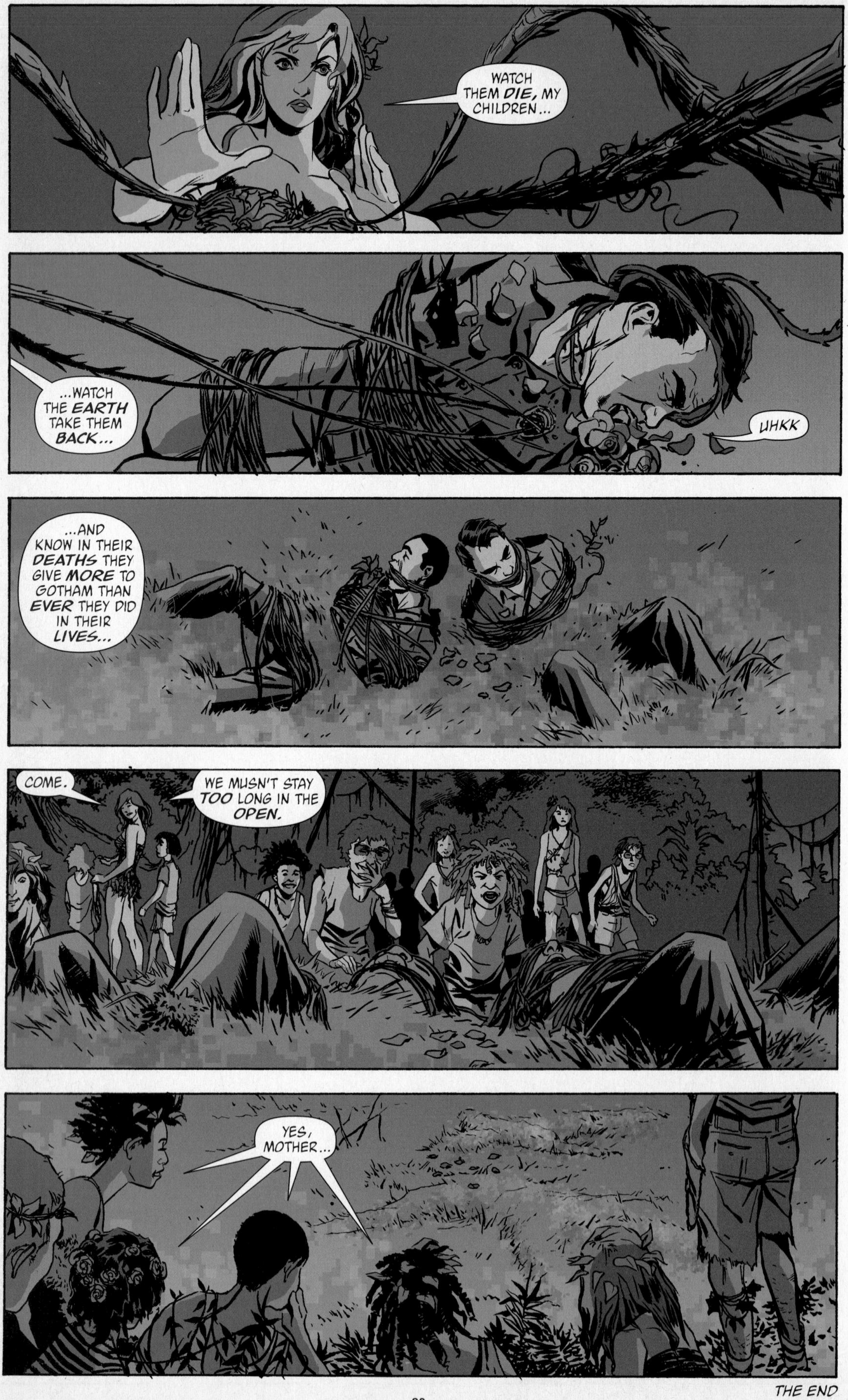
WATCH THEM *DIE*, MY CHILDREN...
...WATCH THE *EARTH* TAKE THEM *BACK*...
UHKK
...AND KNOW IN THEIR *DEATHS* THEY GIVE *MORE* TO GOTHAM THAN *EVER* THEY DID IN THEIR *LIVES*...
COME.
WE MUSN'T STAY *TOO* LONG IN THE *OPEN.*
YES, MOTHER...

THE END

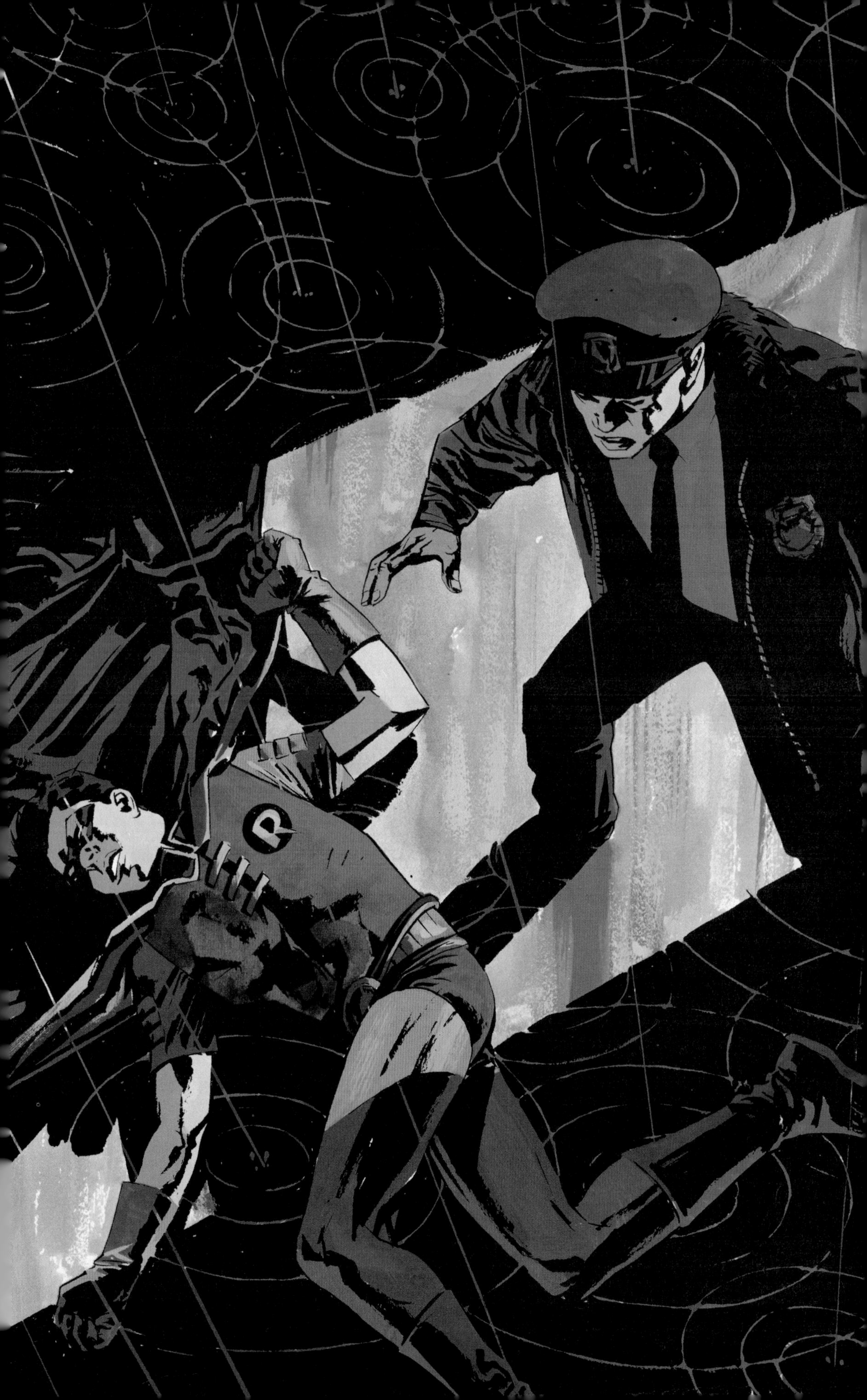

DEAD ROBIN

Written by
ED BRUBAKER & GREG RUCKA
Art by
KANO & STEFANO GAUDIANO
Colors by
LEE LOUGHRIDGE
Letters by
CLEM ROBINS

In an effort to regain control over Gotham following a brutal Gang War, Commissioner Akins outlawed masked vigilantes from roaming the city's streets. Officers are ordered to stop Batman and his crew by any means necessary. The Caped Crusader, not wanting to share his risk of retribution, ordered all of his colleagues to leave Gotham. Robin, along with Batgirl, was banished to Bludhaven, where he patrols the alleys looking for crime... or does he?

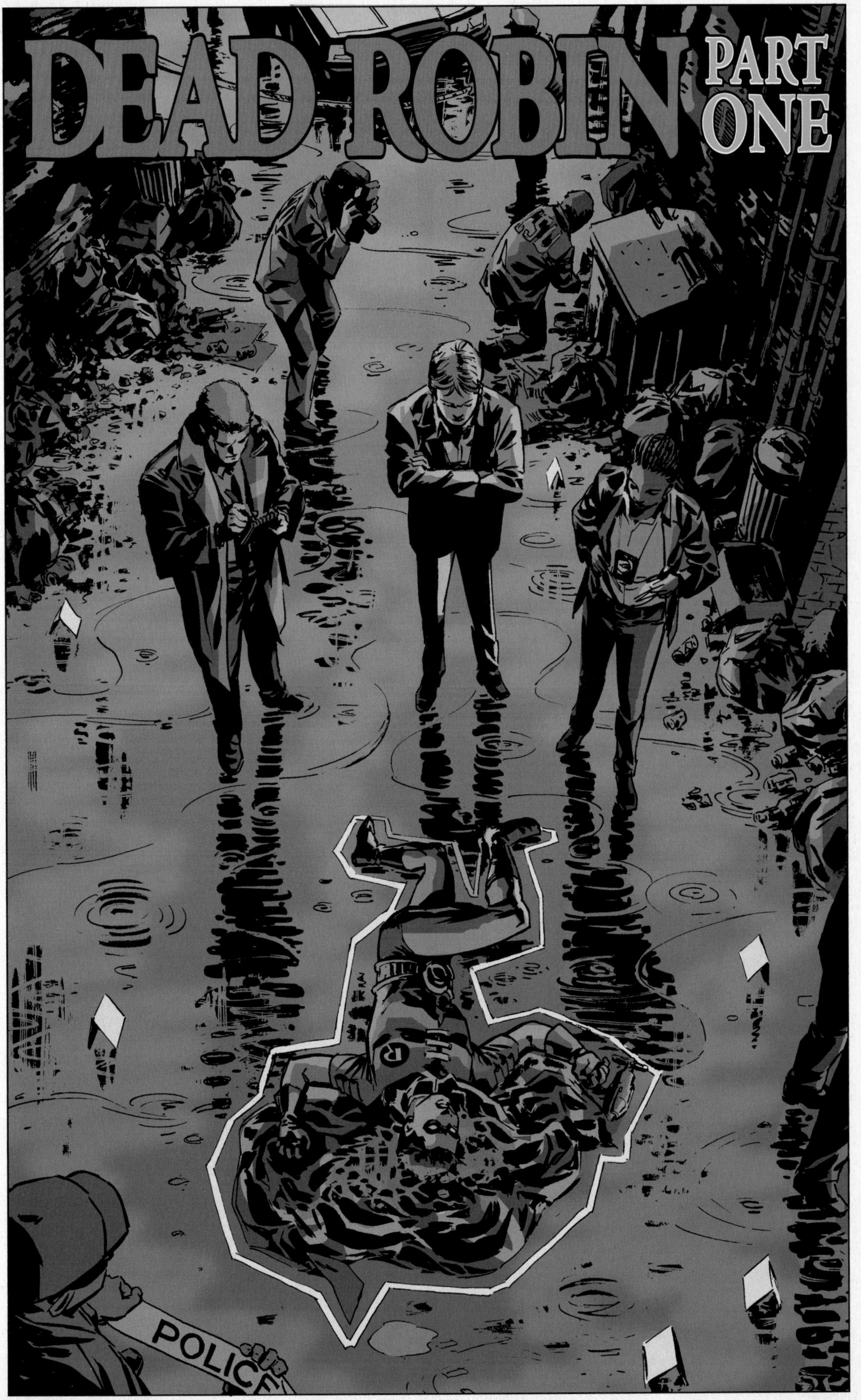
DEAD ROBIN PART ONE
POLICE

IT'S *NOT* HIM.

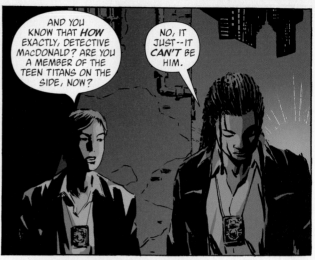

AND YOU KNOW THAT *HOW* EXACTLY, DETECTIVE MACDONALD? ARE YOU A MEMBER OF THE TEEN TITANS ON THE SIDE, NOW?

NO, IT JUST--IT *CAN'T* BE HIM.

SHE'S *RIGHT,* CAPTAIN. IT'S TOO SIMPLE. NO SIGN OF ANYTHING OTHER THAN *IMPACT* INJURIES ON THE BODY; NOT A FACIAL CONTUSION TO SPEAK OF.

WHICH SAYS TO ME HE FELL...YET HE'S GOT HIS *GRAPPLE* THING RIGHT HERE. DOESN'T MAKE SENSE.

HE COULD'VE ENDED UP LYING HERE *ANY* NUMBER OF WAYS, DETECTIVE DRIVER.

THESE PEOPLE *DO* FIGHT ON THOSE ROOFTOPS, *REMEMBER?* HE COULD'VE BEEN *UNCONSCIOUS* WHEN HE WENT OVER THE SIDE.

TRUE...BUT IT STILL FEELS WRONG. THIS *ISN'T* HOW ONE OF *THEM* DIES.

AW, *GOD...*

CAN'T BE *SIXTEEN,* EVEN.

YOU REALIZE, IF THIS *IS* ACTUALLY HIM, THEN EVEN IF THIS IS ACCIDENTAL, THE BAT IS AT *FAULT?*

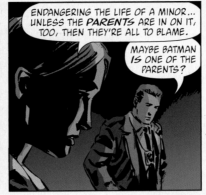

ENDANGERING THE LIFE OF A MINOR... UNLESS THE *PARENTS* ARE IN ON IT, TOO, THEN THEY'RE ALL TO BLAME.

MAYBE BATMAN *IS* ONE OF THE PARENTS?

THERE'S A SCARY THOUGHT.

CAPTAIN SAWYER. DETECTIVES...

COMMISSIONER AKINS.

YOU *DO* REALIZE THERE'S *ALREADY* A MEDIA CIRCUS ACROSS THE STREET?

WONDERFUL.

YEAH, THE UNIFORM MENTIONED THE CAPE ANGLE WHEN HE CALLED IT IN AND POLICE SCANNERS LIT UP ALL OVER TOWN, APPARENTLY.

SO, WHAT ARE WE LOOKING AT? IS IT *ACTUALLY* HIM?

WE DON'T *THINK* SO, SIR... BUT WE CAN'T BE *SURE* AT THIS POINT. THE *GEAR* LOOKS PROFESSIONAL, AT LEAST.

CAUSE OF DEATH?

LOOKING LIKE A SUDDEN CASE OF *CEMENT POISONING,* SIR. SKULL CRACKED OPEN WHEN HE HIT THE PAVEMENT.

WE'LL HAVE TO WAIT FOR THE AUTOPSY FOR ANYTHING ELSE.

SO, THERE'S *NOTHING* TO FEED THE VULTURES WITH, THEN?

SORRY, SIR, NOT UNLESS MONTOYA AND ALLEN FOUND A *BLOODY UMBRELLA* OR A SIGNED *CONFESSION* ON THE ROOF...

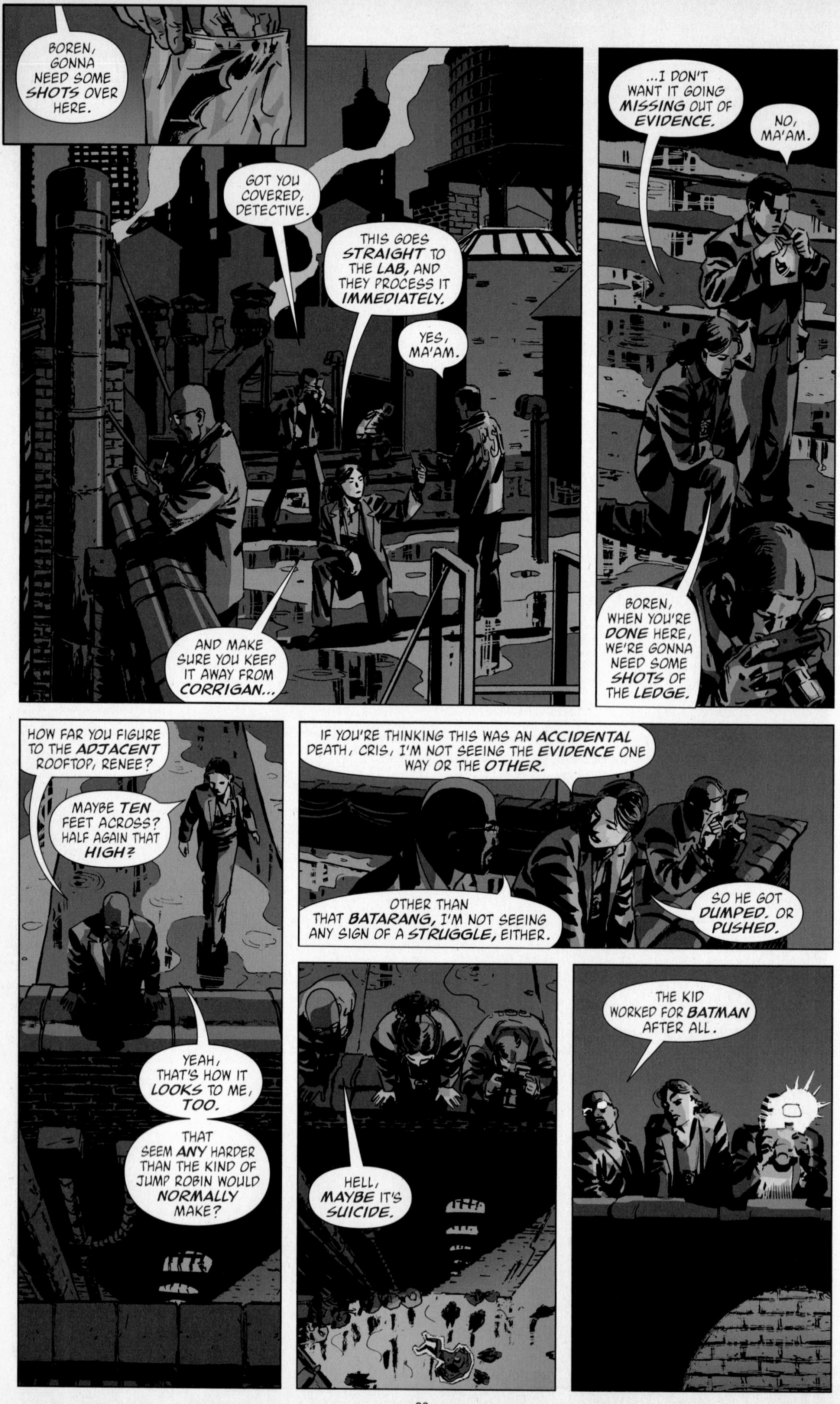
BOREN, GONNA NEED SOME SHOTS OVER HERE.
GOT YOU COVERED, DETECTIVE.
THIS GOES STRAIGHT TO THE LAB, AND THEY PROCESS IT IMMEDIATELY.
YES, MA'AM.
AND MAKE SURE YOU KEEP IT AWAY FROM CORRIGAN...
...I DON'T WANT IT GOING MISSING OUT OF EVIDENCE.
NO, MA'AM.
BOREN, WHEN YOU'RE DONE HERE, WE'RE GONNA NEED SOME SHOTS OF THE LEDGE.
HOW FAR YOU FIGURE TO THE ADJACENT ROOFTOP, RENEE?
MAYBE TEN FEET ACROSS? HALF AGAIN THAT HIGH?
YEAH, THAT'S HOW IT LOOKS TO ME, TOO.
THAT SEEM ANY HARDER THAN THE KIND OF JUMP ROBIN WOULD NORMALLY MAKE?
IF YOU'RE THINKING THIS WAS AN ACCIDENTAL DEATH, CRIS, I'M NOT SEEING THE EVIDENCE ONE WAY OR THE OTHER.
OTHER THAN THAT BATARANG, I'M NOT SEEING ANY SIGN OF A STRUGGLE, EITHER.
SO HE GOT DUMPED. OR PUSHED.
HELL, MAYBE IT'S SUICIDE.
THE KID WORKED FOR BATMAN AFTER ALL.

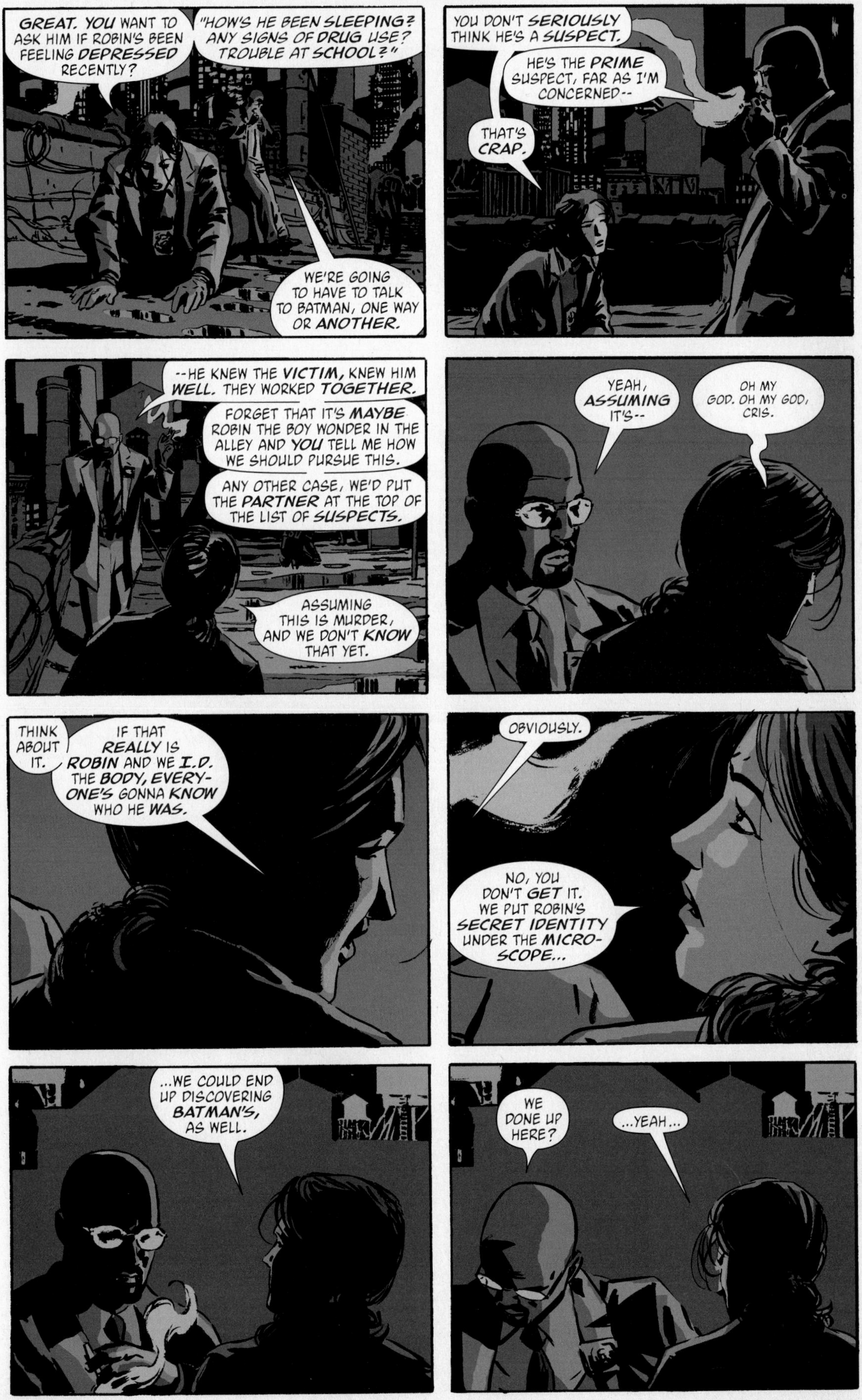
GREAT. YOU WANT TO ASK HIM IF ROBIN'S BEEN FEELING DEPRESSED RECENTLY?
"HOW'S HE BEEN SLEEPING? ANY SIGNS OF DRUG USE? TROUBLE AT SCHOOL?"
WE'RE GOING TO HAVE TO TALK TO BATMAN, ONE WAY OR ANOTHER.
YOU DON'T SERIOUSLY THINK HE'S A SUSPECT.
HE'S THE PRIME SUSPECT, FAR AS I'M CONCERNED--
THAT'S CRAP.
--HE KNEW THE VICTIM, KNEW HIM WELL. THEY WORKED TOGETHER.
FORGET THAT IT'S MAYBE ROBIN THE BOY WONDER IN THE ALLEY AND YOU TELL ME HOW WE SHOULD PURSUE THIS.
ANY OTHER CASE, WE'D PUT THE PARTNER AT THE TOP OF THE LIST OF SUSPECTS.
ASSUMING THIS IS MURDER, AND WE DON'T KNOW THAT YET.
YEAH, ASSUMING IT'S--
OH MY GOD. OH MY GOD, CRIS.
THINK ABOUT IT.
IF THAT REALLY IS ROBIN AND WE I.D. THE BODY, EVERY-ONE'S GONNA KNOW WHO HE WAS.
OBVIOUSLY.
NO, YOU DON'T GET IT. WE PUT ROBIN'S SECRET IDENTITY UNDER THE MICRO-SCOPE...
...WE COULD END UP DISCOVERING BATMAN'S, AS WELL.
WE DONE UP HERE?
...YEAH...

...LET'S SEE WHAT JO AND MARCUS GOT, TAKE IT FROM THERE...

ROBIN'S IN *BLÜDHAVEN.*

THEN *WHO*--

JESUS--

I DON'T *KNOW.*

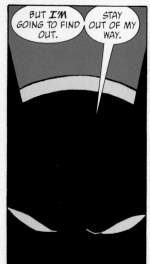

BUT *I'M* GOING TO FIND OUT.

STAY OUT OF MY WAY.

WAIT JUST A *SECOND,* YOU'VE GOT TO *ANSWER*--

BATMAN, *WAIT!*

STAY OUT OF MY WAY.

--IF IT REALLY IS ROBIN, COMMISSIONER?

--CONFIRM THAT THE JOKER IS STILL IN ARKHAM?

--ANY WITNESSES COME FORWARD?

IF YOU'LL LET ME GET A *WORD* IN, I'LL MAKE A STATEMENT.

THANK YOU.

A BODY WAS FOUND A LITTLE OVER AN HOUR AGO IN THE ALLEY BEHIND US. AS MOST OF YOU ALREADY *KNOW*, THAT BODY WAS IN A *ROBIN* COSTUME.

AT THIS EARLY STAGE OF OUR INVESTIGATION, THAT IS THE *ONLY* INFORMATION WE CAN SHARE WITH THE PRESS.

SO, YOU'RE JUST TELLING US WHAT WAS *ALREADY* LEAKED OVER THE *SCANNERS*, THEN, COMMISSIONER?

I COULD ALWAYS *DENY* IT, IF YOU'D PREFER, MR. LIPPMAN. BUT I *TRY* TO TELL THE TRUTH AS OFTEN AS POSSIBLE.

COMMISSIONER! WHAT ABOUT--

DOES THE G.C.P.D. *BELIEVE* THIS BOY IS THE *REAL* ROBIN, COMMISSIONER? OUR VIEWERS DESERVE *THAT* MUCH, AT LEAST.

AT THIS POINT, WE CAN'T *CONFIRM* HIS IDENTITY ONE WAY OR THE *OTHER*, BUT WE'RE

WRRRROOOMM

WRRRROOOOMM

--GETTING THIS?

--YOU SHOOTING, RON? GET THIS! GET THIS!!

SSKRREEEE

WELL, THAT'S JUST *PERFECT*, ISN'T IT?

HE *REALLY* DOESN'T LIKE YOU.

COMMISSIONER! ARE YOU TELLING--

COMMISSIONER! HOW DO YOU--

ARE YOU AWARE THAT THE JOKER HAS SWORN

THE RUMORS OF BREAKOUT AT ARKHAM?

COMMISSIONER! WHAT ABOUT--

COMMISSIONER!

YOU TAKING OFF, SIMON?

OH, *HEY*, DUNNING...YEAH, WE'RE NOT GETTING ANYTHING HERE. MIGHT AS WELL FILE BEFORE THE TV PEOPLE GET TO WORK.

THINK IT'S REALLY *HIM*? ROBIN?

SEEMS A LITTLE OFF TO ME, BUT IN *THIS* TOWN? WHO CAN SAY?

HELL, FOR ALL WE KNOW, BATMAN'S GOT A WHOLE *FLOCK* OF ROBINS. THIS MIGHT'VE BEEN A *TRAINEE* OR SOMETHING.

HUNH, YEAH, *GOOD POINT*. WHAT A WORLD, HUHN?

YOU SAID IT.

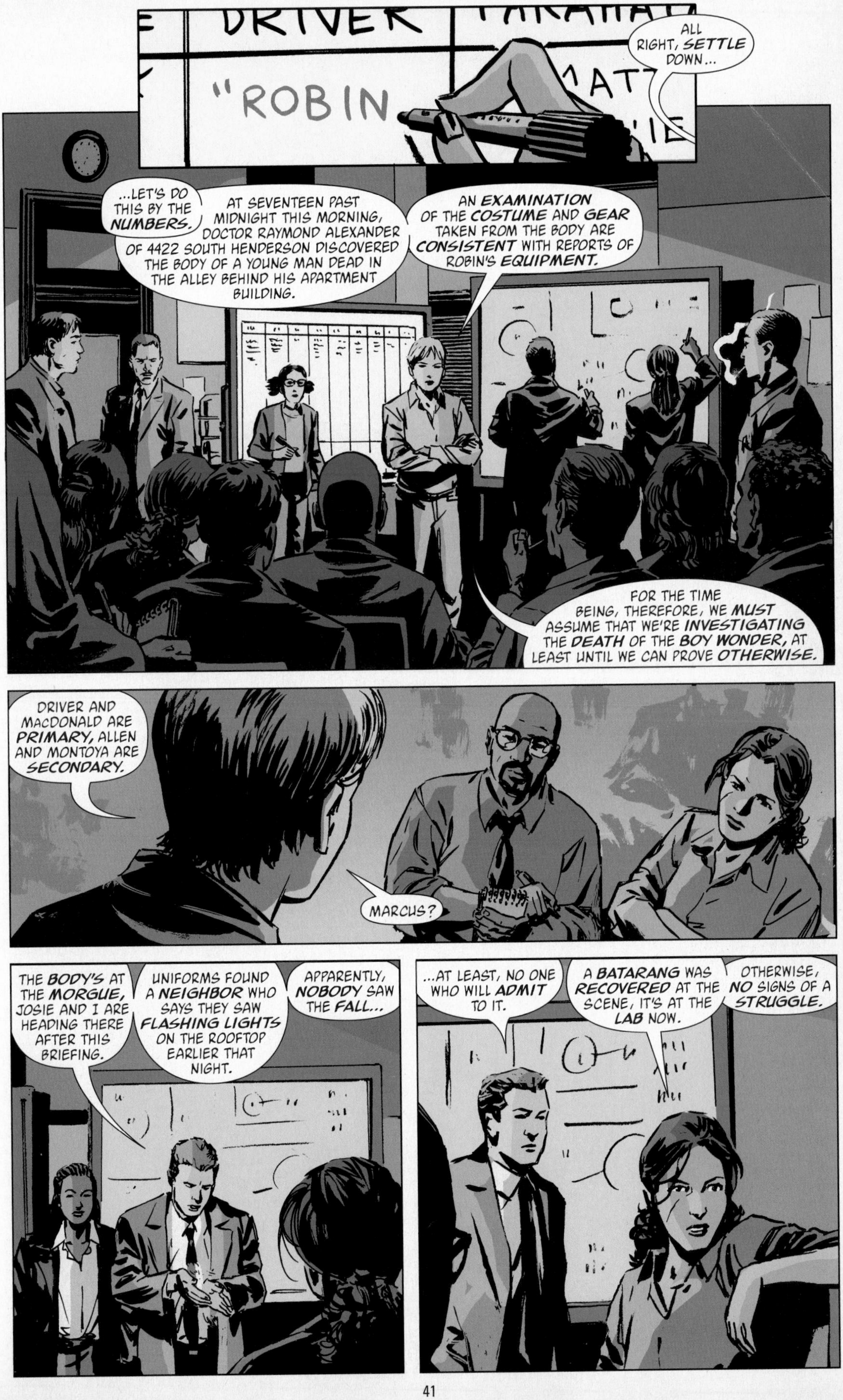
DRIVER
"ROBIN
ALL RIGHT, SETTLE DOWN...
...LET'S DO THIS BY THE NUMBERS.
AT SEVENTEEN PAST MIDNIGHT THIS MORNING, DOCTOR RAYMOND ALEXANDER OF 4422 SOUTH HENDERSON DISCOVERED THE BODY OF A YOUNG MAN DEAD IN THE ALLEY BEHIND HIS APARTMENT BUILDING.
AN EXAMINATION OF THE COSTUME AND GEAR TAKEN FROM THE BODY ARE CONSISTENT WITH REPORTS OF ROBIN'S EQUIPMENT.
FOR THE TIME BEING, THEREFORE, WE MUST ASSUME THAT WE'RE INVESTIGATING THE DEATH OF THE BOY WONDER, AT LEAST UNTIL WE CAN PROVE OTHERWISE.
DRIVER AND MACDONALD ARE PRIMARY, ALLEN AND MONTOYA ARE SECONDARY.
MARCUS?
THE BODY'S AT THE MORGUE, JOSIE AND I ARE HEADING THERE AFTER THIS BRIEFING.
UNIFORMS FOUND A NEIGHBOR WHO SAYS THEY SAW FLASHING LIGHTS ON THE ROOFTOP EARLIER THAT NIGHT.
APPARENTLY, NOBODY SAW THE FALL...
...AT LEAST, NO ONE WHO WILL ADMIT TO IT.
A BATARANG WAS RECOVERED AT THE SCENE, IT'S AT THE LAB NOW.
OTHERWISE, NO SIGNS OF A STRUGGLE.

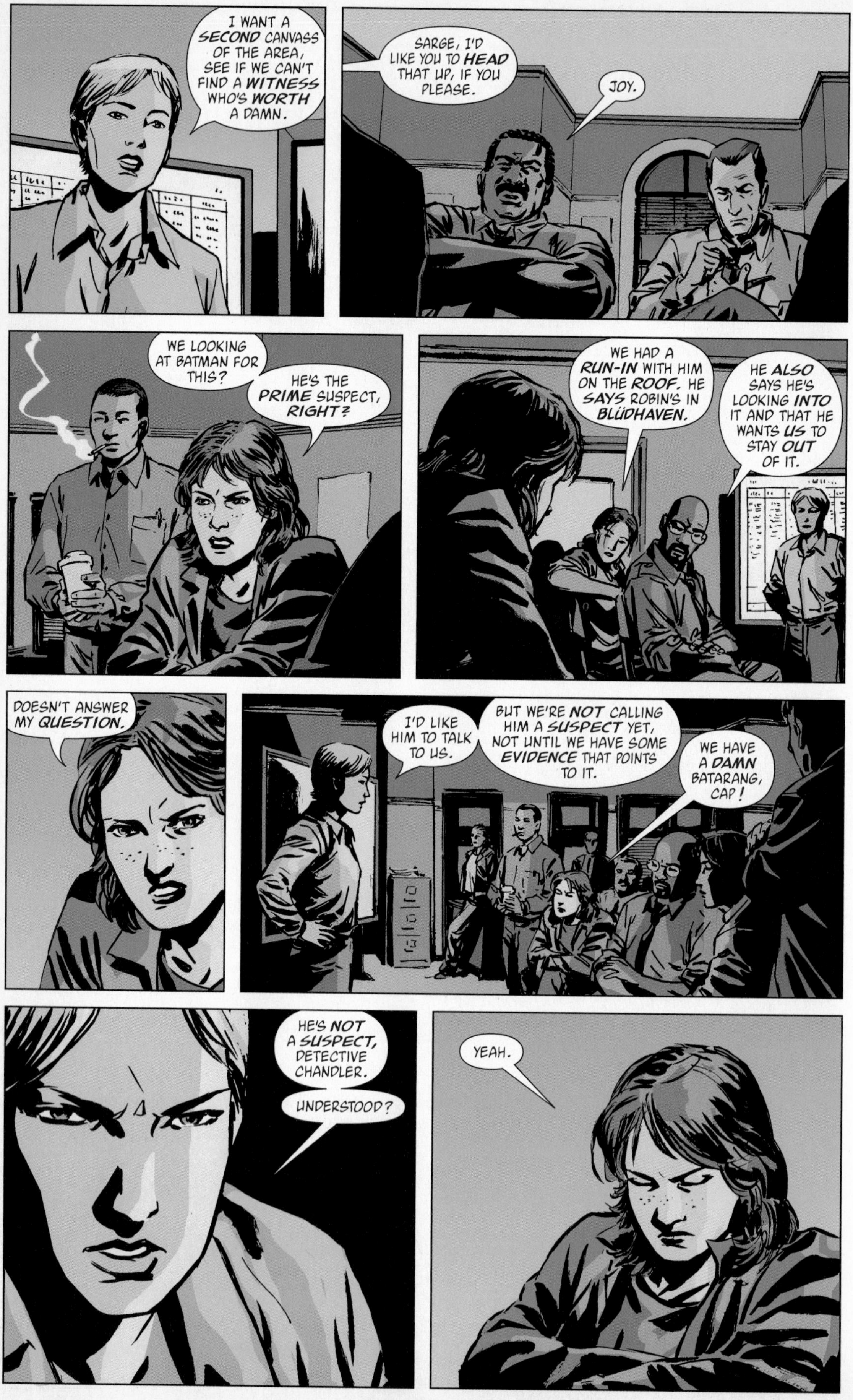
I WANT A SECOND CANVASS OF THE AREA, SEE IF WE CAN'T FIND A WITNESS WHO'S WORTH A DAMN.
SARGE, I'D LIKE YOU TO HEAD THAT UP, IF YOU PLEASE.
JOY.
WE LOOKING AT BATMAN FOR THIS?
HE'S THE PRIME SUSPECT, RIGHT?
WE HAD A RUN-IN WITH HIM ON THE ROOF. HE SAYS ROBIN'S IN BLÜDHAVEN.
HE ALSO SAYS HE'S LOOKING INTO IT AND THAT HE WANTS US TO STAY OUT OF IT.
DOESN'T ANSWER MY QUESTION.
I'D LIKE HIM TO TALK TO US.
BUT WE'RE NOT CALLING HIM A SUSPECT YET, NOT UNTIL WE HAVE SOME EVIDENCE THAT POINTS TO IT.
WE HAVE A DAMN BATARANG, CAP!
HE'S NOT A SUSPECT, DETECTIVE CHANDLER.
UNDERSTOOD?
YEAH.

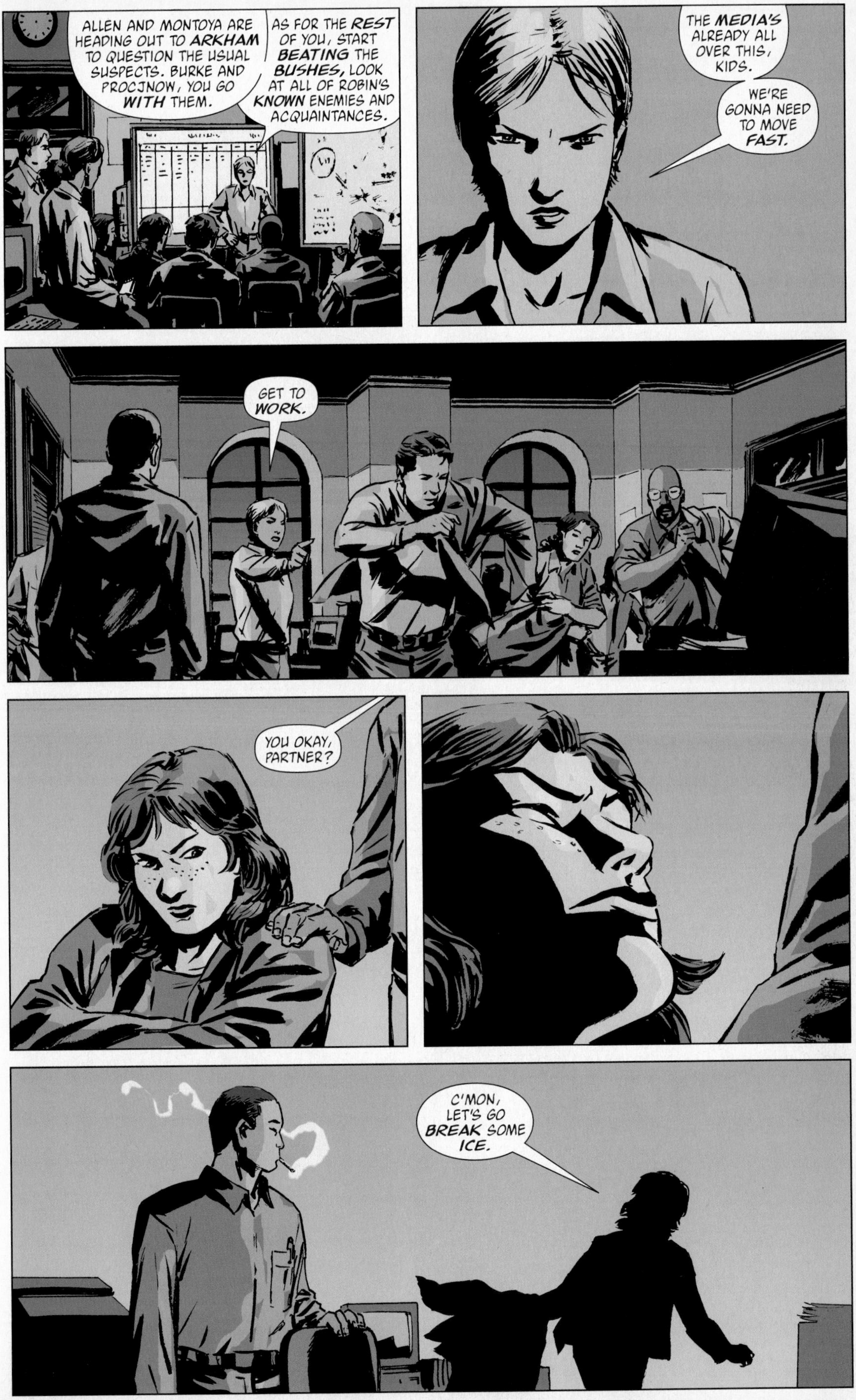
ALLEN AND MONTOYA ARE HEADING OUT TO ARKHAM TO QUESTION THE USUAL SUSPECTS. BURKE AND PROCJNOW, YOU GO WITH THEM.
AS FOR THE REST OF YOU, START BEATING THE BUSHES, LOOK AT ALL OF ROBIN'S KNOWN ENEMIES AND ACQUAINTANCES.
THE MEDIA'S ALREADY ALL OVER THIS, KIDS.
WE'RE GONNA NEED TO MOVE FAST.
GET TO WORK.
YOU OKAY, PARTNER?
C'MON, LET'S GO BREAK SOME ICE.

...BUT YOU DIDN'T HAVE TO OVERSEE EVERYTHING PERSONALLY. YOU COULD STILL BE SLEEPING.

I LOVE THAT YOU JUST *ASSUME* I'M IN *BED* AT TWO A.M., MARCUS... I WAS *ACTUALLY* ON A *DATE*.

--APPRECIATE YOU GETTING THIS PUSHED THROUGH ON THE *NIGHT SHIFT* FOR US, NORA...

KANE COUNTY MORGUE

YOU--YOU--Y...

YOU SHOULD *REALLY* GET THAT STUTTER LOOKED AT.

SO...WHAT'S THE *PROGNOSIS*, BILL?

LOOKING PRETTY STRAIGHTFORWARD, SO FAR.

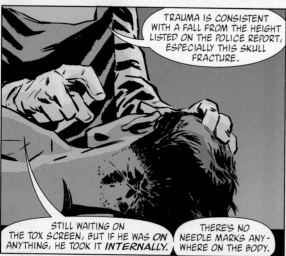

TRAUMA IS CONSISTENT WITH A FALL FROM THE HEIGHT LISTED ON THE POLICE REPORT, ESPECIALLY THIS SKULL FRACTURE.

STILL WAITING ON THE TOX SCREEN, BUT IF HE WAS *ON* ANYTHING, HE TOOK IT *INTERNALLY*.

THERE'S NO NEEDLE MARKS ANY- WHERE ON THE BODY.

IS THERE *ANYTHING* TO TELL US WHETHER THIS IS THE REAL ROBIN OR A FAKE?

HARD TO SAY, DETECTIVE. HE FITS THE *TYPE*, DEFINITELY...

APPEARS IN GOOD SHAPE, PHYSICALLY, AND IS SOMEWHERE AROUND FIFTEEN YEARS OF AGE.

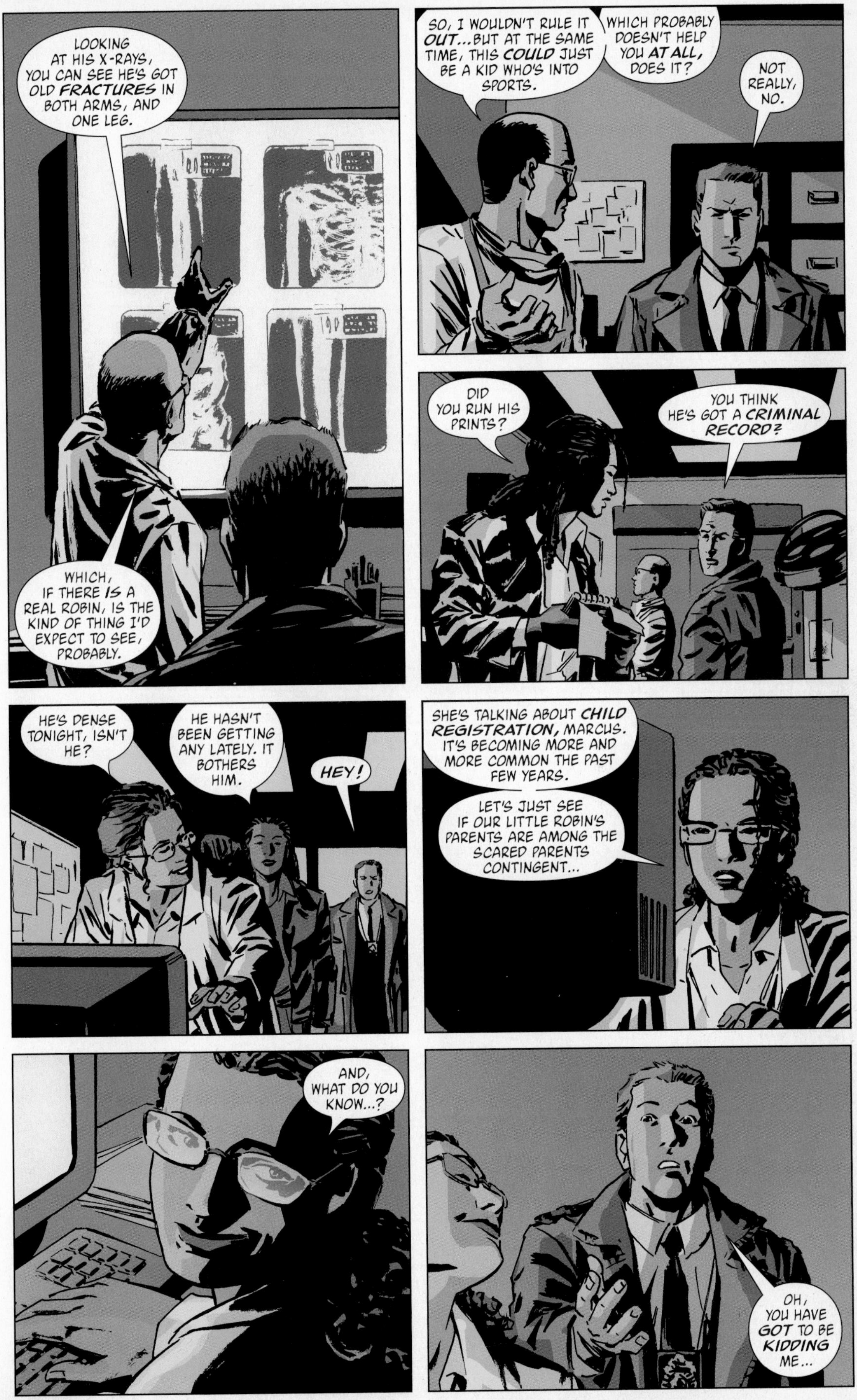
LOOKING AT HIS X-RAYS, YOU CAN SEE HE'S GOT OLD FRACTURES IN BOTH ARMS, AND ONE LEG.
WHICH, IF THERE IS A REAL ROBIN, IS THE KIND OF THING I'D EXPECT TO SEE, PROBABLY.
SO, I WOULDN'T RULE IT OUT...BUT AT THE SAME TIME, THIS COULD JUST BE A KID WHO'S INTO SPORTS.
WHICH PROBABLY DOESN'T HELP YOU AT ALL, DOES IT?
NOT REALLY, NO.
DID YOU RUN HIS PRINTS?
YOU THINK HE'S GOT A CRIMINAL RECORD?
HE'S DENSE TONIGHT, ISN'T HE?
HE HASN'T BEEN GETTING ANY LATELY. IT BOTHERS HIM.
HEY!
SHE'S TALKING ABOUT CHILD REGISTRATION, MARCUS. IT'S BECOMING MORE AND MORE COMMON THE PAST FEW YEARS.
LET'S JUST SEE IF OUR LITTLE ROBIN'S PARENTS ARE AMONG THE SCARED PARENTS CONTINGENT...
AND, WHAT DO YOU KNOW...?
OH, YOU HAVE GOT TO BE KIDDING ME...

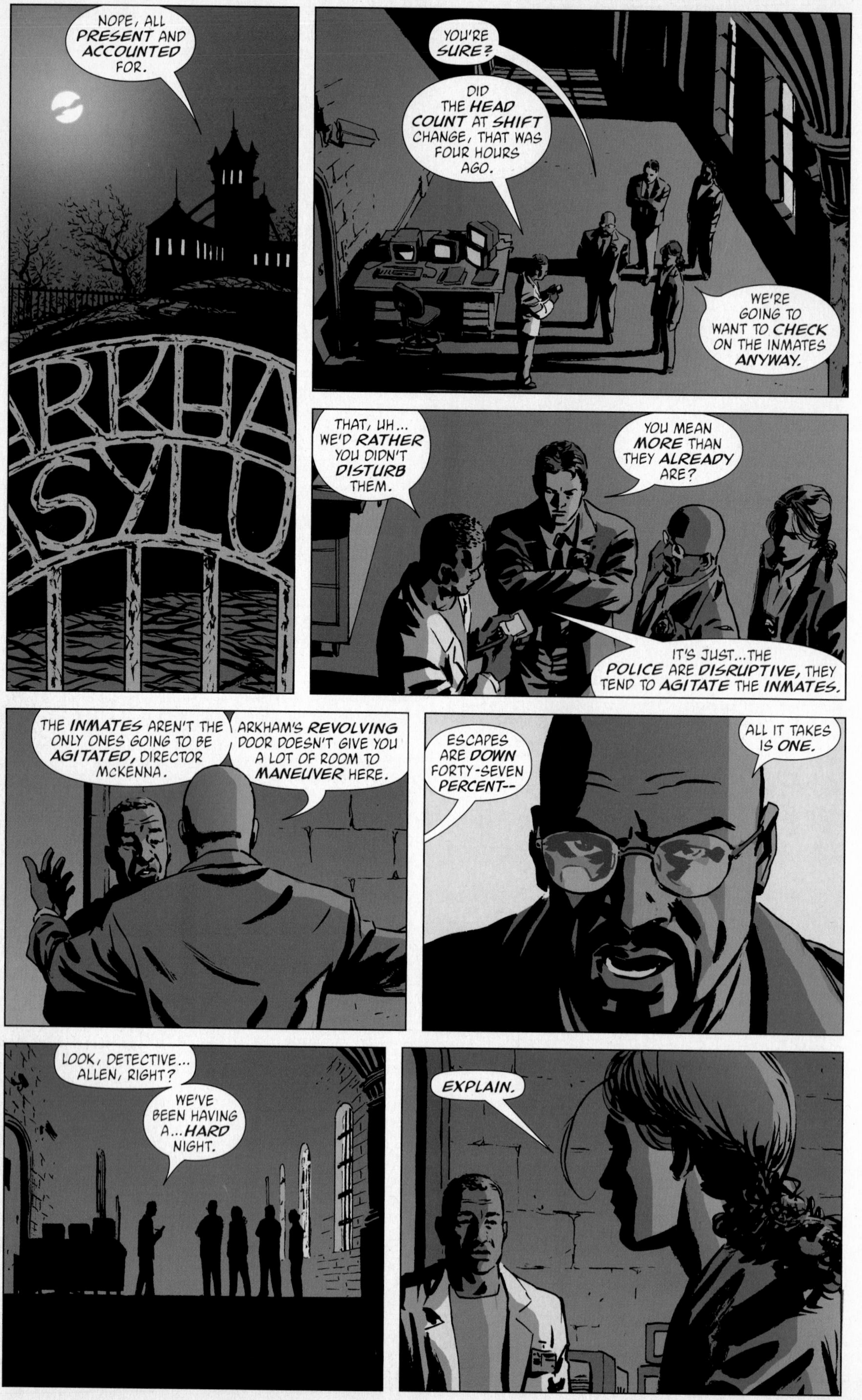
NOPE, ALL PRESENT AND ACCOUNTED FOR.
YOU'RE SURE?
DID THE HEAD COUNT AT SHIFT CHANGE, THAT WAS FOUR HOURS AGO.
WE'RE GOING TO WANT TO CHECK ON THE INMATES ANYWAY.
THAT, UH... WE'D RATHER YOU DIDN'T DISTURB THEM.
YOU MEAN MORE THAN THEY ALREADY ARE?
IT'S JUST...THE POLICE ARE DISRUPTIVE, THEY TEND TO AGITATE THE INMATES.
THE INMATES AREN'T THE ONLY ONES GOING TO BE AGITATED, DIRECTOR McKENNA.
ARKHAM'S REVOLVING DOOR DOESN'T GIVE YOU A LOT OF ROOM TO MANEUVER HERE.
ESCAPES ARE DOWN FORTY-SEVEN PERCENT--
ALL IT TAKES IS ONE.
LOOK, DETECTIVE... ALLEN, RIGHT?
WE'VE BEEN HAVING A...HARD NIGHT.
EXPLAIN.

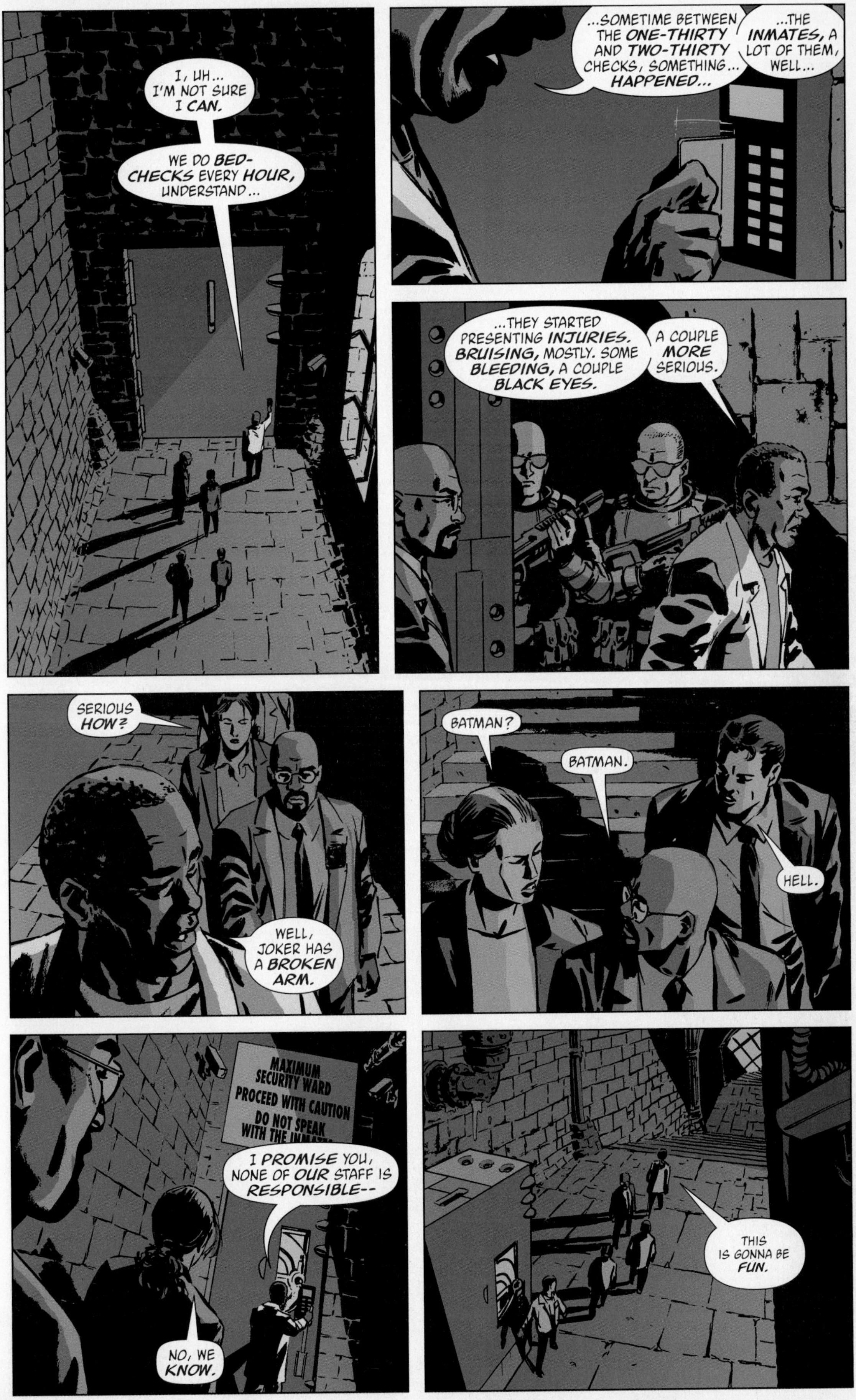
I, UH... I'M NOT SURE I CAN.
WE DO BED-CHECKS EVERY HOUR, UNDERSTAND...
...SOMETIME BETWEEN THE ONE-THIRTY AND TWO-THIRTY CHECKS, SOMETHING... HAPPENED...
...THE INMATES, A LOT OF THEM, WELL...
...THEY STARTED PRESENTING INJURIES. BRUISING, MOSTLY. SOME BLEEDING, A COUPLE BLACK EYES.
A COUPLE MORE SERIOUS.
SERIOUS HOW?
WELL, JOKER HAS A BROKEN ARM.
BATMAN?
BATMAN.
HELL.
MAXIMUM SECURITY WARD
PROCEED WITH CAUTION
DO NOT SPEAK
I PROMISE YOU, NONE OF OUR STAFF IS RESPONSIBLE--
NO, WE KNOW.
THIS IS GONNA BE FUN.

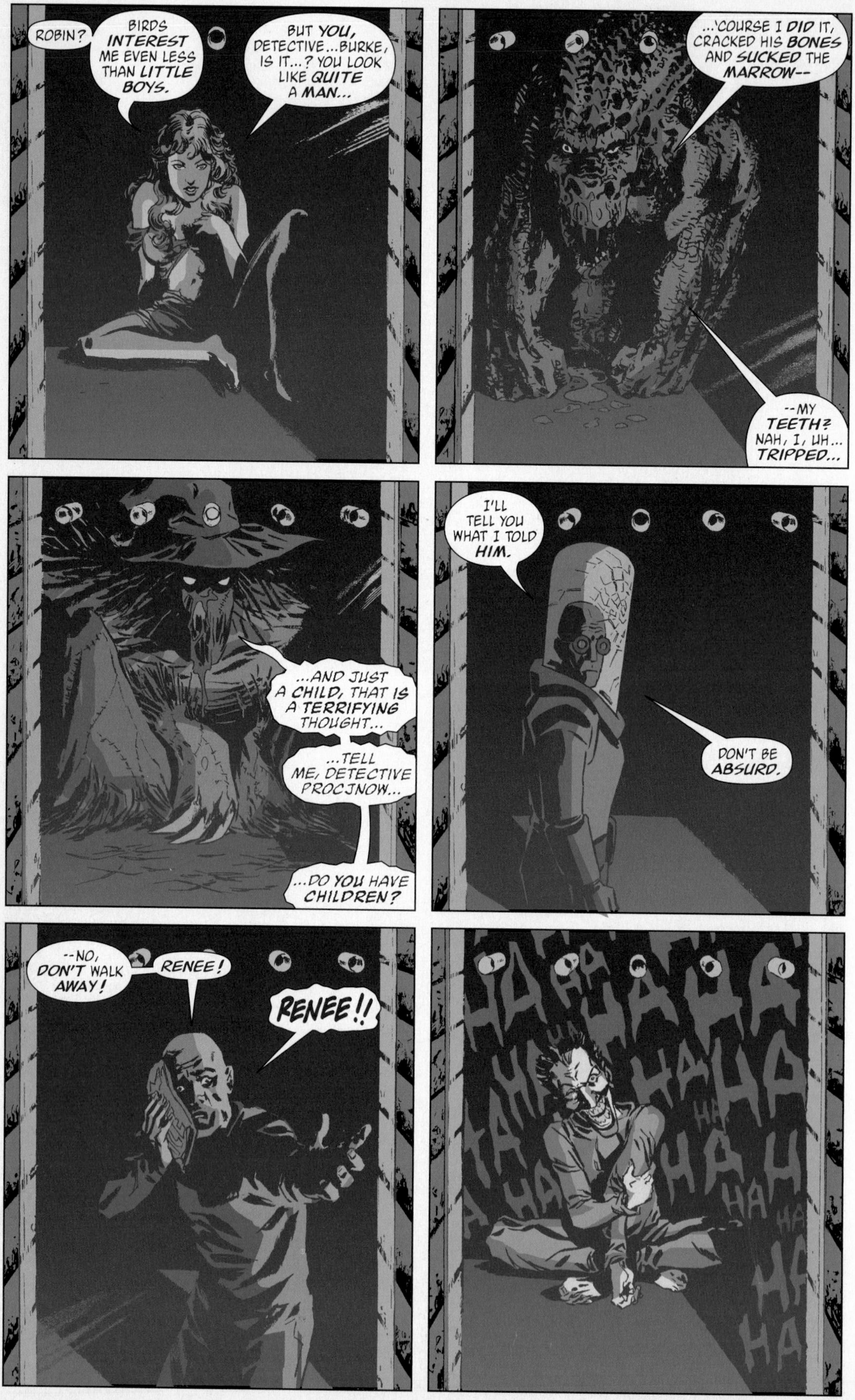
ROBIN?
BIRDS INTEREST ME EVEN LESS THAN LITTLE BOYS.
BUT YOU, DETECTIVE...BURKE, IS IT...? YOU LOOK LIKE QUITE A MAN...
...'COURSE I DID IT, CRACKED HIS BONES AND SUCKED THE MARROW--
--MY TEETH? NAH, I, UH... TRIPPED...
...AND JUST A CHILD, THAT IS A TERRIFYING THOUGHT...
...TELL ME, DETECTIVE PROCJNOW...
...DO YOU HAVE CHILDREN?
I'LL TELL YOU WHAT I TOLD HIM.
DON'T BE ABSURD.
--NO, DON'T WALK AWAY!
RENEE!
RENEE!!
HA HA HA HA HA HA HA HA HA HA HA HA HA HA HA HA HA HA HA HA HA

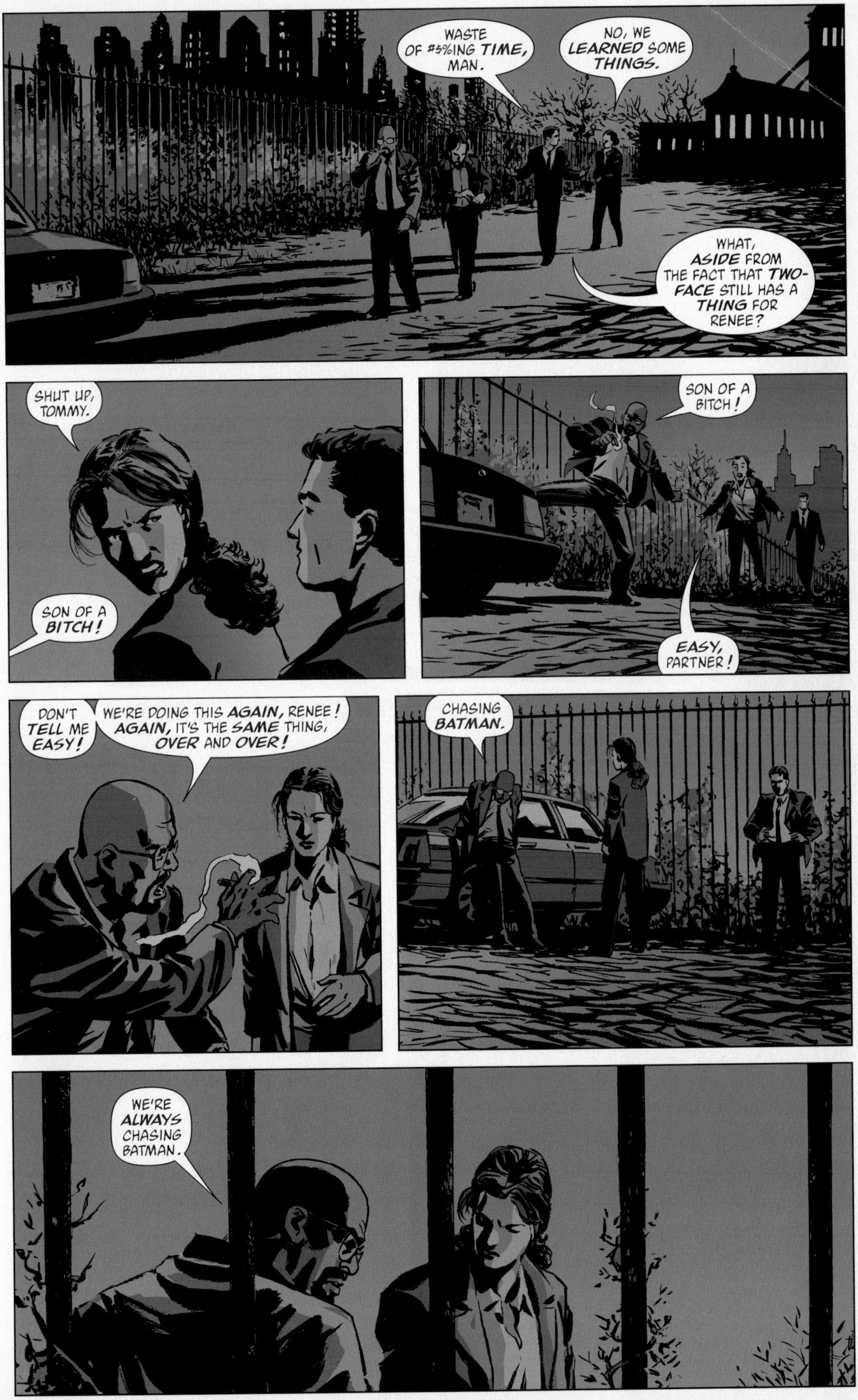
WASTE OF #$%ING TIME, MAN.
NO, WE LEARNED SOME THINGS.
WHAT, ASIDE FROM THE FACT THAT TWO-FACE STILL HAS A THING FOR RENEE?
SHUT UP, TOMMY.
SON OF A BITCH!
SON OF A BITCH!
EASY, PARTNER!
DON'T TELL ME EASY!
WE'RE DOING THIS AGAIN, RENEE! AGAIN, IT'S THE SAME THING, OVER AND OVER!
CHASING BATMAN.
WE'RE ALWAYS CHASING BATMAN.

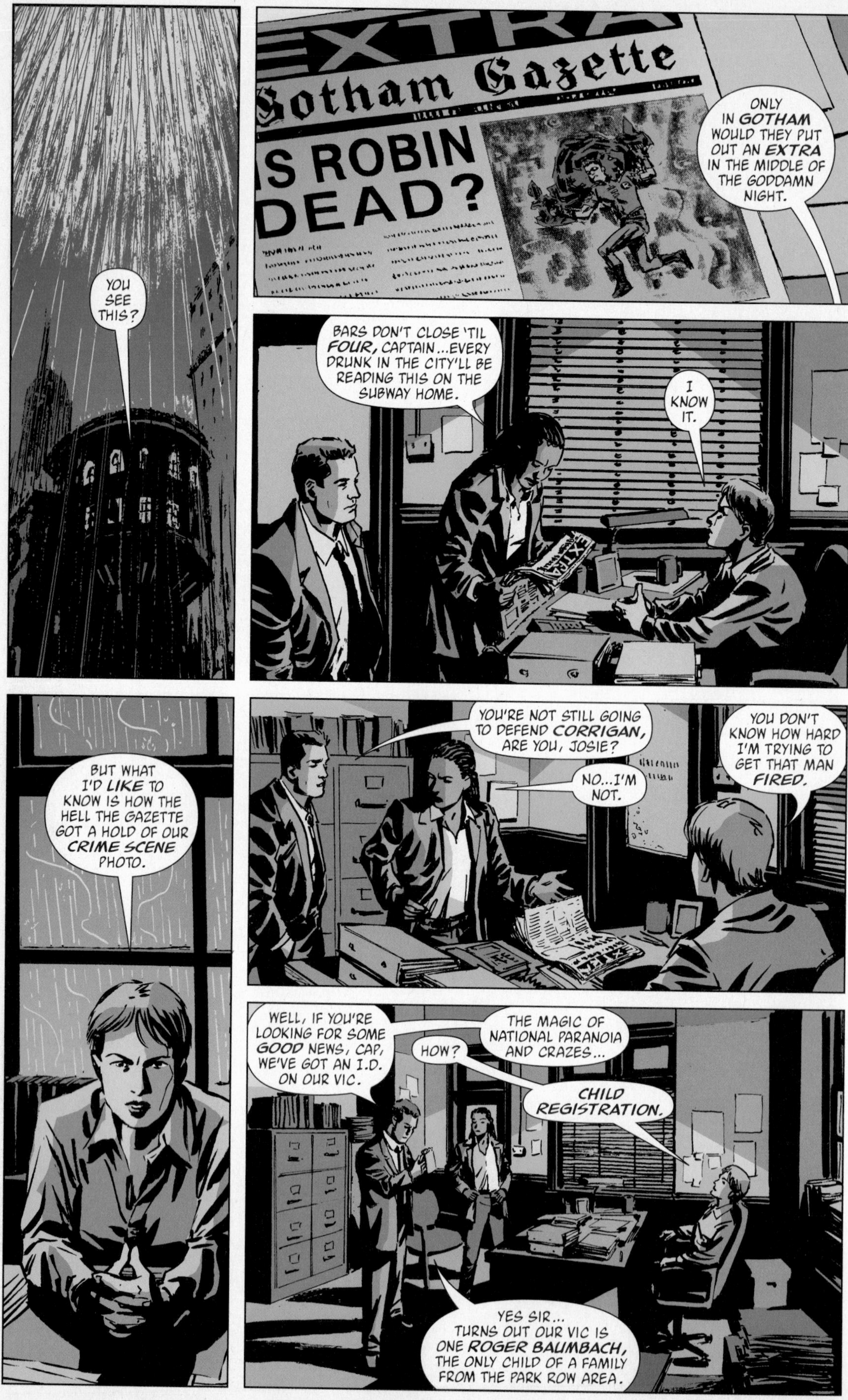

YOU SEE THIS?
EXTRA
Gotham Gazette
IS ROBIN DEAD?
ONLY IN GOTHAM WOULD THEY PUT OUT AN EXTRA IN THE MIDDLE OF THE GODDAMN NIGHT.
BARS DON'T CLOSE 'TIL FOUR, CAPTAIN...EVERY DRUNK IN THE CITY'LL BE READING THIS ON THE SUBWAY HOME.
I KNOW IT.
BUT WHAT I'D LIKE TO KNOW IS HOW THE HELL THE GAZETTE GOT A HOLD OF OUR CRIME SCENE PHOTO.
YOU'RE NOT STILL GOING TO DEFEND CORRIGAN, ARE YOU, JOSIE?
NO...I'M NOT.
YOU DON'T KNOW HOW HARD I'M TRYING TO GET THAT MAN FIRED.
WELL, IF YOU'RE LOOKING FOR SOME GOOD NEWS, CAP, WE'VE GOT AN I.D. ON OUR VIC.
HOW?
THE MAGIC OF NATIONAL PARANOIA AND CRAZES...
CHILD REGISTRATION.
YES SIR... TURNS OUT OUR VIC IS ONE ROGER BAUMBACH, THE ONLY CHILD OF A FAMILY FROM THE PARK ROW AREA.

BUT ACCORDING TO RECORDS THEY'VE ONLY LIVED IN THE CITY LITTLE OVER A YEAR, SO THERE'S *NO WAY* THIS KID IS THE REAL ROBIN.

NO ONE WANTS THAT TO BE TRUE MORE THAN ME, DETECTIVE, BUT WE *CAN'T* MAKE THAT ASSUMPTION.

AS OUR FRIEND SIMON LIPPMAN SO *ELOQUENTLY* POINTS OUT IN THIS ARTICLE, WE HAVE NO WAY OF KNOWING THAT THERE'S ONLY *ONE* ROBIN TO BEGIN WITH.

WHAT, SO ROBIN'S LIKE *LASSIE?*

WE DON'T KNOW, *THAT'S* WHAT I'M SAYING, AND UNTIL WE DO, YOU NEED TO GO TALK TO THE PARENTS OF THE DECEASED...

AND TOMORROW WE'VE GOT TO GET ROBIN'S *KNOWN ASSOCIATES* IN HERE FOR QUESTIONING.

YOU'RE GOING TO HAUL IN A BUNCH OF TEENAGE *SUPER HEROES?* HOW YOU PLANNING TO PULL THAT ONE OFF, CAPTAIN?

I'VE GOT MY WAYS...

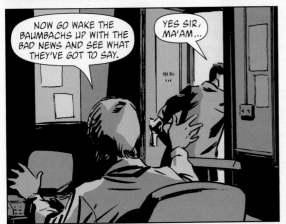

NOW GO WAKE THE BAUMBACHS UP WITH THE BAD NEWS AND SEE WHAT THEY'VE GOT TO SAY.

YES SIR, MA'AM...

LOIS... SORRY TO WAKE YOU. IT'S MAGGIE SAWYER, CALLING FROM GOTHAM.

YEAH, I KNOW, *SORRY...* BUT I NEED A *FAVOR...*

NOW LISTEN, TAKAHATA...I KNOW THIS IS THE PENGUIN'S PLACE, AND HE'S A TOTAL SCUMBAG...BUT LEGALLY, THIS PLACE IS LEGIT.

ICEBERG LOUNGE

SO DON'T GO IN THERE WAVING YOUR GUN AROUND. THIS ISN'T SOME NARCO BUST.

I DID THAT *ONE TIME,* CHANDLER, FOUR *MONTHS* AGO. THINK YOU MIGHT LET IT *DROP* SOMEDAY?

SOMEDAY.

MAYBE.

ANYWAY, I THOUGHT PENGUIN WAS OPERATING OUT OF BLÜDHAVEN THESE DAYS?

HE IS, BUT HE'S STILL GOT THE *ICEBERG,* SO HE'S BACK IN GOTHAM ALL THE TIME. JUST LIKES TO KEEP IT QUIET.

MY SNITCH SAYS HE'S IN TOWN THIS WEEKEND, SO...

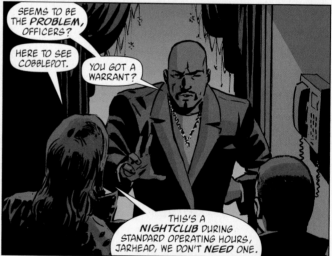

SEEMS TO BE THE *PROBLEM,* OFFICERS?

HERE TO SEE COBBLEPOT.

YOU GOT A WARRANT?

THIS'S A *NIGHTCLUB* DURING STANDARD OPERATING HOURS, JARHEAD, WE DON'T *NEED* ONE.

LEMME CALL AHEAD, ANYWAY.

WHATEVER TURNS YOU ON.

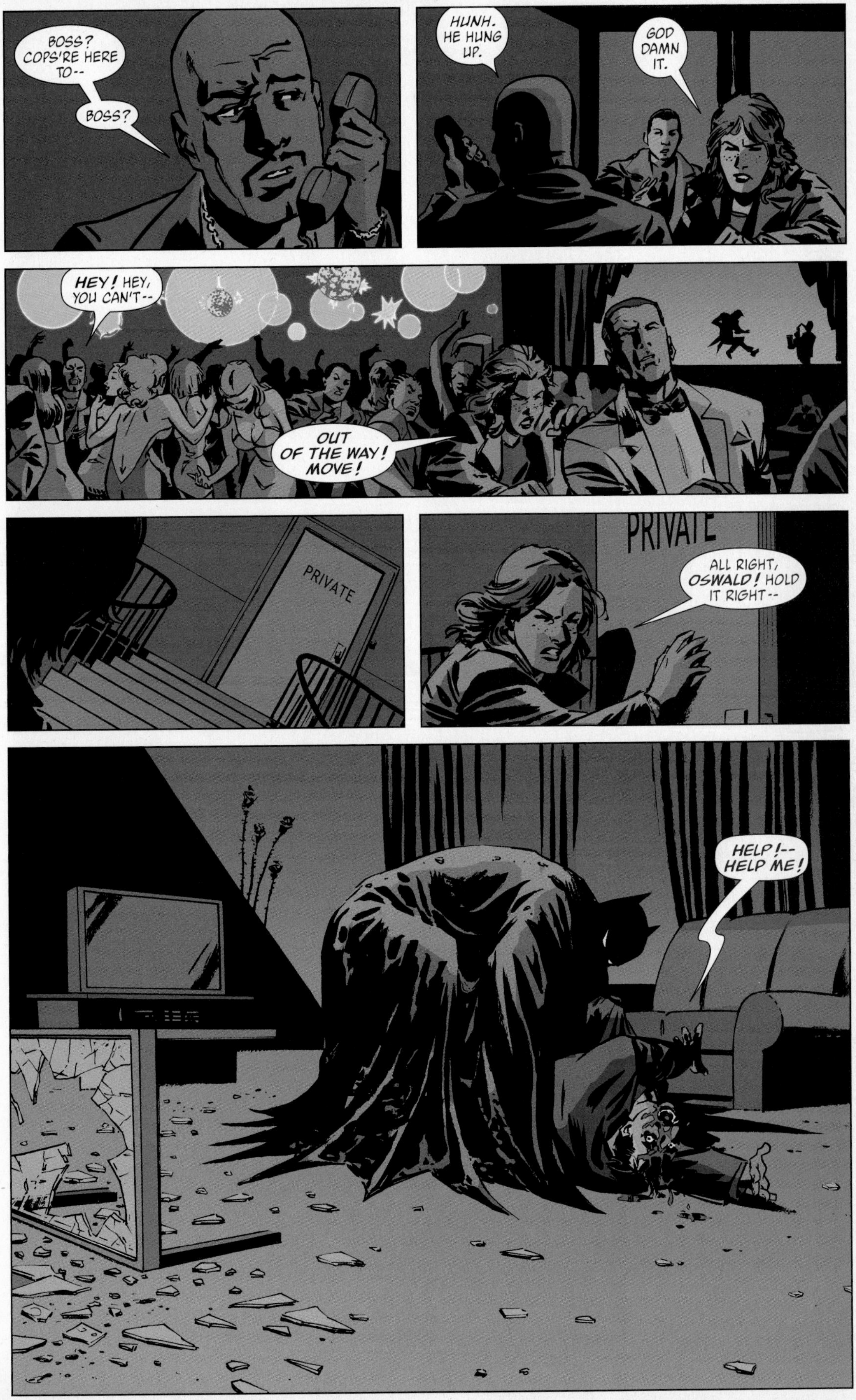
BOSS? COPS'RE HERE TO--
BOSS?
HUNH. HE HUNG UP.
GOD DAMN IT.
HEY! HEY, YOU CAN'T--
OUT OF THE WAY! MOVE!
PRIVATE
PRIVATE
ALL RIGHT, OSWALD! HOLD IT RIGHT--
HELP!-- HELP ME!

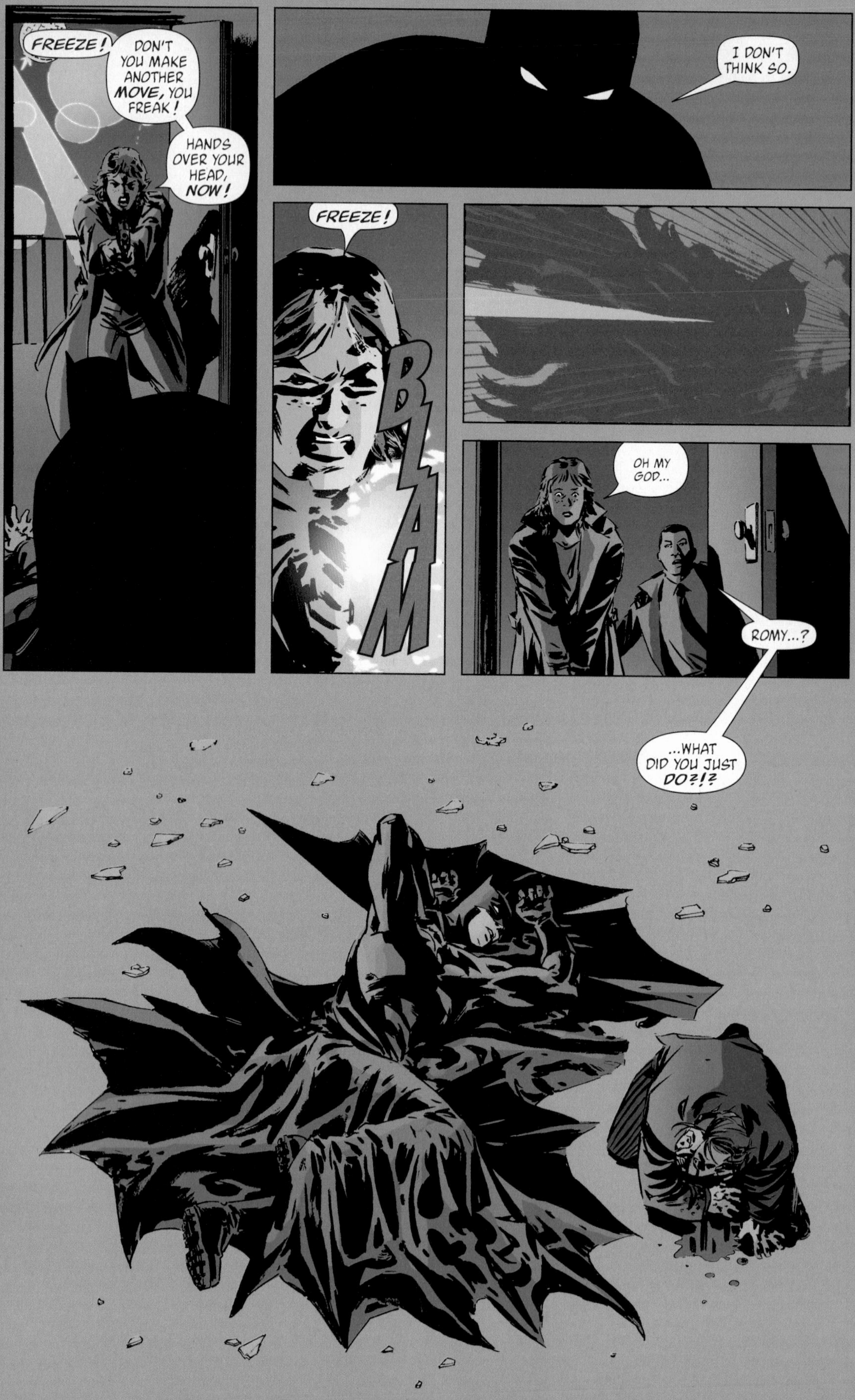
FREEZE!
DON'T YOU MAKE ANOTHER MOVE, YOU FREAK!
HANDS OVER YOUR HEAD, NOW!
I DON'T THINK SO.
FREEZE!
BLAM
OH MY GOD...
ROMY...?
...WHAT DID YOU JUST DO?!?

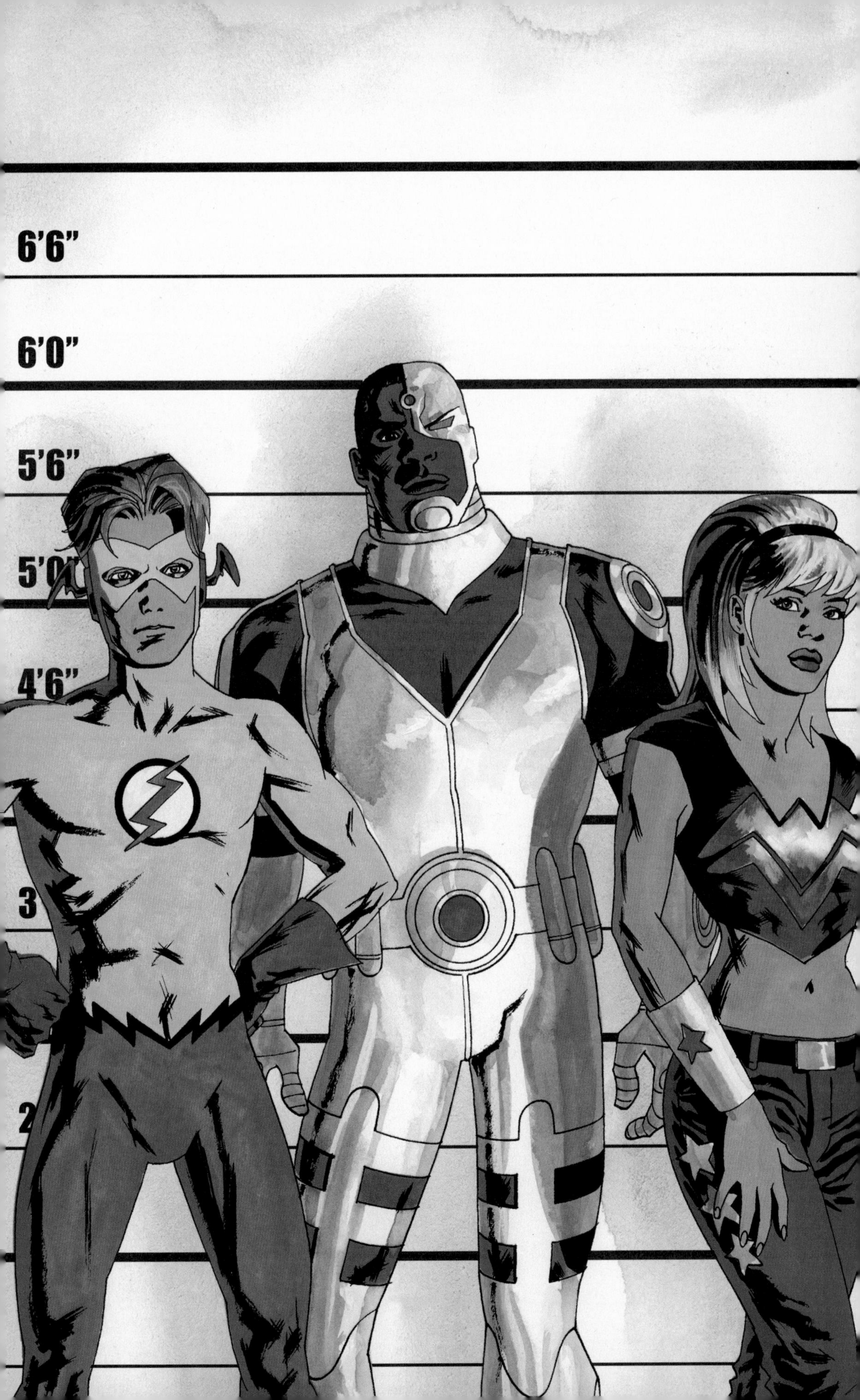
6'6"
6'0"
5'6"
4'6"

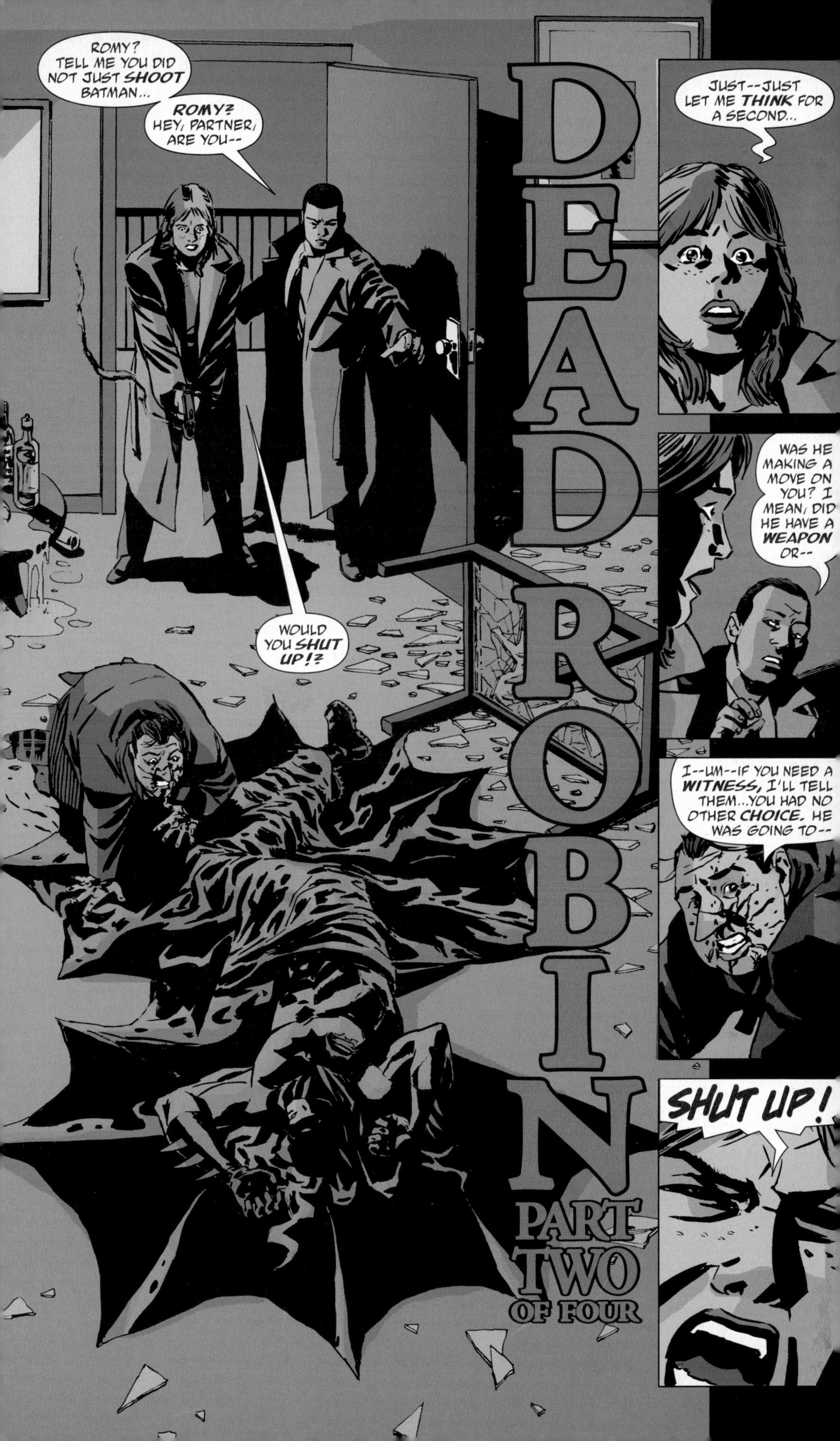
ROMY? TELL ME YOU DID NOT JUST SHOOT BATMAN...
ROMY?! HEY, PARTNER, ARE YOU--
WOULD YOU SHUT UP!?
DEAD ROBIN
PART TWO OF FOUR
JUST--JUST LET ME THINK FOR A SECOND...
WAS HE MAKING A MOVE ON YOU? I MEAN, DID HE HAVE A WEAPON OR--
I--UM--IF YOU NEED A WITNESS, I'LL TELL THEM...YOU HAD NO OTHER CHOICE. HE WAS GOING TO--
SHUT UP!

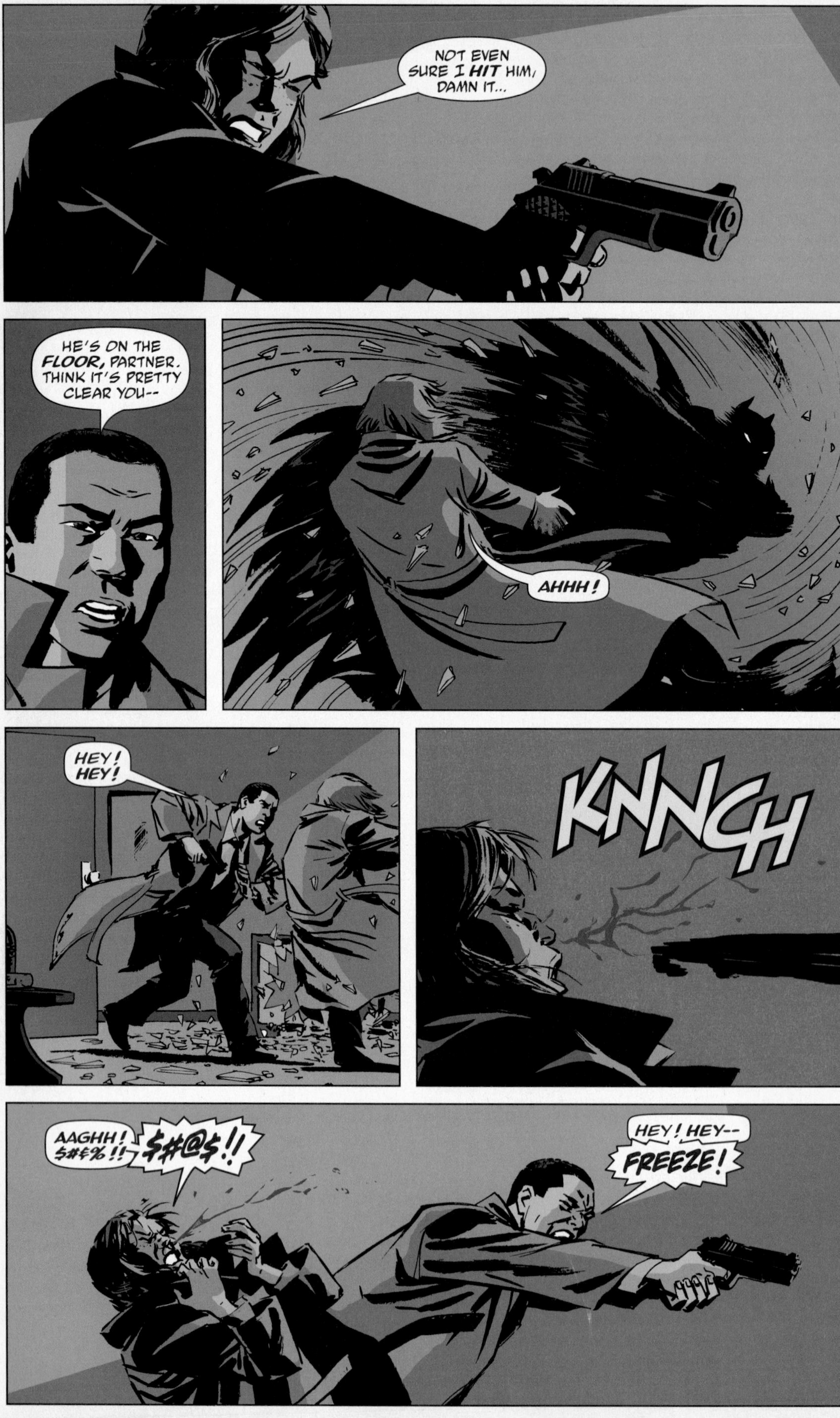
NOT EVEN SURE I HIT HIM, DAMN IT...
HE'S ON THE FLOOR, PARTNER. THINK IT'S PRETTY CLEAR YOU--
AHHH!
HEY! HEY!
KNNCH
AAGHH! $#€% !!
$#@$!!
HEY! HEY--
FREEZE!

#&%! HEY!

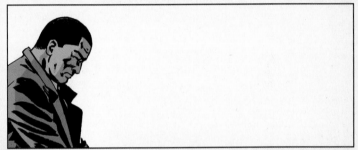

ROMY...LET ME SEE--

LEAVE IT! I'B FINE!

...SHIZ... BY GUN...

WHAT?

THAD BASSARD TOOK BY GUN...

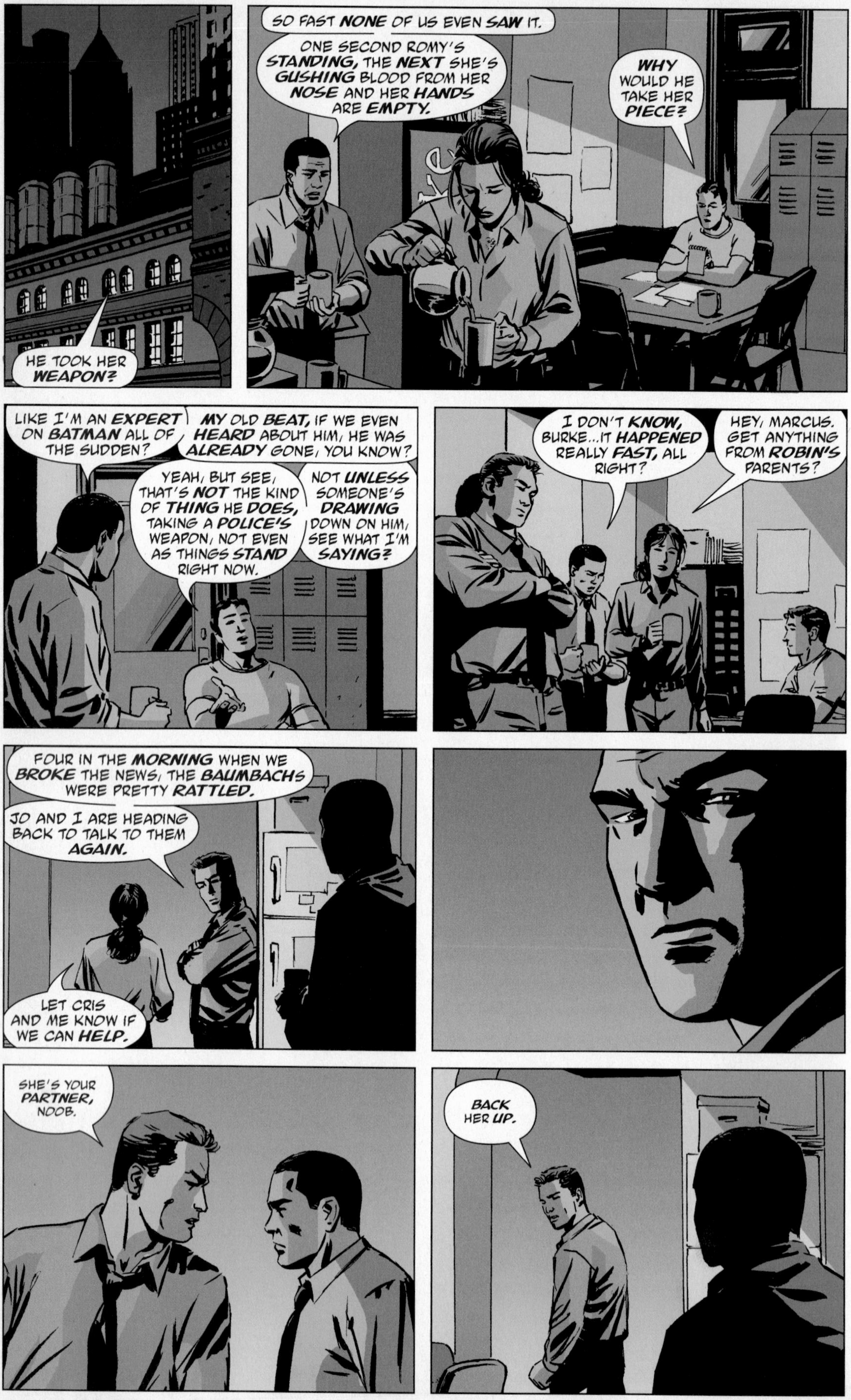
HE TOOK HER WEAPON?
SO FAST NONE OF US EVEN SAW IT.
ONE SECOND ROMY'S STANDING, THE NEXT SHE'S GUSHING BLOOD FROM HER NOSE AND HER HANDS ARE EMPTY.
WHY WOULD HE TAKE HER PIECE?
LIKE I'M AN EXPERT ON BATMAN ALL OF THE SUDDEN?
MY OLD BEAT, IF WE EVEN HEARD ABOUT HIM, HE WAS ALREADY GONE, YOU KNOW?
YEAH, BUT SEE, THAT'S NOT THE KIND OF THING HE DOES, TAKING A POLICE'S WEAPON, NOT EVEN AS THINGS STAND RIGHT NOW.
NOT UNLESS SOMEONE'S DRAWING DOWN ON HIM, SEE WHAT I'M SAYING?
I DON'T KNOW, BURKE...IT HAPPENED REALLY FAST, ALL RIGHT?
HEY, MARCUS. GET ANYTHING FROM ROBIN'S PARENTS?
FOUR IN THE MORNING WHEN WE BROKE THE NEWS, THE BAUMBACHS WERE PRETTY RATTLED.
JO AND I ARE HEADING BACK TO TALK TO THEM AGAIN.
LET CRIS AND ME KNOW IF WE CAN HELP.
SHE'S YOUR PARTNER, NOOB.
BACK HER UP.

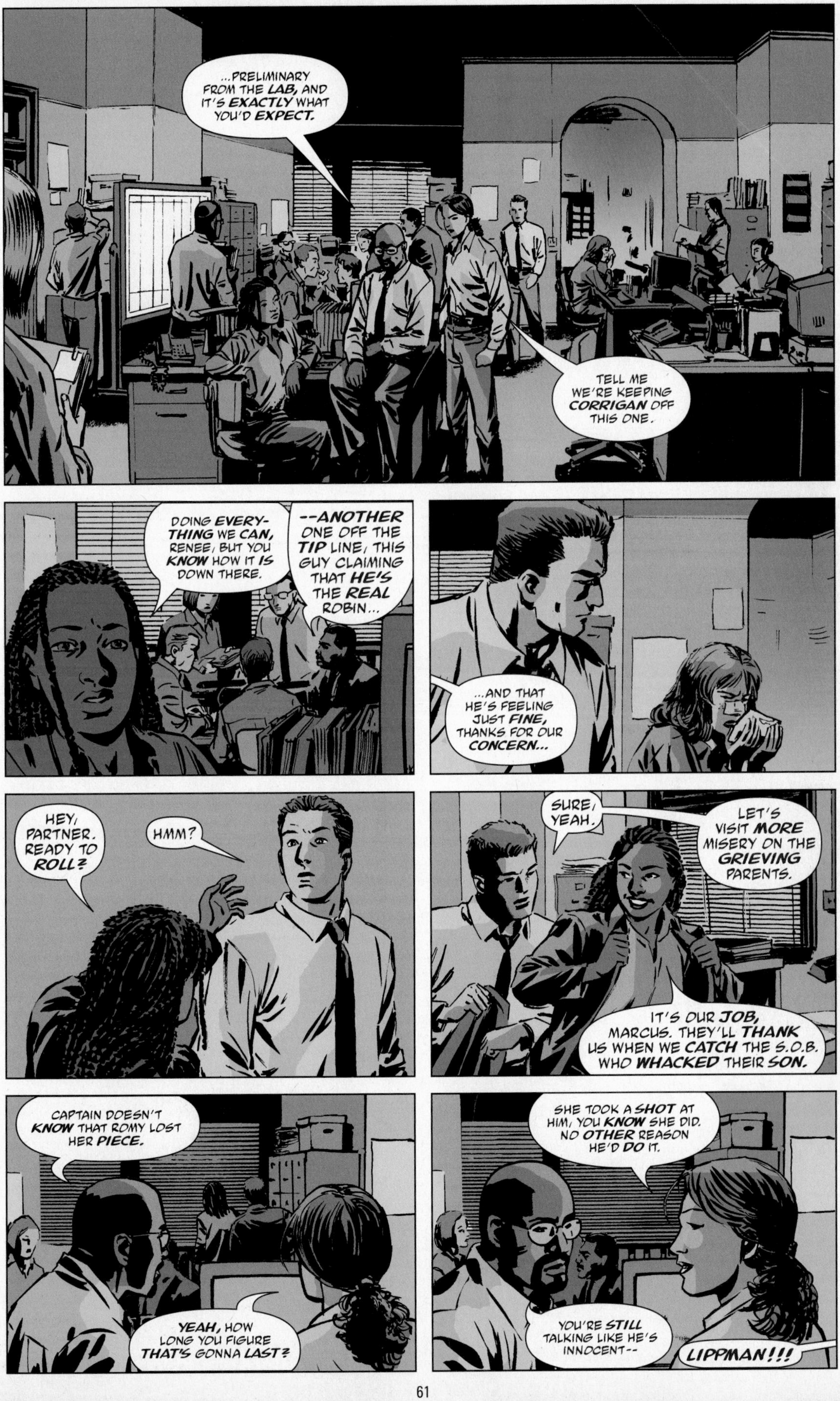

...PRELIMINARY FROM THE LAB, AND IT'S EXACTLY WHAT YOU'D EXPECT.
TELL ME WE'RE KEEPING CORRIGAN OFF THIS ONE.
DOING EVERY-THING WE CAN, RENEE, BUT YOU KNOW HOW IT IS DOWN THERE.
--ANOTHER ONE OFF THE TIP LINE, THIS GUY CLAIMING THAT HE'S THE REAL ROBIN...
...AND THAT HE'S FEELING JUST FINE, THANKS FOR OUR CONCERN...
HEY, PARTNER. READY TO ROLL?
HMM?
SURE, YEAH.
LET'S VISIT MORE MISERY ON THE GRIEVING PARENTS.
IT'S OUR JOB, MARCUS. THEY'LL THANK US WHEN WE CATCH THE S.O.B. WHO WHACKED THEIR SON.
CAPTAIN DOESN'T KNOW THAT ROMY LOST HER PIECE.
YEAH, HOW LONG YOU FIGURE THAT'S GONNA LAST?
SHE TOOK A SHOT AT HIM, YOU KNOW SHE DID. NO OTHER REASON HE'D DO IT.
YOU'RE STILL TALKING LIKE HE'S INNOCENT--
LIPPMAN!!!

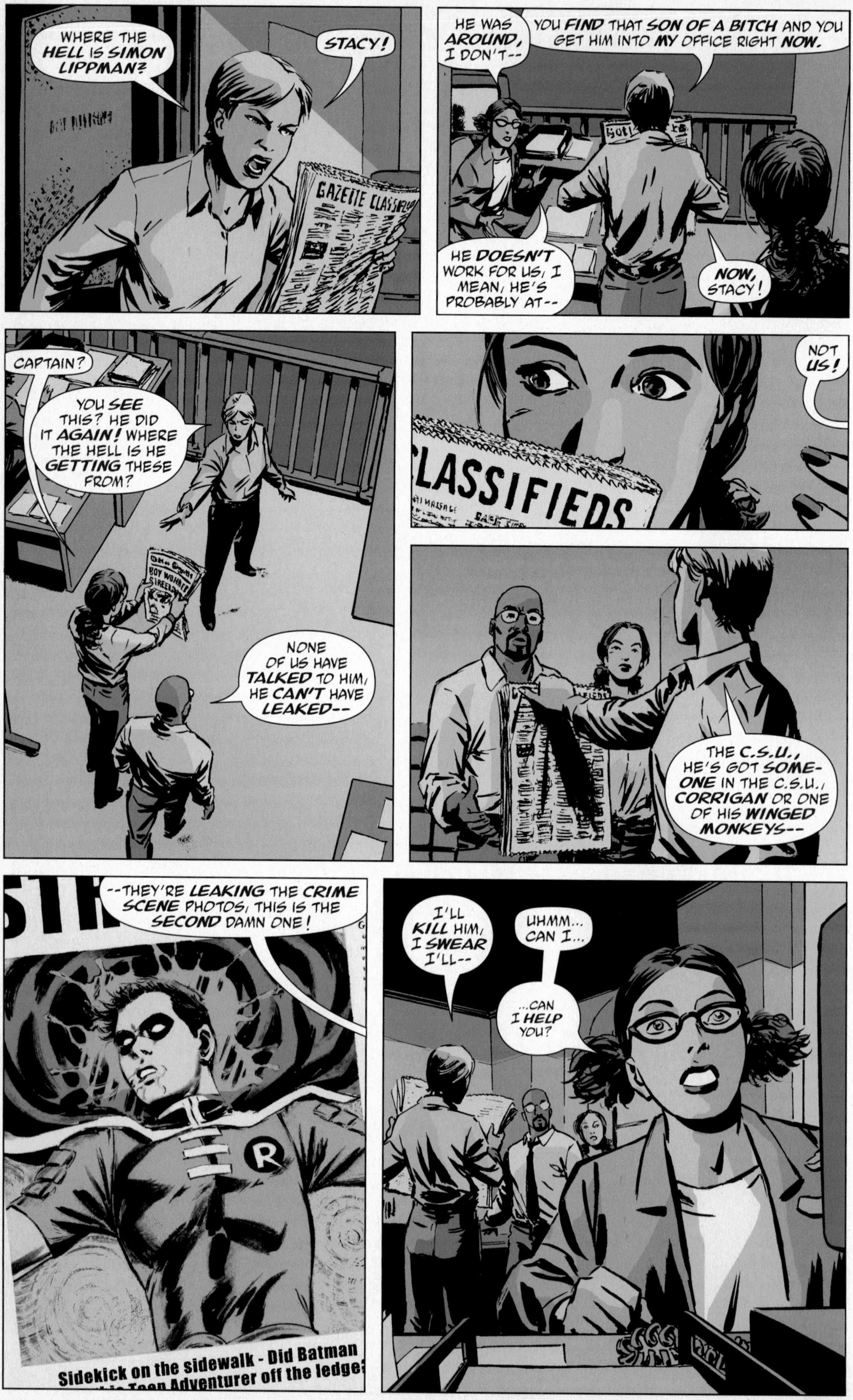
WHERE THE HELL IS SIMON LIPPMAN?
STACY!
GAZETTE CLASSIFIEDS
HE WAS AROUND, I DON'T--
YOU FIND THAT SON OF A BITCH AND YOU GET HIM INTO MY OFFICE RIGHT NOW.
HE DOESN'T WORK FOR US, I MEAN, HE'S PROBABLY AT--
NOW, STACY!
CAPTAIN?
YOU SEE THIS? HE DID IT AGAIN! WHERE THE HELL IS HE GETTING THESE FROM?
BOY WONDER STREET
NONE OF US HAVE TALKED TO HIM, HE CAN'T HAVE LEAKED--
NOT US!
CLASSIFIEDS
THE C.S.U., HE'S GOT SOMEONE IN THE C.S.U., CORRIGAN OR ONE OF HIS WINGED MONKEYS--
--THEY'RE LEAKING THE CRIME SCENE PHOTOS, THIS IS THE SECOND DAMN ONE!
Sidekick on the sidewalk - Did Batman
I'LL KILL HIM, I SWEAR I'LL--
UHMM... CAN I...
...CAN I HELP YOU?

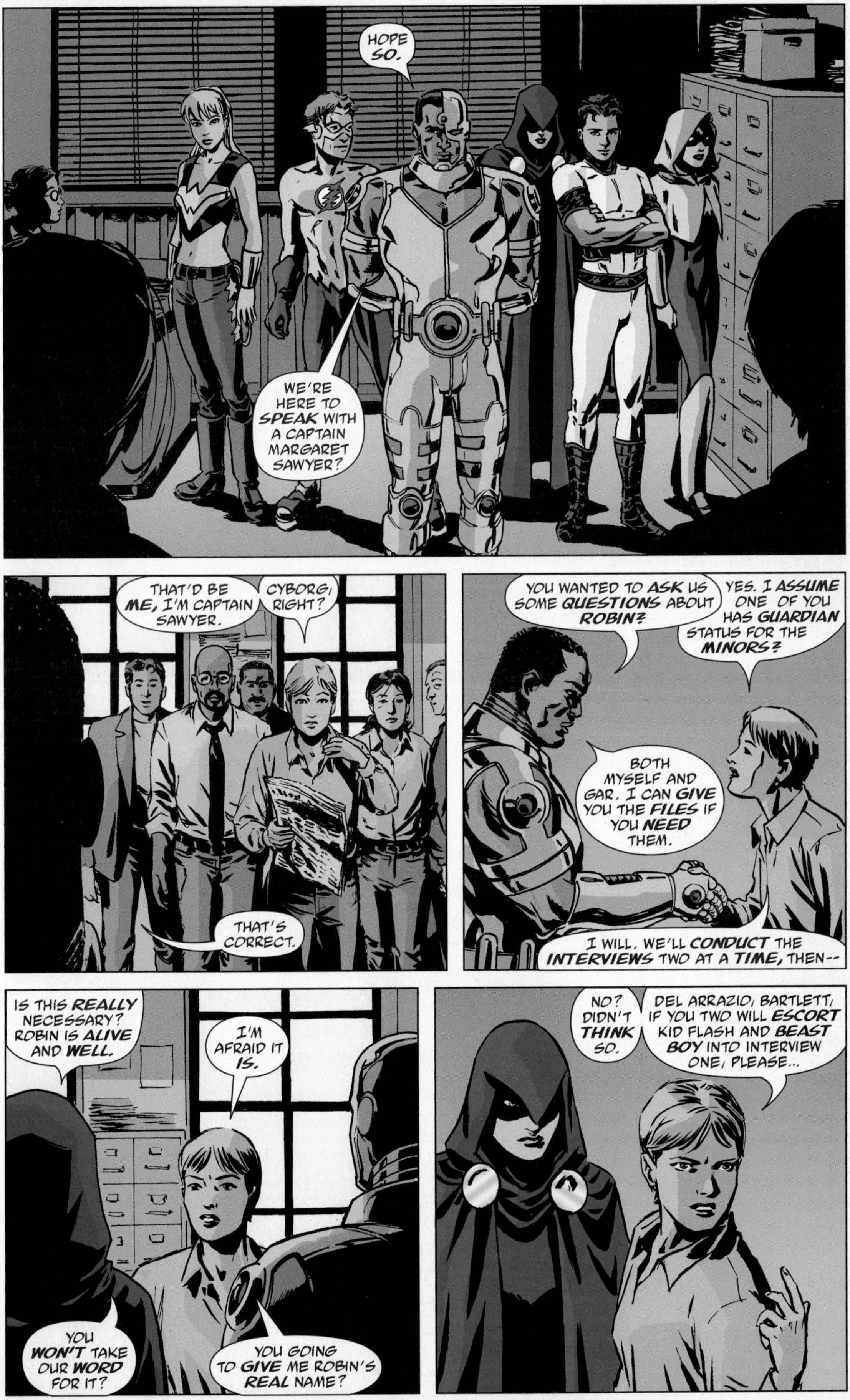
HOPE SO.
WE'RE HERE TO SPEAK WITH A CAPTAIN MARGARET SAWYER?
THAT'D BE ME, I'M CAPTAIN SAWYER.
CYBORG, RIGHT?
THAT'S CORRECT.
YOU WANTED TO ASK US SOME QUESTIONS ABOUT ROBIN?
YES. I ASSUME ONE OF YOU HAS GUARDIAN STATUS FOR THE MINORS?
BOTH MYSELF AND GAR. I CAN GIVE YOU THE FILES IF YOU NEED THEM.
I WILL. WE'LL CONDUCT THE INTERVIEWS TWO AT A TIME, THEN--
IS THIS REALLY NECESSARY? ROBIN IS ALIVE AND WELL.
I'M AFRAID IT IS.
YOU WON'T TAKE OUR WORD FOR IT?
YOU GOING TO GIVE ME ROBIN'S REAL NAME?
NO? DIDN'T THINK SO.
DEL ARRAZIO, BARTLETT, IF YOU TWO WILL ESCORT KID FLASH AND BEAST BOY INTO INTERVIEW ONE, PLEASE...

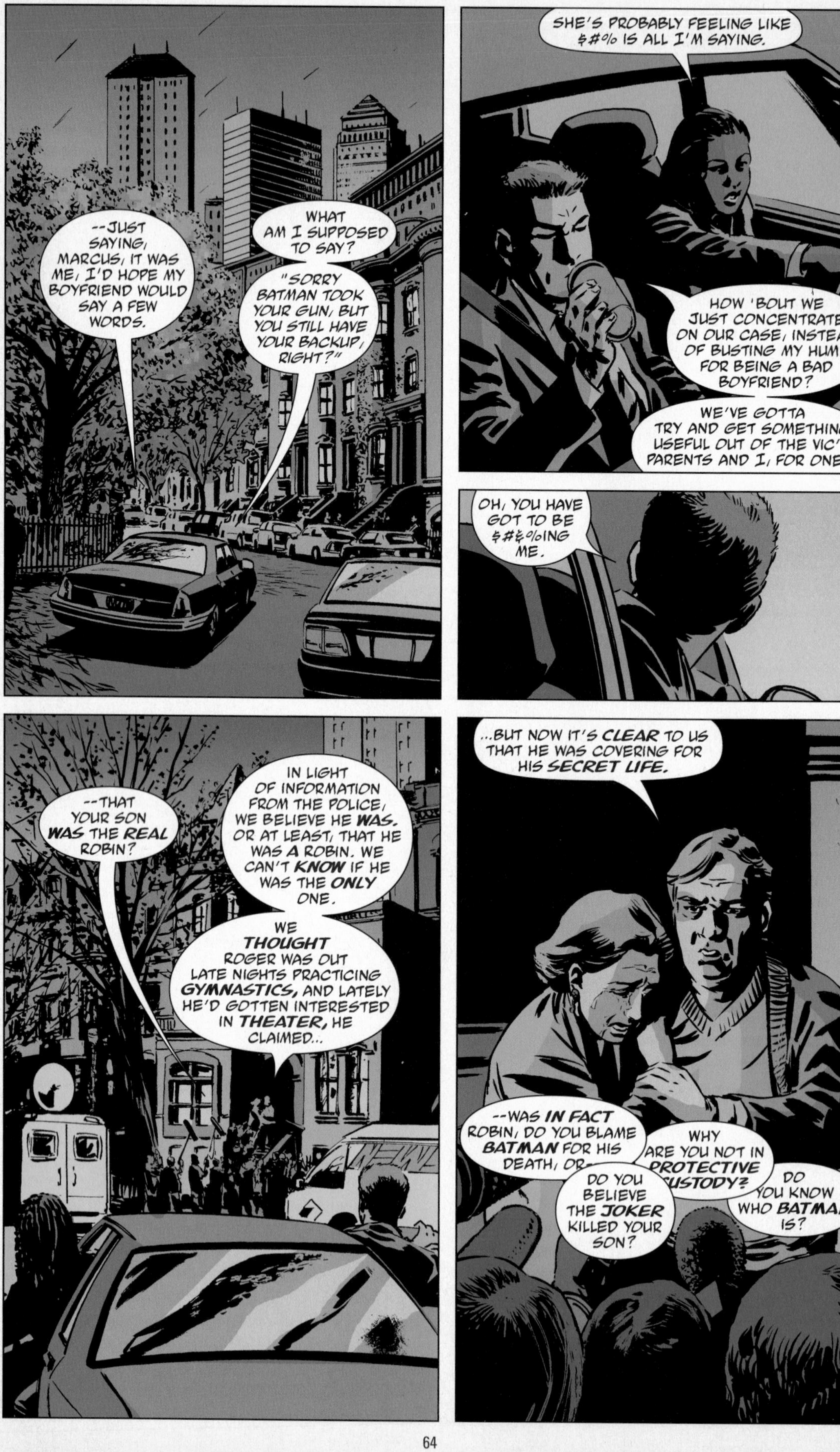
--JUST SAYING, MARCUS, IT WAS ME, I'D HOPE MY BOYFRIEND WOULD SAY A FEW WORDS.
WHAT AM I SUPPOSED TO SAY?
"SORRY BATMAN TOOK YOUR GUN, BUT YOU STILL HAVE YOUR BACKUP, RIGHT?"
SHE'S PROBABLY FEELING LIKE $#% IS ALL I'M SAYING.
HOW 'BOUT WE JUST CONCENTRATE ON OUR CASE, INSTEAD OF BUSTING MY HUMP FOR BEING A BAD BOYFRIEND?
WE'VE GOTTA TRY AND GET SOMETHING USEFUL OUT OF THE VIC'S PARENTS AND I, FOR ONE--
OH, YOU HAVE GOT TO BE $#&%ING ME.
--THAT YOUR SON WAS THE REAL ROBIN?
IN LIGHT OF INFORMATION FROM THE POLICE, WE BELIEVE HE WAS. OR AT LEAST, THAT HE WAS A ROBIN. WE CAN'T KNOW IF HE WAS THE ONLY ONE.
WE THOUGHT ROGER WAS OUT LATE NIGHTS PRACTICING GYMNASTICS, AND LATELY HE'D GOTTEN INTERESTED IN THEATER, HE CLAIMED...
...BUT NOW IT'S CLEAR TO US THAT HE WAS COVERING FOR HIS SECRET LIFE.
--WAS IN FACT ROBIN, DO YOU BLAME BATMAN FOR HIS DEATH, OR--
WHY ARE YOU NOT IN PROTECTIVE CUSTODY?
DO YOU BELIEVE THE JOKER KILLED YOUR SON?
DO YOU KNOW WHO BATMAN IS?

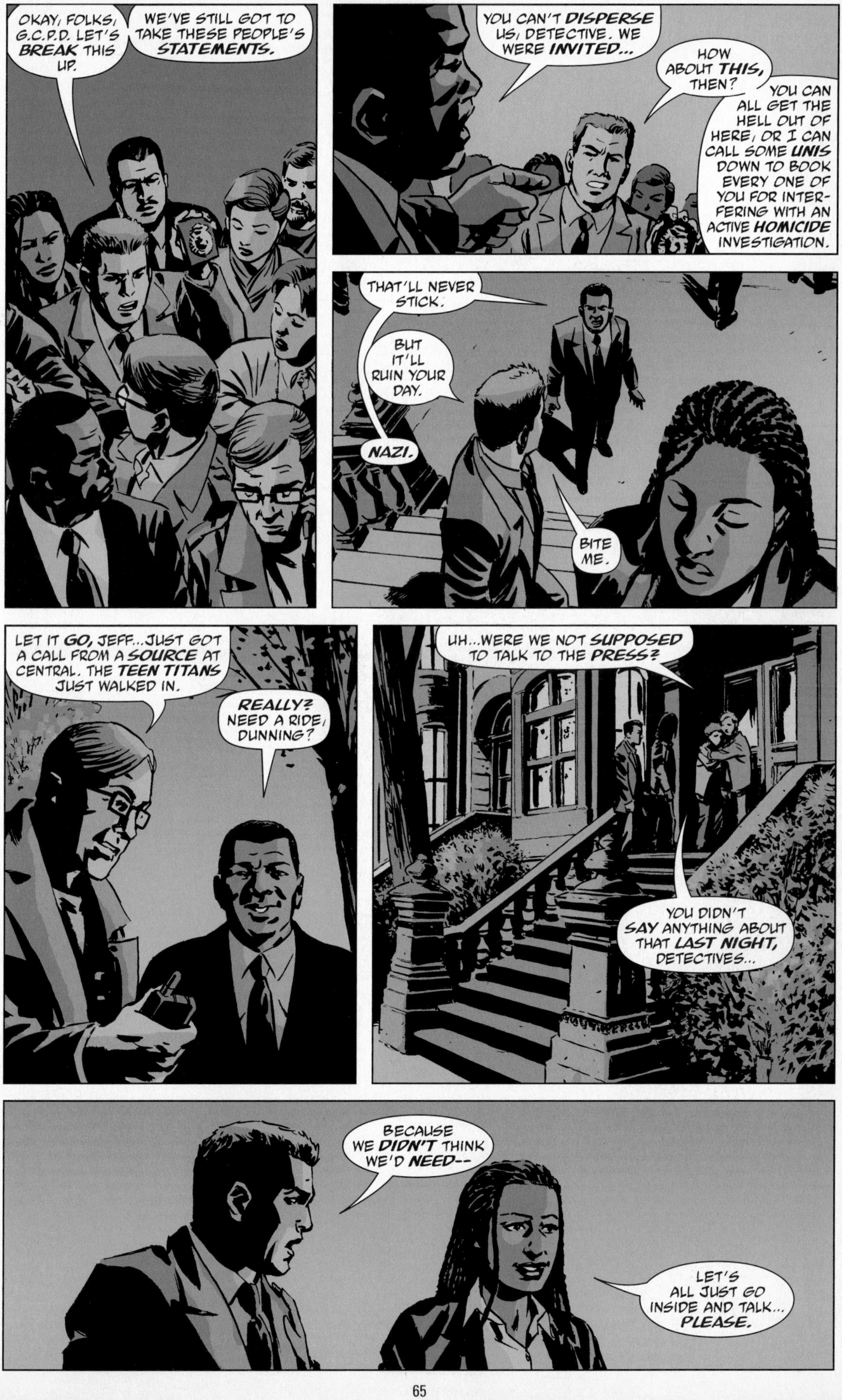
OKAY, FOLKS, G.C.P.D. LET'S BREAK THIS UP.
WE'VE STILL GOT TO TAKE THESE PEOPLE'S STATEMENTS.
YOU CAN'T DISPERSE US, DETECTIVE. WE WERE INVITED...
HOW ABOUT THIS, THEN?
YOU CAN ALL GET THE HELL OUT OF HERE, OR I CAN CALL SOME UNIS DOWN TO BOOK EVERY ONE OF YOU FOR INTERFERING WITH AN ACTIVE HOMICIDE INVESTIGATION.
THAT'LL NEVER STICK.
BUT IT'LL RUIN YOUR DAY.
NAZI.
BITE ME.
LET IT GO, JEFF...JUST GOT A CALL FROM A SOURCE AT CENTRAL. THE TEEN TITANS JUST WALKED IN.
REALLY? NEED A RIDE, DUNNING?
UH...WERE WE NOT SUPPOSED TO TALK TO THE PRESS?
YOU DIDN'T SAY ANYTHING ABOUT THAT LAST NIGHT, DETECTIVES...
BECAUSE WE DIDN'T THINK WE'D NEED--
LET'S ALL JUST GO INSIDE AND TALK... PLEASE.

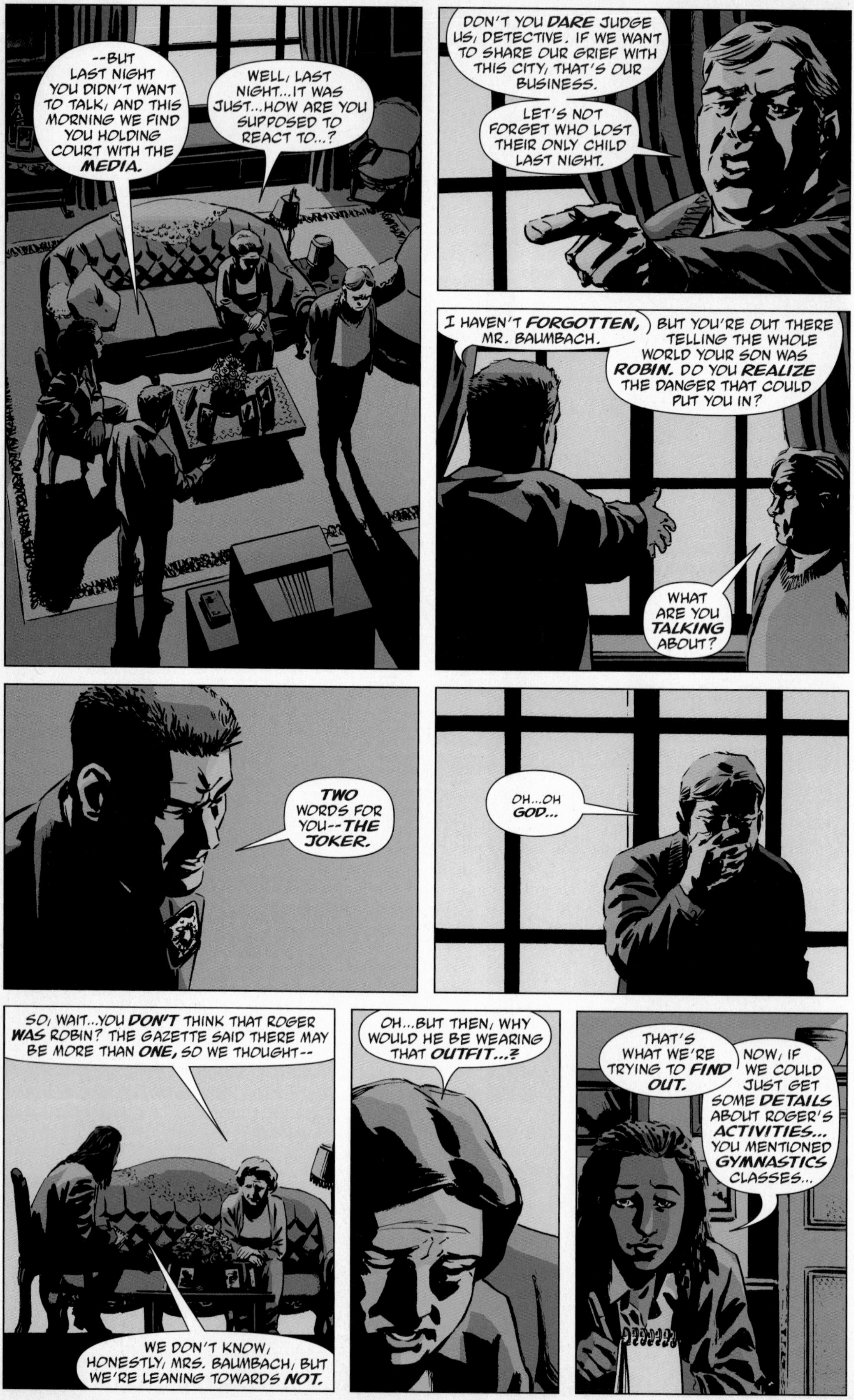
--BUT LAST NIGHT YOU DIDN'T WANT TO TALK, AND THIS MORNING WE FIND YOU HOLDING COURT WITH THE MEDIA.
WELL, LAST NIGHT...IT WAS JUST...HOW ARE YOU SUPPOSED TO REACT TO...?
DON'T YOU DARE JUDGE US, DETECTIVE. IF WE WANT TO SHARE OUR GRIEF WITH THIS CITY, THAT'S OUR BUSINESS.
LET'S NOT FORGET WHO LOST THEIR ONLY CHILD LAST NIGHT.
I HAVEN'T FORGOTTEN, MR. BAUMBACH.
BUT YOU'RE OUT THERE TELLING THE WHOLE WORLD YOUR SON WAS ROBIN. DO YOU REALIZE THE DANGER THAT COULD PUT YOU IN?
WHAT ARE YOU TALKING ABOUT?
TWO WORDS FOR YOU--THE JOKER.
OH...OH GOD...
SO, WAIT...YOU DON'T THINK THAT ROGER WAS ROBIN? THE GAZETTE SAID THERE MAY BE MORE THAN ONE, SO WE THOUGHT--
WE DON'T KNOW, HONESTLY, MRS. BAUMBACH, BUT WE'RE LEANING TOWARDS NOT.
OH...BUT THEN, WHY WOULD HE BE WEARING THAT OUTFIT...?
THAT'S WHAT WE'RE TRYING TO FIND OUT.
NOW, IF WE COULD JUST GET SOME DETAILS ABOUT ROGER'S ACTIVITIES... YOU MENTIONED GYMNASTICS CLASSES...

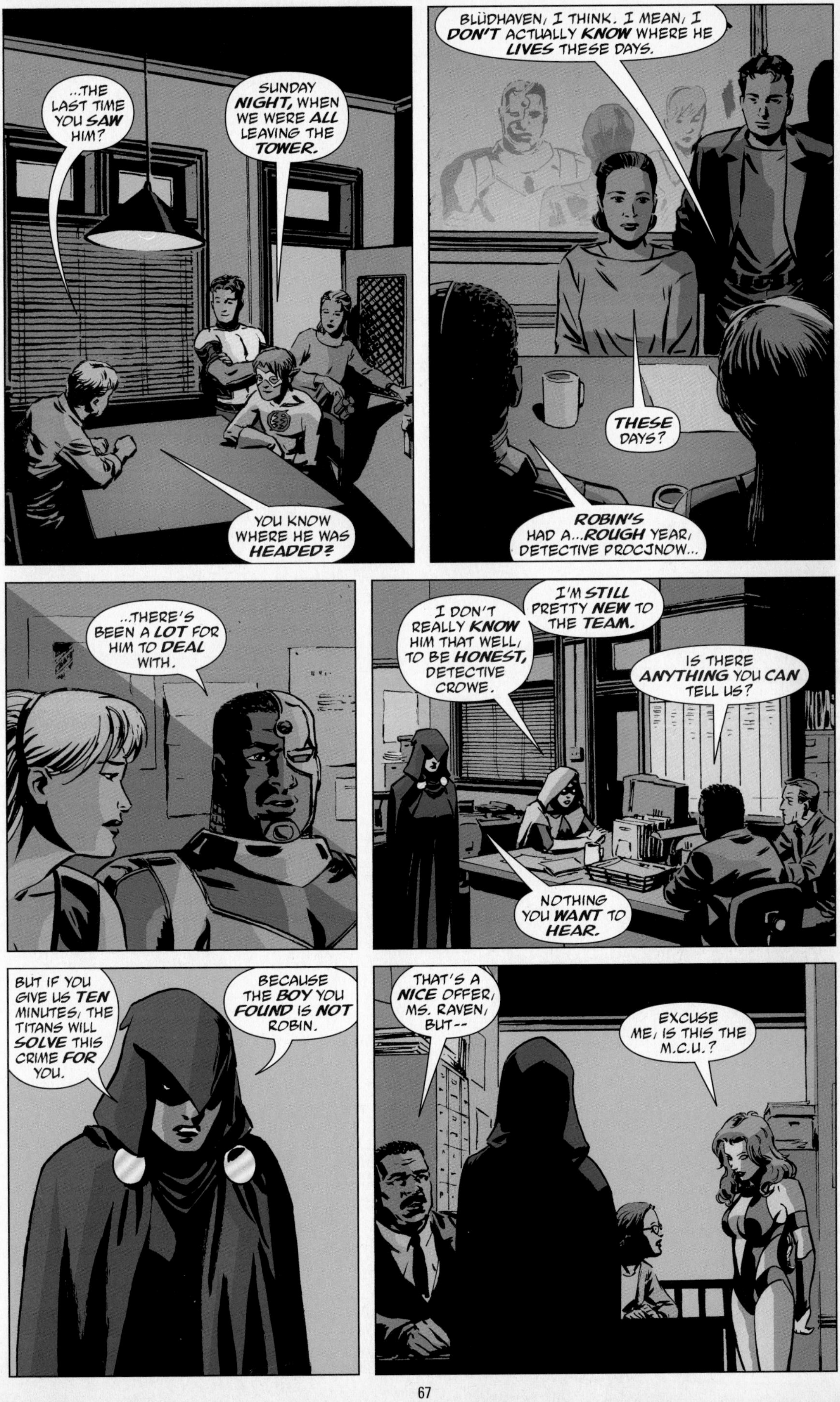
...THE LAST TIME YOU SAW HIM?
SUNDAY NIGHT, WHEN WE WERE ALL LEAVING THE TOWER.
YOU KNOW WHERE HE WAS HEADED?
BLÜDHAVEN, I THINK. I MEAN, I DON'T ACTUALLY KNOW WHERE HE LIVES THESE DAYS.
THESE DAYS?
ROBIN'S HAD A...ROUGH YEAR, DETECTIVE PROCJNOW...
...THERE'S BEEN A LOT FOR HIM TO DEAL WITH.
I DON'T REALLY KNOW HIM THAT WELL, TO BE HONEST, DETECTIVE CROWE.
I'M STILL PRETTY NEW TO THE TEAM.
IS THERE ANYTHING YOU CAN TELL US?
NOTHING YOU WANT TO HEAR.
BECAUSE THE BOY YOU FOUND IS NOT ROBIN.
BUT IF YOU GIVE US TEN MINUTES, THE TITANS WILL SOLVE THIS CRIME FOR YOU.
THAT'S A NICE OFFER, MS. RAVEN, BUT--
EXCUSE ME, IS THIS THE M.C.U.?

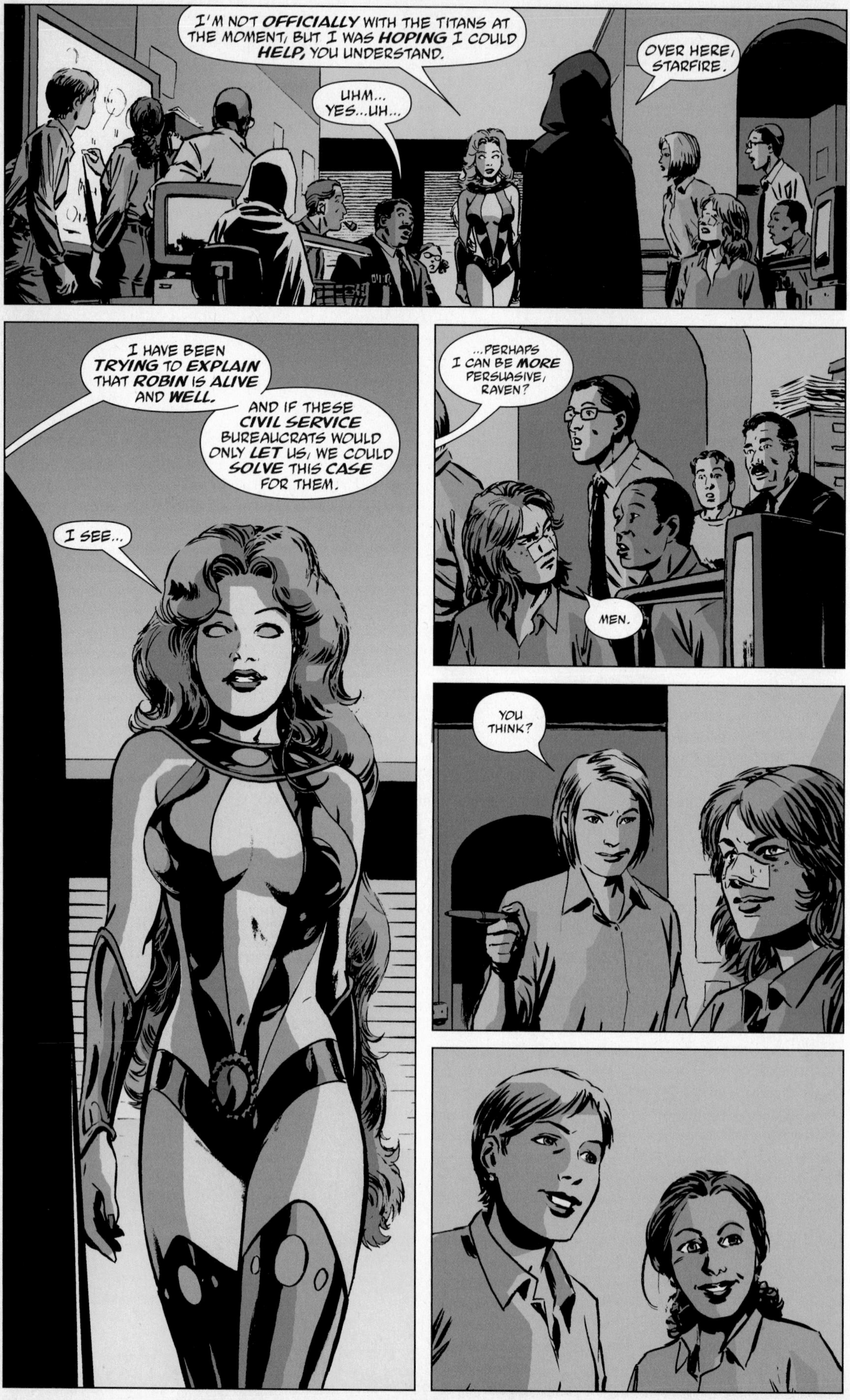
I'M NOT OFFICIALLY WITH THE TITANS AT THE MOMENT, BUT I WAS HOPING I COULD HELP, YOU UNDERSTAND.
UHM... YES...UH...
OVER HERE, STARFIRE.
I HAVE BEEN TRYING TO EXPLAIN THAT ROBIN IS ALIVE AND WELL.
AND IF THESE CIVIL SERVICE BUREAUCRATS WOULD ONLY LET US, WE COULD SOLVE THIS CASE FOR THEM.
I SEE...
...PERHAPS I CAN BE MORE PERSUASIVE, RAVEN?
MEN.
YOU THINK?

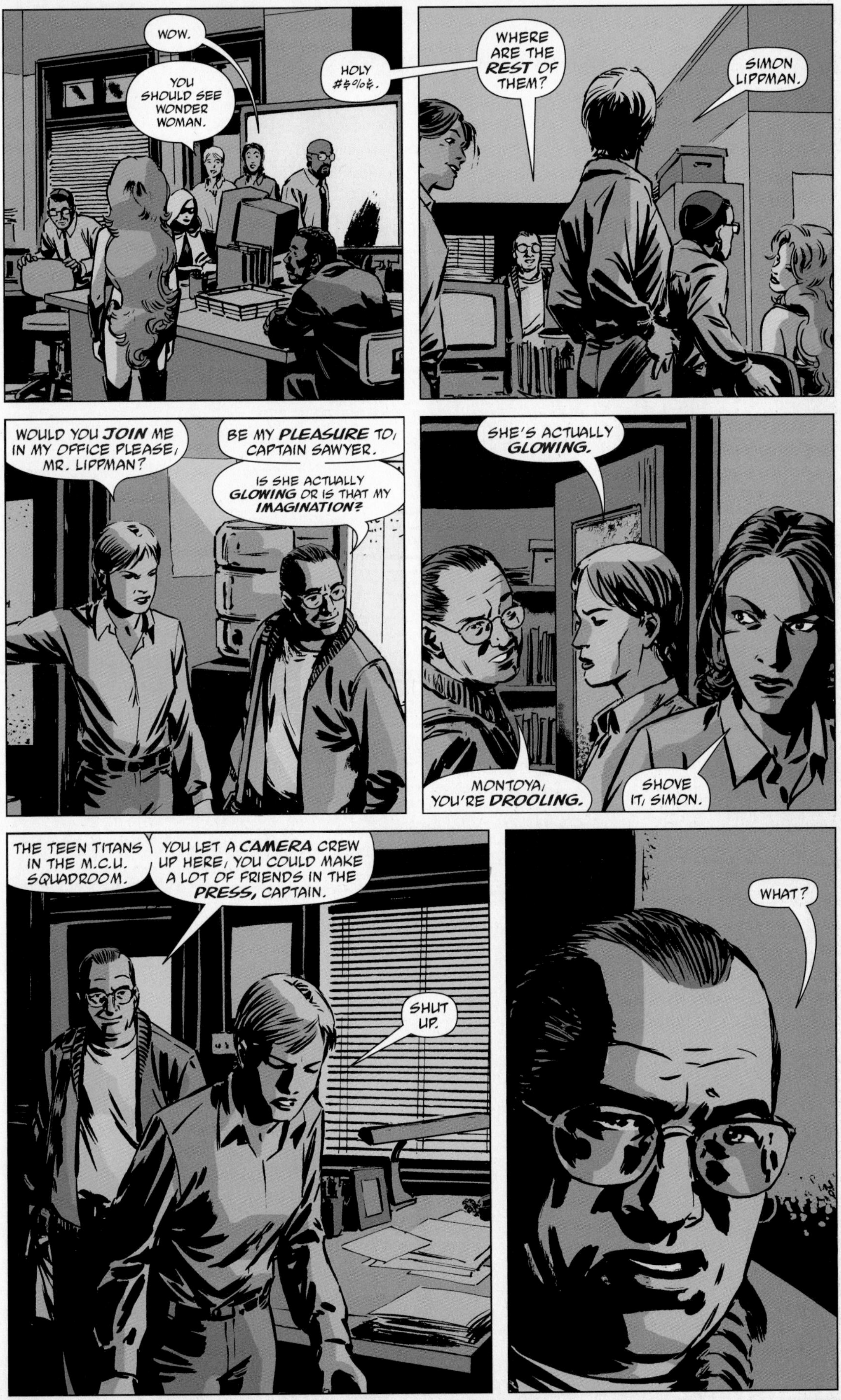
WOW.
YOU SHOULD SEE WONDER WOMAN.
HOLY #$%&.
WHERE ARE THE REST OF THEM?
SIMON LIPPMAN.
WOULD YOU JOIN ME IN MY OFFICE PLEASE, MR. LIPPMAN?
BE MY PLEASURE TO, CAPTAIN SAWYER.
IS SHE ACTUALLY GLOWING OR IS THAT MY IMAGINATION?
SHE'S ACTUALLY GLOWING.
MONTOYA, YOU'RE DROOLING.
SHOVE IT, SIMON.
THE TEEN TITANS IN THE M.C.U. SQUADROOM.
YOU LET A CAMERA CREW UP HERE, YOU COULD MAKE A LOT OF FRIENDS IN THE PRESS, CAPTAIN.
SHUT UP.
WHAT?

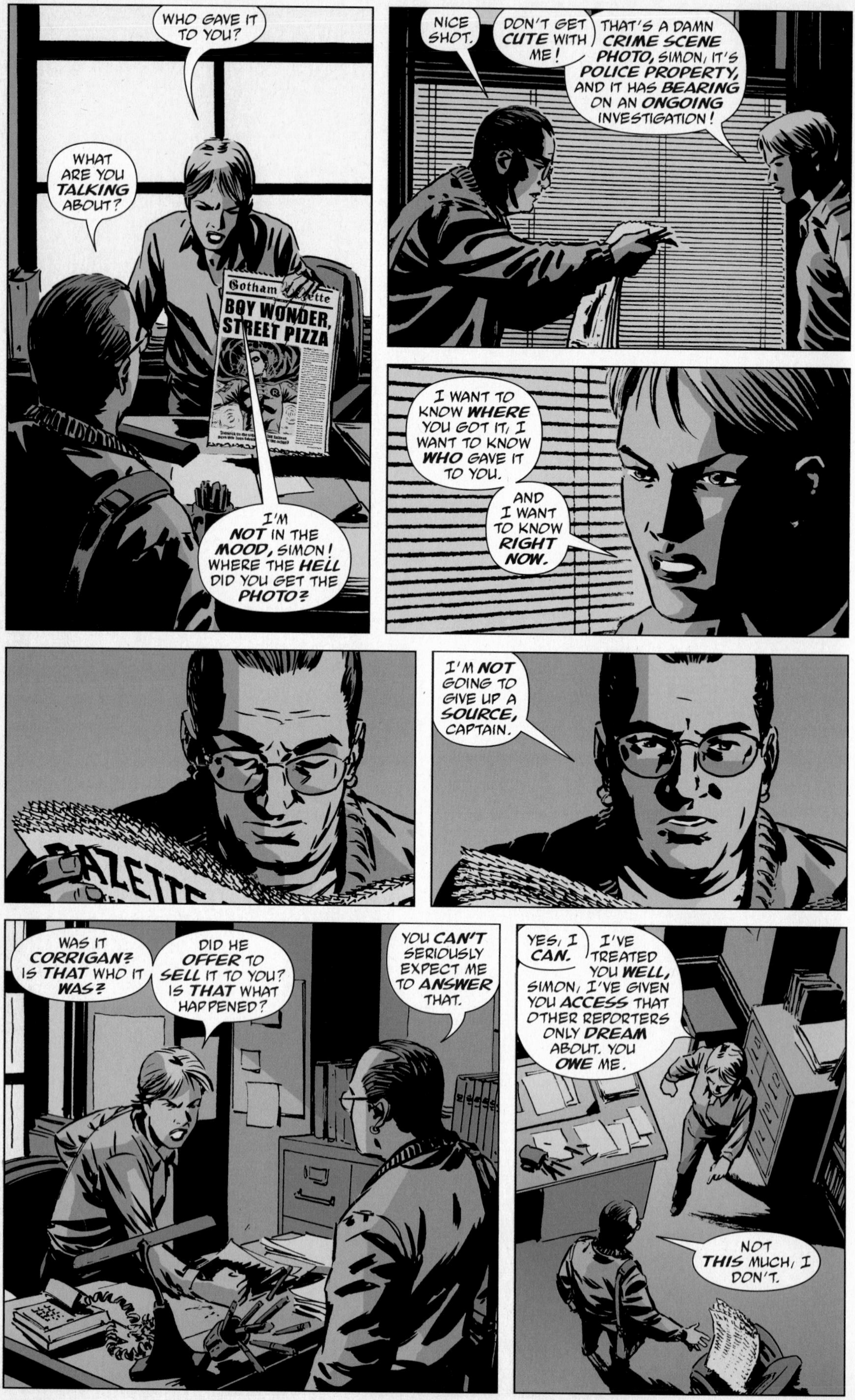
WHO GAVE IT TO YOU?
WHAT ARE YOU TALKING ABOUT?
Gotham Gazette
BOY WONDER, STREET PIZZA
I'M NOT IN THE MOOD, SIMON! WHERE THE HELL DID YOU GET THE PHOTO?
NICE SHOT.
DON'T GET CUTE WITH ME!
THAT'S A DAMN CRIME SCENE PHOTO, SIMON, IT'S POLICE PROPERTY, AND IT HAS BEARING ON AN ONGOING INVESTIGATION!
I WANT TO KNOW WHERE YOU GOT IT, I WANT TO KNOW WHO GAVE IT TO YOU.
AND I WANT TO KNOW RIGHT NOW.
I'M NOT GOING TO GIVE UP A SOURCE, CAPTAIN.
WAS IT CORRIGAN? IS THAT WHO IT WAS?
DID HE OFFER TO SELL IT TO YOU? IS THAT WHAT HAPPENED?
YOU CAN'T SERIOUSLY EXPECT ME TO ANSWER THAT.
YES, I CAN.
I'VE TREATED YOU WELL, SIMON, I'VE GIVEN YOU ACCESS THAT OTHER REPORTERS ONLY DREAM ABOUT. YOU OWE ME.
NOT THIS MUCH, I DON'T.

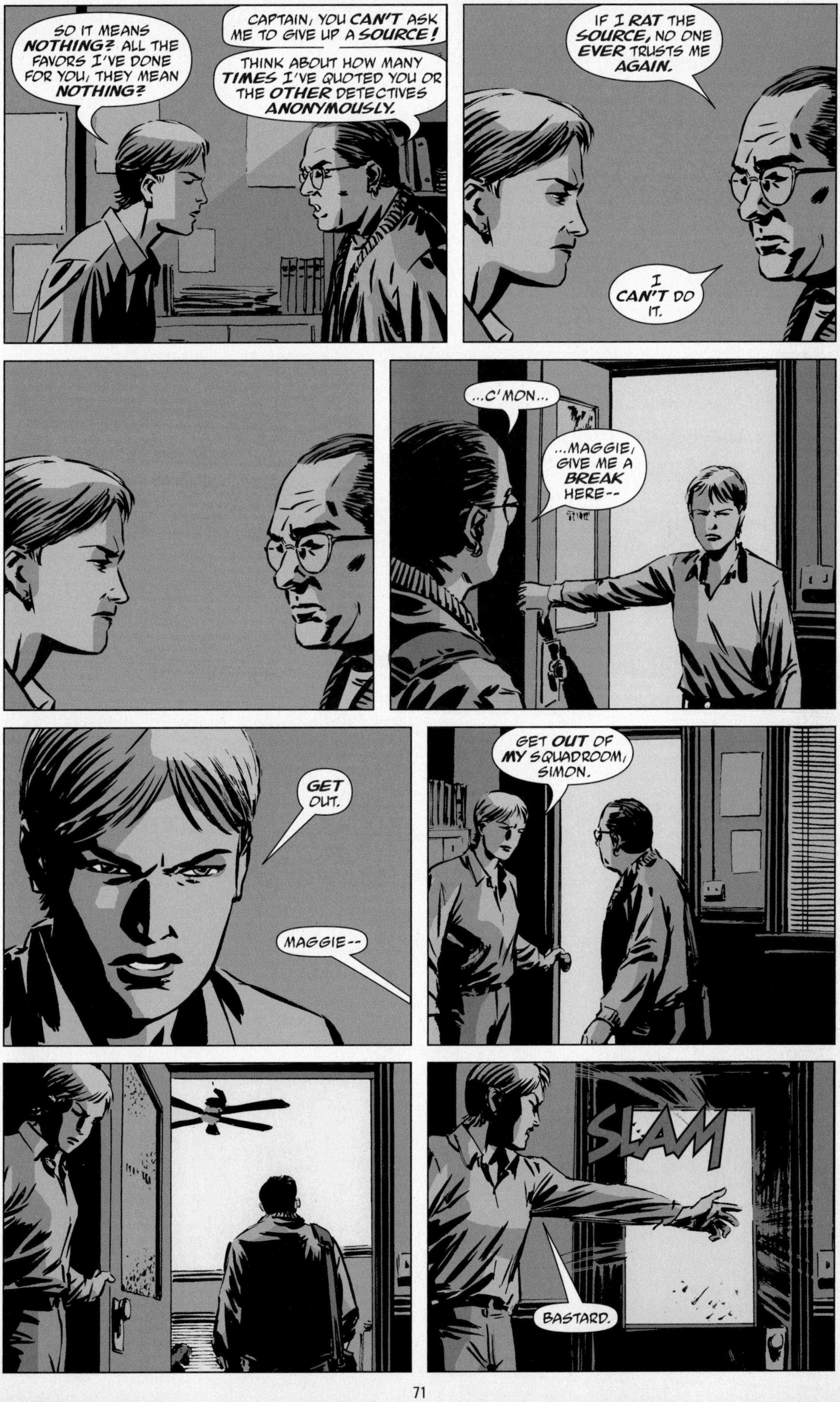
SO IT MEANS NOTHING? ALL THE FAVORS I'VE DONE FOR YOU, THEY MEAN NOTHING?
CAPTAIN, YOU CAN'T ASK ME TO GIVE UP A SOURCE!
THINK ABOUT HOW MANY TIMES I'VE QUOTED YOU OR THE OTHER DETECTIVES ANONYMOUSLY.
IF I RAT THE SOURCE, NO ONE EVER TRUSTS ME AGAIN.
I CAN'T DO IT.
...C'MON...
...MAGGIE, GIVE ME A BREAK HERE--
GET OUT.
MAGGIE--
GET OUT OF MY SQUADROOM, SIMON.
SLAM
BASTARD.

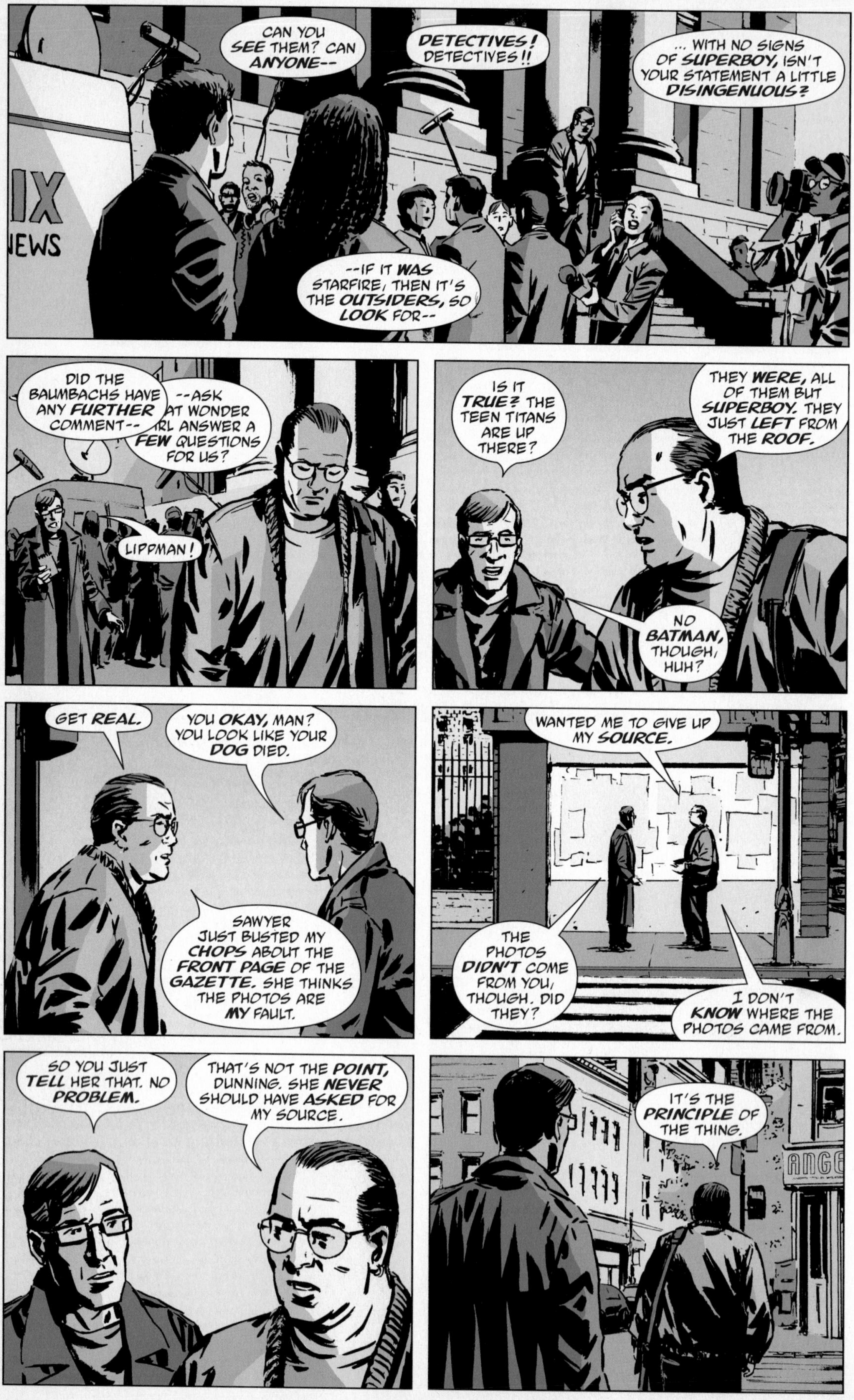

CAN YOU SEE THEM? CAN ANYONE--
DETECTIVES! DETECTIVES!!
... WITH NO SIGNS OF SUPERBOY, ISN'T YOUR STATEMENT A LITTLE DISINGENUOUS?
--IF IT WAS STARFIRE, THEN IT'S THE OUTSIDERS, SO LOOK FOR--
DID THE BAUMBACHS HAVE ANY FURTHER COMMENT--
--ASK AT WONDER IRL ANSWER A FEW QUESTIONS FOR US?
LIPPMAN!
IS IT TRUE? THE TEEN TITANS ARE UP THERE?
THEY WERE, ALL OF THEM BUT SUPERBOY. THEY JUST LEFT FROM THE ROOF.
NO BATMAN, THOUGH, HUH?
GET REAL.
YOU OKAY, MAN? YOU LOOK LIKE YOUR DOG DIED.
SAWYER JUST BUSTED MY CHOPS ABOUT THE FRONT PAGE OF THE GAZETTE. SHE THINKS THE PHOTOS ARE MY FAULT.
WANTED ME TO GIVE UP MY SOURCE.
THE PHOTOS DIDN'T COME FROM YOU, THOUGH. DID THEY?
I DON'T KNOW WHERE THE PHOTOS CAME FROM.
SO YOU JUST TELL HER THAT. NO PROBLEM.
THAT'S NOT THE POINT, DUNNING. SHE NEVER SHOULD HAVE ASKED FOR MY SOURCE.
IT'S THE PRINCIPLE OF THE THING.

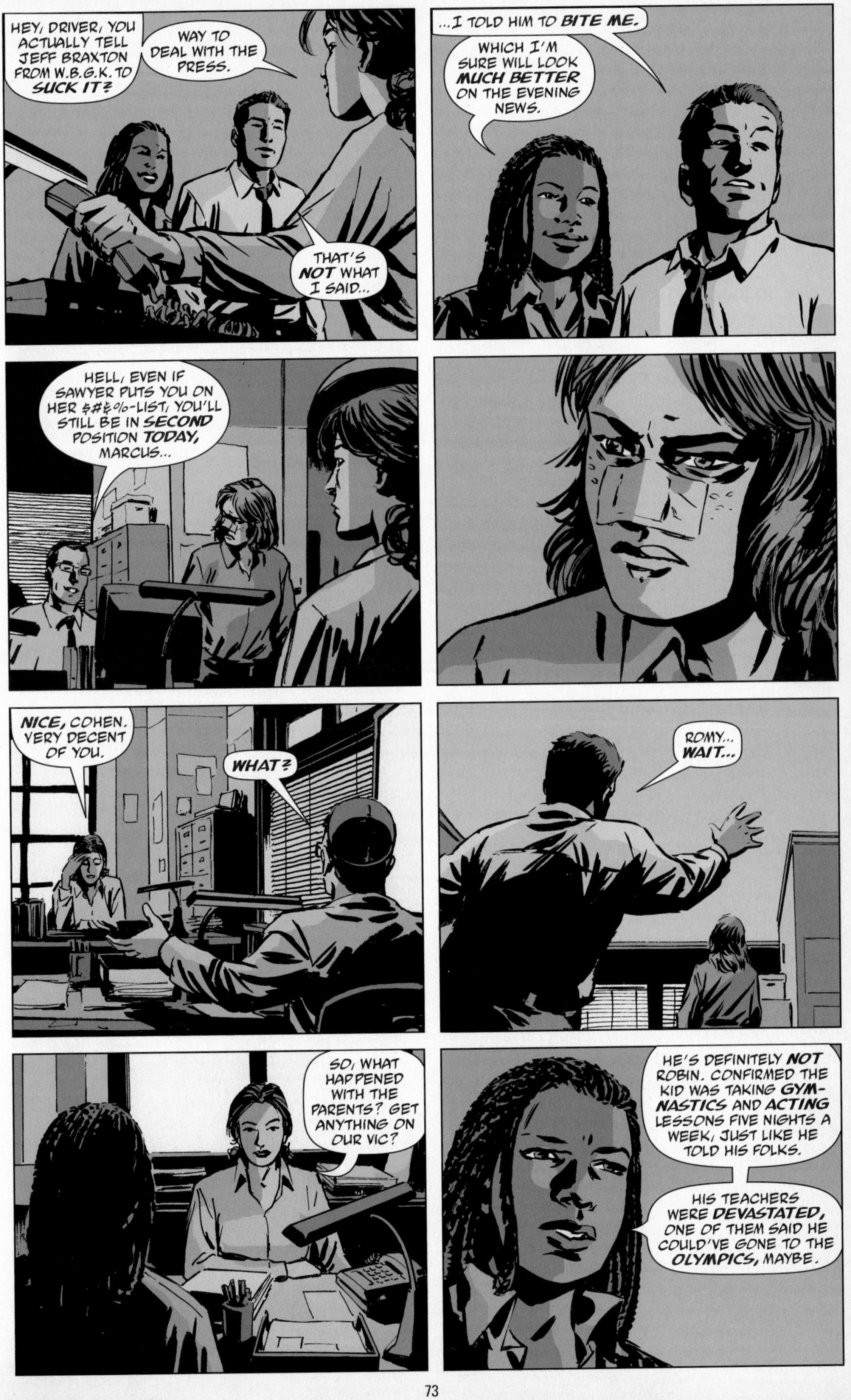
HEY, DRIVER, YOU ACTUALLY TELL JEFF BRAXTON FROM W.B.G.K. TO SUCK IT?
WAY TO DEAL WITH THE PRESS.
THAT'S NOT WHAT I SAID...
...I TOLD HIM TO BITE ME.
WHICH I'M SURE WILL LOOK MUCH BETTER ON THE EVENING NEWS.
HELL, EVEN IF SAWYER PUTS YOU ON HER $#&%-LIST, YOU'LL STILL BE IN SECOND POSITION TODAY, MARCUS...
NICE, COHEN. VERY DECENT OF YOU.
WHAT?
ROMY... WAIT...
SO, WHAT HAPPENED WITH THE PARENTS? GET ANYTHING ON OUR VIC?
HE'S DEFINITELY NOT ROBIN. CONFIRMED THE KID WAS TAKING GYMNASTICS AND ACTING LESSONS FIVE NIGHTS A WEEK, JUST LIKE HE TOLD HIS FOLKS.
HIS TEACHERS WERE DEVASTATED, ONE OF THEM SAID HE COULD'VE GONE TO THE OLYMPICS, MAYBE.

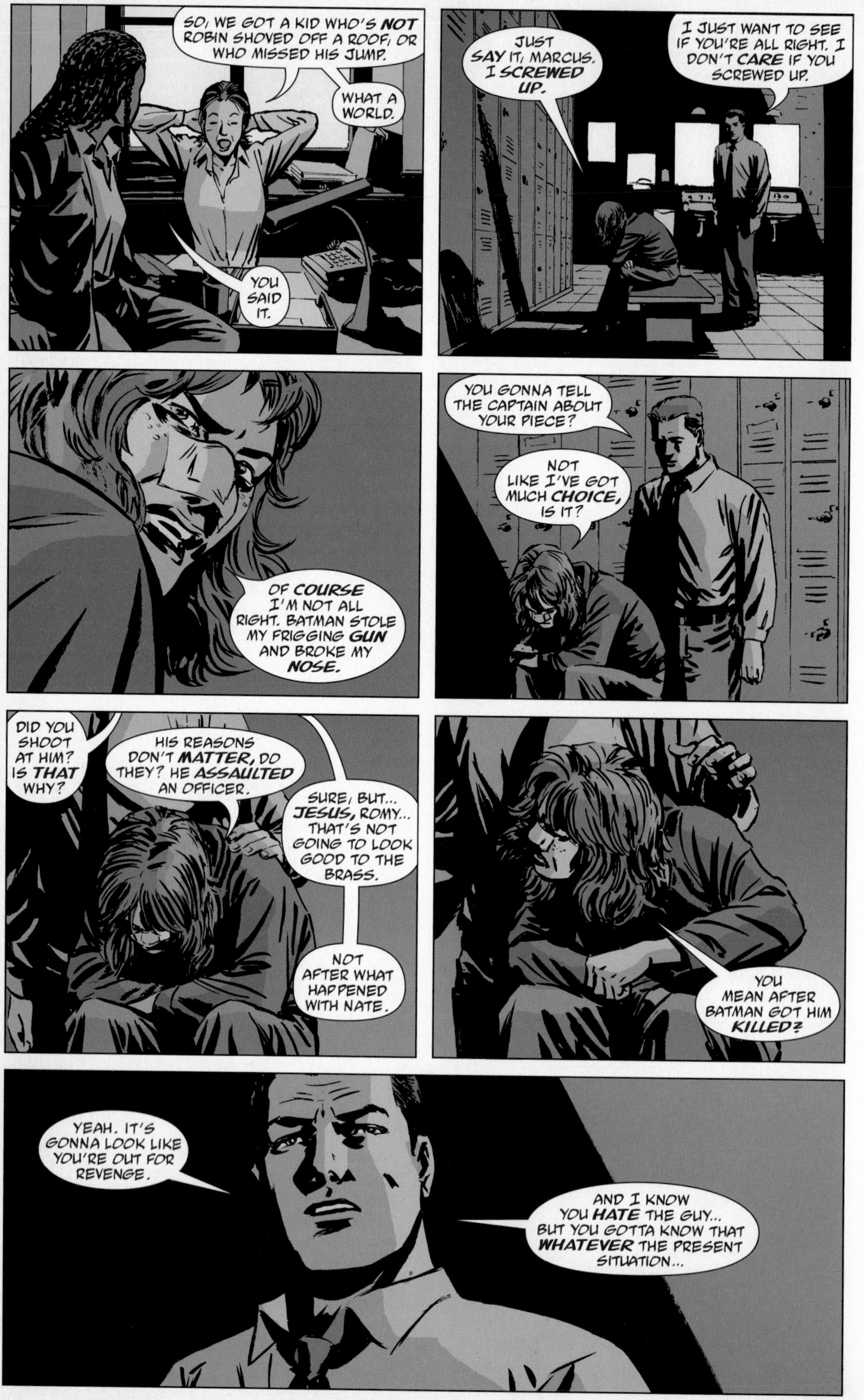
SO, WE GOT A KID WHO'S **NOT** ROBIN SHOVED OFF A ROOF, OR WHO MISSED HIS JUMP.
WHAT A WORLD.
YOU SAID IT.
JUST **SAY** IT, MARCUS. I **SCREWED UP.**
I JUST WANT TO SEE IF YOU'RE ALL RIGHT. I DON'T **CARE** IF YOU SCREWED UP.
OF **COURSE** I'M NOT ALL RIGHT. BATMAN STOLE MY FRIGGING **GUN** AND BROKE MY **NOSE.**
YOU GONNA TELL THE CAPTAIN ABOUT YOUR PIECE?
NOT LIKE I'VE GOT MUCH **CHOICE,** IS IT?
DID YOU SHOOT AT HIM? IS **THAT** WHY?
HIS REASONS DON'T **MATTER,** DO THEY? HE **ASSAULTED** AN OFFICER.
SURE, BUT... **JESUS,** ROMY... THAT'S NOT GOING TO LOOK GOOD TO THE BRASS.
NOT AFTER WHAT HAPPENED WITH NATE.
YOU MEAN AFTER BATMAN GOT HIM **KILLED?**
YEAH. IT'S GONNA LOOK LIKE YOU'RE OUT FOR REVENGE.
AND I KNOW YOU **HATE** THE GUY... BUT YOU GOTTA KNOW THAT **WHATEVER** THE PRESENT SITUATION...

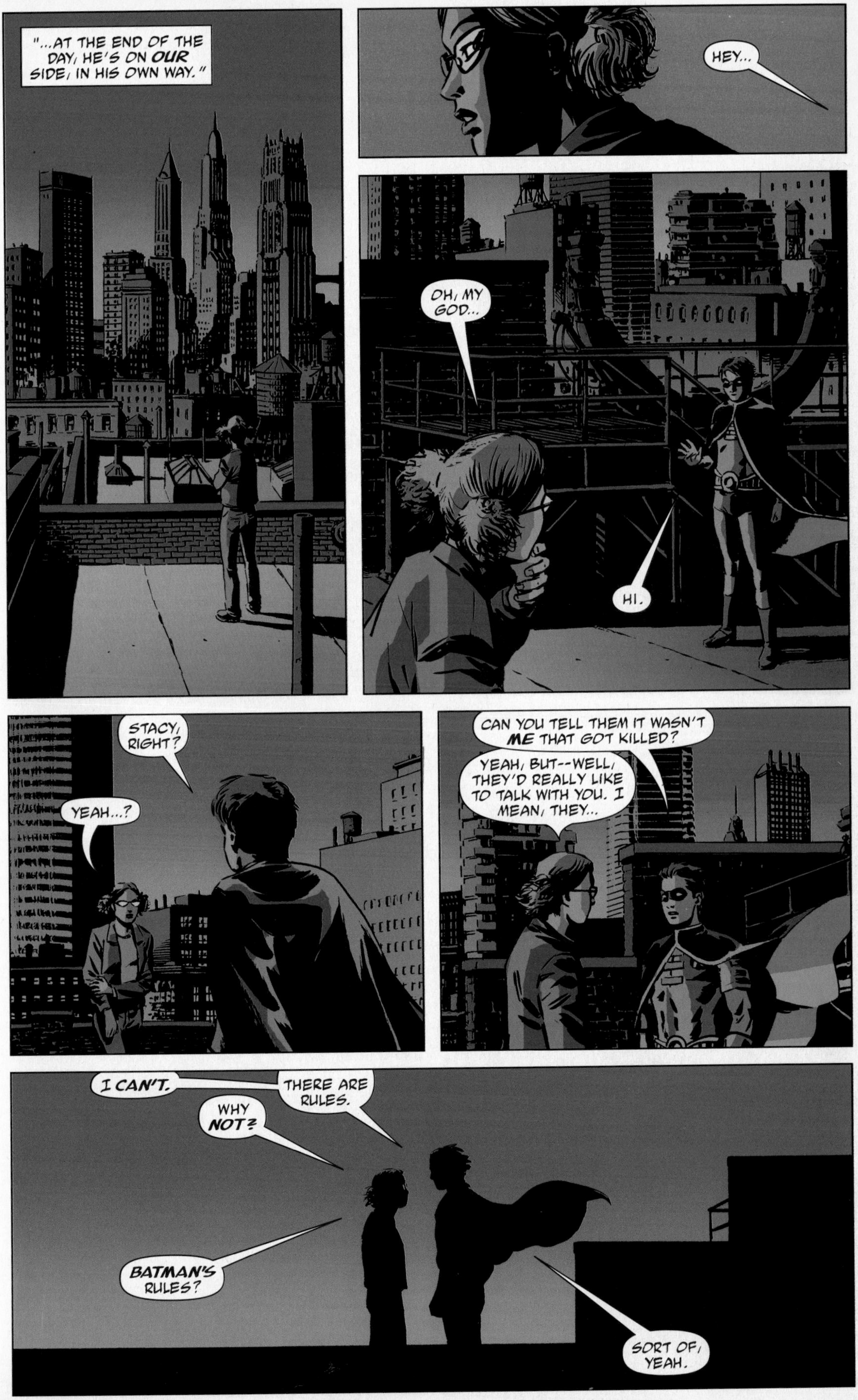
"...AT THE END OF THE DAY, HE'S ON OUR SIDE, IN HIS OWN WAY."
HEY...
OH, MY GOD...
HI.
STACY, RIGHT?
YEAH...?
CAN YOU TELL THEM IT WASN'T ME THAT GOT KILLED?
YEAH, BUT--WELL, THEY'D REALLY LIKE TO TALK WITH YOU. I MEAN, THEY...
I CAN'T.
THERE ARE RULES.
WHY NOT?
BATMAN'S RULES?
SORT OF, YEAH.

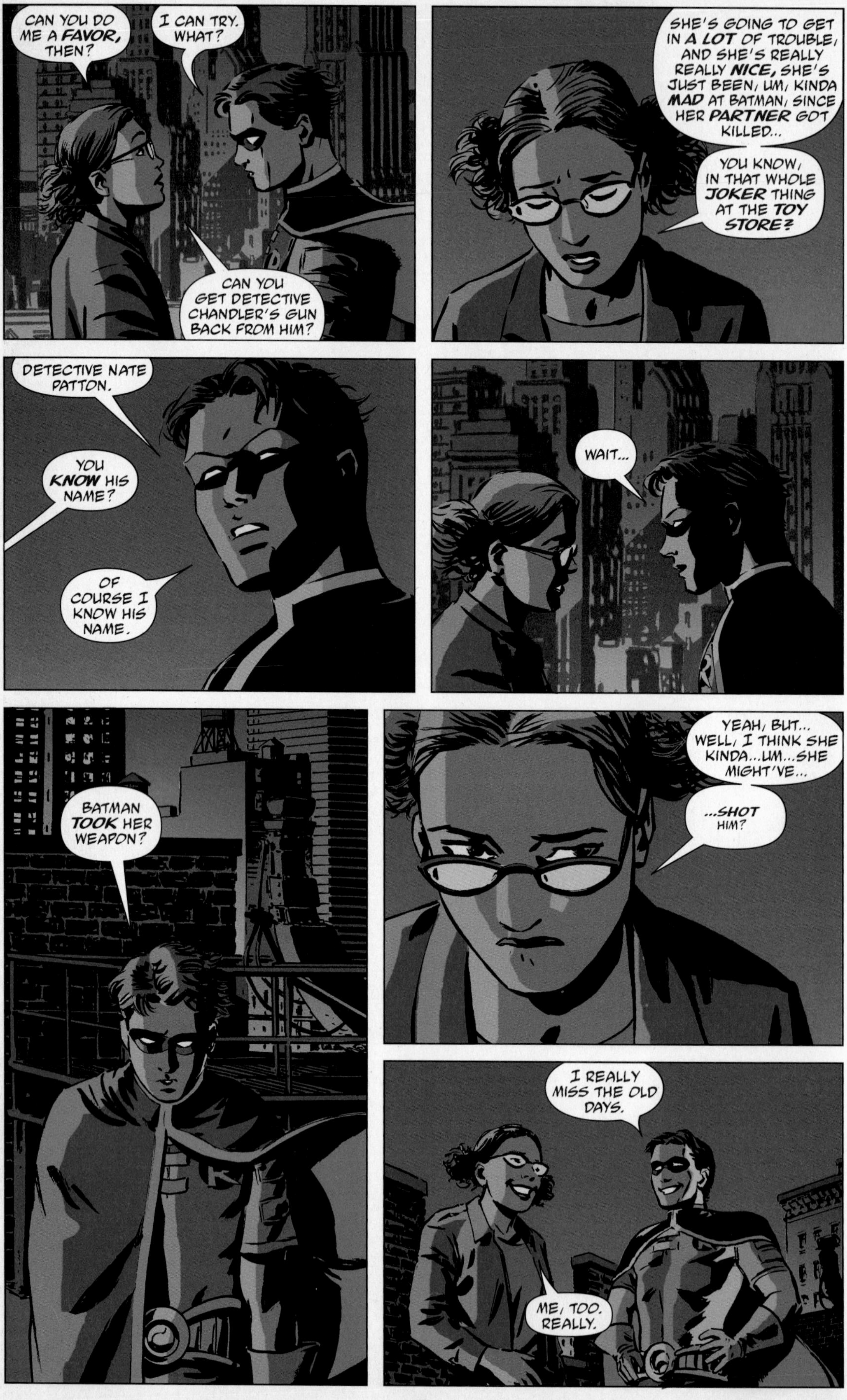
CAN YOU DO ME A **FAVOR,** THEN?
I CAN TRY. WHAT?
CAN YOU GET DETECTIVE CHANDLER'S GUN BACK FROM HIM?
SHE'S GOING TO GET IN **A LOT** OF TROUBLE, AND SHE'S REALLY REALLY **NICE,** SHE'S JUST BEEN, UM, KINDA **MAD** AT BATMAN, SINCE HER **PARTNER** GOT KILLED...
YOU KNOW, IN THAT WHOLE **JOKER** THING AT THE **TOY STORE?**
DETECTIVE NATE PATTON.
YOU **KNOW** HIS NAME?
OF COURSE I KNOW HIS NAME.
WAIT...
BATMAN **TOOK** HER WEAPON?
YEAH, BUT... WELL, I THINK SHE KINDA...UM...SHE MIGHT'VE...
...SHOT HIM?
I REALLY MISS THE OLD DAYS.
ME, TOO. REALLY.

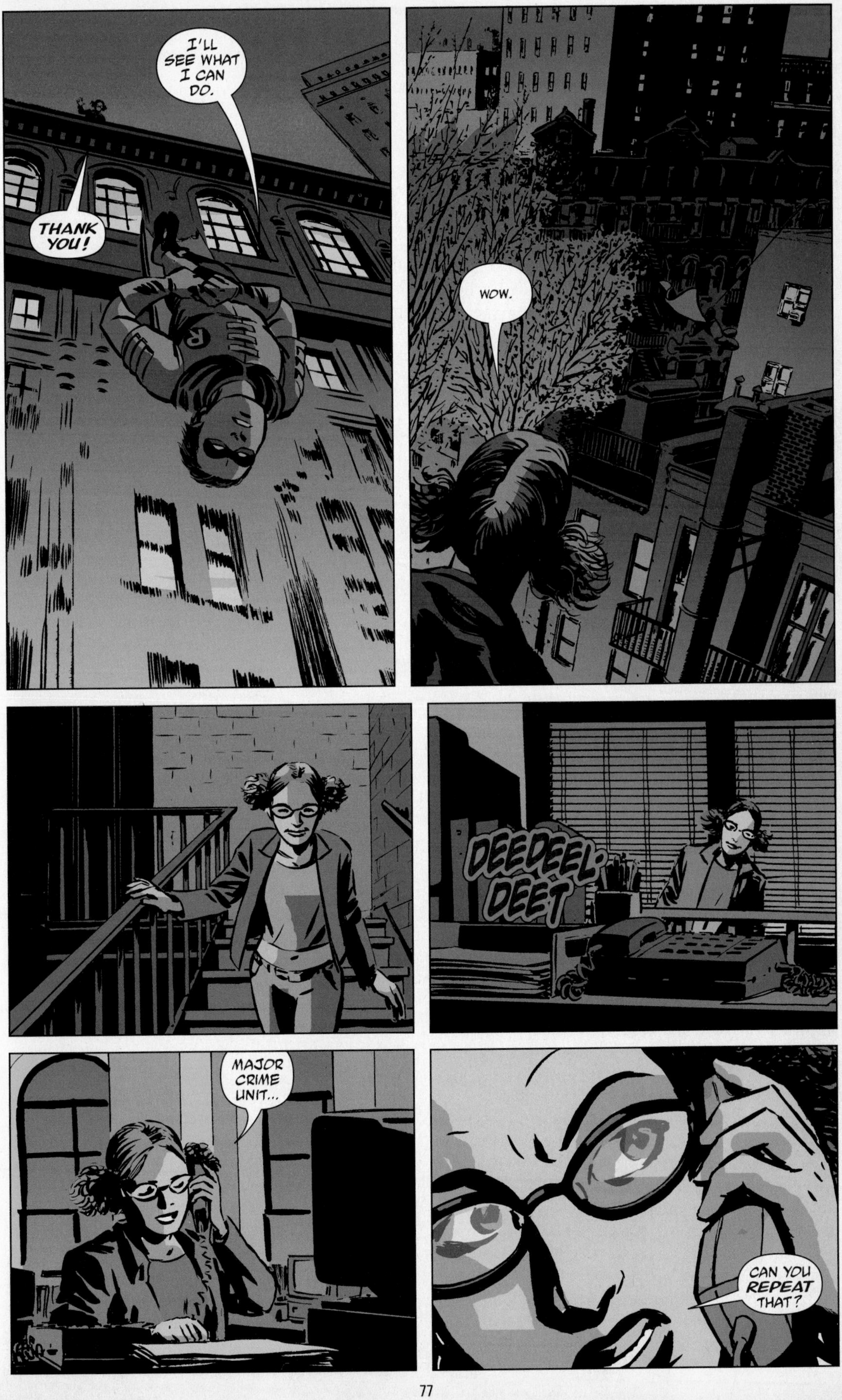
I'LL SEE WHAT I CAN DO.
THANK YOU!
WOW.
DEEDEEL-DEET
MAJOR CRIME UNIT...
CAN YOU REPEAT THAT?

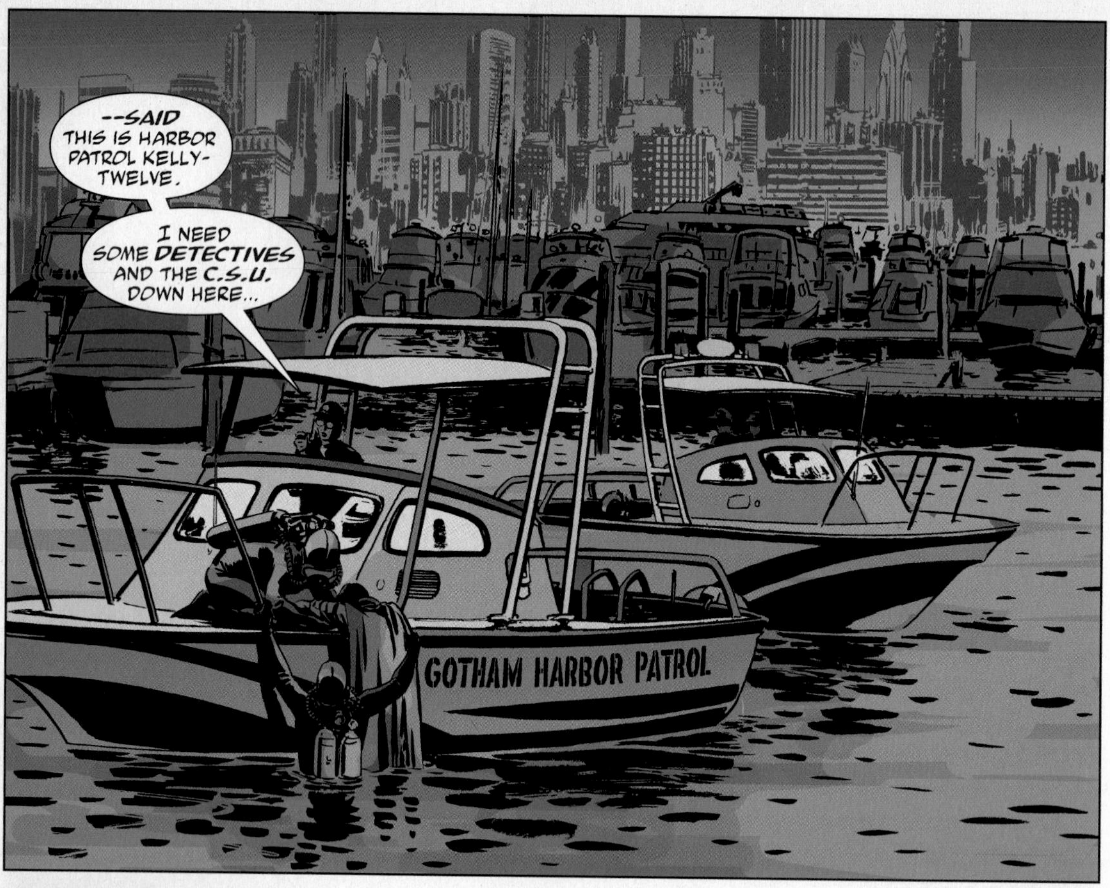
--SAID THIS IS HARBOR PATROL KELLY-TWELVE.
I NEED SOME DETECTIVES AND THE C.S.U. DOWN HERE...
GOTHAM HARBOR PATROL

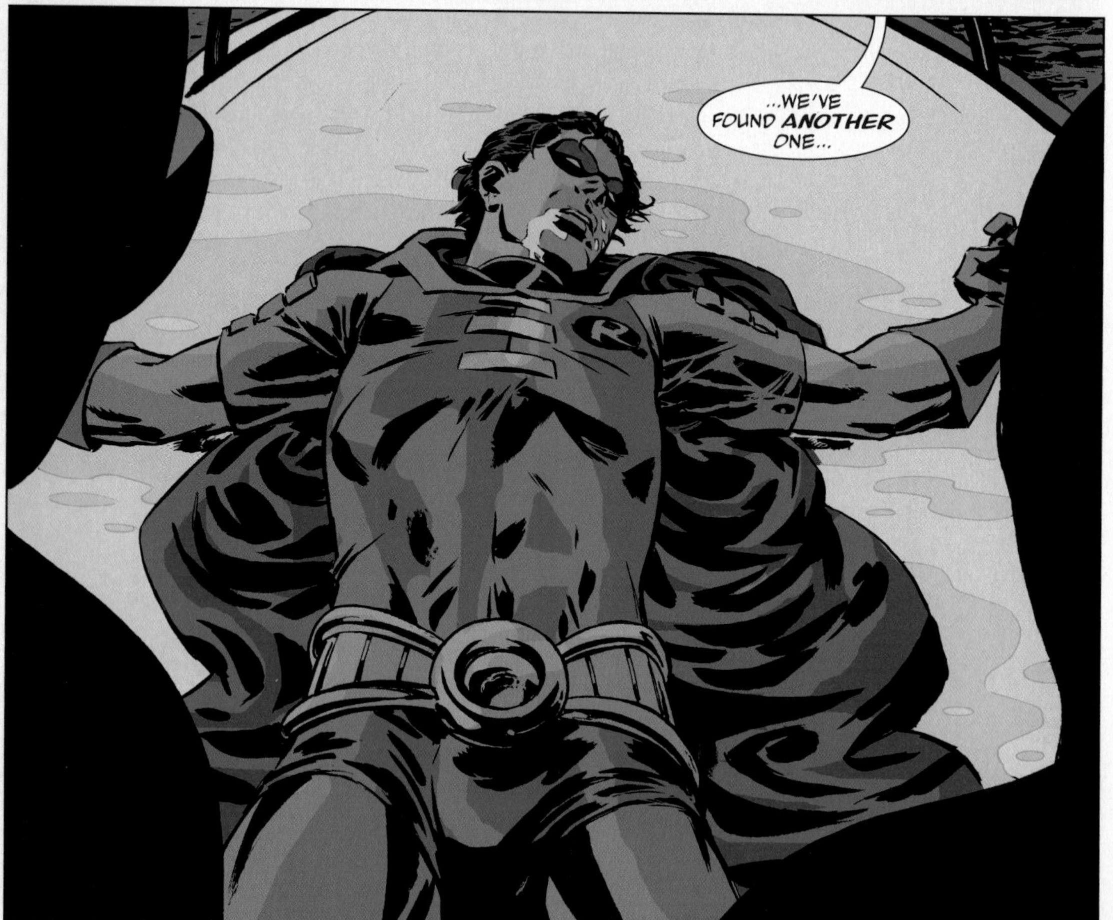
...WE'VE FOUND ANOTHER ONE...

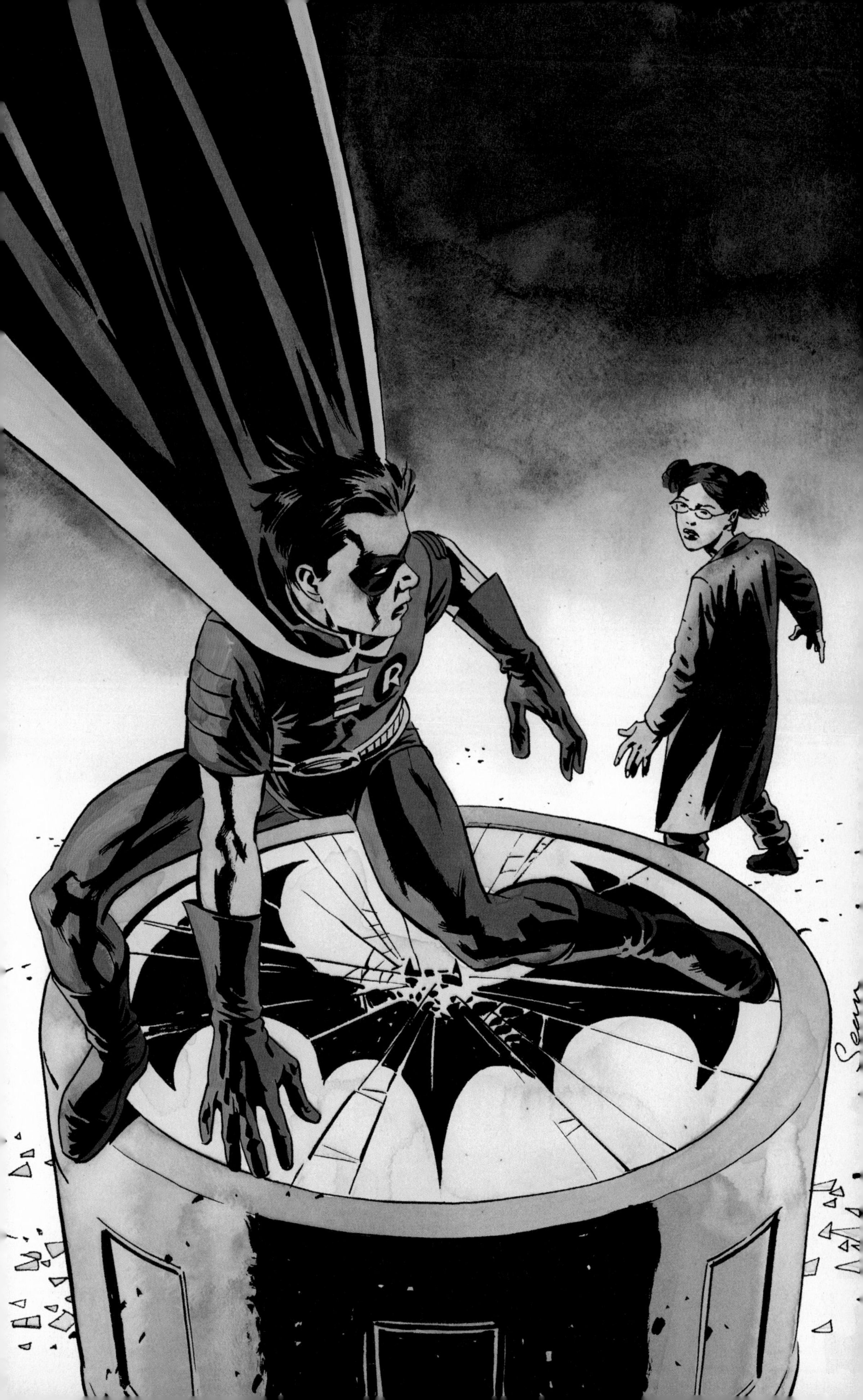
Sean

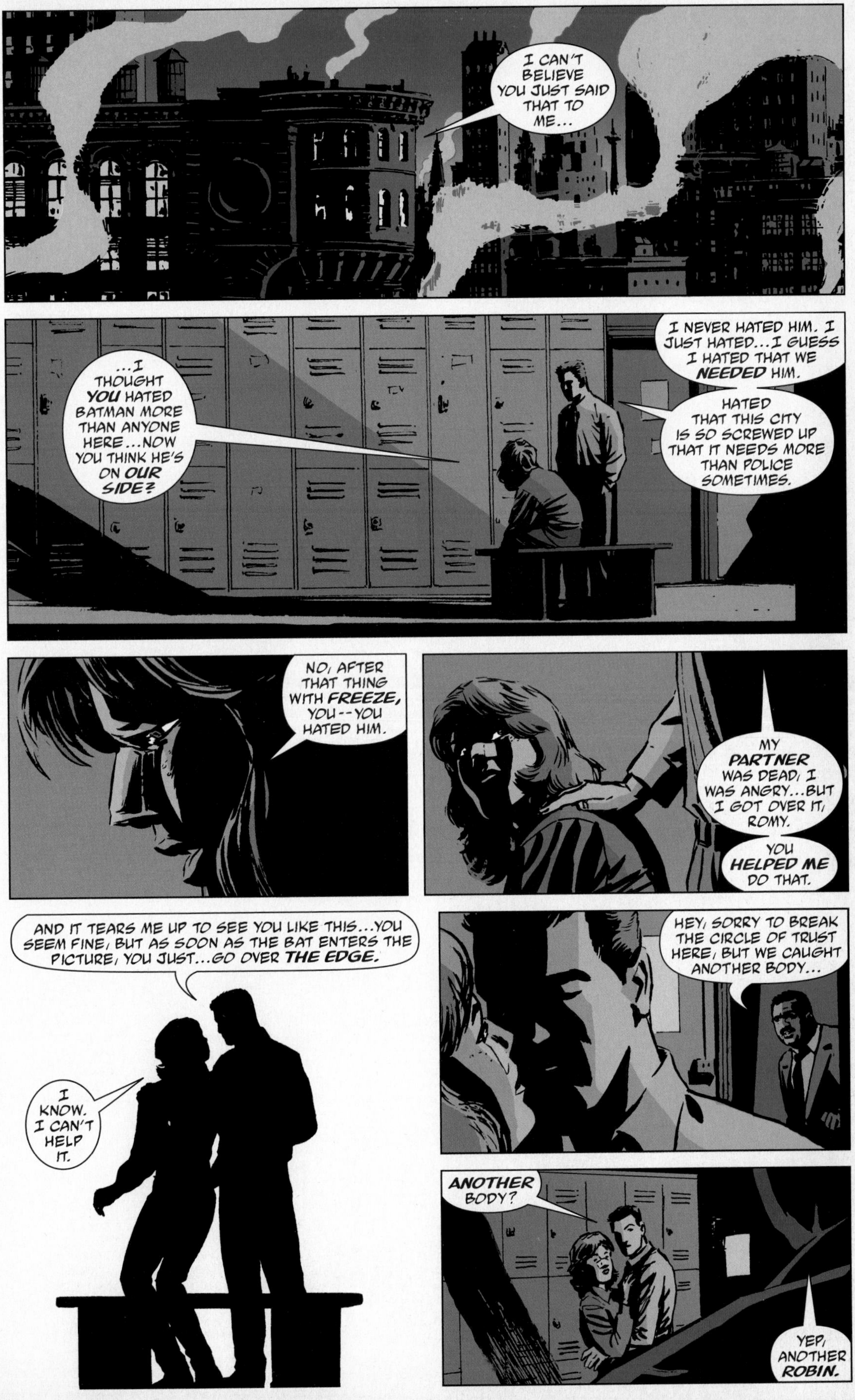
I CAN'T BELIEVE YOU JUST SAID THAT TO ME...
...I THOUGHT **YOU** HATED BATMAN MORE THAN ANYONE HERE...NOW YOU THINK HE'S ON **OUR SIDE**?
I NEVER HATED HIM. I JUST HATED...I GUESS I HATED THAT WE **NEEDED** HIM.
HATED THAT THIS CITY IS SO SCREWED UP THAT IT NEEDS MORE THAN POLICE SOMETIMES.
NO, AFTER THAT THING WITH **FREEZE,** YOU--YOU HATED HIM.
MY **PARTNER** WAS DEAD, I WAS ANGRY...BUT I GOT OVER IT, ROMY.
YOU **HELPED ME** DO THAT.
AND IT TEARS ME UP TO SEE YOU LIKE THIS...YOU SEEM FINE, BUT AS SOON AS THE BAT ENTERS THE PICTURE, YOU JUST...GO OVER **THE EDGE.**
I KNOW. I CAN'T HELP IT.
HEY, SORRY TO BREAK THE CIRCLE OF TRUST HERE, BUT WE CAUGHT ANOTHER BODY...
ANOTHER BODY?
YEP, ANOTHER **ROBIN.**

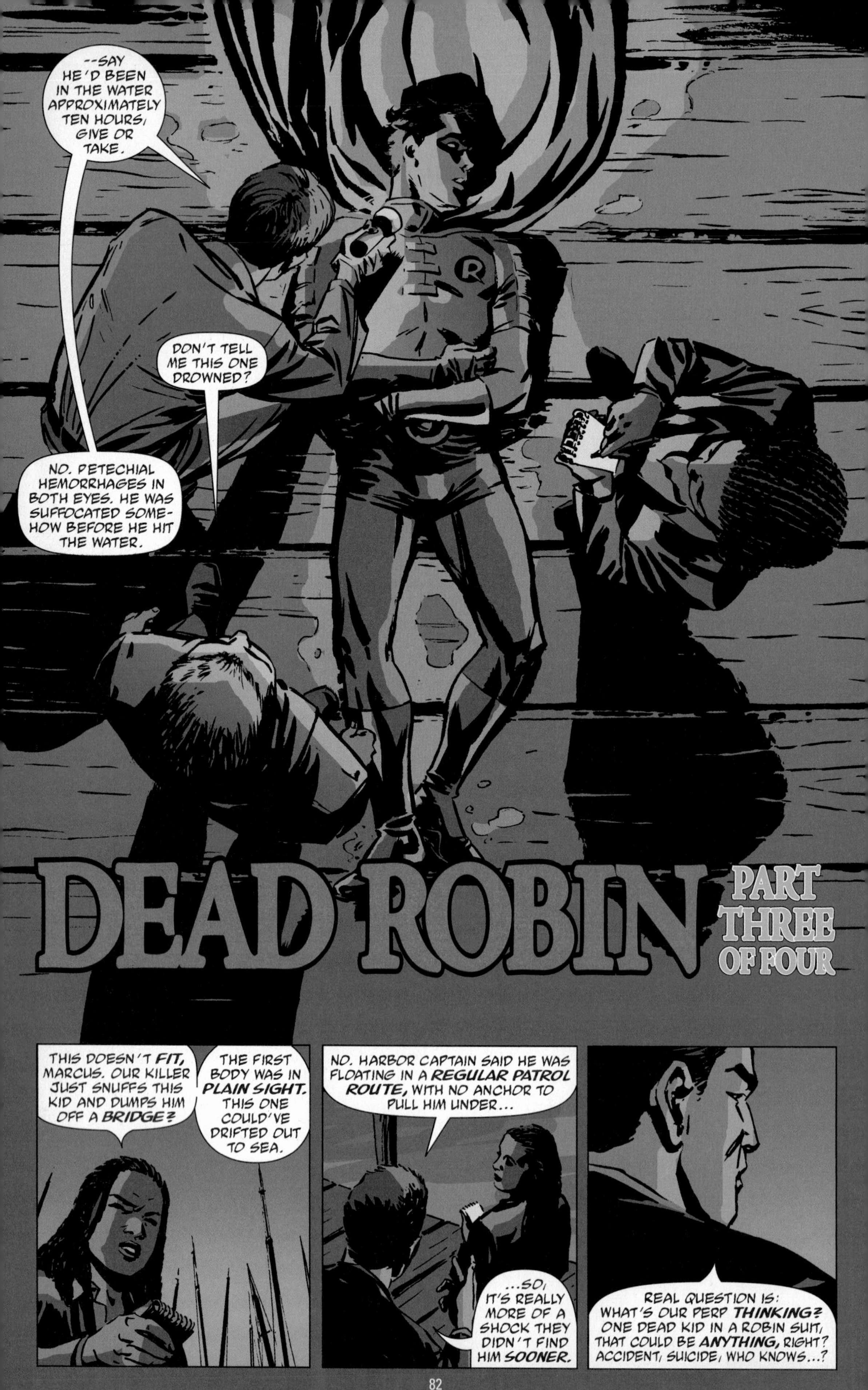
--SAY HE'D BEEN IN THE WATER APPROXIMATELY TEN HOURS, GIVE OR TAKE.
DON'T TELL ME THIS ONE DROWNED?
NO. PETECHIAL HEMORRHAGES IN BOTH EYES. HE WAS SUFFOCATED SOME-HOW BEFORE HE HIT THE WATER.
DEAD ROBIN
PART THREE OF FOUR
THIS DOESN'T **FIT,** MARCUS. OUR KILLER JUST SNUFFS THIS KID AND DUMPS HIM OFF A **BRIDGE?**
THE FIRST BODY WAS IN **PLAIN SIGHT.** THIS ONE COULD'VE DRIFTED OUT TO SEA.
NO. HARBOR CAPTAIN SAID HE WAS FLOATING IN A **REGULAR PATROL ROUTE,** WITH NO ANCHOR TO PULL HIM UNDER...
...SO, IT'S REALLY MORE OF A SHOCK THEY DIDN'T FIND HIM **SOONER.**
REAL QUESTION IS: WHAT'S OUR PERP **THINKING?** ONE DEAD KID IN A ROBIN SUIT, THAT COULD BE **ANYTHING,** RIGHT? ACCIDENT, SUICIDE, WHO KNOWS...?

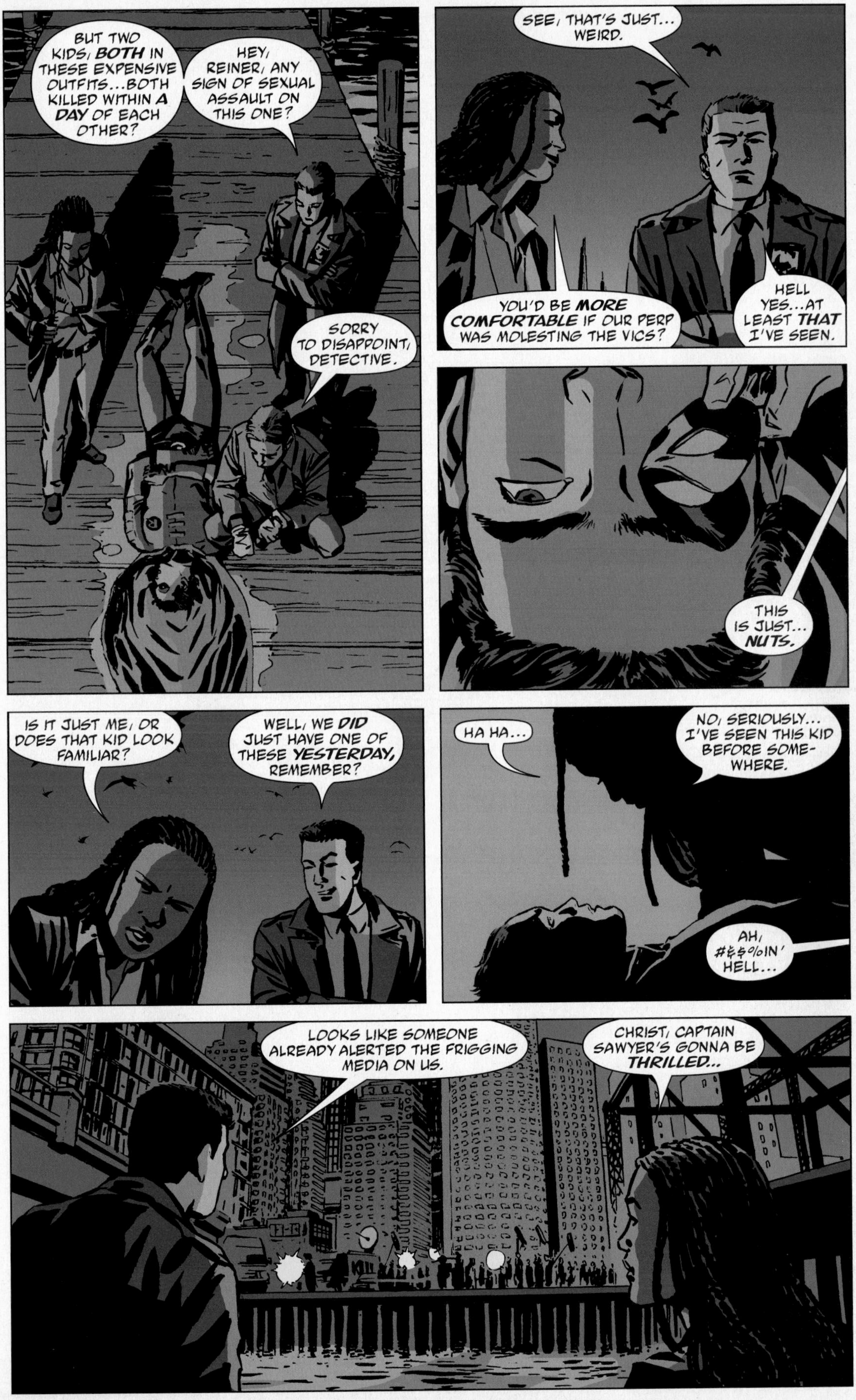
BUT TWO KIDS, BOTH IN THESE EXPENSIVE OUTFITS...BOTH KILLED WITHIN A DAY OF EACH OTHER?
HEY, REINER, ANY SIGN OF SEXUAL ASSAULT ON THIS ONE?
SORRY TO DISAPPOINT, DETECTIVE.
SEE, THAT'S JUST... WEIRD.
YOU'D BE MORE COMFORTABLE IF OUR PERP WAS MOLESTING THE VICS?
HELL YES...AT LEAST THAT I'VE SEEN.
THIS IS JUST... NUTS.
IS IT JUST ME, OR DOES THAT KID LOOK FAMILIAR?
WELL, WE DID JUST HAVE ONE OF THESE YESTERDAY, REMEMBER?
HA HA...
NO, SERIOUSLY... I'VE SEEN THIS KID BEFORE SOME-WHERE.
AH, #&$%IN' HELL...
LOOKS LIKE SOMEONE ALREADY ALERTED THE FRIGGING MEDIA ON US.
CHRIST, CAPTAIN SAWYER'S GONNA BE THRILLED...

MOTHER*%5¢!

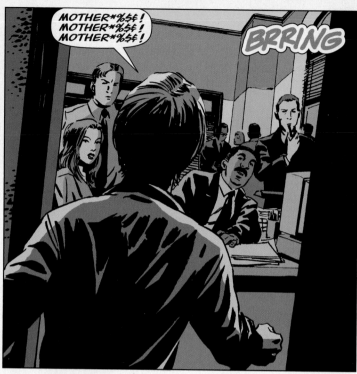

MOTHER*%5¢!
MOTHER*%5¢!
MOTHER*%5¢!

BRRING

BRRING BRRING

CAPTAIN! THE **PHONES** WON'T **STOP** RINGING!

I'VE GOT **KLEX** HERE, THEY WANT TO KNOW IF WE CAN **CONFIRM** A **SECOND** DEAD ROBIN --

NO *%5#ING COMMENT!

EVERY-ONE GOT THAT?

YES, MA'AM.

YES, CAPTAIN.

GOT IT.

YES'M.

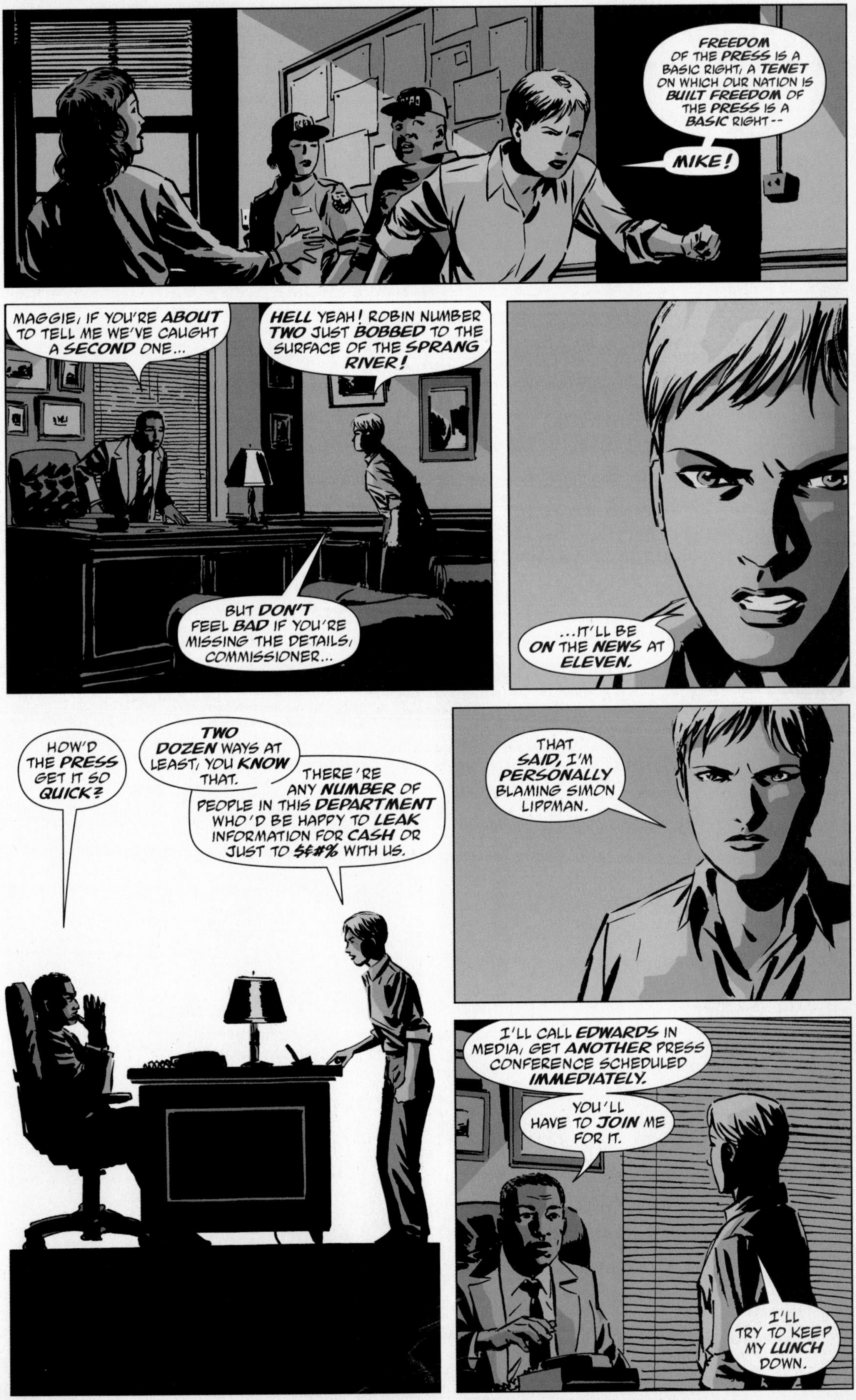

FREEDOM OF THE PRESS IS A BASIC RIGHT, A TENET ON WHICH OUR NATION IS BUILT FREEDOM OF THE PRESS IS A BASIC RIGHT--
MIKE!
MAGGIE, IF YOU'RE ABOUT TO TELL ME WE'VE CAUGHT A SECOND ONE...
HELL YEAH! ROBIN NUMBER TWO JUST BOBBED TO THE SURFACE OF THE SPRANG RIVER!
BUT DON'T FEEL BAD IF YOU'RE MISSING THE DETAILS, COMMISSIONER...
...IT'LL BE ON THE NEWS AT ELEVEN.
HOW'D THE PRESS GET IT SO QUICK?
TWO DOZEN WAYS AT LEAST, YOU KNOW THAT.
THERE'RE ANY NUMBER OF PEOPLE IN THIS DEPARTMENT WHO'D BE HAPPY TO LEAK INFORMATION FOR CASH OR JUST TO $&#% WITH US.
THAT SAID, I'M PERSONALLY BLAMING SIMON LIPPMAN.
I'LL CALL EDWARDS IN MEDIA, GET ANOTHER PRESS CONFERENCE SCHEDULED IMMEDIATELY.
YOU'LL HAVE TO JOIN ME FOR IT.
I'LL TRY TO KEEP MY LUNCH DOWN.

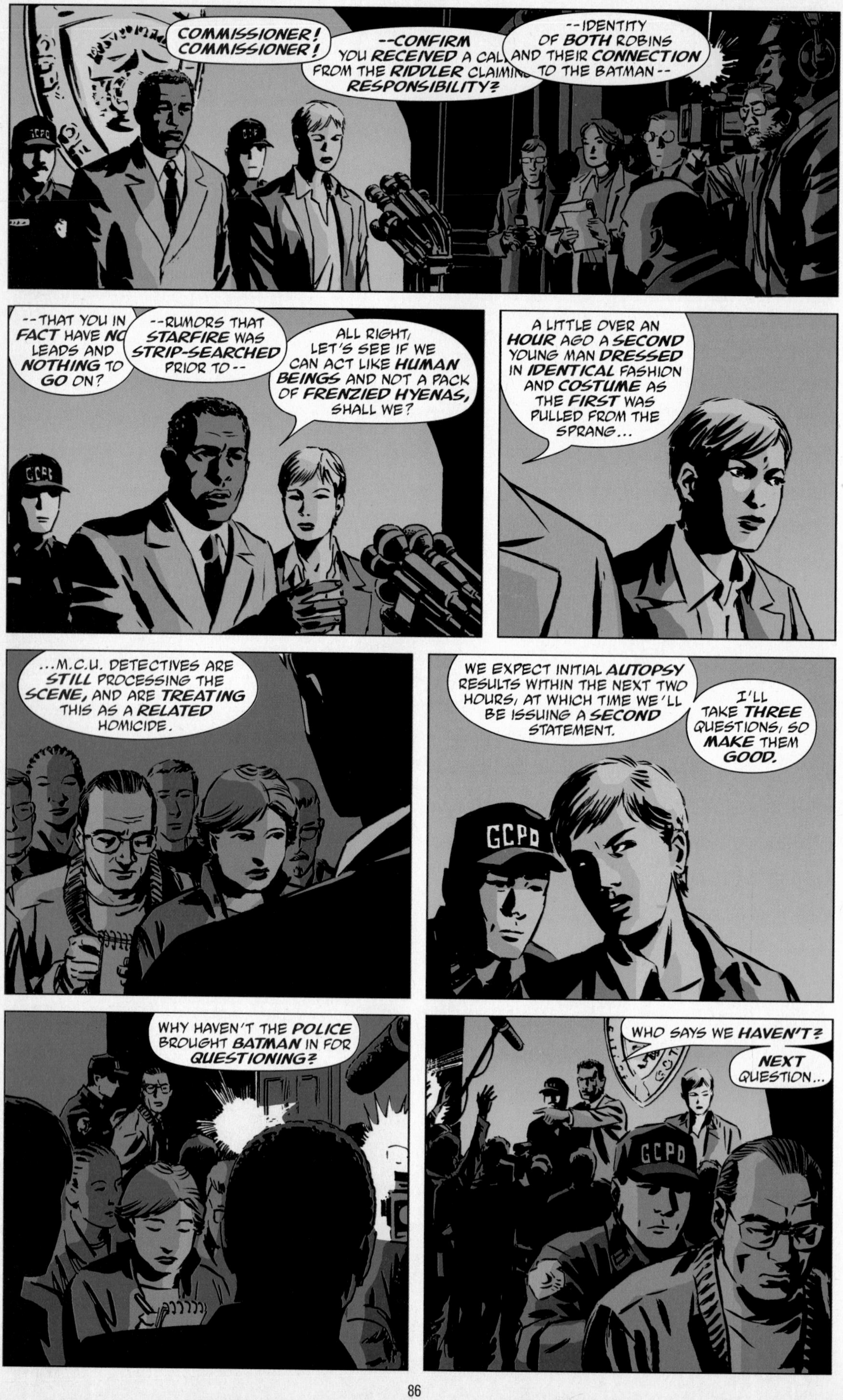

COMMISSIONER! COMMISSIONER!
--CONFIRM YOU RECEIVED A CAL FROM THE RIDDLER CLAIMIN RESPONSIBILITY?
--IDENTITY OF BOTH ROBINS AND THEIR CONNECTION TO THE BATMAN--
--THAT YOU IN FACT HAVE NO LEADS AND NOTHING TO GO ON?
--RUMORS THAT STARFIRE WAS STRIP-SEARCHED PRIOR TO--
ALL RIGHT, LET'S SEE IF WE CAN ACT LIKE HUMAN BEINGS AND NOT A PACK OF FRENZIED HYENAS, SHALL WE?
A LITTLE OVER AN HOUR AGO A SECOND YOUNG MAN DRESSED IN IDENTICAL FASHION AND COSTUME AS THE FIRST WAS PULLED FROM THE SPRANG...
...M.C.U. DETECTIVES ARE STILL PROCESSING THE SCENE, AND ARE TREATING THIS AS A RELATED HOMICIDE.
WE EXPECT INITIAL AUTOPSY RESULTS WITHIN THE NEXT TWO HOURS, AT WHICH TIME WE'LL BE ISSUING A SECOND STATEMENT.
I'LL TAKE THREE QUESTIONS, SO MAKE THEM GOOD.
GCPD
WHY HAVEN'T THE POLICE BROUGHT BATMAN IN FOR QUESTIONING?
WHO SAYS WE HAVEN'T?
NEXT QUESTION...
GCPD

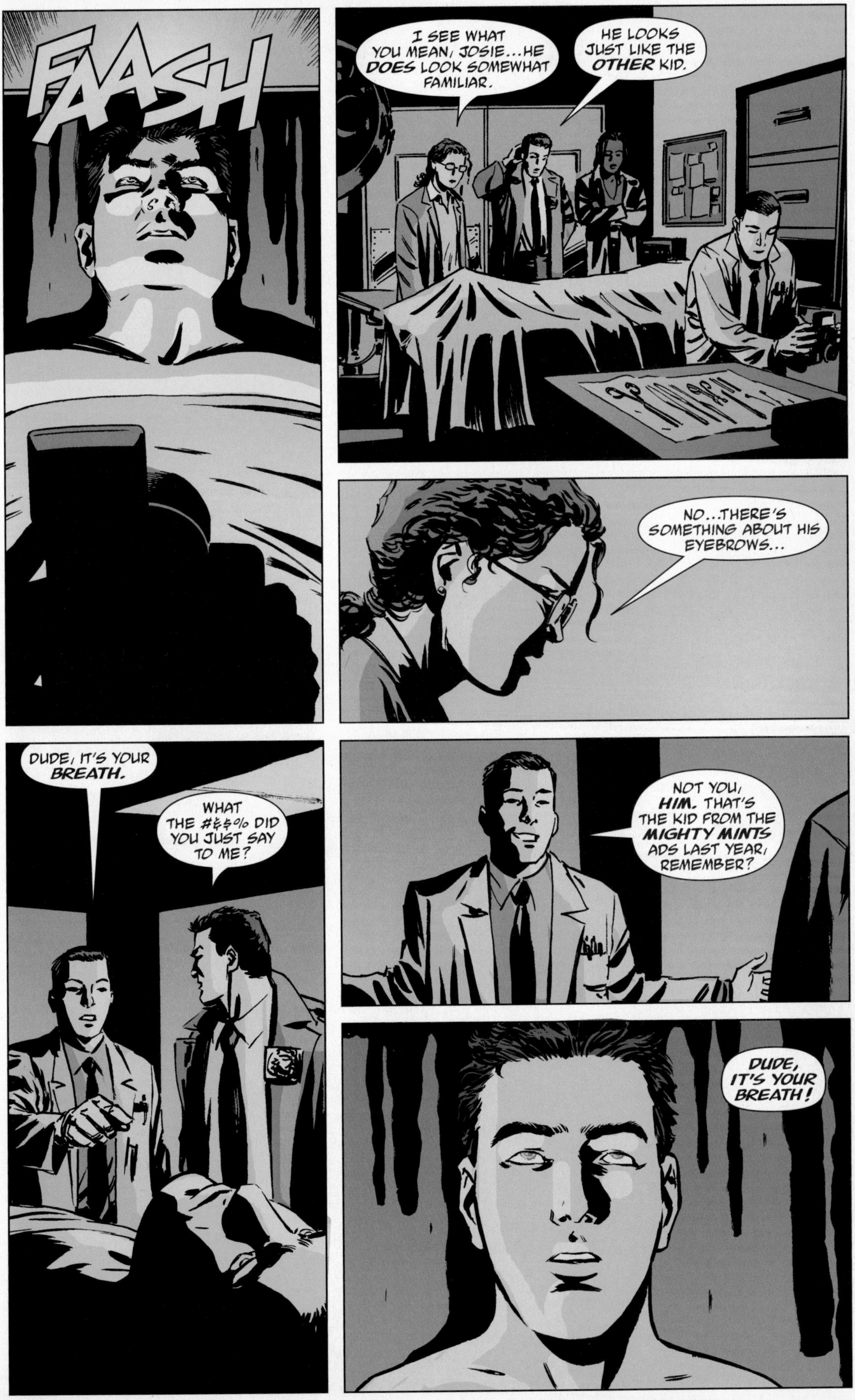
FAASH
I SEE WHAT YOU MEAN, JOSIE... HE DOES LOOK SOMEWHAT FAMILIAR.
HE LOOKS JUST LIKE THE OTHER KID.
NO...THERE'S SOMETHING ABOUT HIS EYEBROWS...
DUDE, IT'S YOUR BREATH.
WHAT THE #&$% DID YOU JUST SAY TO ME?
NOT YOU, HIM. THAT'S THE KID FROM THE MIGHTY MINTS ADS LAST YEAR, REMEMBER?
DUDE, IT'S YOUR BREATH!

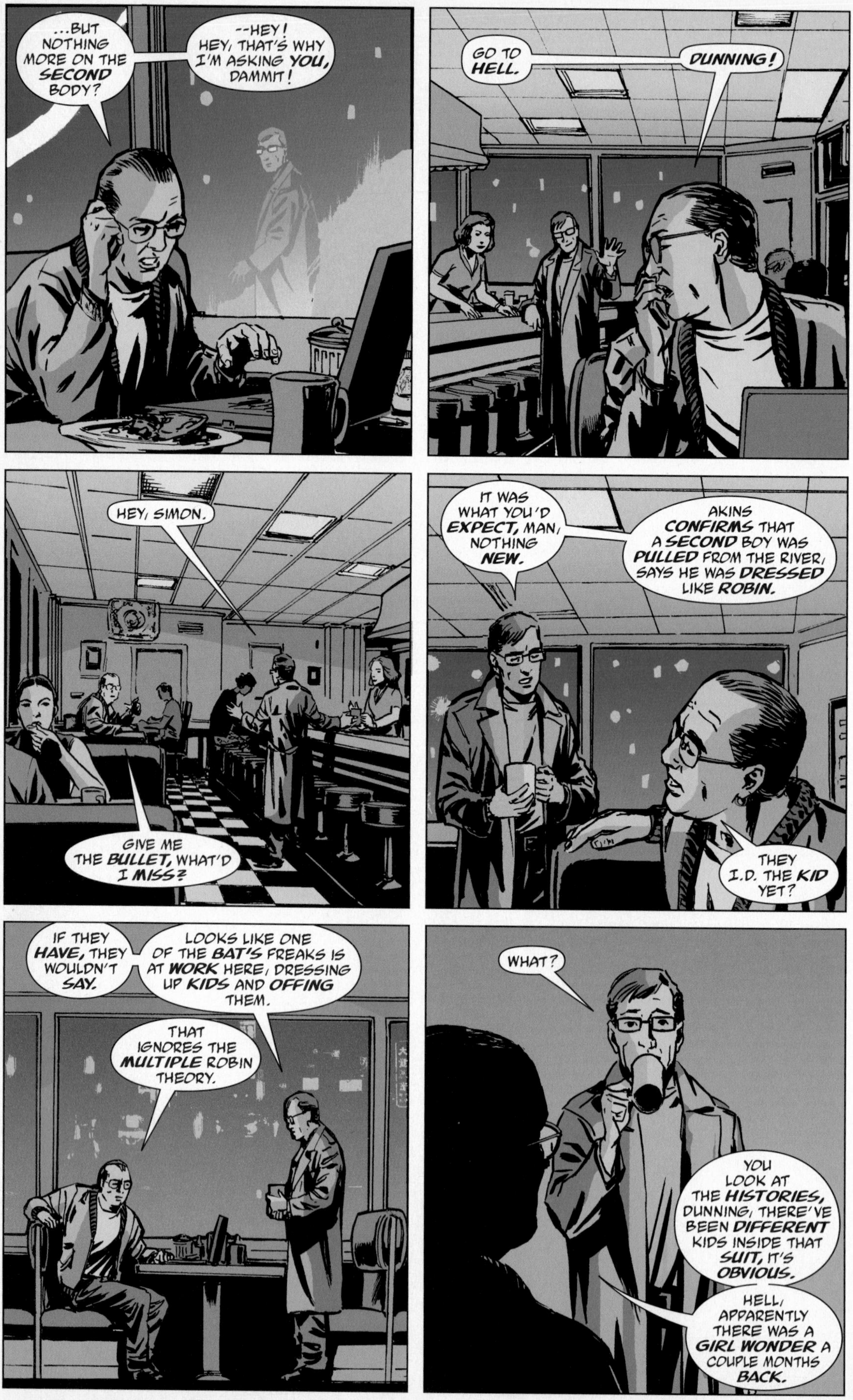
...BUT NOTHING MORE ON THE SECOND BODY?
--HEY! HEY, THAT'S WHY I'M ASKING YOU, DAMMIT!
GO TO HELL.
DUNNING!
HEY, SIMON.
GIVE ME THE BULLET, WHAT'D I MISS?
IT WAS WHAT YOU'D EXPECT, MAN, NOTHING NEW.
AKINS CONFIRMS THAT A SECOND BOY WAS PULLED FROM THE RIVER, SAYS HE WAS DRESSED LIKE ROBIN.
THEY I.D. THE KID YET?
IF THEY HAVE, THEY WOULDN'T SAY.
LOOKS LIKE ONE OF THE BAT'S FREAKS IS AT WORK HERE, DRESSING UP KIDS AND OFFING THEM.
THAT IGNORES THE MULTIPLE ROBIN THEORY.
WHAT?
YOU LOOK AT THE HISTORIES, DUNNING, THERE'VE BEEN DIFFERENT KIDS INSIDE THAT SUIT, IT'S OBVIOUS.
HELL, APPARENTLY THERE WAS A GIRL WONDER A COUPLE MONTHS BACK.

YOU THINK THESE KIDS ARE THE *REAL* THING?

I'M SAYING IT'S *POSSIBLE.*

THING IS, THERE'S *NO* KNOWN *HISTORY* OF *MULTIPLE* ROBINS BEING ACTIVE AT THE *SAME* TIME.

C'MON, *TELL* ME. THEY SAY *ANYTHING* ELSE?

THEY HAVE ANY *SUSPECTS,* AT LEAST?

NOTHING, MAN. THEY'RE *STONEWALLED,* YOU CAN TELL.

SAWYER MUST *REALLY* WANT YOUR *HEAD* IN A *SACK* TO HAVE YOU EJECTED FROM THE *CONFERENCE* LIKE THAT.

YEAH, YOU *DON'T* WANT TO PISS HER *OFF.*

WHY DON'T YOU *JUST* TELL HER THE *PHOTOS* WEREN'T YOUR *FAULT?*

I ALREADY TOLD YOU, IT'S THE *PRINCIPLE.*

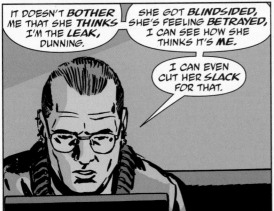

IT DOESN'T *BOTHER* ME THAT SHE *THINKS* I'M THE *LEAK,* DUNNING.

SHE GOT *BLINDSIDED,* SHE'S FEELING *BETRAYED,* I CAN SEE HOW SHE THINKS IT'S *ME.*

I CAN EVEN CUT HER *SLACK* FOR THAT.

BUT SHE *EXPECTED* ME TO GIVE UP A *SOURCE.*

SHE SHOULD *KNOW* ME BETTER THAN THAT BY *NOW,* Y'KNOW?

YOU'RE *OLD SCHOOL,* LIPPMAN, YOU KNOW THAT?

NO SCHOOL LIKE THE OLD SCHOOL, MAN.

HAVE A *NIGHT,* DUNNING.

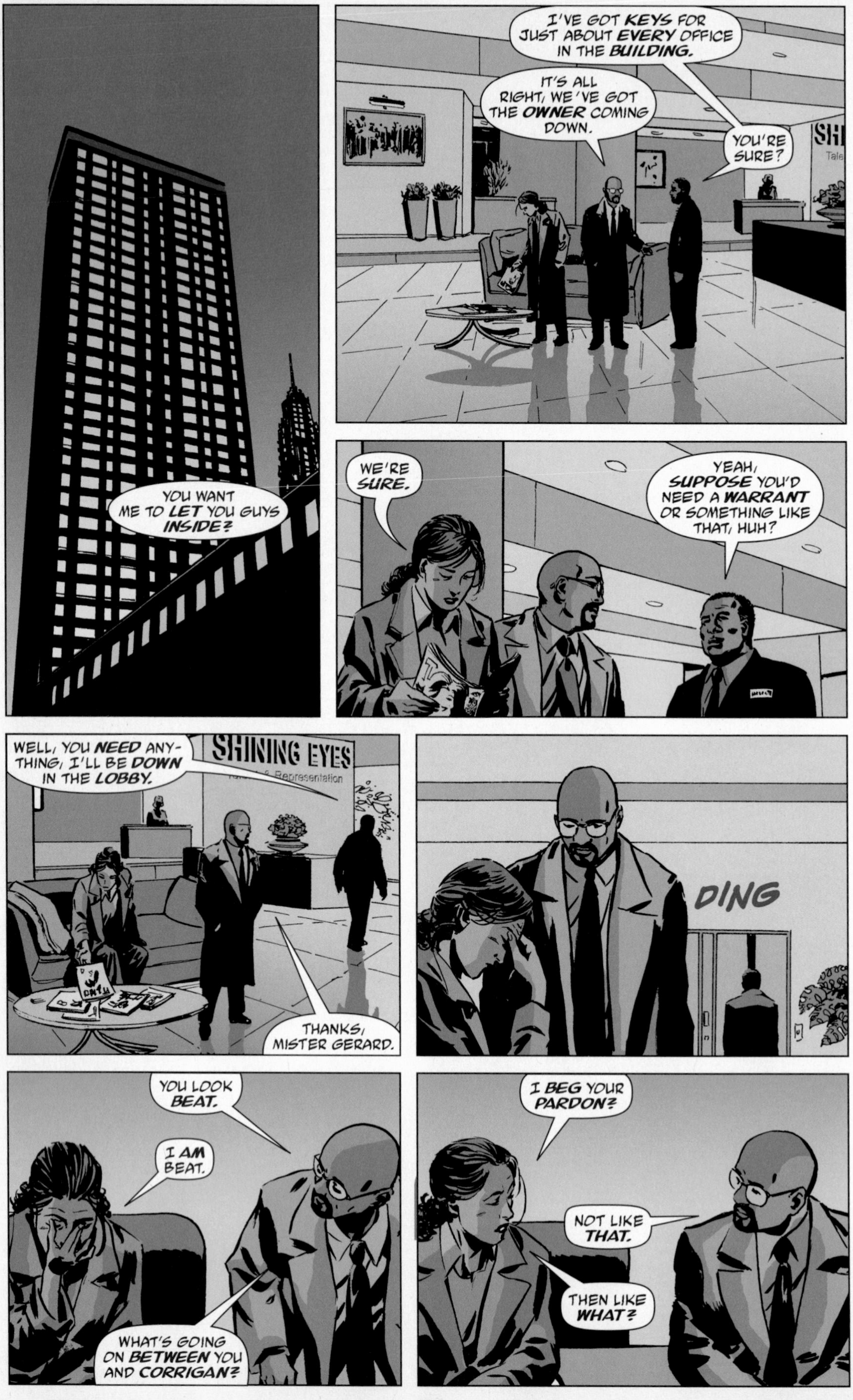
YOU WANT ME TO LET YOU GUYS INSIDE?
I'VE GOT KEYS FOR JUST ABOUT EVERY OFFICE IN THE BUILDING.
IT'S ALL RIGHT, WE'VE GOT THE OWNER COMING DOWN.
YOU'RE SURE?
WE'RE SURE.
YEAH, SUPPOSE YOU'D NEED A WARRANT OR SOMETHING LIKE THAT, HUH?
WELL, YOU NEED ANYTHING, I'LL BE DOWN IN THE LOBBY.
SHINING EYES
THANKS, MISTER GERARD.
DING
YOU LOOK BEAT.
I AM BEAT.
WHAT'S GOING ON BETWEEN YOU AND CORRIGAN?
I BEG YOUR PARDON?
NOT LIKE THAT.
THEN LIKE WHAT?

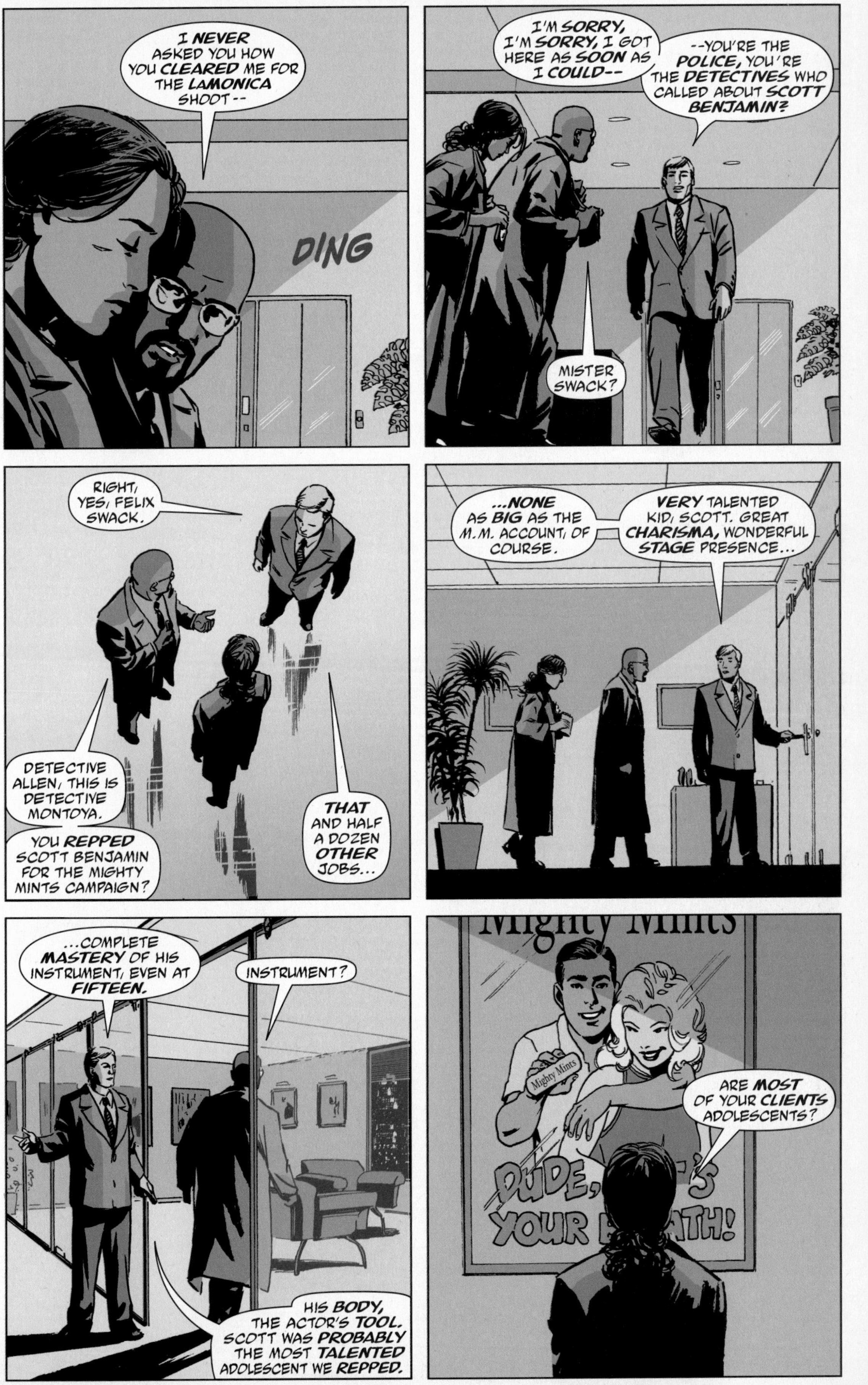
I NEVER ASKED YOU HOW YOU CLEARED ME FOR THE LAMONICA SHOOT --
DING
I'M SORRY, I'M SORRY, I GOT HERE AS SOON AS I COULD--
--YOU'RE THE POLICE, YOU'RE THE DETECTIVES WHO CALLED ABOUT SCOTT BENJAMIN?
MISTER SWACK?
RIGHT, YES, FELIX SWACK.
DETECTIVE ALLEN, THIS IS DETECTIVE MONTOYA.
YOU REPPED SCOTT BENJAMIN FOR THE MIGHTY MINTS CAMPAIGN?
THAT AND HALF A DOZEN OTHER JOBS...
VERY TALENTED KID, SCOTT. GREAT CHARISMA, WONDERFUL STAGE PRESENCE...
...NONE AS BIG AS THE M.M. ACCOUNT, OF COURSE.
...COMPLETE MASTERY OF HIS INSTRUMENT, EVEN AT FIFTEEN.
INSTRUMENT?
HIS BODY, THE ACTOR'S TOOL. SCOTT WAS PROBABLY THE MOST TALENTED ADOLESCENT WE REPPED.
Mighty Mints
Mighty Mints
ARE MOST OF YOUR CLIENTS ADOLESCENTS?

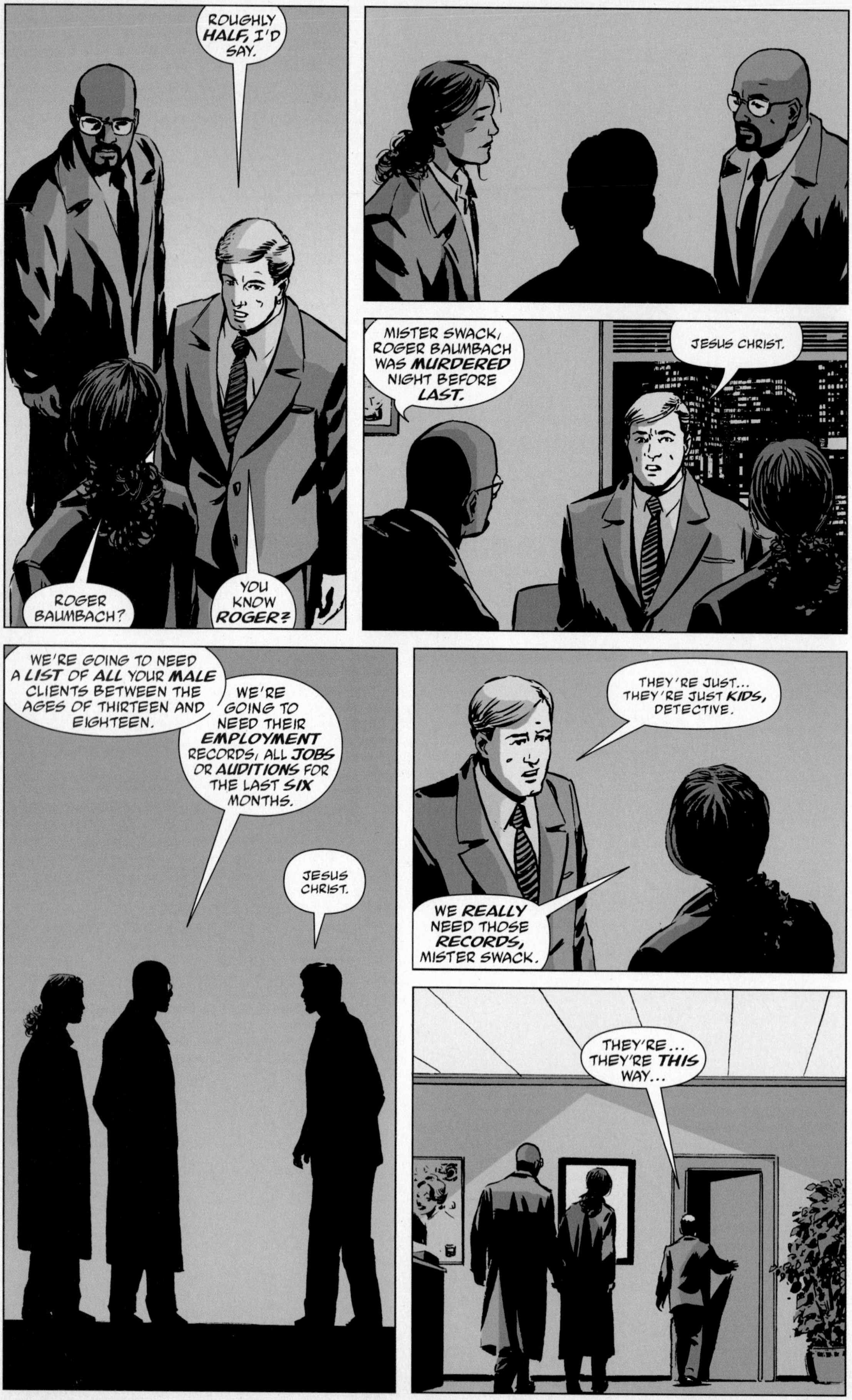
ROUGHLY HALF, I'D SAY.
ROGER BAUMBACH?
YOU KNOW ROGER?
MISTER SWACK, ROGER BAUMBACH WAS MURDERED NIGHT BEFORE LAST.
JESUS CHRIST.
WE'RE GOING TO NEED A LIST OF ALL YOUR MALE CLIENTS BETWEEN THE AGES OF THIRTEEN AND EIGHTEEN.
WE'RE GOING TO NEED THEIR EMPLOYMENT RECORDS, ALL JOBS OR AUDITIONS FOR THE LAST SIX MONTHS.
JESUS CHRIST.
THEY'RE JUST... THEY'RE JUST KIDS, DETECTIVE.
WE REALLY NEED THOSE RECORDS, MISTER SWACK.
THEY'RE... THEY'RE THIS WAY...

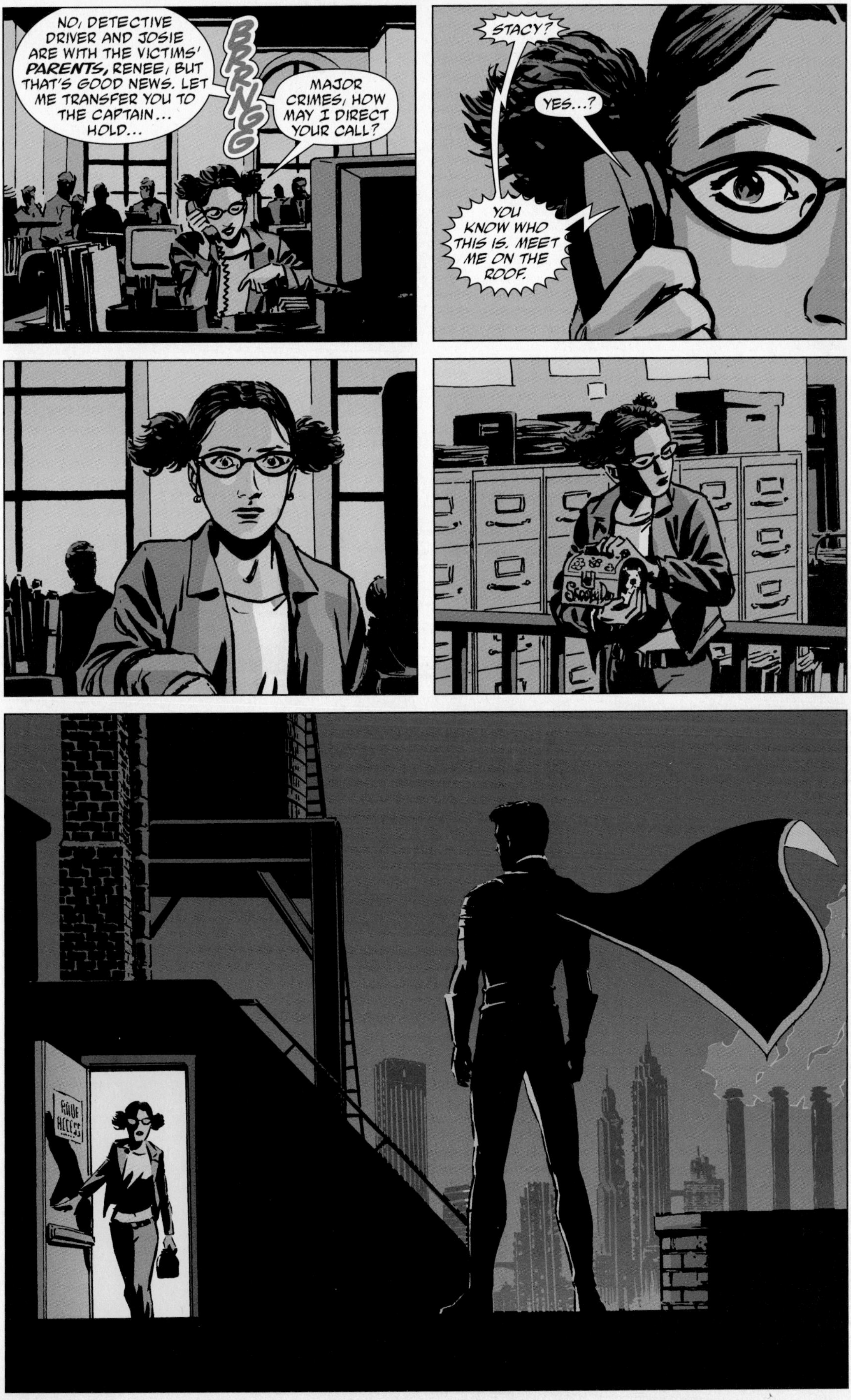
NO, DETECTIVE DRIVER AND JOSIE ARE WITH THE VICTIMS' **PARENTS,** RENEE, BUT THAT'S GOOD NEWS. LET ME TRANSFER YOU TO THE CAPTAIN... HOLD...
BRRNGG
MAJOR CRIMES, HOW MAY I DIRECT YOUR CALL?
STACY?
YES...?
YOU KNOW WHO THIS IS. MEET ME ON THE ROOF.

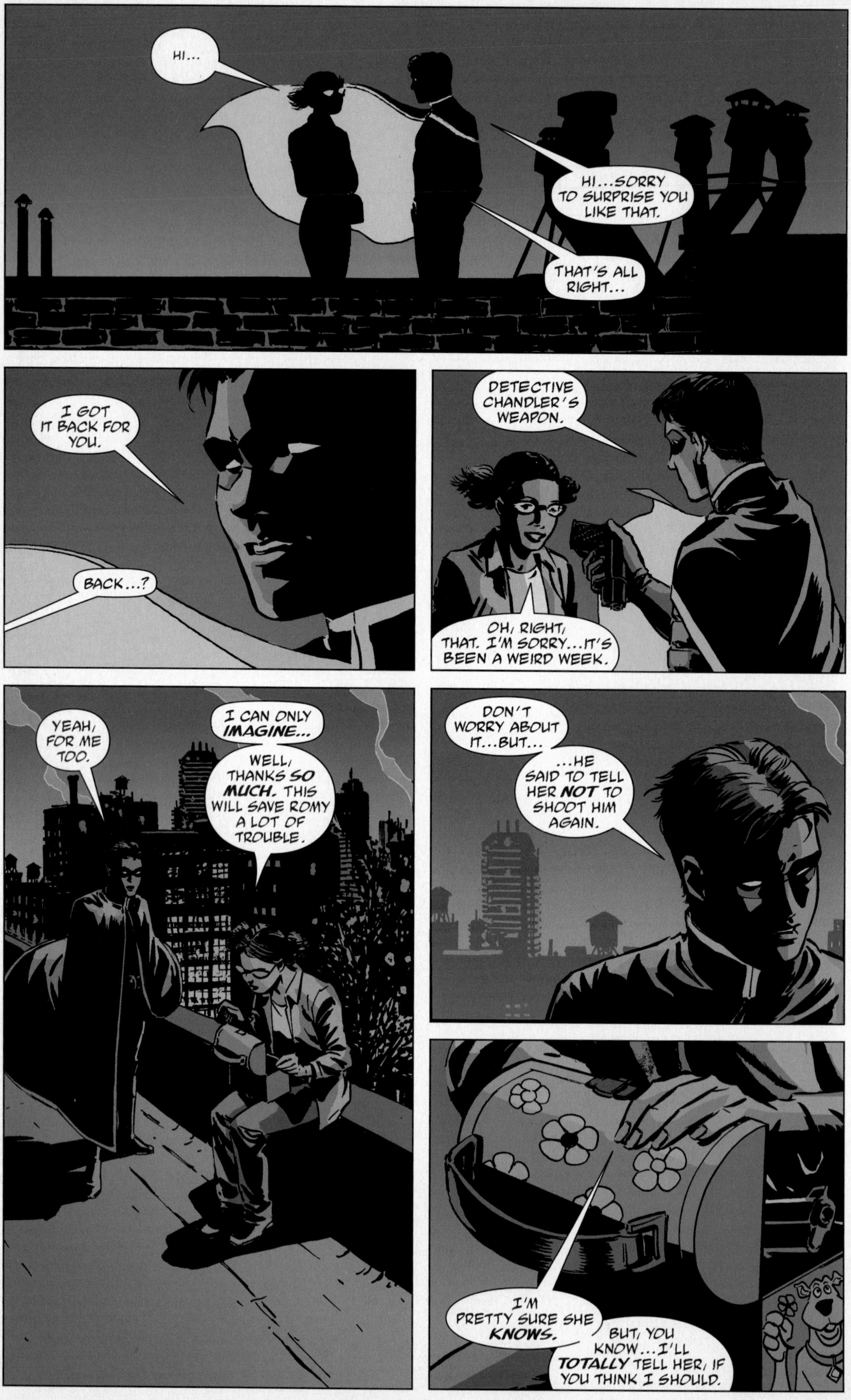
HI...
HI...SORRY TO SURPRISE YOU LIKE THAT.
THAT'S ALL RIGHT...
I GOT IT BACK FOR YOU.
BACK...?
DETECTIVE CHANDLER'S WEAPON.
OH, RIGHT, THAT. I'M SORRY...IT'S BEEN A WEIRD WEEK.
YEAH, FOR ME TOO.
I CAN ONLY IMAGINE...
WELL, THANKS SO MUCH. THIS WILL SAVE ROMY A LOT OF TROUBLE.
DON'T WORRY ABOUT IT...BUT...
...HE SAID TO TELL HER NOT TO SHOOT HIM AGAIN.
I'M PRETTY SURE SHE KNOWS.
BUT, YOU KNOW...I'LL TOTALLY TELL HER, IF YOU THINK I SHOULD.

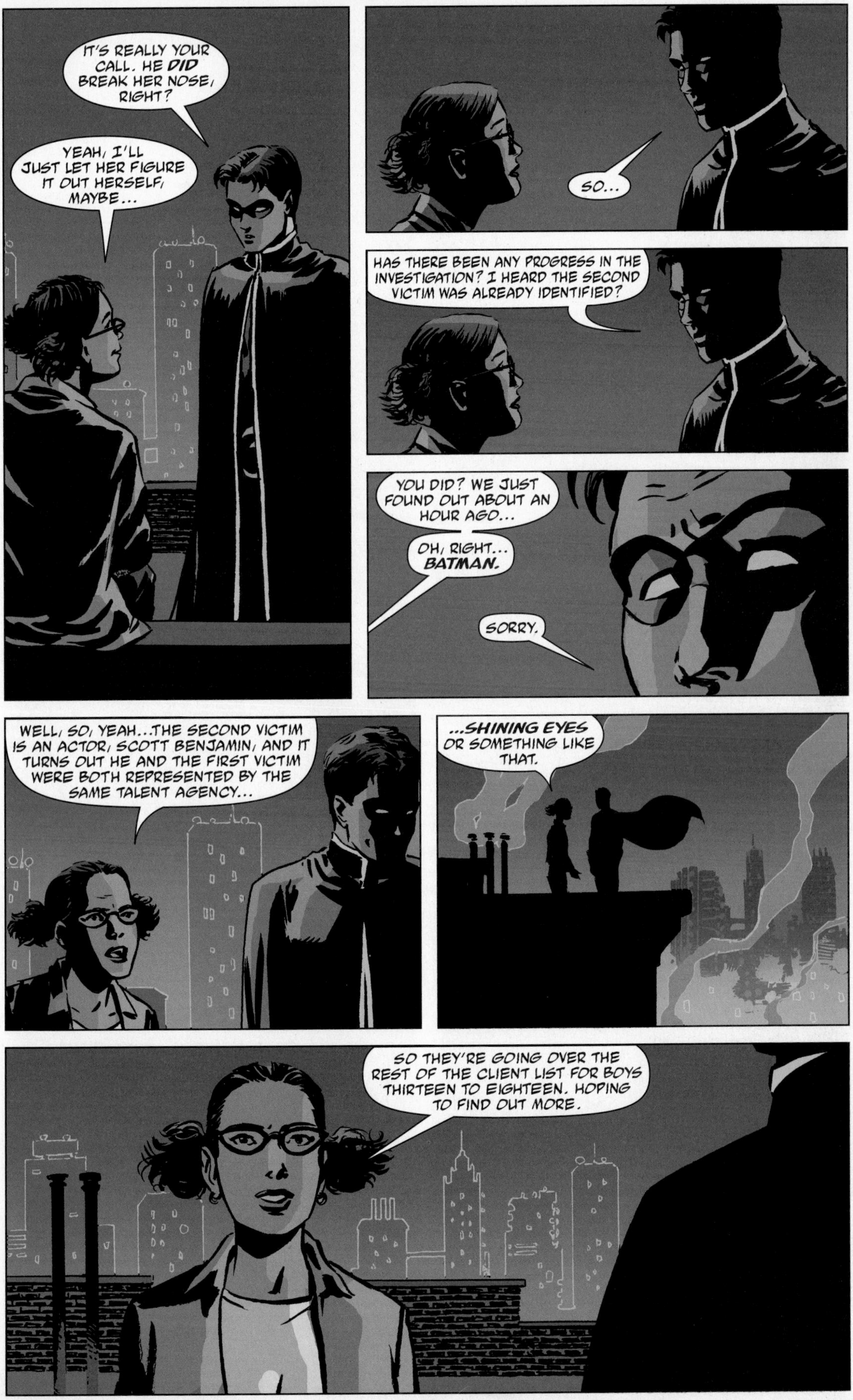
IT'S REALLY YOUR CALL. HE DID BREAK HER NOSE, RIGHT?
YEAH, I'LL JUST LET HER FIGURE IT OUT HERSELF, MAYBE...
SO...
HAS THERE BEEN ANY PROGRESS IN THE INVESTIGATION? I HEARD THE SECOND VICTIM WAS ALREADY IDENTIFIED?
YOU DID? WE JUST FOUND OUT ABOUT AN HOUR AGO...
OH, RIGHT... BATMAN.
SORRY.
WELL, SO, YEAH...THE SECOND VICTIM IS AN ACTOR, SCOTT BENJAMIN, AND IT TURNS OUT HE AND THE FIRST VICTIM WERE BOTH REPRESENTED BY THE SAME TALENT AGENCY...
...SHINING EYES OR SOMETHING LIKE THAT.
SO THEY'RE GOING OVER THE REST OF THE CLIENT LIST FOR BOYS THIRTEEN TO EIGHTEEN. HOPING TO FIND OUT MORE.

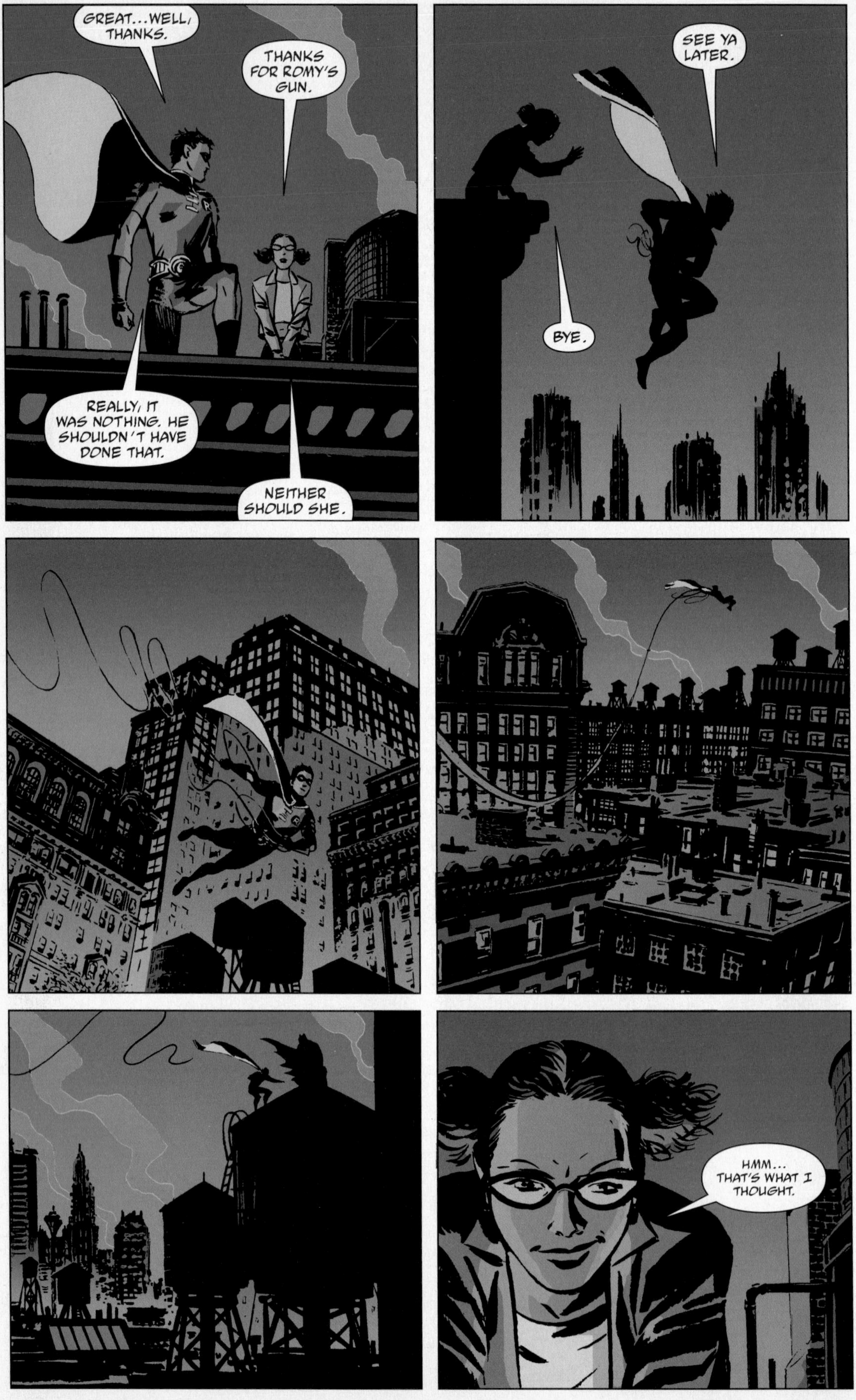
GREAT...WELL, THANKS.
THANKS FOR ROMY'S GUN.
REALLY, IT WAS NOTHING. HE SHOULDN'T HAVE DONE THAT.
NEITHER SHOULD SHE.
SEE YA LATER.
BYE.
HMM... THAT'S WHAT I THOUGHT.

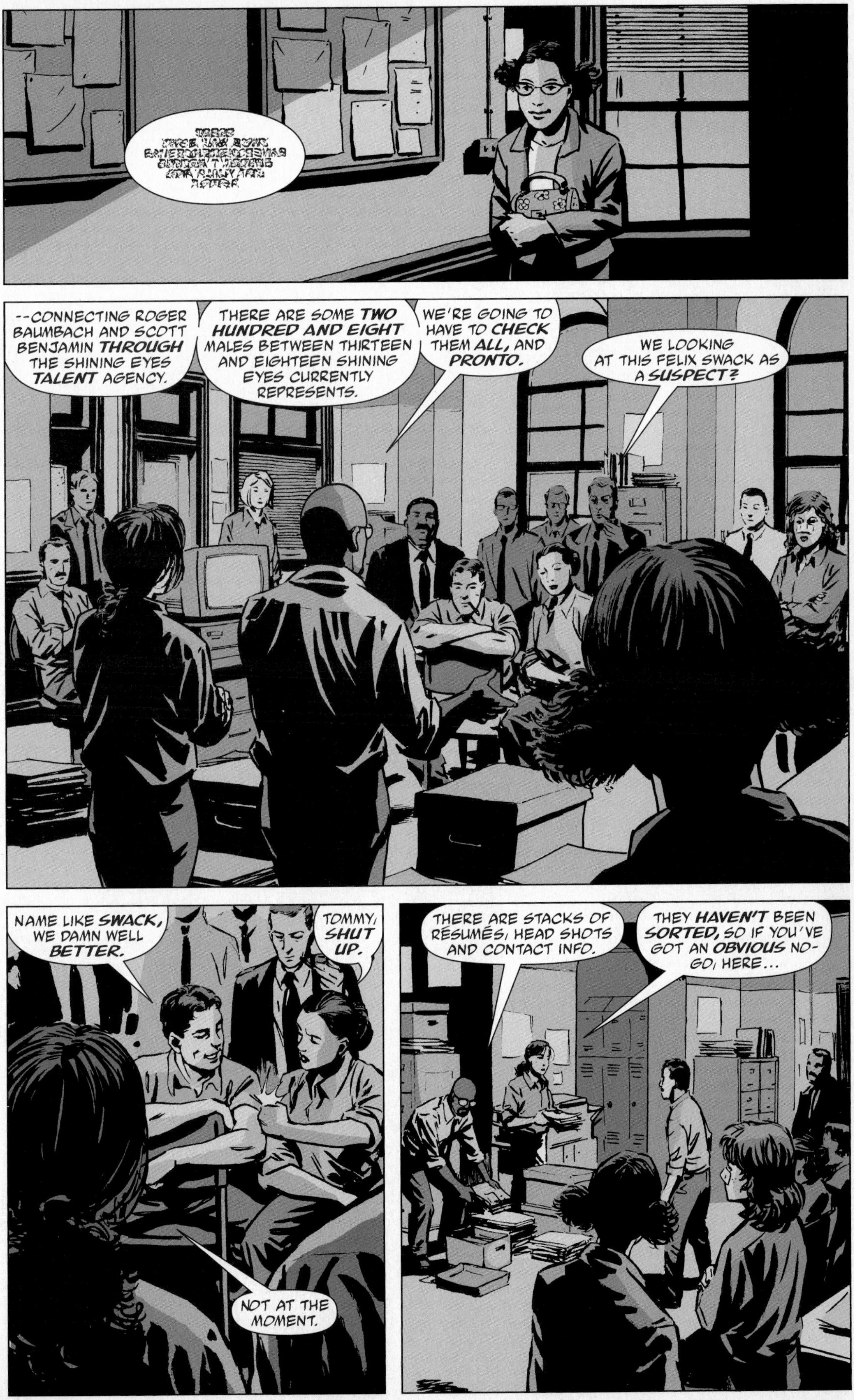
--CONNECTING ROGER BAUMBACH AND SCOTT BENJAMIN THROUGH THE SHINING EYES TALENT AGENCY.
THERE ARE SOME TWO HUNDRED AND EIGHT MALES BETWEEN THIRTEEN AND EIGHTEEN SHINING EYES CURRENTLY REPRESENTS.
WE'RE GOING TO HAVE TO CHECK THEM ALL, AND PRONTO.
WE LOOKING AT THIS FELIX SWACK AS A SUSPECT?
NAME LIKE SWACK, WE DAMN WELL BETTER.
TOMMY, SHUT UP.
NOT AT THE MOMENT.
THERE ARE STACKS OF RÉSUMÉS, HEAD SHOTS AND CONTACT INFO.
THEY HAVEN'T BEEN SORTED, SO IF YOU'VE GOT AN OBVIOUS NO-GO, HERE...

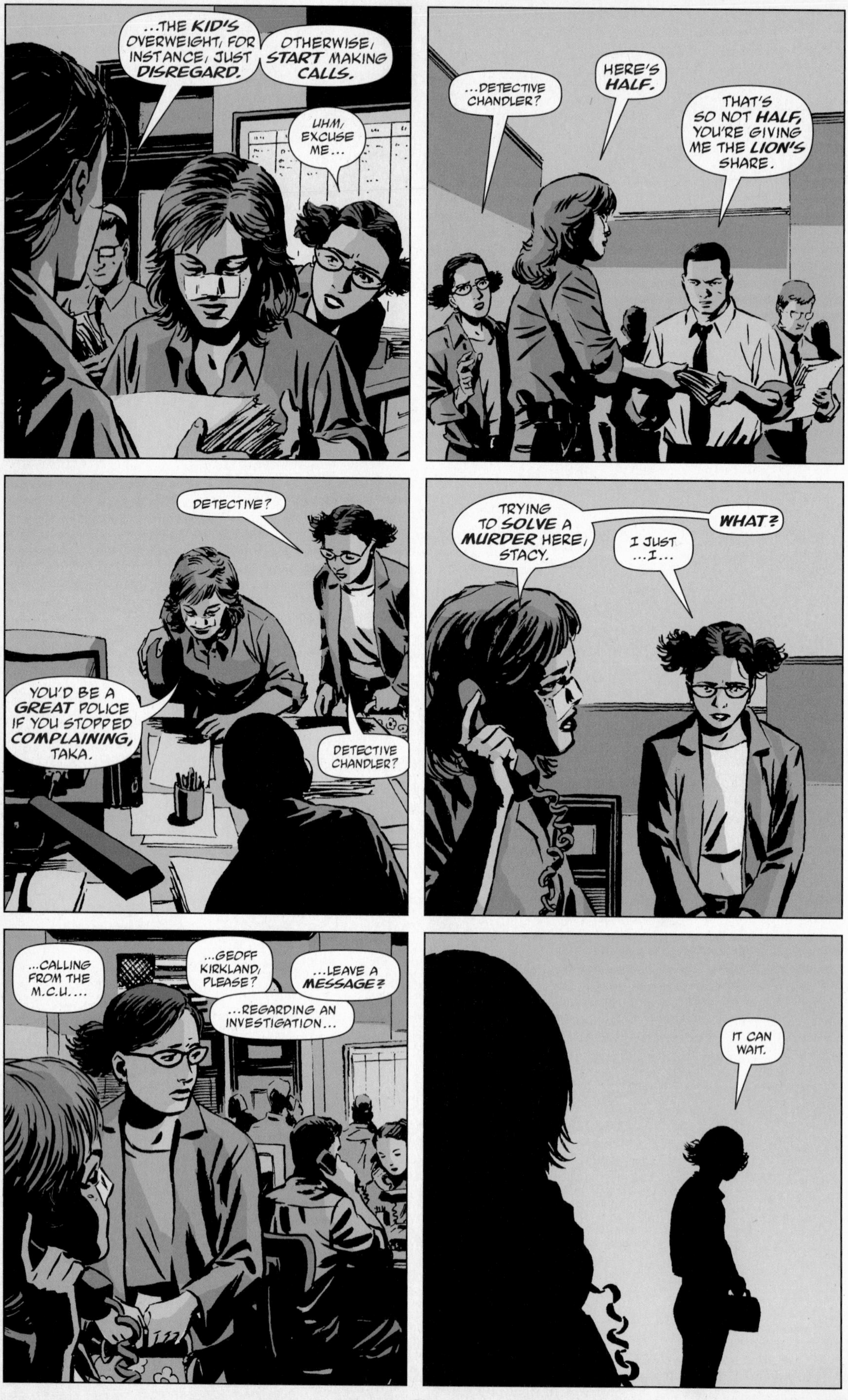
...THE KID'S OVERWEIGHT, FOR INSTANCE, JUST DISREGARD.
OTHERWISE, START MAKING CALLS.
UHM, EXCUSE ME...
...DETECTIVE CHANDLER?
HERE'S HALF.
THAT'S SO NOT HALF, YOU'RE GIVING ME THE LION'S SHARE.
DETECTIVE?
YOU'D BE A GREAT POLICE IF YOU STOPPED COMPLAINING, TAKA.
DETECTIVE CHANDLER?
TRYING TO SOLVE A MURDER HERE, STACY.
WHAT?
I JUST ...I...
...CALLING FROM THE M.C.U....
...GEOFF KIRKLAND, PLEASE?
...LEAVE A MESSAGE?
...REGARDING AN INVESTIGATION...
IT CAN WAIT.

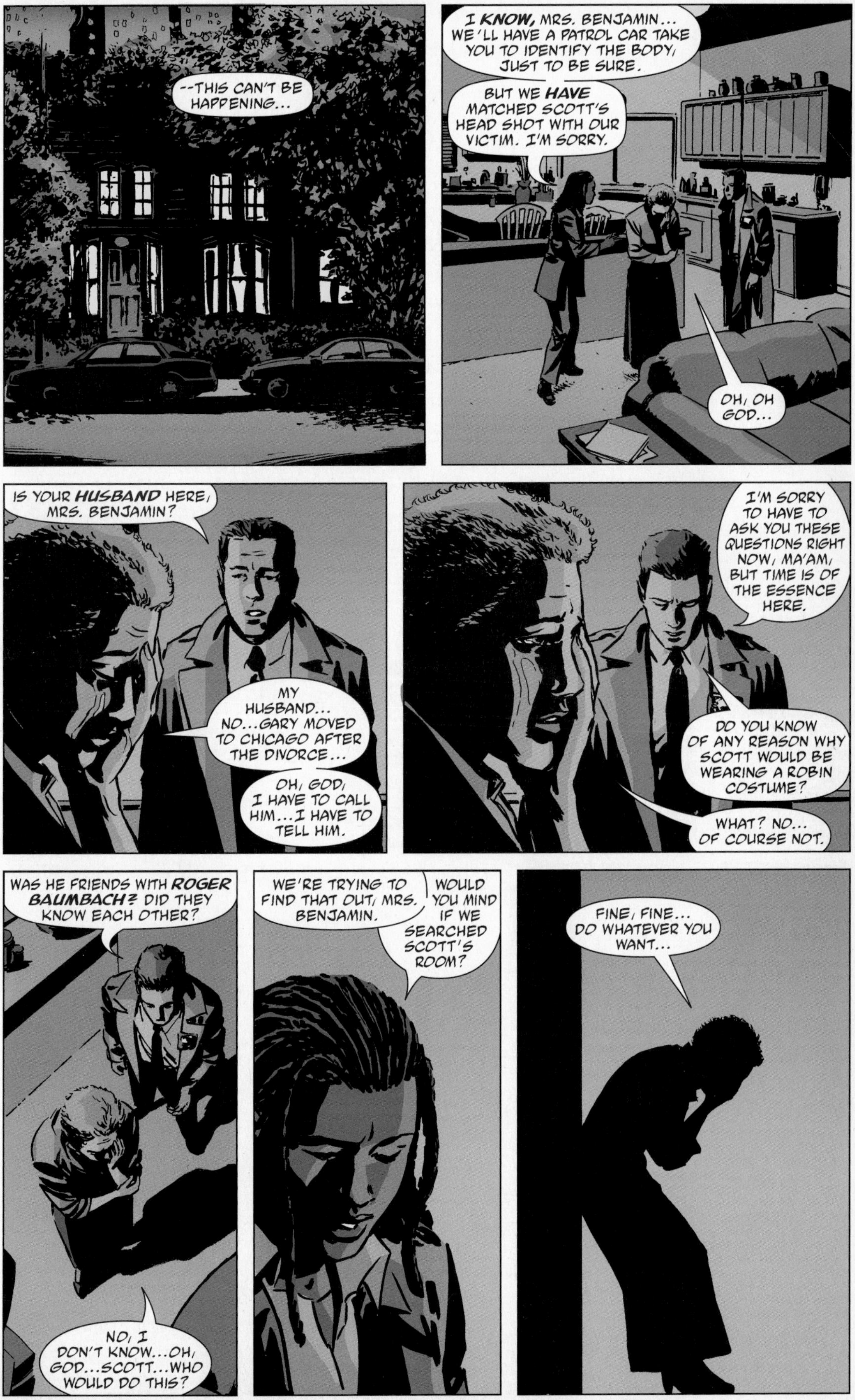
--THIS CAN'T BE HAPPENING...
I KNOW, MRS. BENJAMIN... WE'LL HAVE A PATROL CAR TAKE YOU TO IDENTIFY THE BODY, JUST TO BE SURE.
BUT WE HAVE MATCHED SCOTT'S HEAD SHOT WITH OUR VICTIM. I'M SORRY.
OH, OH GOD...
IS YOUR HUSBAND HERE, MRS. BENJAMIN?
MY HUSBAND... NO...GARY MOVED TO CHICAGO AFTER THE DIVORCE...
OH, GOD, I HAVE TO CALL HIM...I HAVE TO TELL HIM.
I'M SORRY TO HAVE TO ASK YOU THESE QUESTIONS RIGHT NOW, MA'AM, BUT TIME IS OF THE ESSENCE HERE.
DO YOU KNOW OF ANY REASON WHY SCOTT WOULD BE WEARING A ROBIN COSTUME?
WHAT? NO... OF COURSE NOT.
WAS HE FRIENDS WITH ROGER BAUMBACH? DID THEY KNOW EACH OTHER?
NO, I DON'T KNOW...OH, GOD...SCOTT...WHO WOULD DO THIS?
WE'RE TRYING TO FIND THAT OUT, MRS. BENJAMIN.
WOULD YOU MIND IF WE SEARCHED SCOTT'S ROOM?
FINE, FINE... DO WHATEVER YOU WANT...

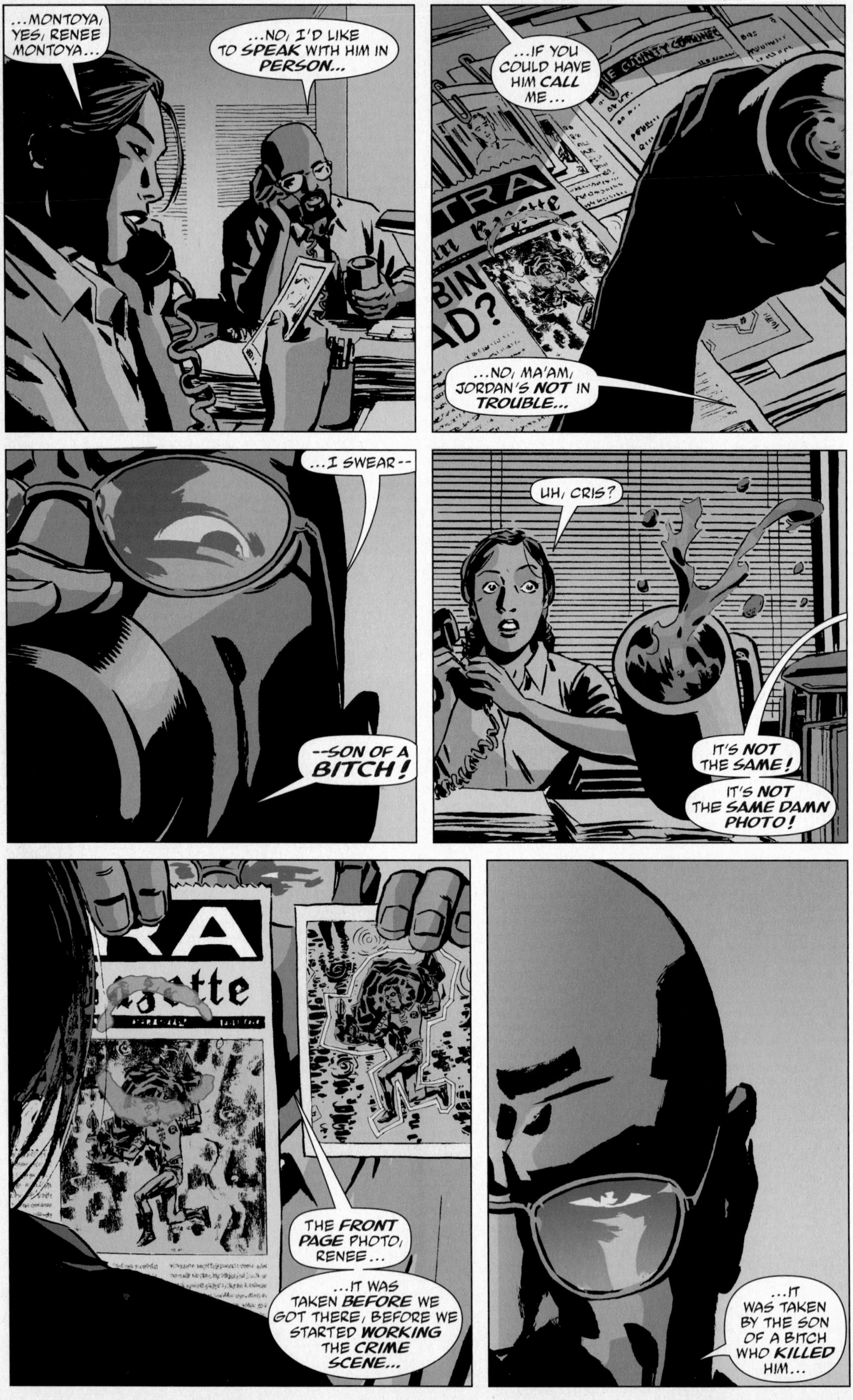
...MONTOYA, YES, RENEE MONTOYA...
...NO, I'D LIKE TO SPEAK WITH HIM IN PERSON...
...IF YOU COULD HAVE HIM CALL ME...
...NO, MA'AM, JORDAN'S NOT IN TROUBLE...
...I SWEAR--
--SON OF A BITCH!
UH, CRIS?
IT'S NOT THE SAME!
IT'S NOT THE SAME DAMN PHOTO!
THE FRONT PAGE PHOTO, RENEE...
...IT WAS TAKEN BEFORE WE GOT THERE, BEFORE WE STARTED WORKING THE CRIME SCENE...
...IT WAS TAKEN BY THE SON OF A BITCH WHO KILLED HIM...

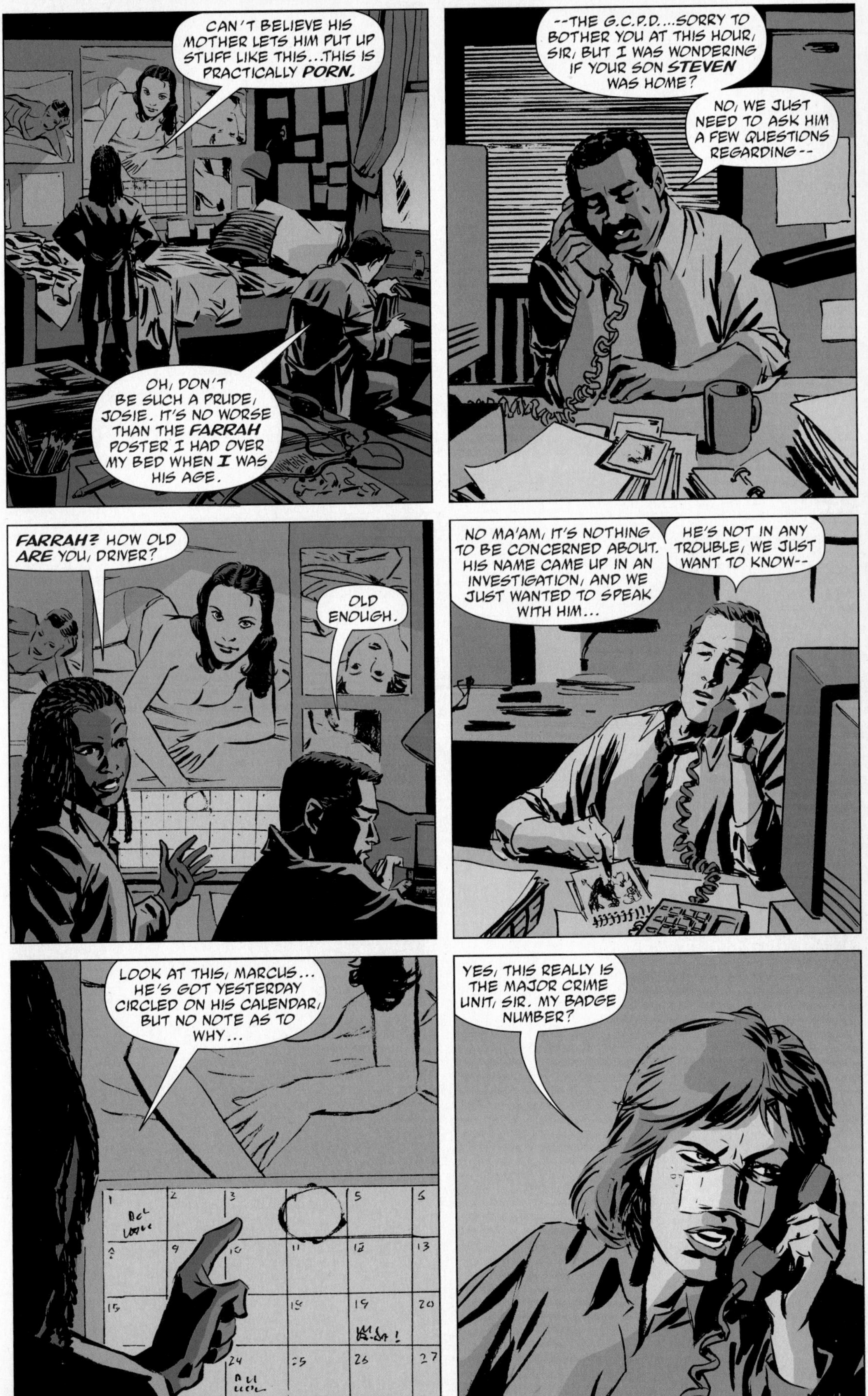
CAN'T BELIEVE HIS MOTHER LETS HIM PUT UP STUFF LIKE THIS...THIS IS PRACTICALLY PORN.
OH, DON'T BE SUCH A PRUDE, JOSIE. IT'S NO WORSE THAN THE FARRAH POSTER I HAD OVER MY BED WHEN I WAS HIS AGE.
--THE G.C.P.D....SORRY TO BOTHER YOU AT THIS HOUR, SIR, BUT I WAS WONDERING IF YOUR SON STEVEN WAS HOME?
NO, WE JUST NEED TO ASK HIM A FEW QUESTIONS REGARDING--
FARRAH? HOW OLD ARE YOU, DRIVER?
OLD ENOUGH.
NO MA'AM, IT'S NOTHING TO BE CONCERNED ABOUT. HIS NAME CAME UP IN AN INVESTIGATION, AND WE JUST WANTED TO SPEAK WITH HIM...
HE'S NOT IN ANY TROUBLE, WE JUST WANT TO KNOW--
LOOK AT THIS, MARCUS... HE'S GOT YESTERDAY CIRCLED ON HIS CALENDAR, BUT NO NOTE AS TO WHY...
YES, THIS REALLY IS THE MAJOR CRIME UNIT, SIR. MY BADGE NUMBER?

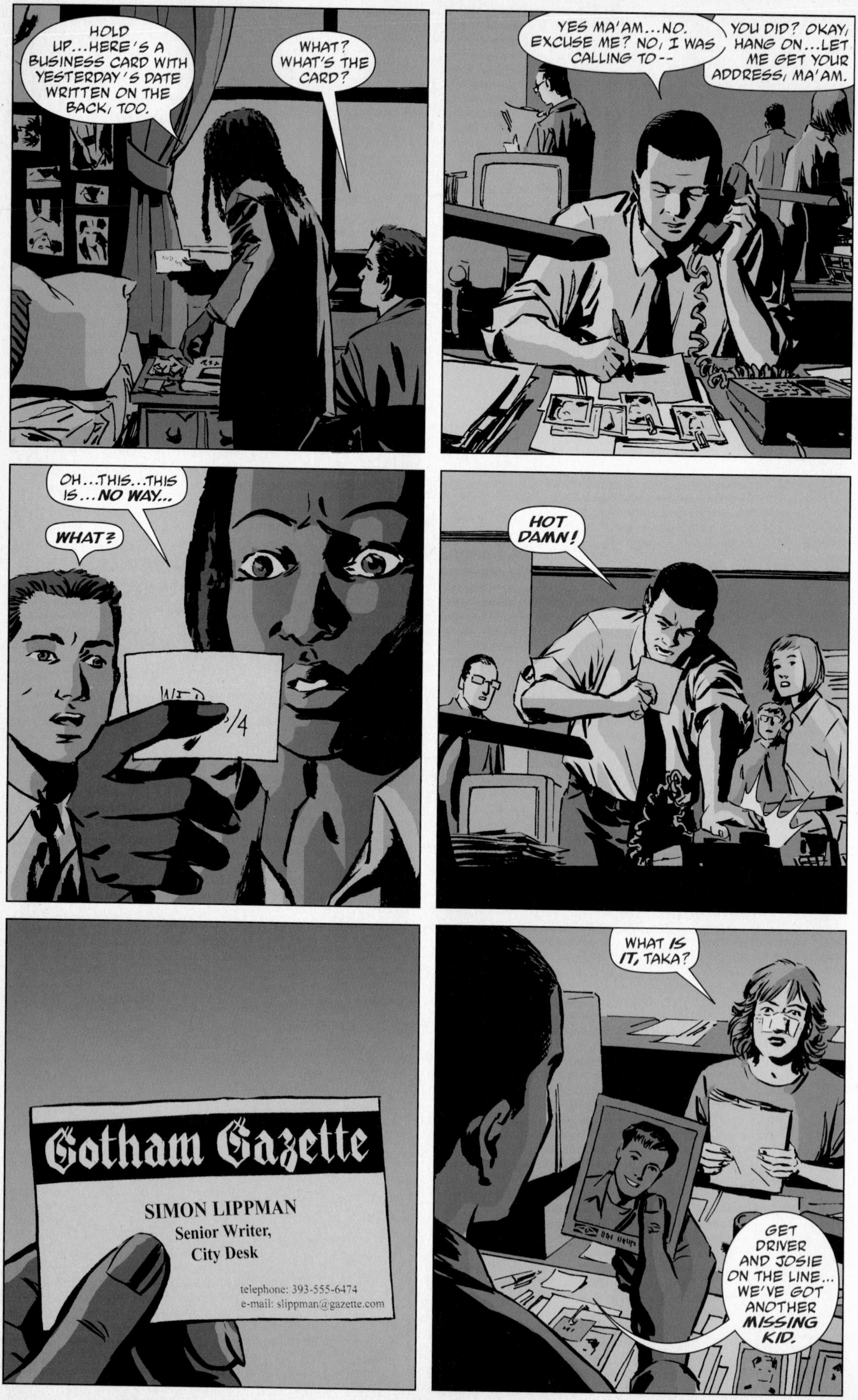
HOLD UP...HERE'S A BUSINESS CARD WITH YESTERDAY'S DATE WRITTEN ON THE BACK, TOO.
WHAT? WHAT'S THE CARD?
YES MA'AM...NO. EXCUSE ME? NO, I WAS CALLING TO--
YOU DID? OKAY, HANG ON...LET ME GET YOUR ADDRESS, MA'AM.
OH...THIS...THIS IS...NO WAY...
WHAT?
HOT DAMN!
Gotham Gazette
SIMON LIPPMAN
Senior Writer,
City Desk
telephone: 393-555-6474
e-mail: slippman@gazette.com
WHAT IS IT, TAKA?
GET DRIVER AND JOSIE ON THE LINE... WE'VE GOT ANOTHER MISSING KID.

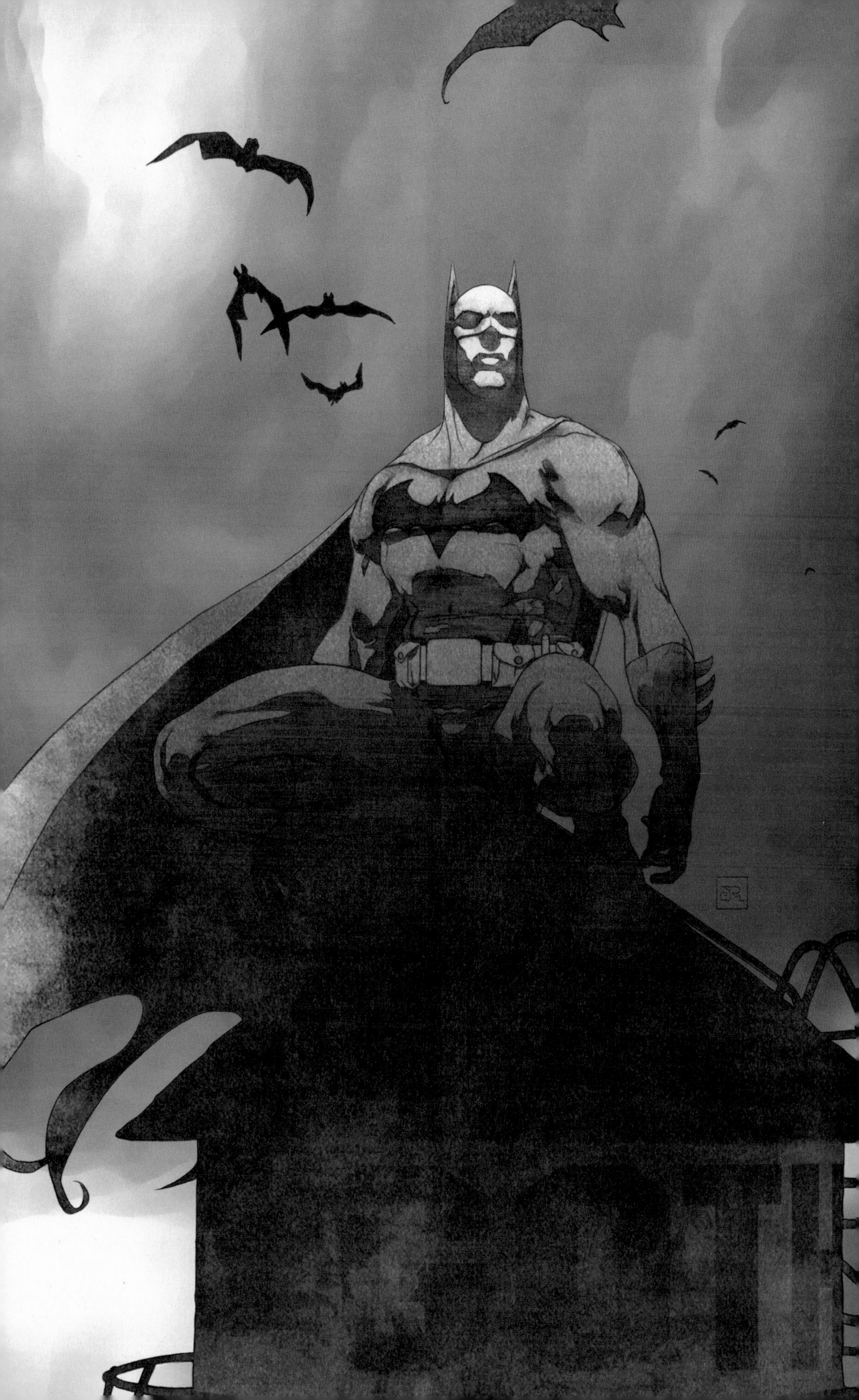

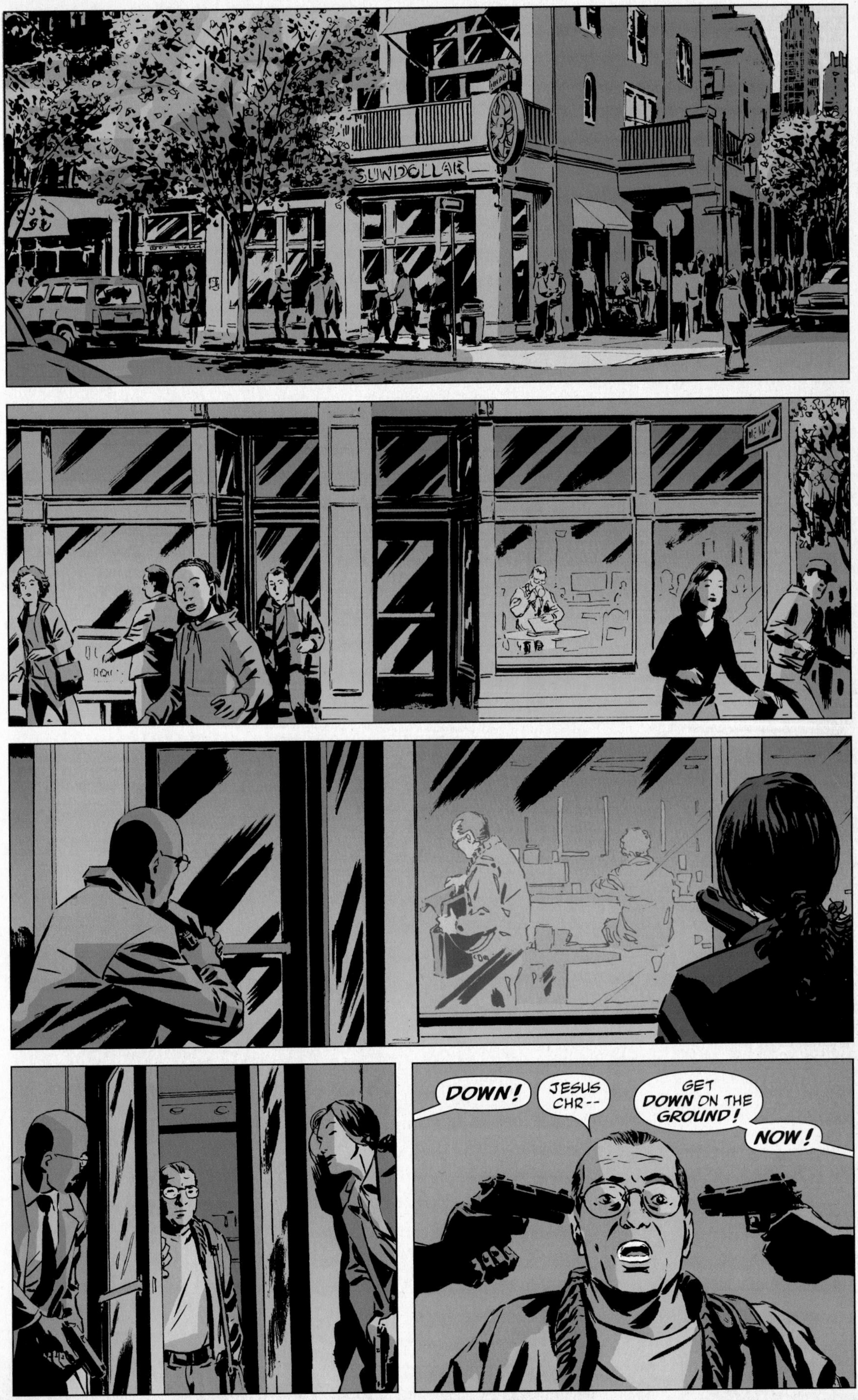
SUNDOLLAR
DOWN!
JESUS CHR--
GET DOWN ON THE GROUND!
NOW!

WH-WHAT THE HELL--
SHUT UP, LIPPMAN!
SIMON LIPPMAN, YOU ARE UNDER ARREST FOR THE MURDER OF SCOTT BENJAMIN!
WHAT?!?
GUYS, C'MON, IF SAWYER'S STILL--
YOU HAVE THE RIGHT TO REMAIN SILENT...
NHHN!
IF YOU GIVE UP YOUR RIGHT TO SILENCE, ANYTHING YOU SAY CAN BE USED AGAINST YOU...
THIS IS SERIOUSLY *$#¢ED UP.
...AND I'D CONSIDER EXERCISING IT RIGHT ABOUT NOW, SIMON.
GCPD

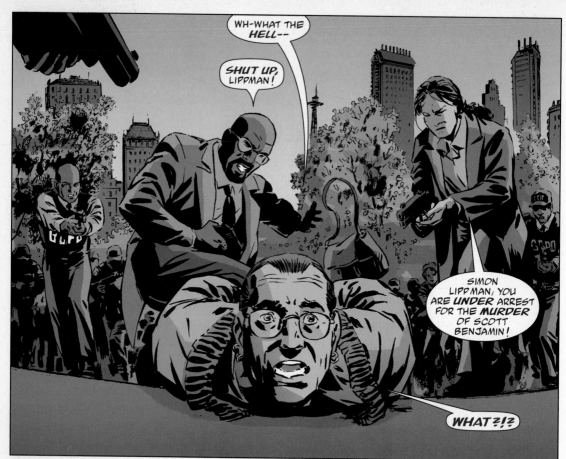

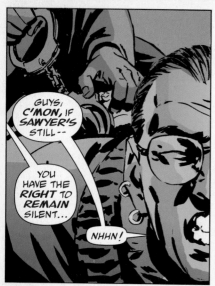

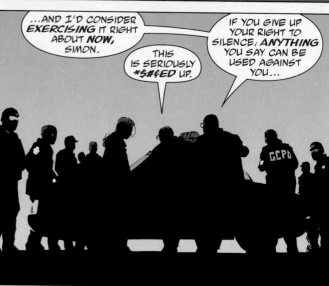

DEAD ROBIN

CONCLUSION

...RADIOED IT IN THAT THEY'VE GOT **LIPPMAN** IN **CUSTODY** AND ARE ON THE WAY HERE.

ASSUMING THAT HE'S **NOT** GOING TO GIVE IT UP--AND IT'S **GOTHAM**, SO I THINK WE ALL KNOW IT'S A **SAFE** ASSUMPTION-- THAT MEANS WE'VE GOT A **THIRD** KID OUT THERE SOMEWHERE.

KID'S NAME IS **ZACK WESTON**, SIXTEEN, FROM THE HEIGHTS.

DEL ARRAZIO AND BARTLETT ARE ON THEIR WAY TO TALK TO THE **PARENTS** AS WE SPEAK.

ZACK'S PARENTS **REPORTED** HIM **MISSING** YESTERDAY, WHICH PUTS THE **CLOCK** AT ROUGHLY **FIFTY HOURS** SINCE HE WAS **LAST SEEN**.

ASSUMING HE'S **STILL** ALIVE, WE NEED TO **FIND** HIM.

ASSUMING HE **ISN'T**...

...WE NEED TO FIND THE **BODY**.

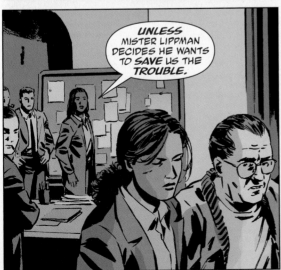

UNLESS MISTER LIPPMAN DECIDES HE WANTS TO **SAVE** US THE **TROUBLE**.

THIS IS ALL A **MISTAKE**.

NO, THE **MISTAKE** WAS **TRUSTING** YOU IN THE **FIRST** PLACE...

...BUT WE'RE AIMING TO CORRECT THAT ONE.

DAMMIT, MAGGIE! I DIDN'T SCREW YOU GUYS!

AND I SURE AS HELL HAVEN'T KILLED ANYONE!

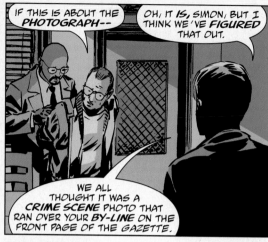

IF THIS IS ABOUT THE PHOTOGRAPH--

OH, IT IS, SIMON, BUT I THINK WE'VE FIGURED THAT OUT.

WE ALL THOUGHT IT WAS A CRIME SCENE PHOTO THAT RAN OVER YOUR BY-LINE ON THE FRONT PAGE OF THE GAZETTE.

FIGURED YOU'D BOUGHT IT OFF OF CORRIGAN, THAT EITHER HE OR ONE OF HIS BUNKIES WAS YOUR SOURCE.

BUT THEY WEREN'T, WERE THEY? BECAUSE THE GAZETTE'S PHOTO WASN'T OUR PHOTO AT ALL...

...IT WAS A DIFFERENT ONE ALTOGETHER, TAKEN BEFORE WE EVEN ARRIVED...

...TAKEN BY SOMEONE WHO WAS ON THE ROOF AT THE TIME OF THE MURDER.

AND YOU THINK IT WAS ME?

I THINK IT'S A HELL OF A PHOTO TO RUN OVER YOUR BY-LINE, SIMON.

AND YOU'VE ALWAYS HAD A NOSE FOR A GOOD STORY.

SO MAYBE YOU DECIDED TO MAKE ONE ALL YOUR OWN.

I DON'T KNOW WHERE THE PHOTO CAME FROM!

TWO DAYS AGO YOU WERE GOING ON AND ON ABOUT HOW I COULDN'T ASK YOU TO GIVE UP A SOURCE.

WHICH STORY IS IT, SIMON?

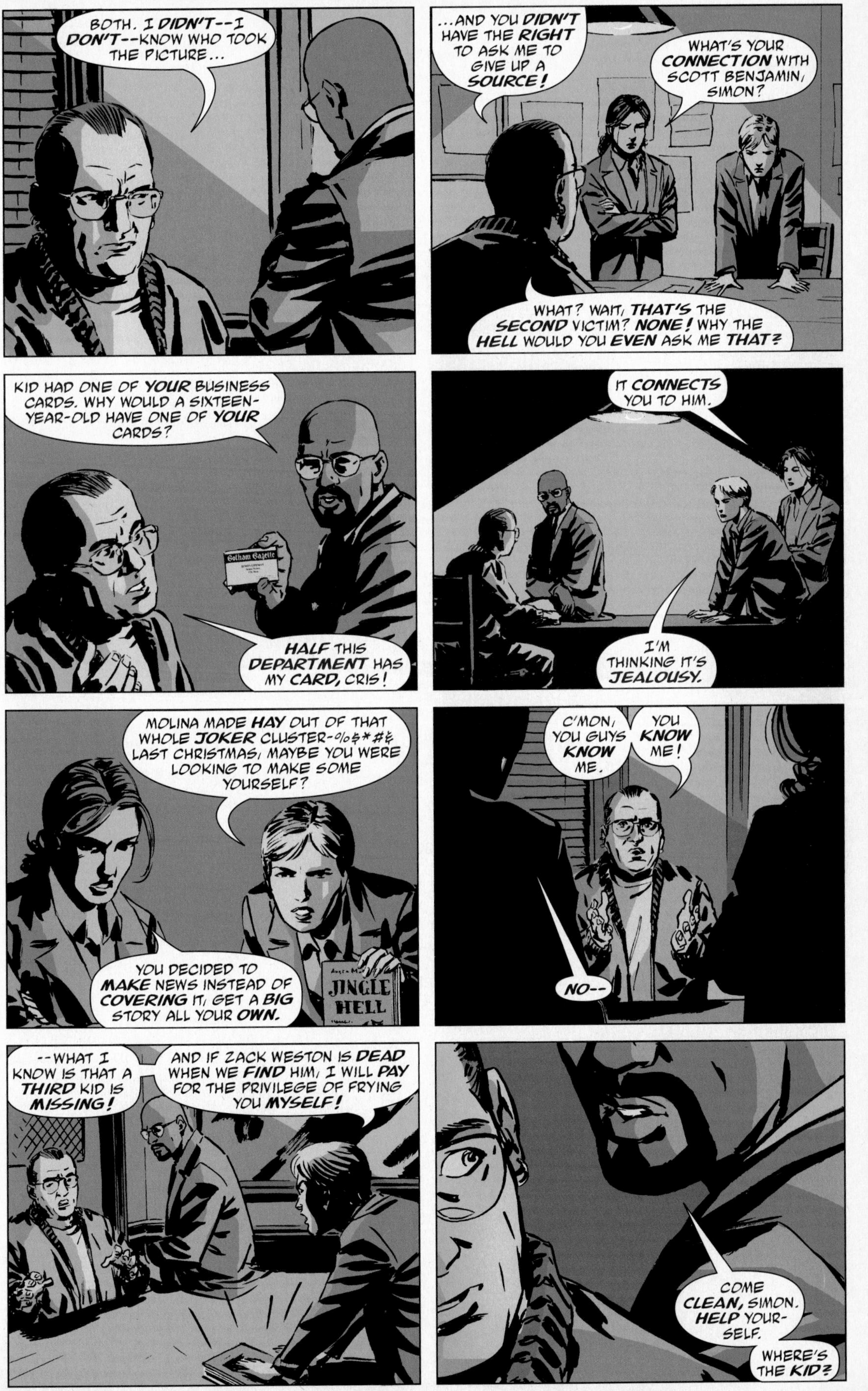
BOTH. I DIDN'T--I DON'T--KNOW WHO TOOK THE PICTURE...
...AND YOU DIDN'T HAVE THE RIGHT TO ASK ME TO GIVE UP A SOURCE!
WHAT'S YOUR CONNECTION WITH SCOTT BENJAMIN, SIMON?
WHAT? WAIT, THAT'S THE SECOND VICTIM? NONE! WHY THE HELL WOULD YOU EVEN ASK ME THAT?
KID HAD ONE OF YOUR BUSINESS CARDS. WHY WOULD A SIXTEEN-YEAR-OLD HAVE ONE OF YOUR CARDS?
Gotham Gazette
HALF THIS DEPARTMENT HAS MY CARD, CRIS!
IT CONNECTS YOU TO HIM.
I'M THINKING IT'S JEALOUSY.
MOLINA MADE HAY OUT OF THAT WHOLE JOKER CLUSTER-%$*#& LAST CHRISTMAS, MAYBE YOU WERE LOOKING TO MAKE SOME YOURSELF?
YOU DECIDED TO MAKE NEWS INSTEAD OF COVERING IT, GET A BIG STORY ALL YOUR OWN.
JINGLE HELL
NO--
C'MON, YOU GUYS KNOW ME.
YOU KNOW ME!
--WHAT I KNOW IS THAT A THIRD KID IS MISSING!
AND IF ZACK WESTON IS DEAD WHEN WE FIND HIM, I WILL PAY FOR THE PRIVILEGE OF FRYING YOU MYSELF!
COME CLEAN, SIMON. HELP YOURSELF.
WHERE'S THE KID?

HEY, UH... ROMY?

ON THE PHONE, STACY.

YEAH, BUT I'VE GOT--

EXCUSE ME?

YES?

WHO ARE THE DETECTIVES IN CHARGE OF THE DEAD ROBINS CASE?

THAT WOULD BE DETECTIVES DRIVER AND MACDONALD. I'M SORRY, AREN'T YOU *PRESS*?

YEAH, JUST *FREELANCE*, BUT... I NEED TO TALK TO DRIVER AND MACDONALD.

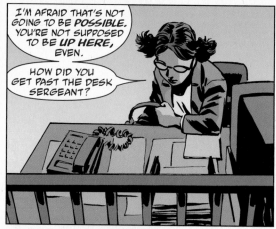

I'M AFRAID THAT'S NOT GOING TO BE *POSSIBLE*. YOU'RE NOT SUPPOSED TO BE *UP HERE*, EVEN.

HOW DID YOU GET PAST THE DESK SERGEANT?

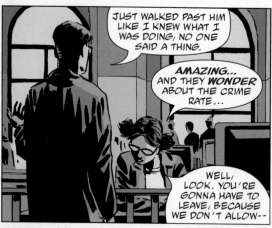

JUST WALKED PAST HIM LIKE I KNEW WHAT I WAS DOING, NO ONE SAID A THING.

AMAZING... AND THEY *WONDER* ABOUT THE CRIME RATE...

WELL, LOOK. YOU'RE GONNA HAVE TO LEAVE, BECAUSE WE DON'T ALLOW--

I NEED TO SEE THEM ABOUT *THIS*.

EADMONTE ACADEMY GOTHAM

Zack Weston

ZACK WESTON NO. 7652-5085-08   NOT VALID FOR USE OFF CAMPUS

Zack Weston

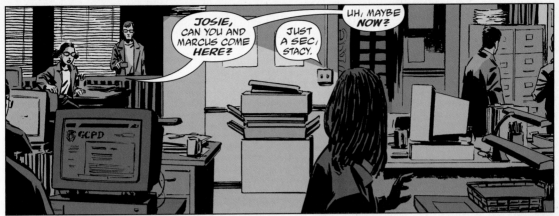

JOSIE, CAN YOU AND MARCUS COME *HERE?*

JUST A SEC, STACY.

UH, MAYBE *NOW?*

STACY? WHAT'S GOING ON?

I UNDERSTAND YOU'VE TAKEN *SIMON LIPPMAN* INTO CUSTODY?

I'M SORRY. WHO ARE *YOU?*

STACE, WHO *IS* THIS?

HE'S GOT--

YOU'VE GOT THE WRONG MAN, DETECTIVE.

MOTHER$#%--

--YOU THE GOD'S HONEST *TRUTH* HERE, MAGGIE.

--IS THE *KID,* YOU SONNUVABICH! WHERE IS HE?!

...WHAT THE *HELL?*

WHAT'D YOU DO WITH THE KID, YOU SICK--

DETECTIVES!

WHAT THE *HELL* IS GOING ON HERE?

SON OF A BITCH JUST WALKED IN WITH ZACK WESTON'S *SCHOOL I.D. CARD.*

WE'VE GOT THE *WRONG* GUY IN THE *BOX,* CAPTAIN.

WHAT?

IT'S *THIS* HUMP.

WHAT?

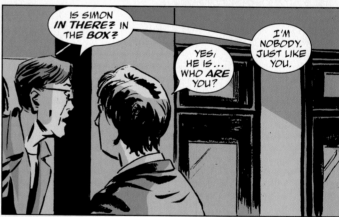

IS SIMON *IN THERE?* IN THE *BOX?*

YES, HE IS... WHO *ARE* YOU?

I'M *NOBODY.* JUST LIKE YOU.

BUT I'M A FRIEND OF SIMON'S. AND I'D LIKE TO TALK TO HIM.

GIVE HIM AN *EXCLUSIVE* FOR ALL HIS TROUBLE.

I DON'T LIKE THIS ONE BIT.

THAT'S WHY YOU'RE **SECOND SHIFT**, DETECTIVE.

I COULD **NOT** TELL.

HEY, I **GOT** THE GUY.

-- ANY CHANCE YOU COULD LEAVE US ALONE? I'M **SURE** YOU'LL BE **RECORDING** THIS, ANYWAY.

'FRAID NOT, MR. DUNNING. CONSIDER US **BODYGUARDS**...WHAT YOU JUST PUT YOUR **FRIEND** HERE THROUGH, YOU MAY **NEED** ONE.

I'M SURE THAT'S NOT... TRUE?

SIMON?

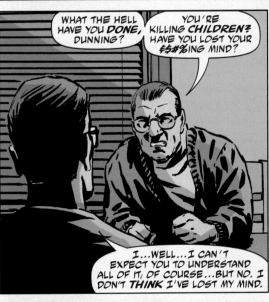

WHAT THE HELL HAVE YOU **DONE**, DUNNING?

YOU'RE KILLING **CHILDREN?** HAVE YOU LOST YOUR £$#%ING MIND?

I...WELL...I CAN'T EXPECT YOU TO UNDERSTAND ALL OF IT, OF COURSE...BUT NO. I DON'T **THINK** I'VE LOST MY MIND.

THEN **WHY?**

IT'S KIND OF COMPLICATED --

WHY SET ME UP? WE WERE **FRIENDS**, JACK.

WE STILL ARE. I **CAME DOWN** AS SOON AS I **HEARD** THEY ARRESTED YOU.

I JUST WANTED TO BE SURE YOU'D BE HERE...FOR THE STORY.

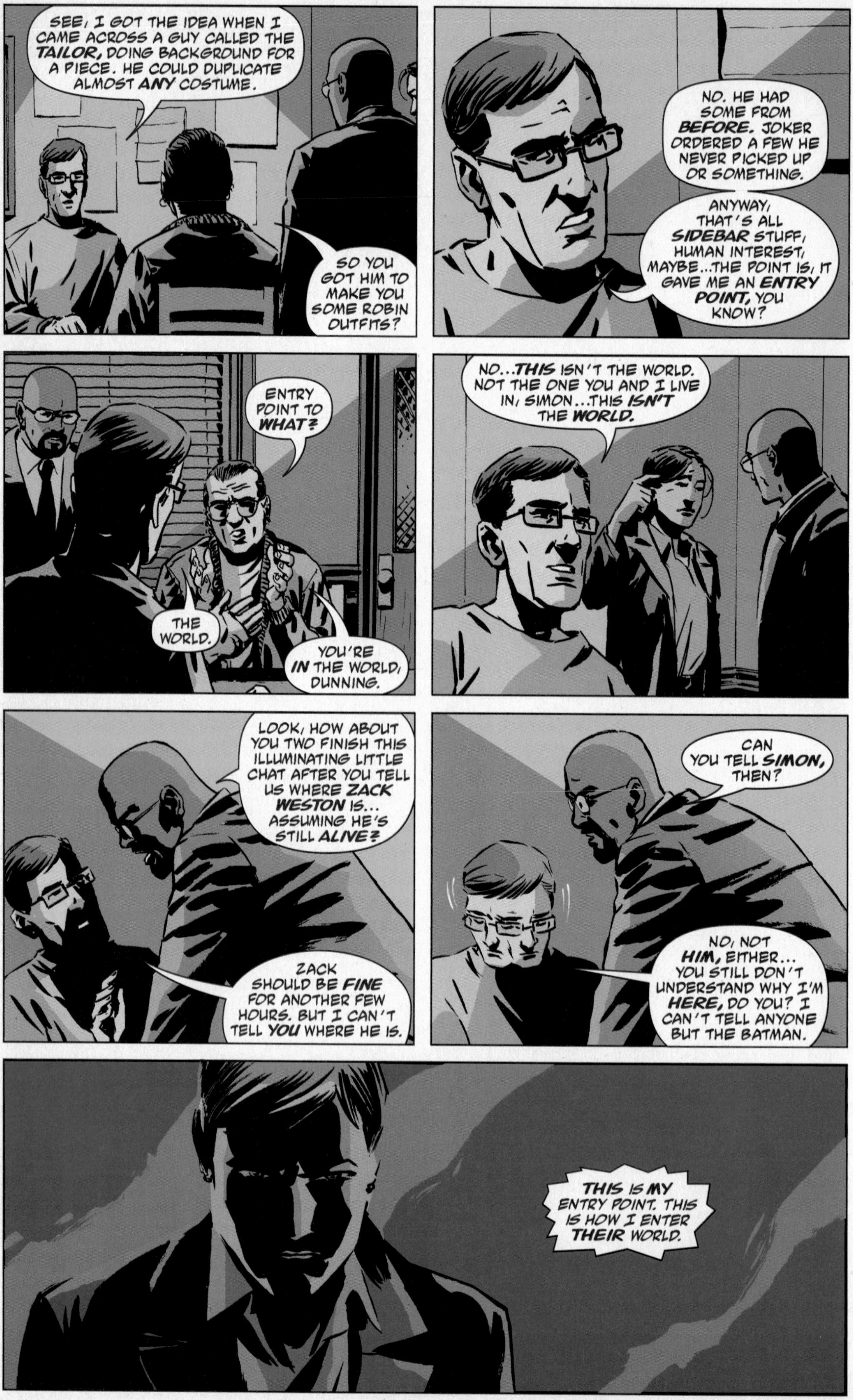
SEE, I GOT THE IDEA WHEN I CAME ACROSS A GUY CALLED THE TAILOR, DOING BACKGROUND FOR A PIECE. HE COULD DUPLICATE ALMOST ANY COSTUME.
SO YOU GOT HIM TO MAKE YOU SOME ROBIN OUTFITS?
NO. HE HAD SOME FROM BEFORE. JOKER ORDERED A FEW HE NEVER PICKED UP OR SOMETHING.
ANYWAY, THAT'S ALL SIDEBAR STUFF, HUMAN INTEREST, MAYBE...THE POINT IS, IT GAVE ME AN ENTRY POINT, YOU KNOW?
ENTRY POINT TO WHAT?
THE WORLD.
YOU'RE IN THE WORLD, DUNNING.
NO...THIS ISN'T THE WORLD. NOT THE ONE YOU AND I LIVE IN, SIMON...THIS ISN'T THE WORLD.
LOOK, HOW ABOUT YOU TWO FINISH THIS ILLUMINATING LITTLE CHAT AFTER YOU TELL US WHERE ZACK WESTON IS... ASSUMING HE'S STILL ALIVE?
ZACK SHOULD BE FINE FOR ANOTHER FEW HOURS. BUT I CAN'T TELL YOU WHERE HE IS.
CAN YOU TELL SIMON, THEN?
NO, NOT HIM, EITHER... YOU STILL DON'T UNDERSTAND WHY I'M HERE, DO YOU? I CAN'T TELL ANYONE BUT THE BATMAN.
THIS IS MY ENTRY POINT. THIS IS HOW I ENTER THEIR WORLD.

C'MON, CAPTAIN, WE **KNOW** HOW THIS **ENDS**...

WAIT, MARCUS.

I JUST--

NO **GODDAMN** WAY!

LOWER YOUR **VOICE** AND **CLOSE** THE **DOOR**.

YOU **CANNOT** SERIOUSLY **CONSIDER** THIS, CAPTAIN!

TELL ME THIS IS **NOT** AN **OPTION**, HERE!

WHY THE HELL **NOT?**

WE **DO** THIS, WE **GIVE** DUNNING WHAT HE **WANTS**, MARCUS! WE END UP **VALIDATING** HIS **CRIME!**

THAT HAPPENS AND IT'LL BE **LET'S MAKE A DEAL** EVERY TIME WE RUN AN **INTERROGATION!**

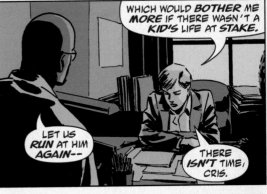

WHICH WOULD **BOTHER** ME **MORE** IF THERE WASN'T A **KID'S** LIFE AT **STAKE**.

LET US **RUN** AT HIM **AGAIN**--

THERE ISN'T TIME, CRIS.

YOU **HEARD** DUNNING. HE'S GIVING ZACK WESTON A FEW HOURS TO **LIVE**, ON THE **OUTSIDE**.

COULD BE HE'S **BLUFFING**, CAPTAIN?

YOU **REALLY** WANT TO **TAKE** THAT **CHANCE?**

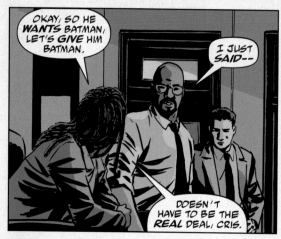

OKAY, SO HE **WANTS** BATMAN, LET'S **GIVE** HIM BATMAN.

I JUST **SAID**--

DOESN'T HAVE TO BE THE **REAL DEAL**, CRIS.

WHAT, YOU **FIGURE** I SHOULD JUST **SHOOT** OVER TO THIS **TAILOR'S** PLACE, GET MYSELF A **BATMAN** COSTUME?

DRESS UP AND TRY TO MAKE DUNNING **WET** HIMSELF?

YEAH, ON **SECOND** THOUGHT IT'S PROBABLY **NOT** SUCH A **GOOD** IDEA...

...ROMY MIGHT **TRY** TO **BUST A CAP** IN YOUR ASS.

YEAH, WELL, HE'D HAVE TO GIVE HER **WEAPON** BACK, **FIRST.**

WHAT WAS **THAT?**

OH, HELL.

NICE ONE, RENEE.

DID I **HEAR** THAT **RIGHT?** DID DETECTIVE CHANDLER TAKE A **SHOT** AT BATMAN?

DID BATMAN **TAKE** HER DUTY WEAPON?

IT'S **NOT** WHAT YOU **THINK,** CAPTAIN--

YOU HAVE **NO** IDEA **WHAT** I THINK, DETECTIVE DRIVER!

JESUS CHRIST, SHE'S A **POLICE!** SHE DOESN'T GO **SHOOTING** AT PEOPLE BECAUSE SHE DOESN'T **LIKE** THEM!

HE BROKE HER NOSE, **DIDN'T** HE?

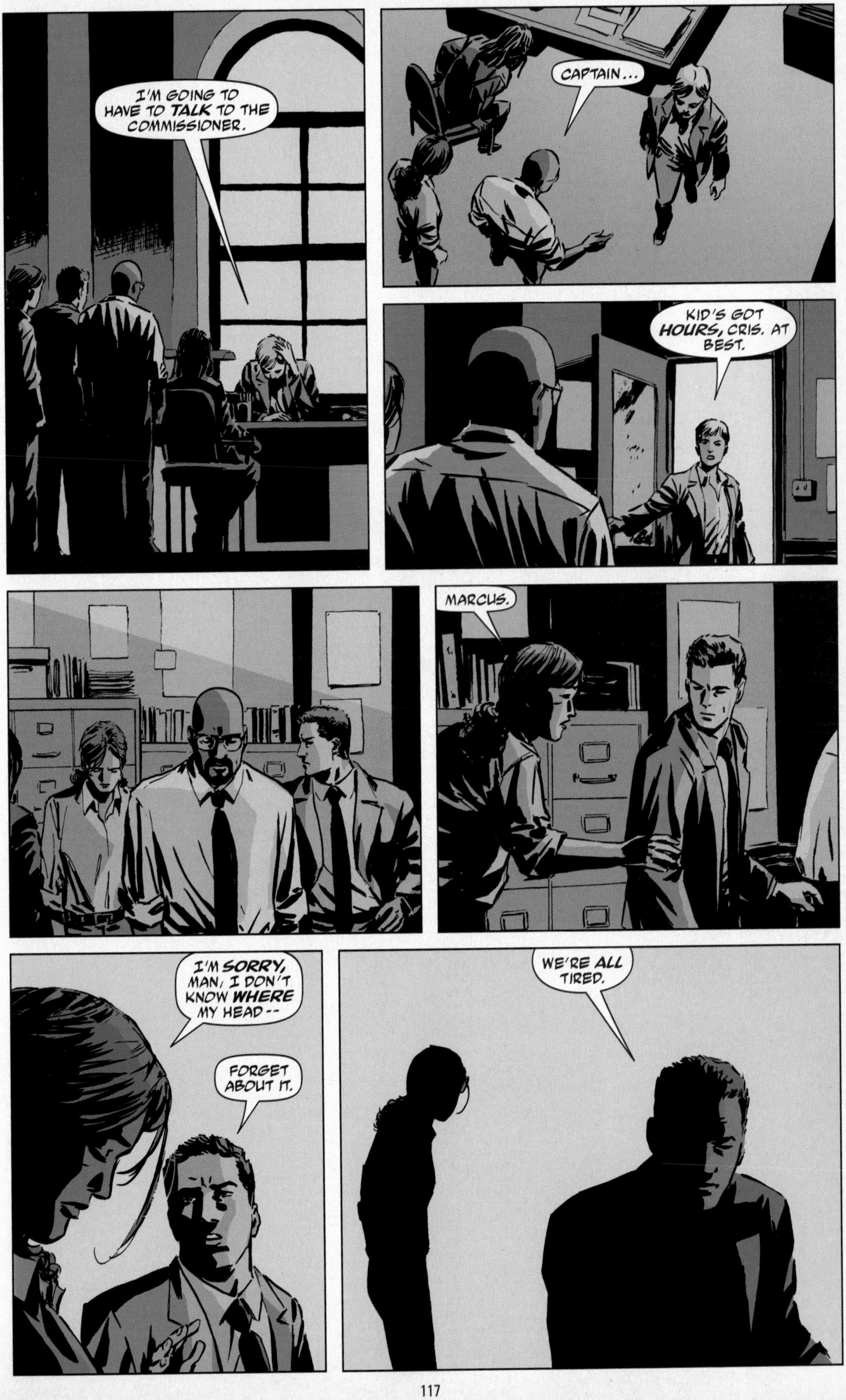

I'M GOING TO HAVE TO TALK TO THE COMMISSIONER.
CAPTAIN...
KID'S GOT HOURS, CRIS. AT BEST.
MARCUS.
I'M SORRY, MAN, I DON'T KNOW WHERE MY HEAD--
FORGET ABOUT IT.
WE'RE ALL TIRED.

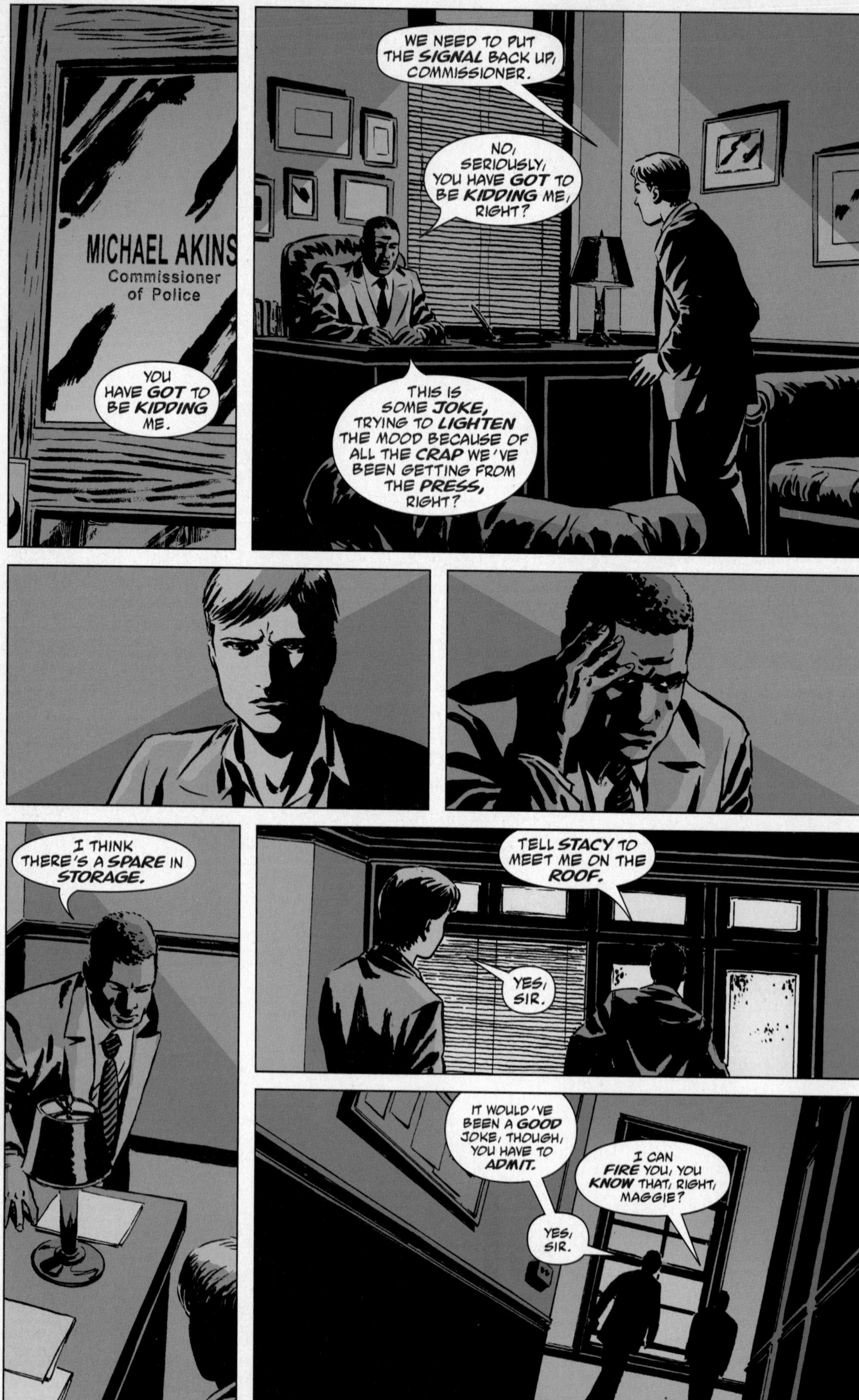
MICHAEL AKINS
Commissioner
of Police
YOU HAVE GOT TO BE KIDDING ME.
WE NEED TO PUT THE SIGNAL BACK UP, COMMISSIONER.
NO, SERIOUSLY, YOU HAVE GOT TO BE KIDDING ME, RIGHT?
THIS IS SOME JOKE, TRYING TO LIGHTEN THE MOOD BECAUSE OF ALL THE CRAP WE'VE BEEN GETTING FROM THE PRESS, RIGHT?
I THINK THERE'S A SPARE IN STORAGE.
TELL STACY TO MEET ME ON THE ROOF.
YES, SIR.
IT WOULD'VE BEEN A GOOD JOKE, THOUGH, YOU HAVE TO ADMIT.
I CAN FIRE YOU, YOU KNOW THAT, RIGHT, MAGGIE?
YES, SIR.

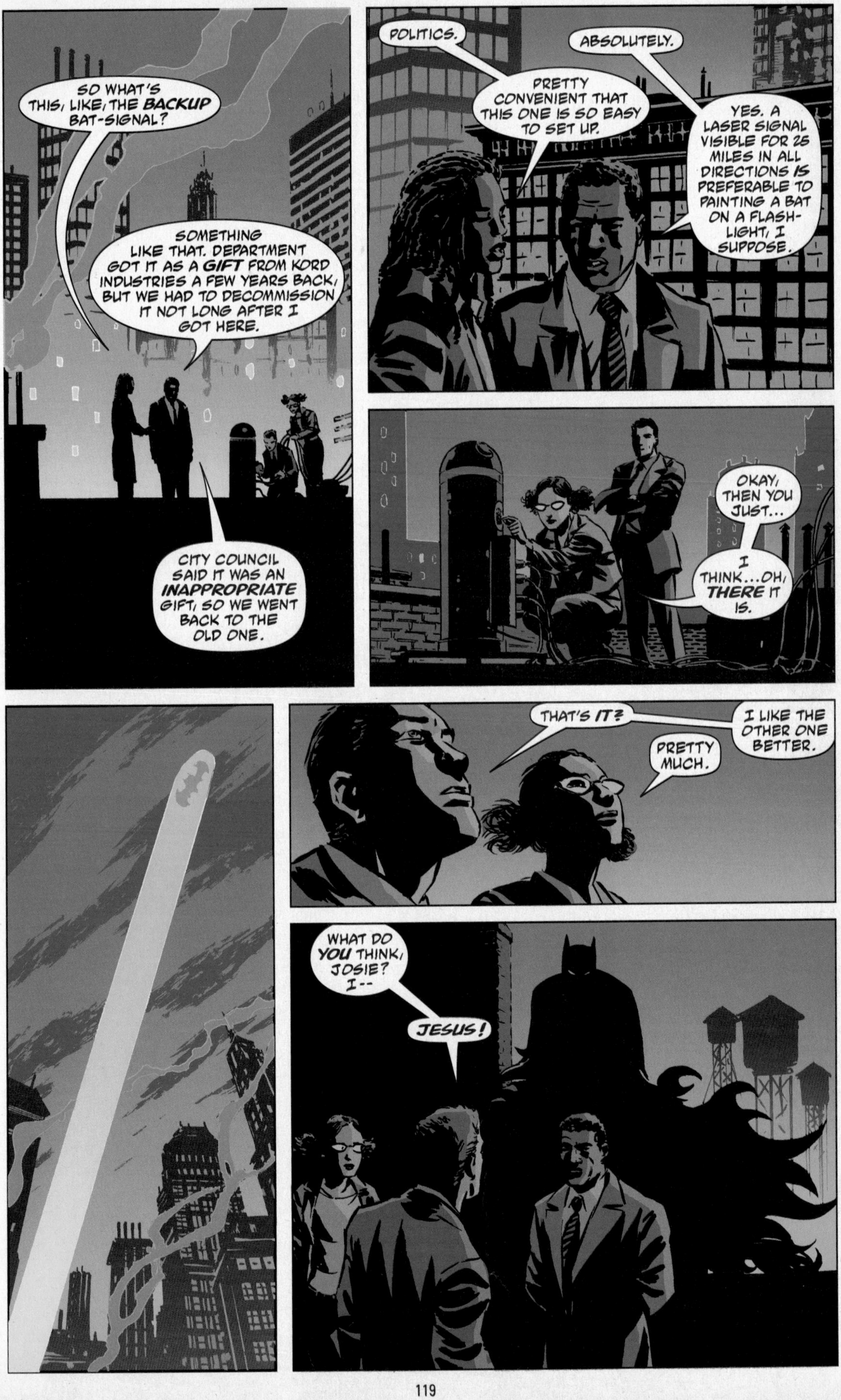
SO WHAT'S THIS, LIKE, THE BACKUP BAT-SIGNAL?
SOMETHING LIKE THAT. DEPARTMENT GOT IT AS A GIFT FROM KORD INDUSTRIES A FEW YEARS BACK, BUT WE HAD TO DECOMMISSION IT NOT LONG AFTER I GOT HERE.
CITY COUNCIL SAID IT WAS AN INAPPROPRIATE GIFT, SO WE WENT BACK TO THE OLD ONE.
POLITICS.
ABSOLUTELY.
PRETTY CONVENIENT THAT THIS ONE IS SO EASY TO SET UP.
YES. A LASER SIGNAL VISIBLE FOR 25 MILES IN ALL DIRECTIONS IS PREFERABLE TO PAINTING A BAT ON A FLASH-LIGHT, I SUPPOSE.
OKAY, THEN YOU JUST...
I THINK...OH, THERE IT IS.
THAT'S IT?
PRETTY MUCH.
I LIKE THE OTHER ONE BETTER.
WHAT DO YOU THINK, JOSIE? I--
JESUS!

THAT WAS QUICK. DID YOU ACTUALLY *WAIT* FOR THE SIGNAL, OR DO YOU HAVE *LISTENING DEVICES* IN MY OFFICE?

IS THERE A *REASON* YOU LIT THAT?

YOU THINK I'D *WASTE* MY RESOURCES ON YOU IF THERE WASN'T A *DAMN GOOD* REASON?

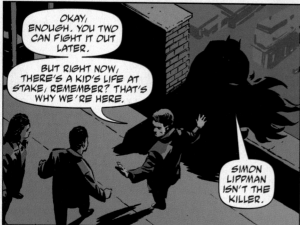

OKAY, ENOUGH. YOU TWO CAN FIGHT IT OUT LATER.

BUT RIGHT NOW, THERE'S A KID'S LIFE AT STAKE, REMEMBER? THAT'S WHY WE'RE HERE.

SIMON LIPPMAN ISN'T THE KILLER.

WE *KNOW* THAT. WE'VE GOT THE *REAL* PERP DOWNSTAIRS, AND THE THIRD VIC IS STILL BREATHING FOR NOW. BUT HE WON'T SAY *WHERE* HE IS...

YES, HE'LL ONLY GIVE *THAT* PIECE OF INFORMATION TO *YOU.*

KILL THE LIGHTS IN THE SQUAD ROOM... *AND* THE BOX.

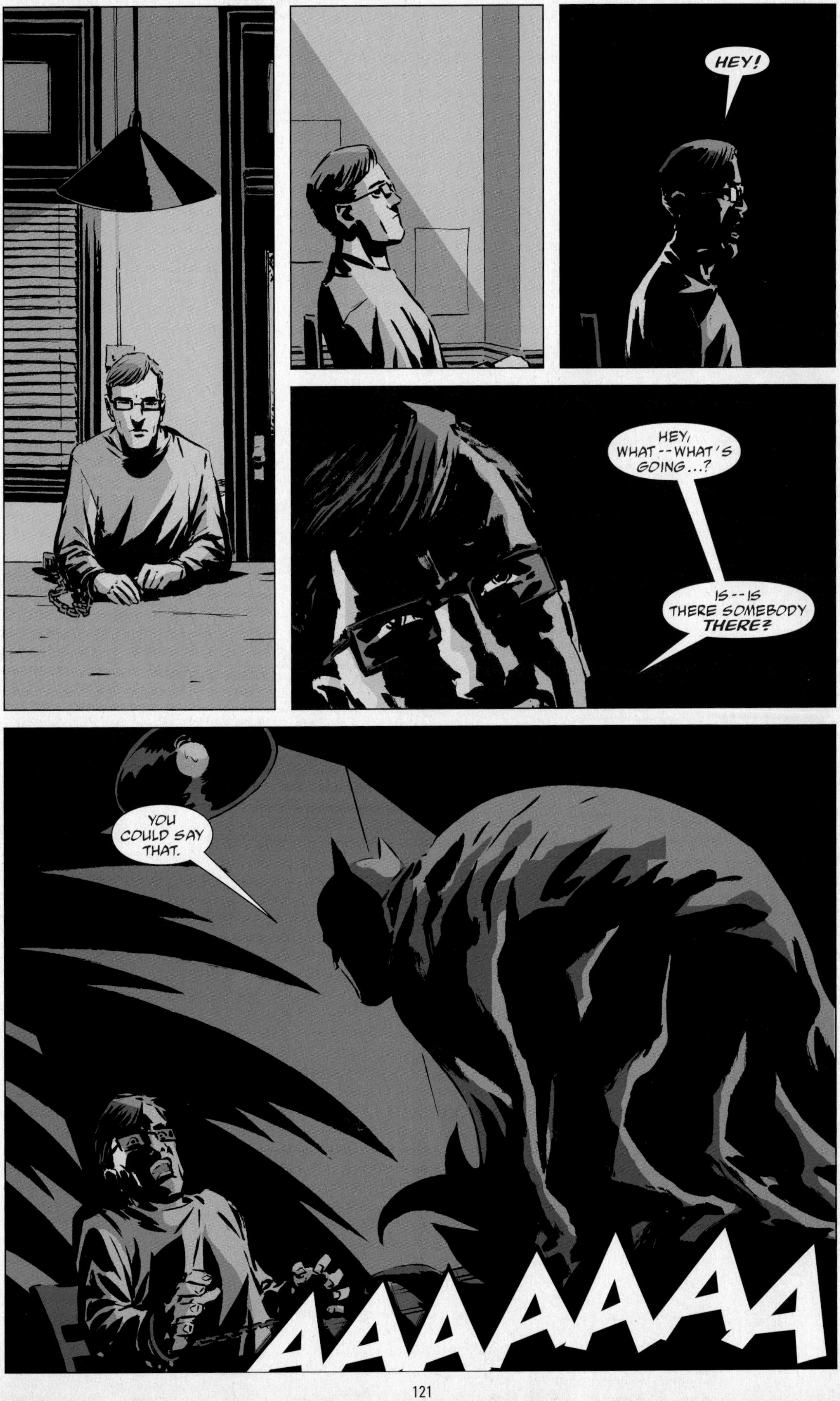
HEY!
HEY, WHAT--WHAT'S GOING...?
IS--IS THERE SOMEBODY THERE?
YOU COULD SAY THAT.
AAAAAA

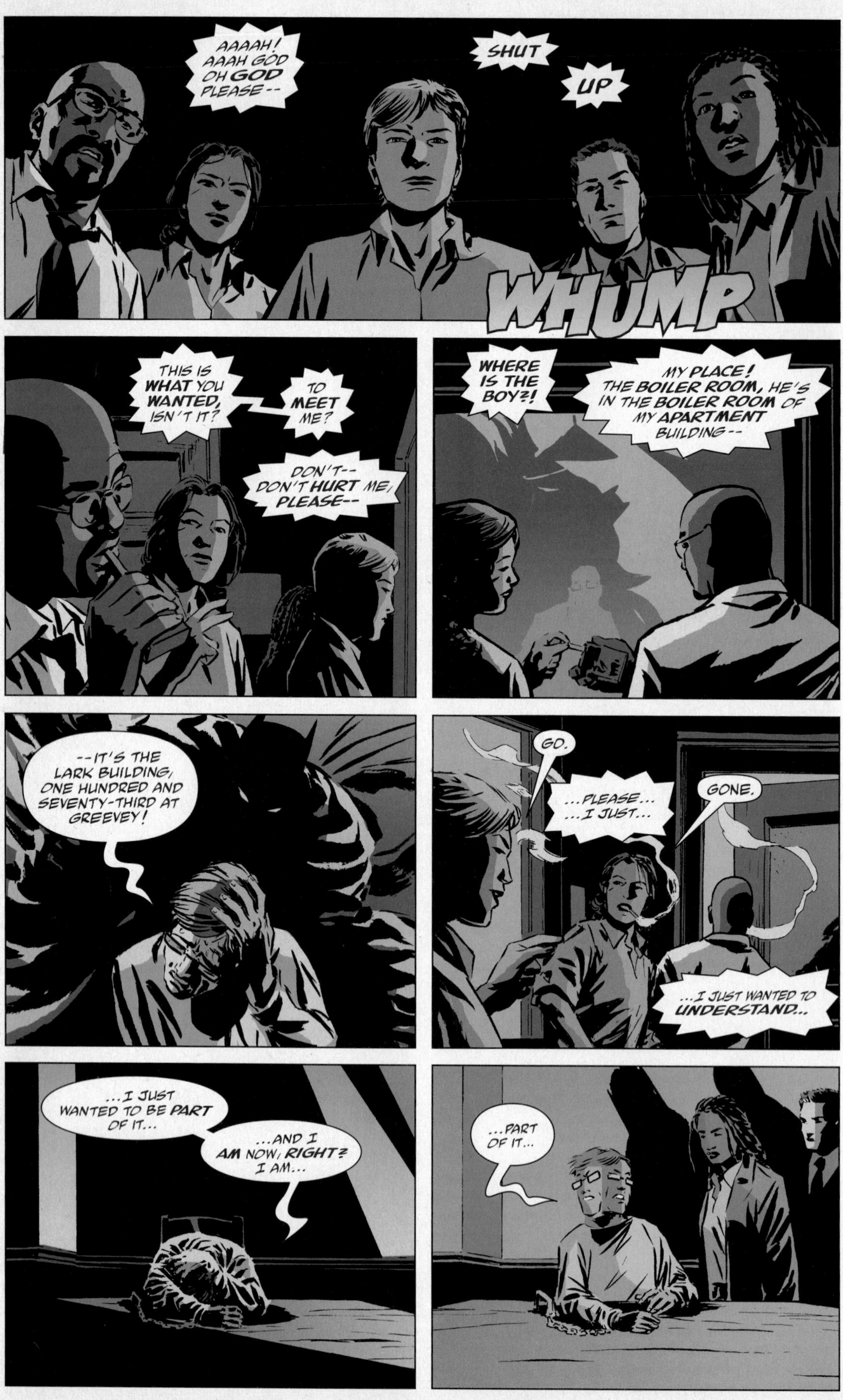
AAAAH! AAAH GOD OH GOD PLEASE--
SHUT
UP
WHUMP
THIS IS WHAT YOU WANTED, ISN'T IT?
TO MEET ME?
DON'T-- DON'T HURT ME, PLEASE--
WHERE IS THE BOY?!
MY PLACE! THE BOILER ROOM, HE'S IN THE BOILER ROOM OF MY APARTMENT BUILDING--
--IT'S THE LARK BUILDING, ONE HUNDRED AND SEVENTY-THIRD AT GREEVEY!
GO.
...PLEASE... ...I JUST...
GONE.
...I JUST WANTED TO UNDERSTAND...
...I JUST WANTED TO BE PART OF IT...
...AND I AM NOW, RIGHT? I AM...
...PART OF IT...

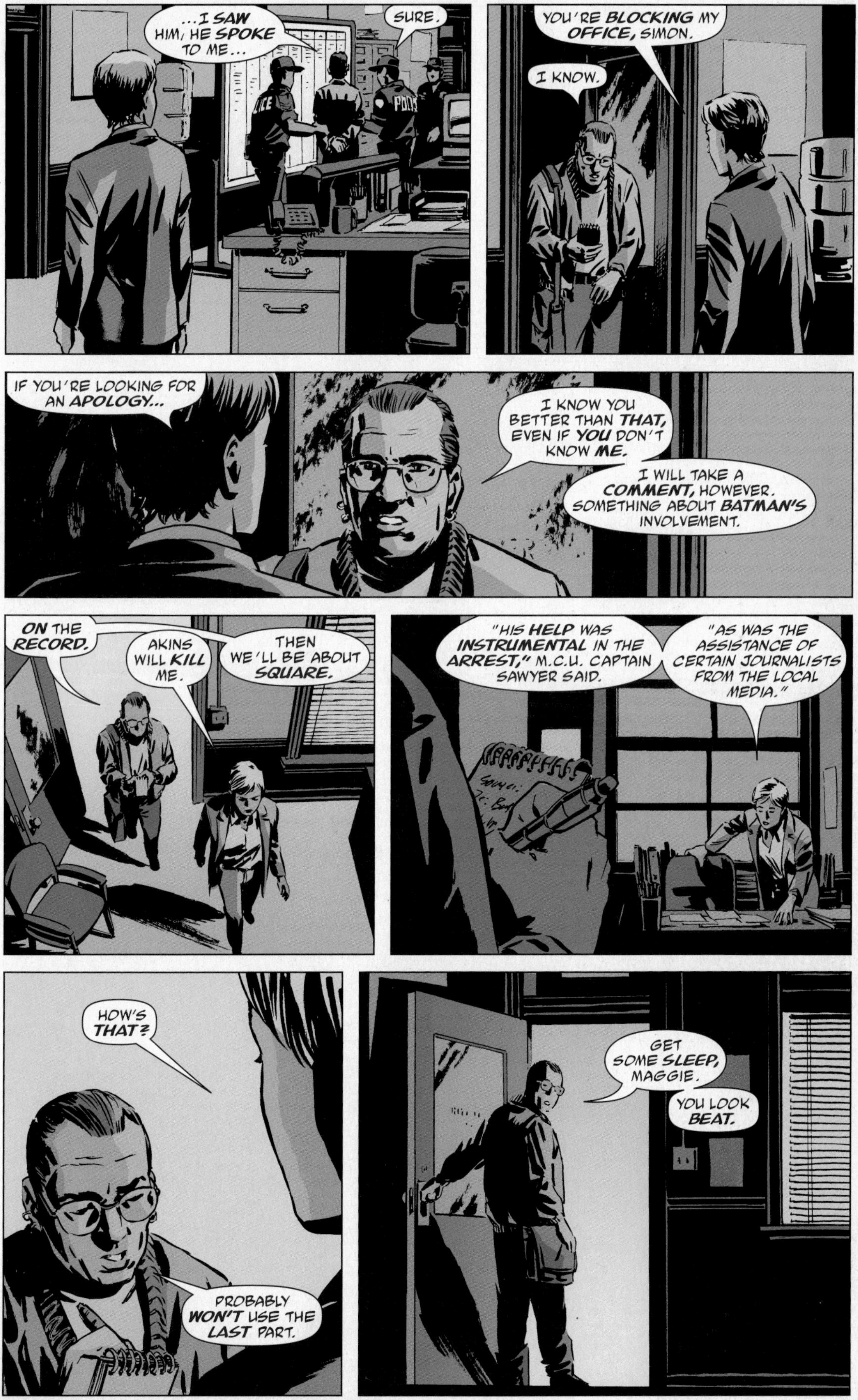
...I SAW HIM, HE SPOKE TO ME...
SURE.
YOU'RE BLOCKING MY OFFICE, SIMON.
I KNOW.
IF YOU'RE LOOKING FOR AN APOLOGY...
I KNOW YOU BETTER THAN THAT, EVEN IF YOU DON'T KNOW ME.
I WILL TAKE A COMMENT, HOWEVER. SOMETHING ABOUT BATMAN'S INVOLVEMENT.
ON THE RECORD.
AKINS WILL KILL ME.
THEN WE'LL BE ABOUT SQUARE.
"HIS HELP WAS INSTRUMENTAL IN THE ARREST," M.C.U. CAPTAIN SAWYER SAID.
"AS WAS THE ASSISTANCE OF CERTAIN JOURNALISTS FROM THE LOCAL MEDIA."
HOW'S THAT?
PROBABLY WON'T USE THE LAST PART.
GET SOME SLEEP, MAGGIE.
YOU LOOK BEAT.

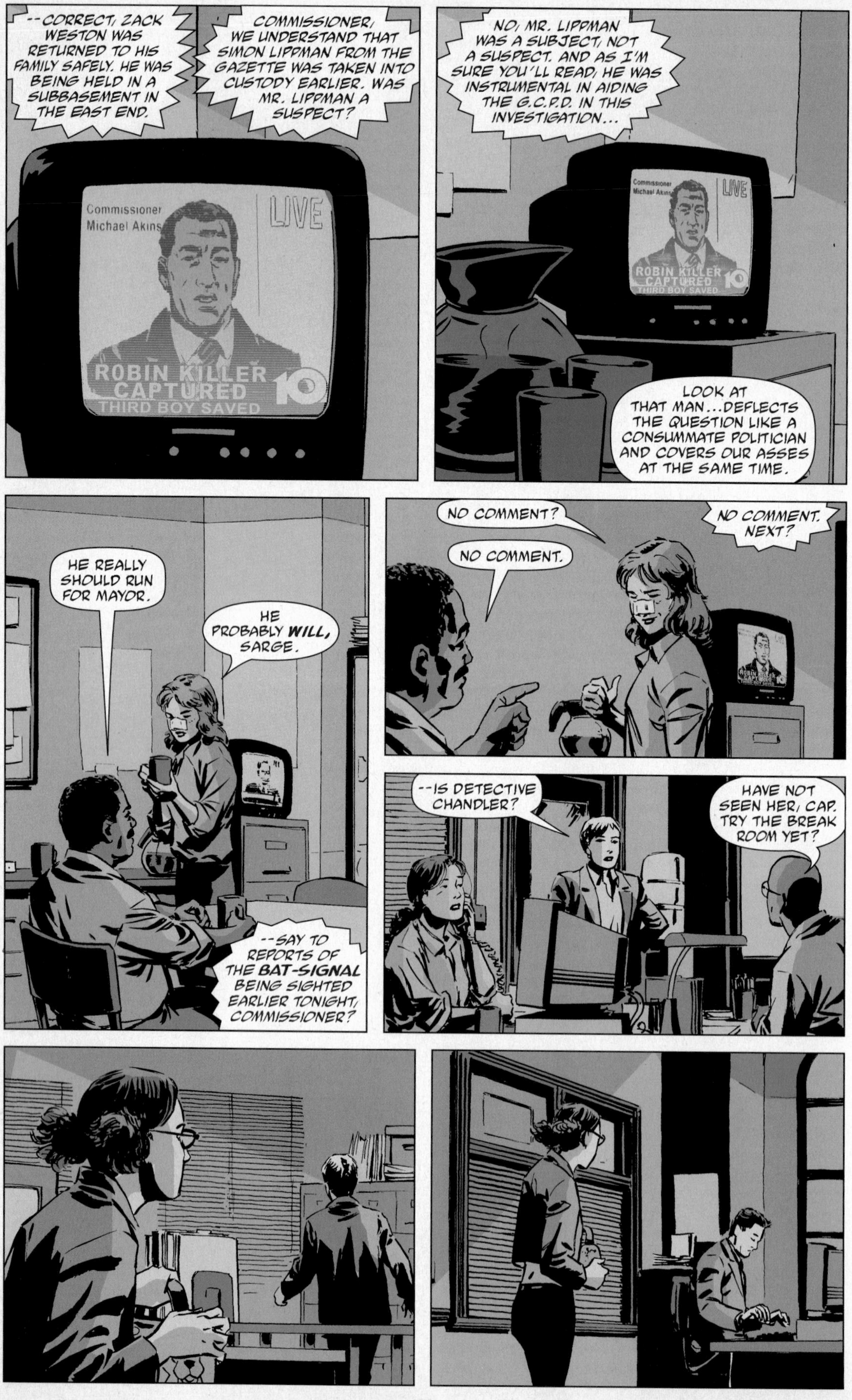
--CORRECT, ZACK WESTON WAS RETURNED TO HIS FAMILY SAFELY. HE WAS BEING HELD IN A SUBBASEMENT IN THE EAST END.
COMMISSIONER, WE UNDERSTAND THAT SIMON LIPPMAN FROM THE GAZETTE WAS TAKEN INTO CUSTODY EARLIER. WAS MR. LIPPMAN A SUSPECT?
Commissioner Michael Akins
LIVE
ROBIN KILLER CAPTURED
THIRD BOY SAVED
10
NO, MR. LIPPMAN WAS A SUBJECT, NOT A SUSPECT. AND AS I'M SURE YOU'LL READ, HE WAS INSTRUMENTAL IN AIDING THE G.C.P.D. IN THIS INVESTIGATION...
LOOK AT THAT MAN...DEFLECTS THE QUESTION LIKE A CONSUMMATE POLITICIAN AND COVERS OUR ASSES AT THE SAME TIME.
HE REALLY SHOULD RUN FOR MAYOR.
HE PROBABLY **WILL,** SARGE.
--SAY TO REPORTS OF THE **BAT-SIGNAL** BEING SIGHTED EARLIER TONIGHT, COMMISSIONER?
NO COMMENT?
NO COMMENT.
NO COMMENT. NEXT?
--IS DETECTIVE CHANDLER?
HAVE NOT SEEN HER, CAP. TRY THE BREAK ROOM YET?

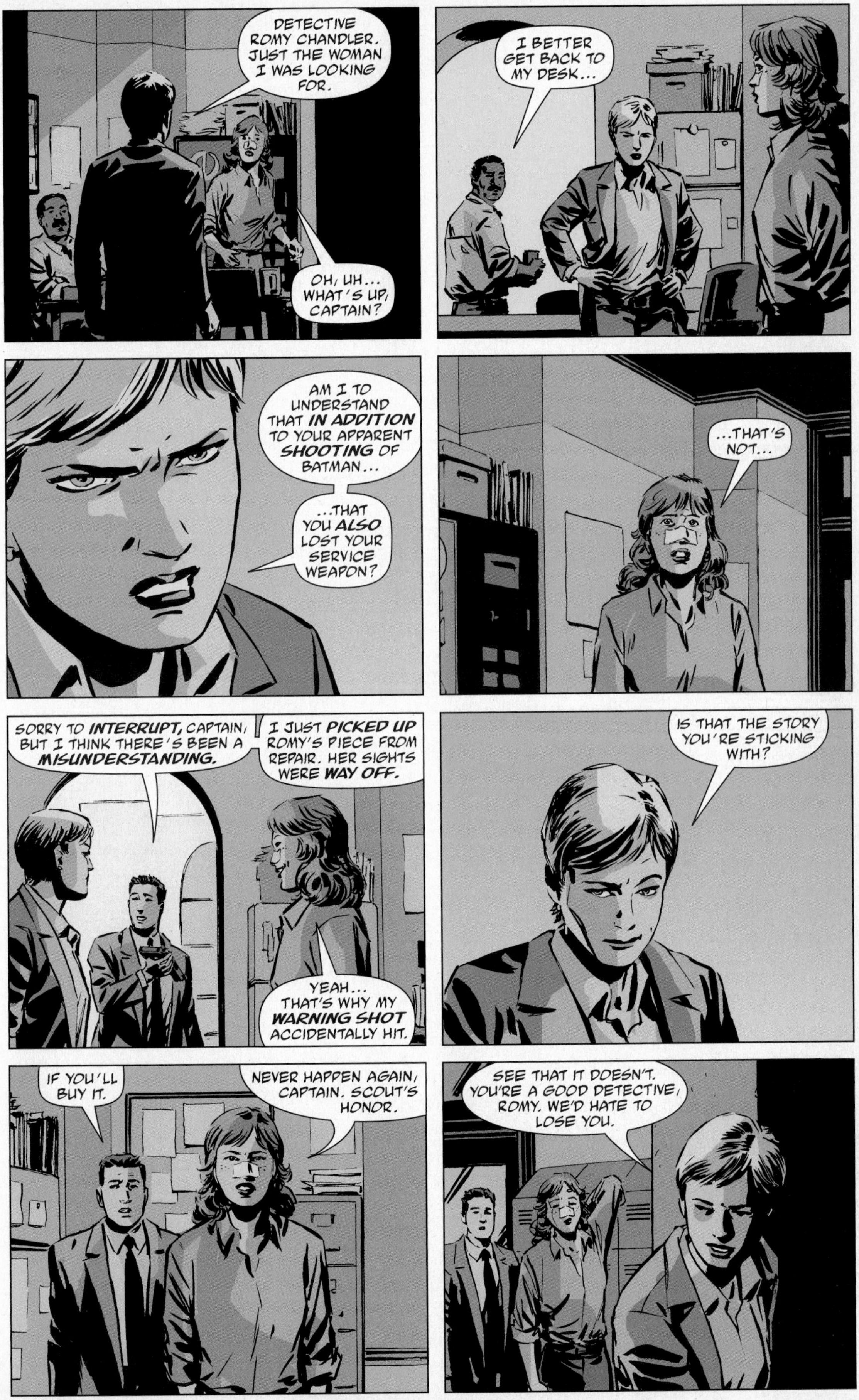

DETECTIVE ROMY CHANDLER. JUST THE WOMAN I WAS LOOKING FOR.
OH, UH... WHAT'S UP, CAPTAIN?
I BETTER GET BACK TO MY DESK...
AM I TO UNDERSTAND THAT IN ADDITION TO YOUR APPARENT SHOOTING OF BATMAN...
...THAT YOU ALSO LOST YOUR SERVICE WEAPON?
...THAT'S NOT...
SORRY TO INTERRUPT, CAPTAIN, BUT I THINK THERE'S BEEN A MISUNDERSTANDING.
I JUST PICKED UP ROMY'S PIECE FROM REPAIR. HER SIGHTS WERE WAY OFF.
YEAH... THAT'S WHY MY WARNING SHOT ACCIDENTALLY HIT.
IS THAT THE STORY YOU'RE STICKING WITH?
IF YOU'LL BUY IT.
NEVER HAPPEN AGAIN, CAPTAIN. SCOUT'S HONOR.
SEE THAT IT DOESN'T. YOU'RE A GOOD DETECTIVE, ROMY. WE'D HATE TO LOSE YOU.

STACY GOT IT FROM ROBIN.

I KNOW.

DAMN.

WHAT *IS* IT WITH THIS CITY...?

IT'S A LOVE/HATE THING, ROMY...

THERE'S A LOT HERE TO LOVE...THAT YOU WON'T FIND IN ANY OTHER CITY IN THE WORLD...

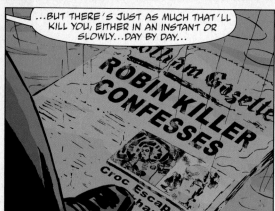

...BUT THERE'S JUST AS MUCH THAT'LL KILL YOU, EITHER IN AN INSTANT OR SLOWLY...DAY BY DAY...

ROBIN KILLER CONFESSES

Croc Escapes

BUT WHAT ARE YOU GONNA DO? *QUIT? LEAVE?*

NO...THIS IS MY *CITY.*

I COULD SOONER LEAVE *YOU.*

HEY!

AND THAT'S *NOT* GOING TO HAPPEN, MARCUS...

LET'S GO HOME.

THE END

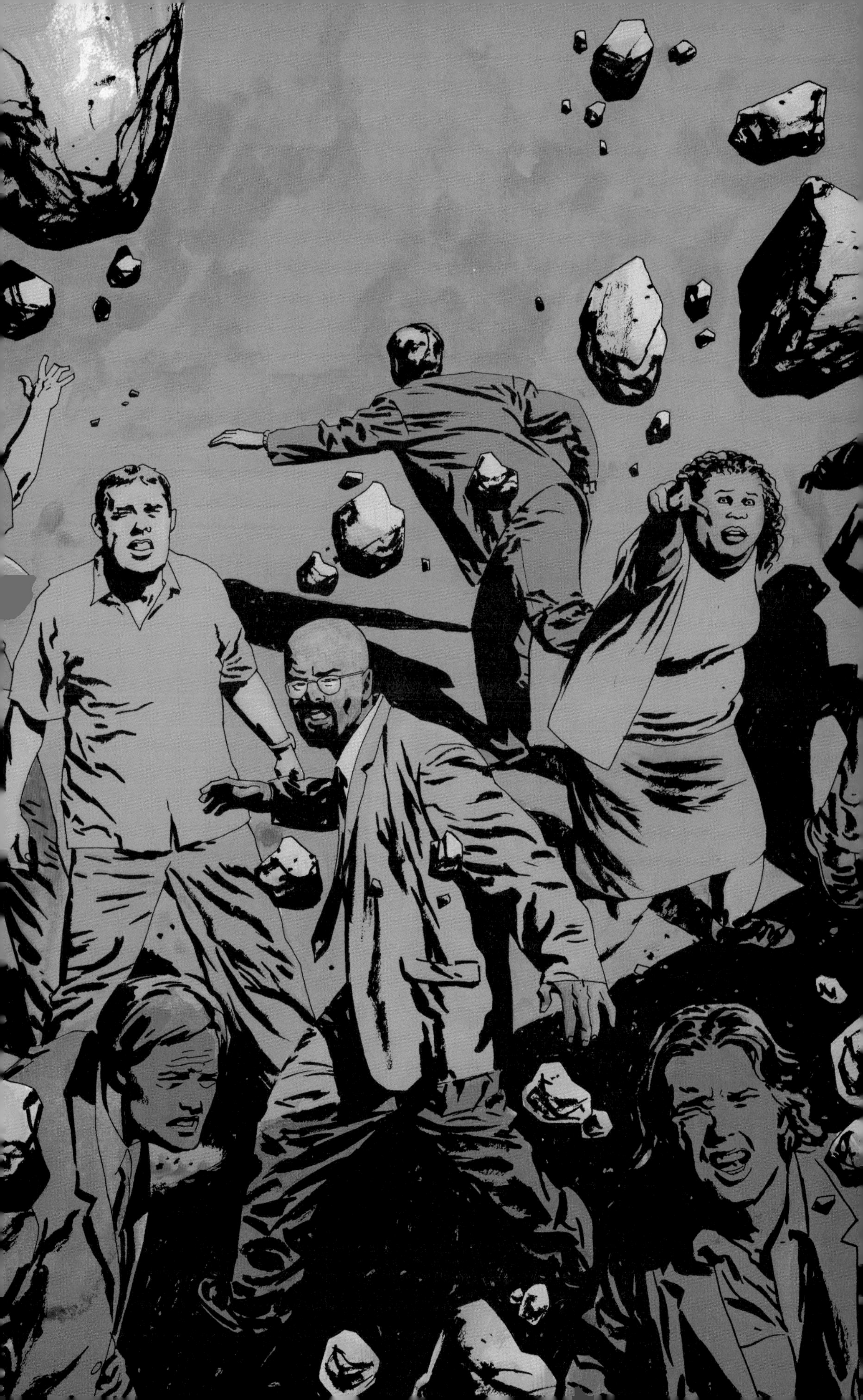

SUNDAY BLOODY SUNDAY

Written by
GREG RUCKA
Art by
STEVE LIEBER
Colors by
LEE LOUGHRIDGE
Letters by
CLEM ROBINS

The cosmic cataclysm known as the Infinite Crisis is wreaking havoc
all across the Galaxy. As an-all-too powerful madman is molding the laws
of nature and physics like clay, the properties of magic are also changing,
and all of the wielders of magic are losing control of their powers. The most
powerful of all the supernatural guardians is the Spectre — the living spirit
of vengeance. The Spectre relies on a human host for moral guidance, but
has been without one for too long. Whoever he chooses as his next host will
become the arbiter of morality for all humankind.

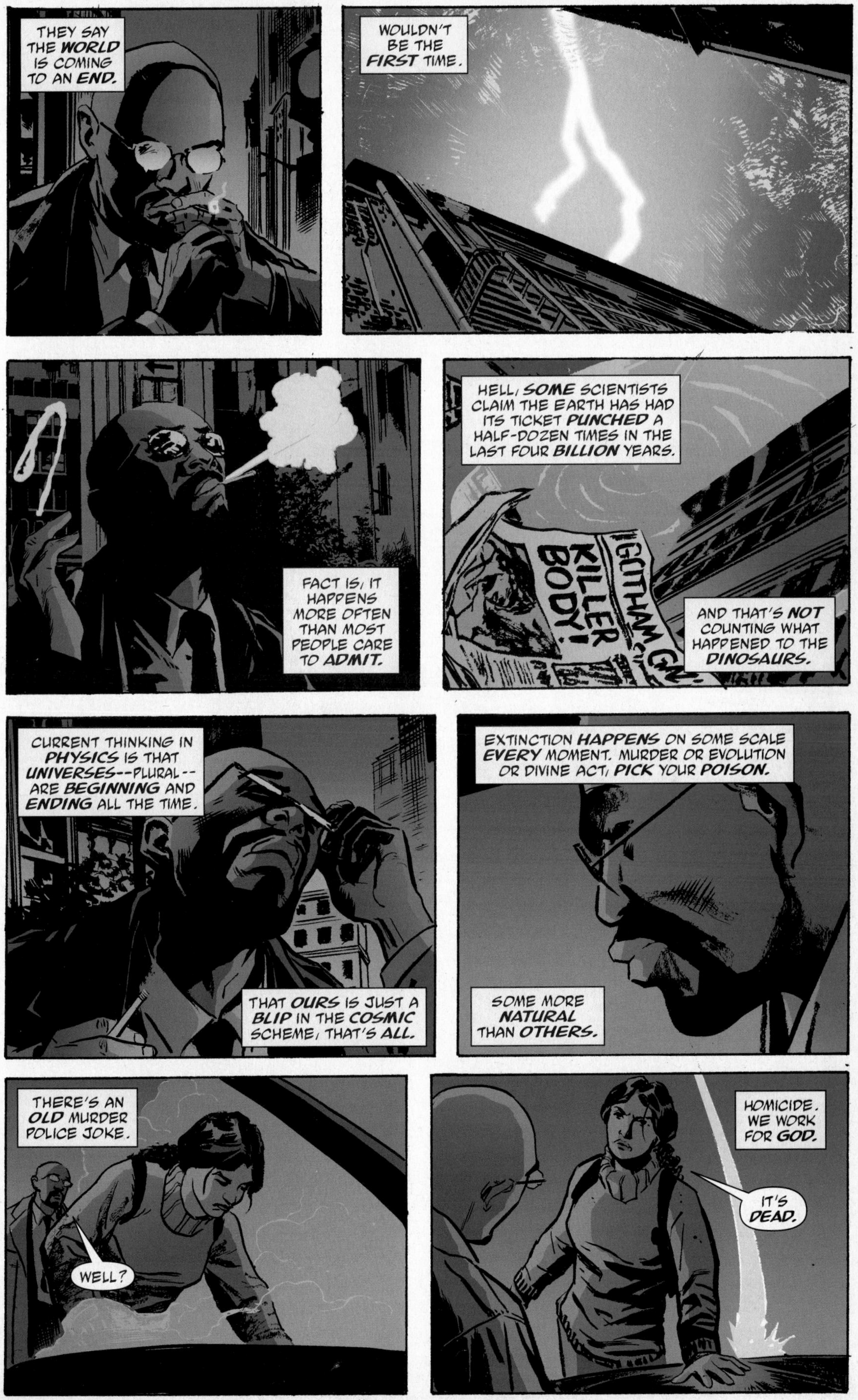
THEY SAY THE WORLD IS COMING TO AN END.
WOULDN'T BE THE FIRST TIME.
FACT IS, IT HAPPENS MORE OFTEN THAN MOST PEOPLE CARE TO ADMIT.
HELL, SOME SCIENTISTS CLAIM THE EARTH HAS HAD ITS TICKET PUNCHED A HALF-DOZEN TIMES IN THE LAST FOUR BILLION YEARS.
GOTHAM
KILLER BODY!
AND THAT'S NOT COUNTING WHAT HAPPENED TO THE DINOSAURS.
CURRENT THINKING IN PHYSICS IS THAT UNIVERSES--PLURAL--ARE BEGINNING AND ENDING ALL THE TIME.
THAT OURS IS JUST A BLIP IN THE COSMIC SCHEME, THAT'S ALL.
EXTINCTION HAPPENS ON SOME SCALE EVERY MOMENT. MURDER OR EVOLUTION OR DIVINE ACT, PICK YOUR POISON.
SOME MORE NATURAL THAN OTHERS.
THERE'S AN OLD MURDER POLICE JOKE.
WELL?
HOMICIDE. WE WORK FOR GOD.
IT'S DEAD.

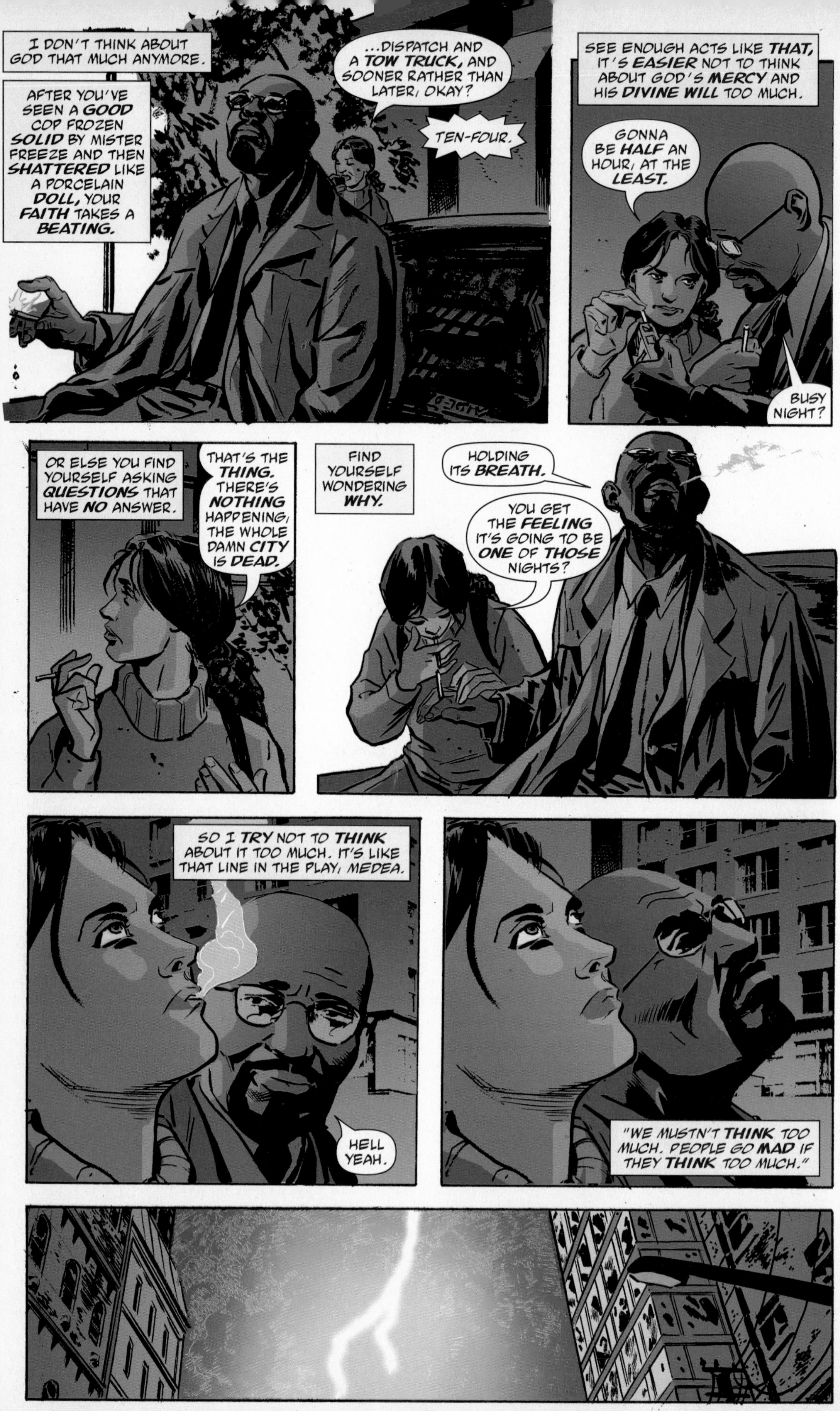
I DON'T THINK ABOUT GOD THAT MUCH ANYMORE.
AFTER YOU'VE SEEN A GOOD COP FROZEN SOLID BY MISTER FREEZE AND THEN SHATTERED LIKE A PORCELAIN DOLL, YOUR FAITH TAKES A BEATING.
...DISPATCH AND A TOW TRUCK, AND SOONER RATHER THAN LATER, OKAY?
TEN-FOUR.
SEE ENOUGH ACTS LIKE THAT, IT'S EASIER NOT TO THINK ABOUT GOD'S MERCY AND HIS DIVINE WILL TOO MUCH.
GONNA BE HALF AN HOUR, AT THE LEAST.
BUSY NIGHT?
OR ELSE YOU FIND YOURSELF ASKING QUESTIONS THAT HAVE NO ANSWER.
THAT'S THE THING. THERE'S NOTHING HAPPENING, THE WHOLE DAMN CITY IS DEAD.
FIND YOURSELF WONDERING WHY.
HOLDING ITS BREATH.
YOU GET THE FEELING IT'S GOING TO BE ONE OF THOSE NIGHTS?
SO I TRY NOT TO THINK ABOUT IT TOO MUCH. IT'S LIKE THAT LINE IN THE PLAY, MEDEA.
HELL YEAH.
"WE MUSTN'T THINK TOO MUCH. PEOPLE GO MAD IF THEY THINK TOO MUCH."

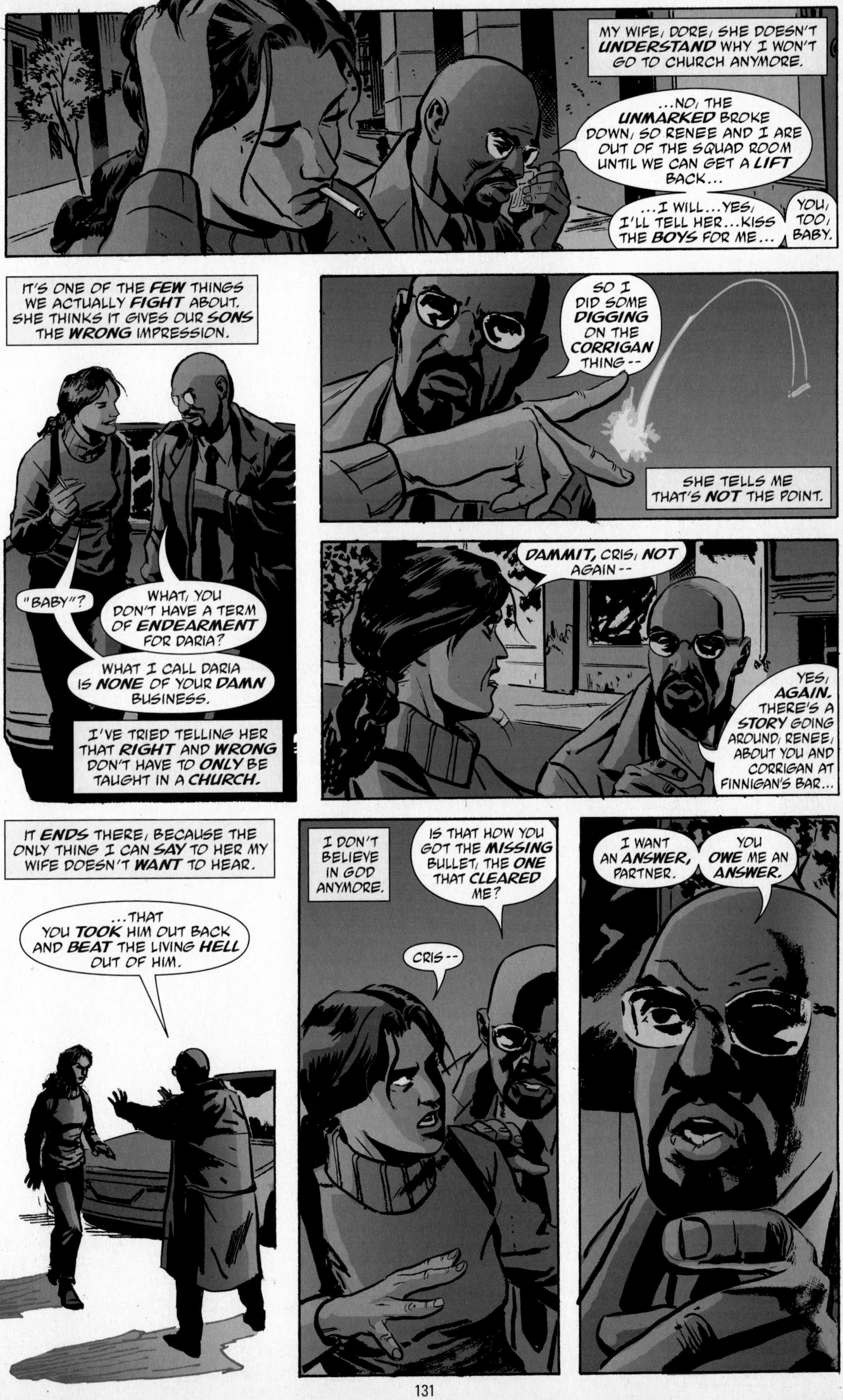

MY WIFE, DORE, SHE DOESN'T UNDERSTAND WHY I WON'T GO TO CHURCH ANYMORE.
...NO, THE UNMARKED BROKE DOWN, SO RENEE AND I ARE OUT OF THE SQUAD ROOM UNTIL WE CAN GET A LIFT BACK...
...I WILL...YES, I'LL TELL HER...KISS THE BOYS FOR ME...
YOU, TOO, BABY.
IT'S ONE OF THE FEW THINGS WE ACTUALLY FIGHT ABOUT. SHE THINKS IT GIVES OUR SONS THE WRONG IMPRESSION.
"BABY"?
WHAT, YOU DON'T HAVE A TERM OF ENDEARMENT FOR DARIA?
WHAT I CALL DARIA IS NONE OF YOUR DAMN BUSINESS.
I'VE TRIED TELLING HER THAT RIGHT AND WRONG DON'T HAVE TO ONLY BE TAUGHT IN A CHURCH.
SO I DID SOME DIGGING ON THE CORRIGAN THING--
SHE TELLS ME THAT'S NOT THE POINT.
DAMMIT, CRIS, NOT AGAIN--
YES, AGAIN. THERE'S A STORY GOING AROUND, RENEE, ABOUT YOU AND CORRIGAN AT FINNIGAN'S BAR...
IT ENDS THERE, BECAUSE THE ONLY THING I CAN SAY TO HER MY WIFE DOESN'T WANT TO HEAR.
...THAT YOU TOOK HIM OUT BACK AND BEAT THE LIVING HELL OUT OF HIM.
I DON'T BELIEVE IN GOD ANYMORE.
IS THAT HOW YOU GOT THE MISSING BULLET, THE ONE THAT CLEARED ME?
CRIS--
I WANT AN ANSWER, PARTNER.
YOU OWE ME AN ANSWER.

RENEE MONTOYA'S BEEN MY **PARTNER** FOR **YEARS** NOW.

CORRIGAN **SOLD** IT, I HAD TO FIND OUT WHO **TO**, AND HE **WASN'T** TALKING.

I **DID** WHAT I **HAD** TO, CRIS.

IN MANY WAYS, SHE KNOWS ME **BETTER** THAN MY OWN **WIFE**.

GOD **DAMMIT**, RENEE! WHAT THE HELL WERE YOU **THINKING**?

WE'RE **NOT** GOING TO **HAVE** THIS--

IN MANY WAYS, I KNOW **HER** BETTER THAN HER **LOVER**, DARIA.

I DON'T KNOW IF DARIA'S **SEEN** IT.

NO, WE **ARE** GOING TO HAVE THIS CONVERSATION!

GET **OFF** OF ME!

I **KNOW** FOR A **FACT** THAT CAPTAIN SAWYER **HASN'T**.

BY **BEATING** CORRIGAN DOWN, YOU **KILLED** ANY CHANCE OF **US** OR I.A.D. **EVER** MAKING A **CASE** AGAINST THAT **ROTTEN** SON OF A BITCH.

ARE YOU **OUT** OF YOUR **MIND**, RENEE?

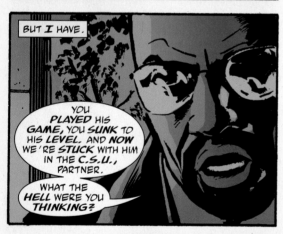

BUT **I** HAVE.

YOU **PLAYED** HIS **GAME**, YOU **SUNK** TO HIS **LEVEL**. AND **NOW** WE'RE **STUCK** WITH HIM IN THE C.S.U., PARTNER.

WHAT THE **HELL** WERE YOU **THINKING**?

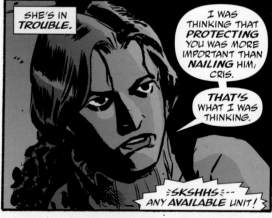

SHE'S IN **TROUBLE**.

I WAS **THINKING** THAT **PROTECTING** YOU WAS MORE IMPORTANT THAN **NAILING** HIM, CRIS.

THAT'S WHAT I WAS THINKING.

=SKSHHS=-- ANY **AVAILABLE** UNIT!

IT **STARTED** AFTER THE THING WITH **TWO-FACE**.

TEN-THREE! TEN-THREE, CATHEDRAL SQUARE!

MULTIPLE FREAKS, WE'VE GOT--

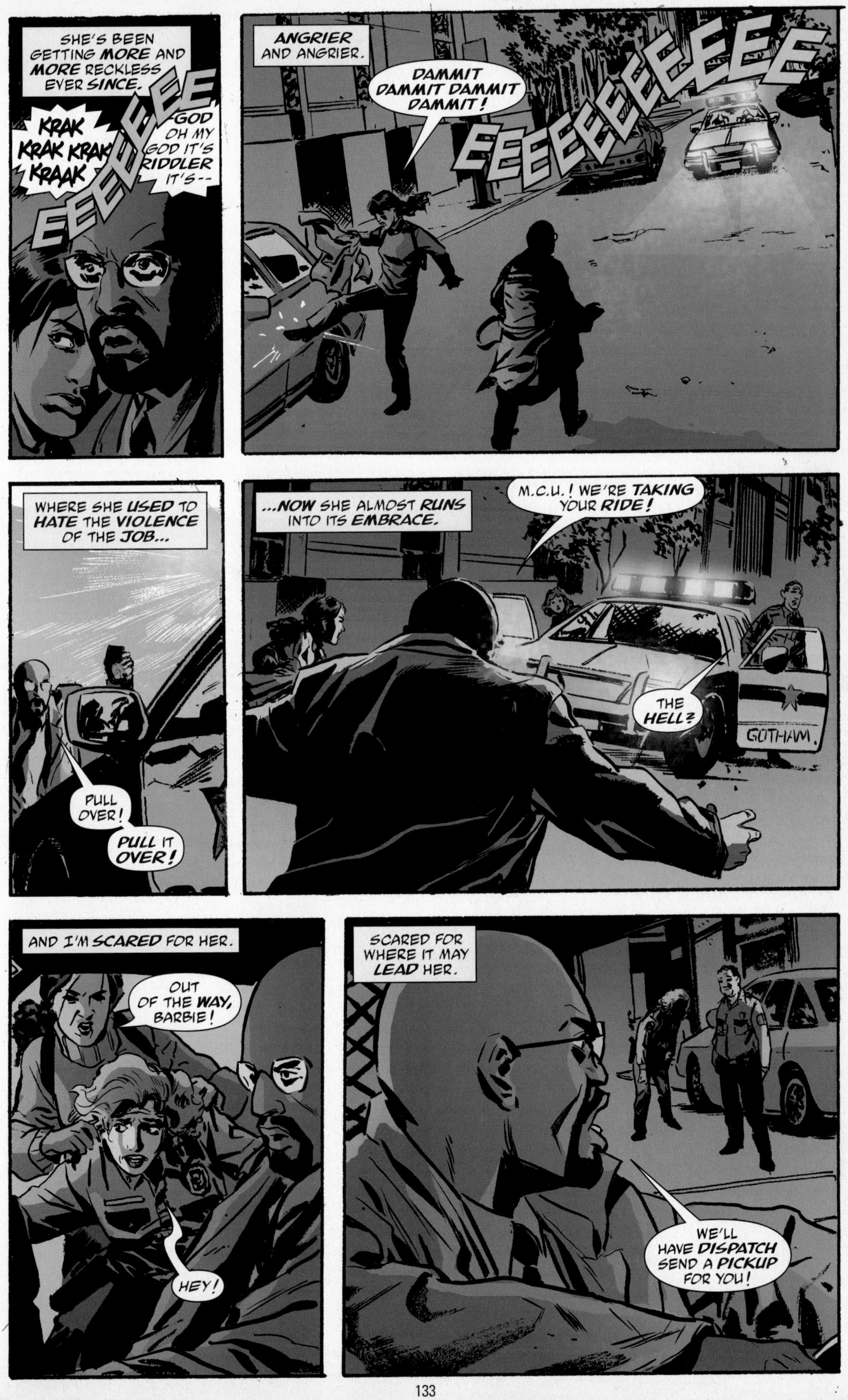
SHE'S BEEN GETTING MORE AND MORE RECKLESS EVER SINCE.
KRAK KRAK KRAK KRAAK
EEEEEEE
-GOD OH MY GOD IT'S RIDDLER IT'S--
ANGRIER AND ANGRIER.
DAMMIT DAMMIT DAMMIT DAMMIT!
EEEEEEEEEEEEEEEE
WHERE SHE USED TO HATE THE VIOLENCE OF THE JOB...
PULL OVER!
PULL IT OVER!
...NOW SHE ALMOST RUNS INTO ITS EMBRACE.
M.C.U.! WE'RE TAKING YOUR RIDE!
THE HELL?
GOTHAM
AND I'M SCARED FOR HER.
OUT OF THE WAY, BARBIE!
HEY!
SCARED FOR WHERE IT MAY LEAD HER.
WE'LL HAVE DISPATCH SEND A PICKUP FOR YOU!

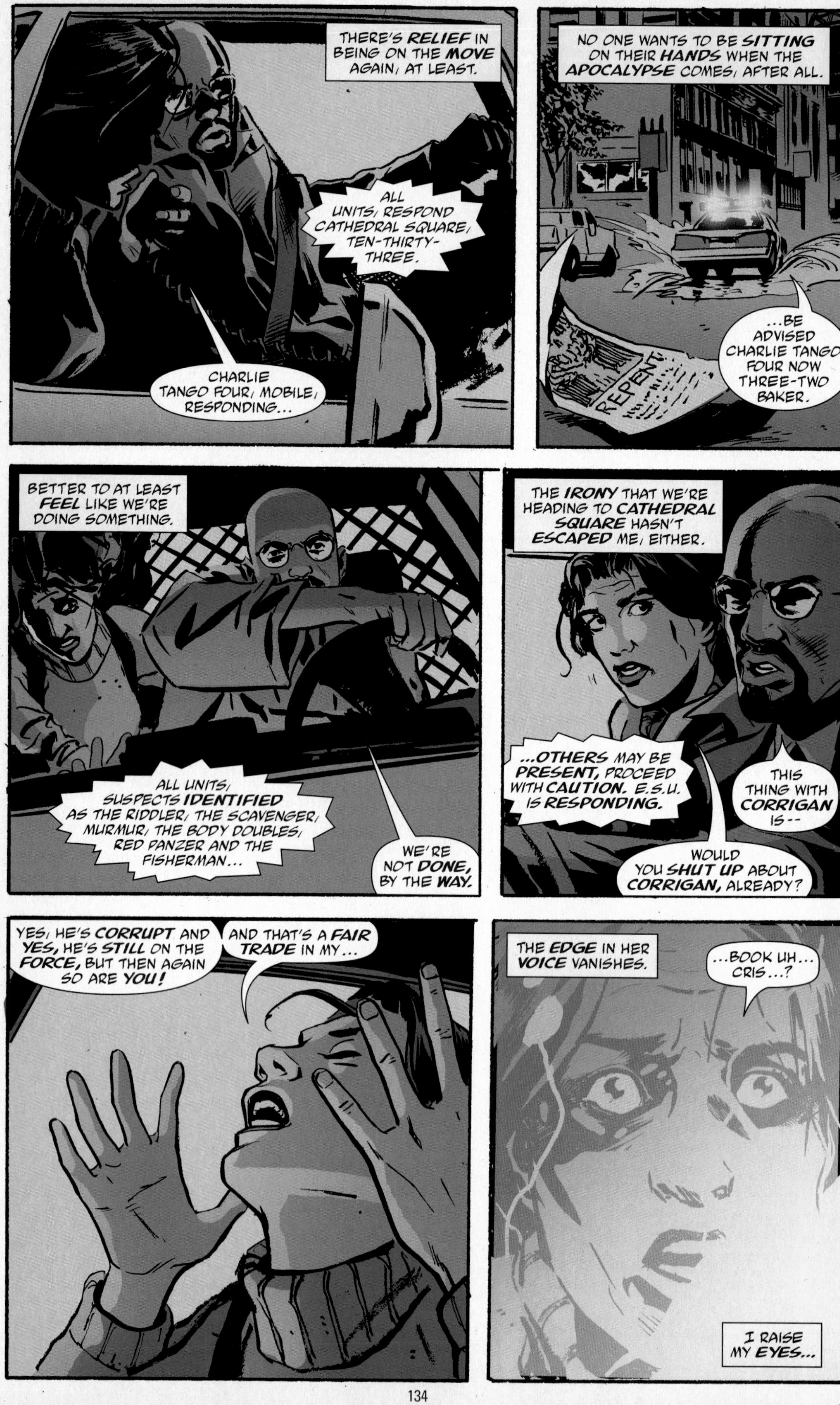
THERE'S RELIEF IN BEING ON THE MOVE AGAIN, AT LEAST.
ALL UNITS, RESPOND CATHEDRAL SQUARE, TEN-THIRTY-THREE.
CHARLIE TANGO FOUR, MOBILE, RESPONDING...
NO ONE WANTS TO BE SITTING ON THEIR HANDS WHEN THE APOCALYPSE COMES, AFTER ALL.
REPENT
...BE ADVISED CHARLIE TANGO FOUR NOW THREE-TWO BAKER.
BETTER TO AT LEAST FEEL LIKE WE'RE DOING SOMETHING.
ALL UNITS, SUSPECTS IDENTIFIED AS THE RIDDLER, THE SCAVENGER, MURMUR, THE BODY DOUBLES, RED PANZER AND THE FISHERMAN...
WE'RE NOT DONE, BY THE WAY.
THE IRONY THAT WE'RE HEADING TO CATHEDRAL SQUARE HASN'T ESCAPED ME, EITHER.
...OTHERS MAY BE PRESENT, PROCEED WITH CAUTION. E.S.U. IS RESPONDING.
THIS THING WITH CORRIGAN IS--
WOULD YOU SHUT UP ABOUT CORRIGAN, ALREADY?
YES, HE'S CORRUPT AND YES, HE'S STILL ON THE FORCE, BUT THEN AGAIN SO ARE YOU!
AND THAT'S A FAIR TRADE IN MY...
THE EDGE IN HER VOICE VANISHES.
...BOOK UH... CRIS...?
I RAISE MY EYES...

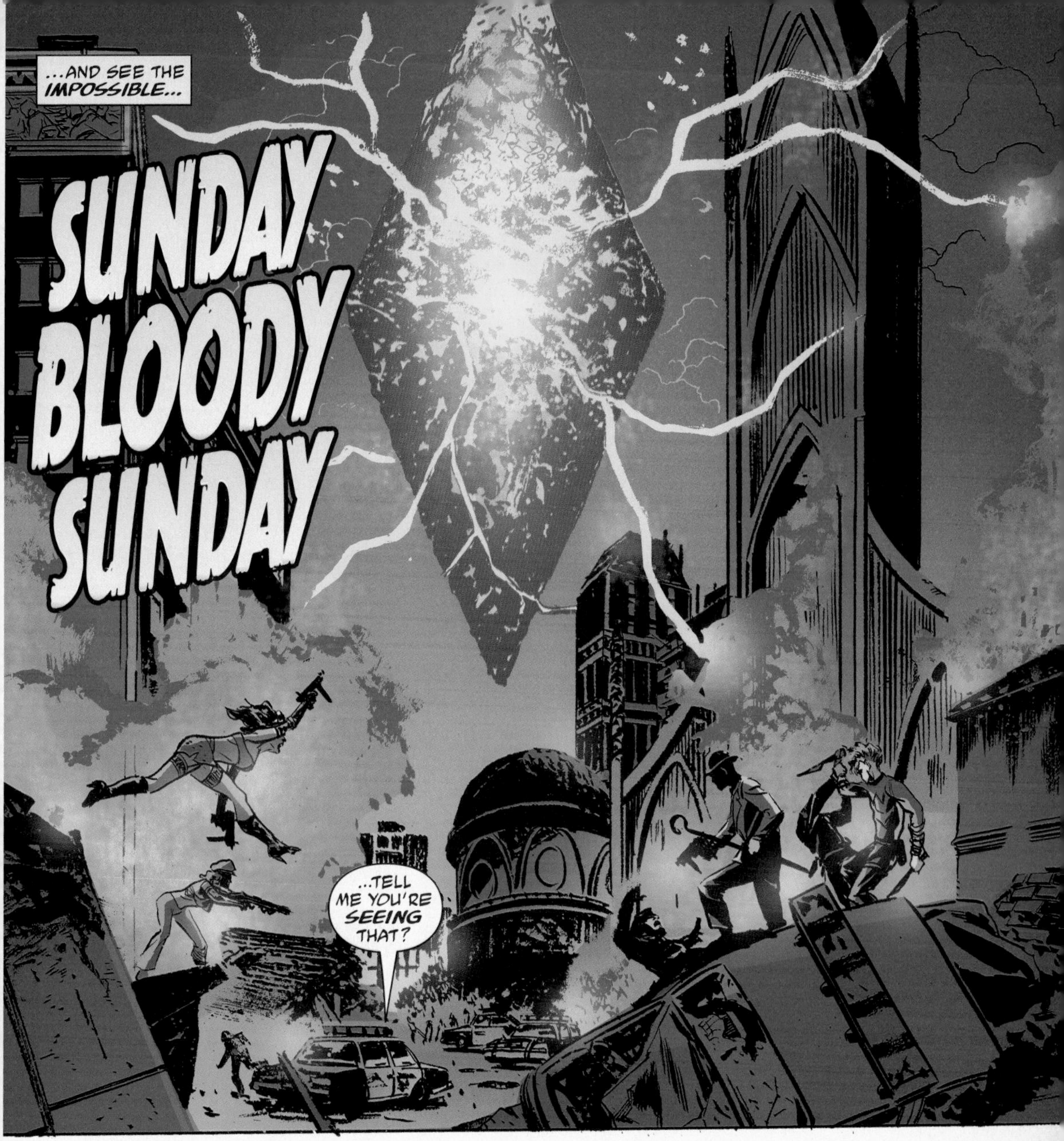
...AND SEE THE IMPOSSIBLE...
SUNDAY BLOODY SUNDAY
...TELL ME YOU'RE SEEING THAT?

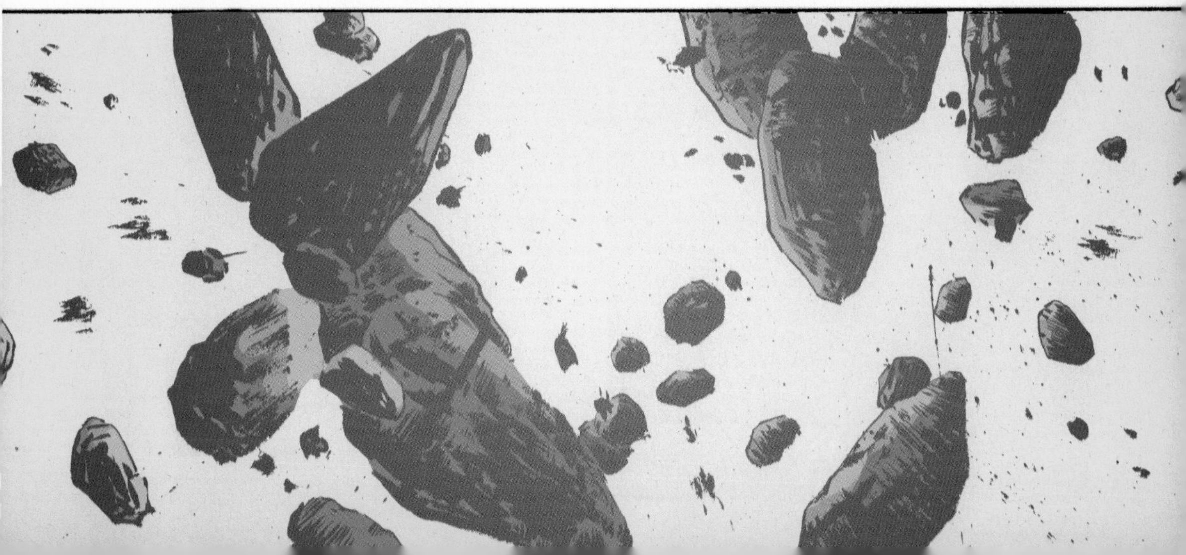

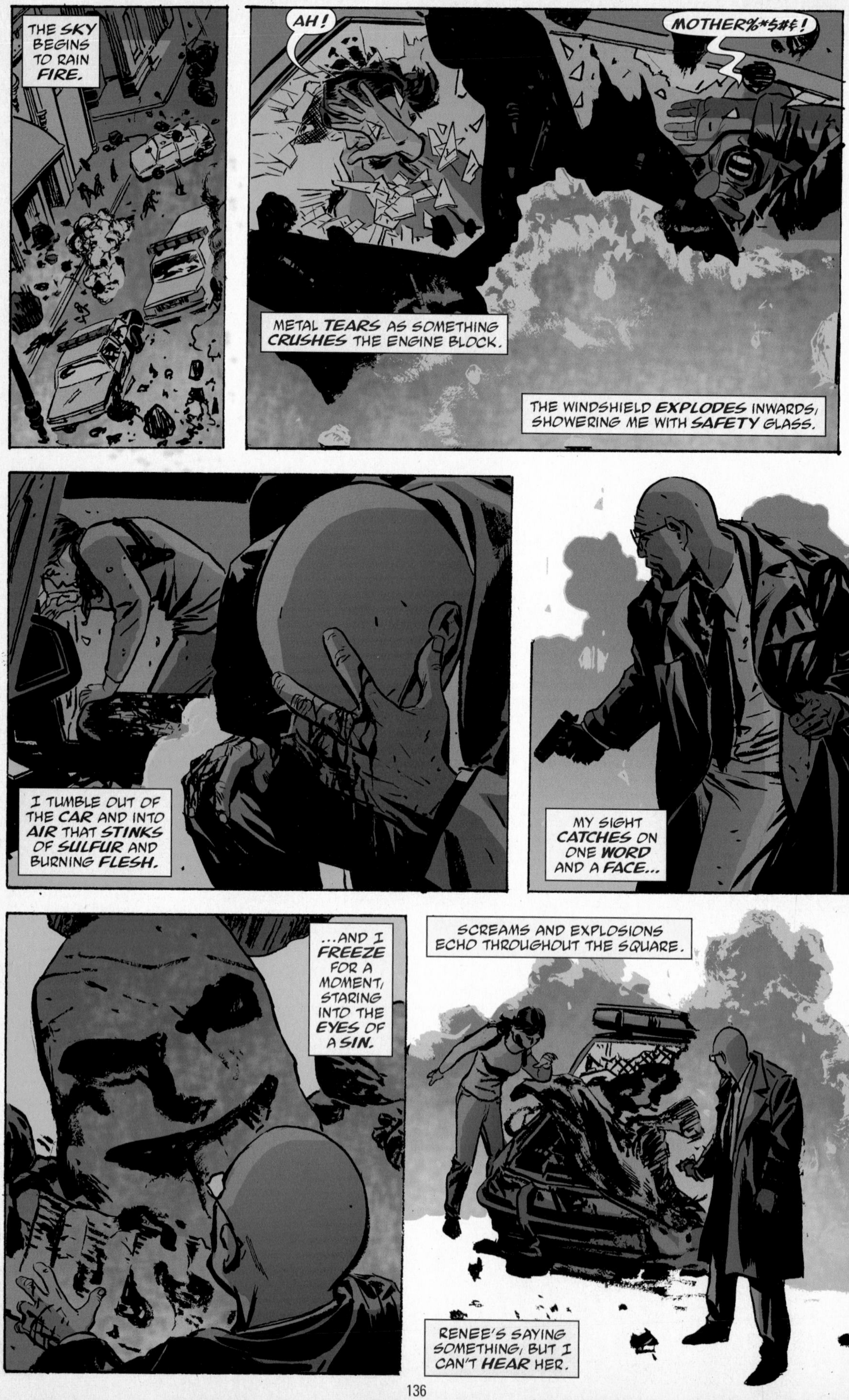
THE SKY BEGINS TO RAIN FIRE.
AH!
MOTHER%*$#¢!
METAL TEARS AS SOMETHING CRUSHES THE ENGINE BLOCK.
THE WINDSHIELD EXPLODES INWARDS, SHOWERING ME WITH SAFETY GLASS.
I TUMBLE OUT OF THE CAR AND INTO AIR THAT STINKS OF SULFUR AND BURNING FLESH.
MY SIGHT CATCHES ON ONE WORD AND A FACE...
...AND I FREEZE FOR A MOMENT, STARING INTO THE EYES OF A SIN.
SCREAMS AND EXPLOSIONS ECHO THROUGHOUT THE SQUARE.
RENEE'S SAYING SOMETHING, BUT I CAN'T HEAR HER.

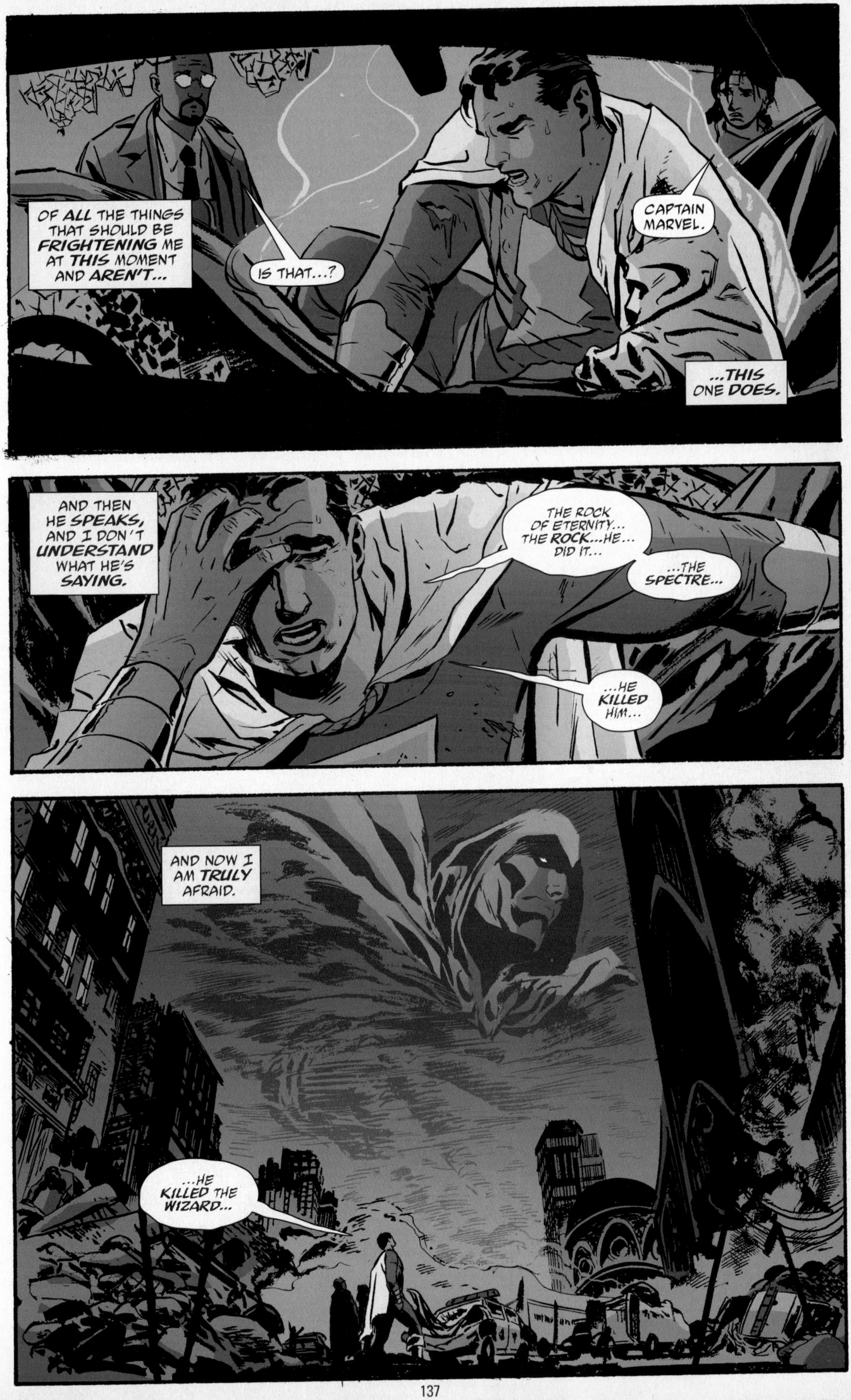
OF ALL THE THINGS THAT SHOULD BE FRIGHTENING ME AT THIS MOMENT AND AREN'T...
IS THAT...?
CAPTAIN MARVEL.
...THIS ONE DOES.
AND THEN HE SPEAKS, AND I DON'T UNDERSTAND WHAT HE'S SAYING.
THE ROCK OF ETERNITY... THE ROCK...HE... DID IT...
...THE SPECTRE...
...HE KILLED HIM...
AND NOW I AM TRULY AFRAID.
...HE KILLED THE WIZARD...

THE THINGS I'VE SEEN, SO MANY THINGS...

...BATMAN IN THE NIGHT SKY AND THE JOKER IN THE BOX AND MURDER A THOUSAND TIMES OVER...

...BUT NOTHING LIKE THIS, NOTHING EVER LIKE THIS...

WHAT... WHAT IS THAT...?

THE SPECTRE, THE AGENT OF DIVINE VENGEANCE.

BUT HE'S GONE MAD, HE'S UNRAVELING ALL MAGICK--

HNH!

RENEE MAKES A NOISE, IT'S THE SOUND I IMAGINE A SHARK WOULD MAKE WHEN IT SMELLS BLOOD IN THE WATER--

PARTNER?

BASTARDS BASTARDS--

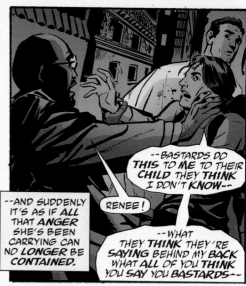

--AND SUDDENLY IT'S AS IF ALL THAT ANGER SHE'S BEEN CARRYING CAN NO LONGER BE CONTAINED.

RENEE!

--BASTARDS DO THIS TO ME TO THEIR CHILD THEY THINK I DON'T KNOW--

--WHAT THEY THINK THEY'RE SAYING BEHIND MY BACK WHAT ALL OF YOU THINK YOU SAY YOU BASTARDS--

I'VE GOT JUST LONG ENOUGH TO SEE THE IRONY IN BEING KILLED BY MY BEST FRIEND...

--I'LL KILL YOU, I'LL £*%#ING SON OF A--

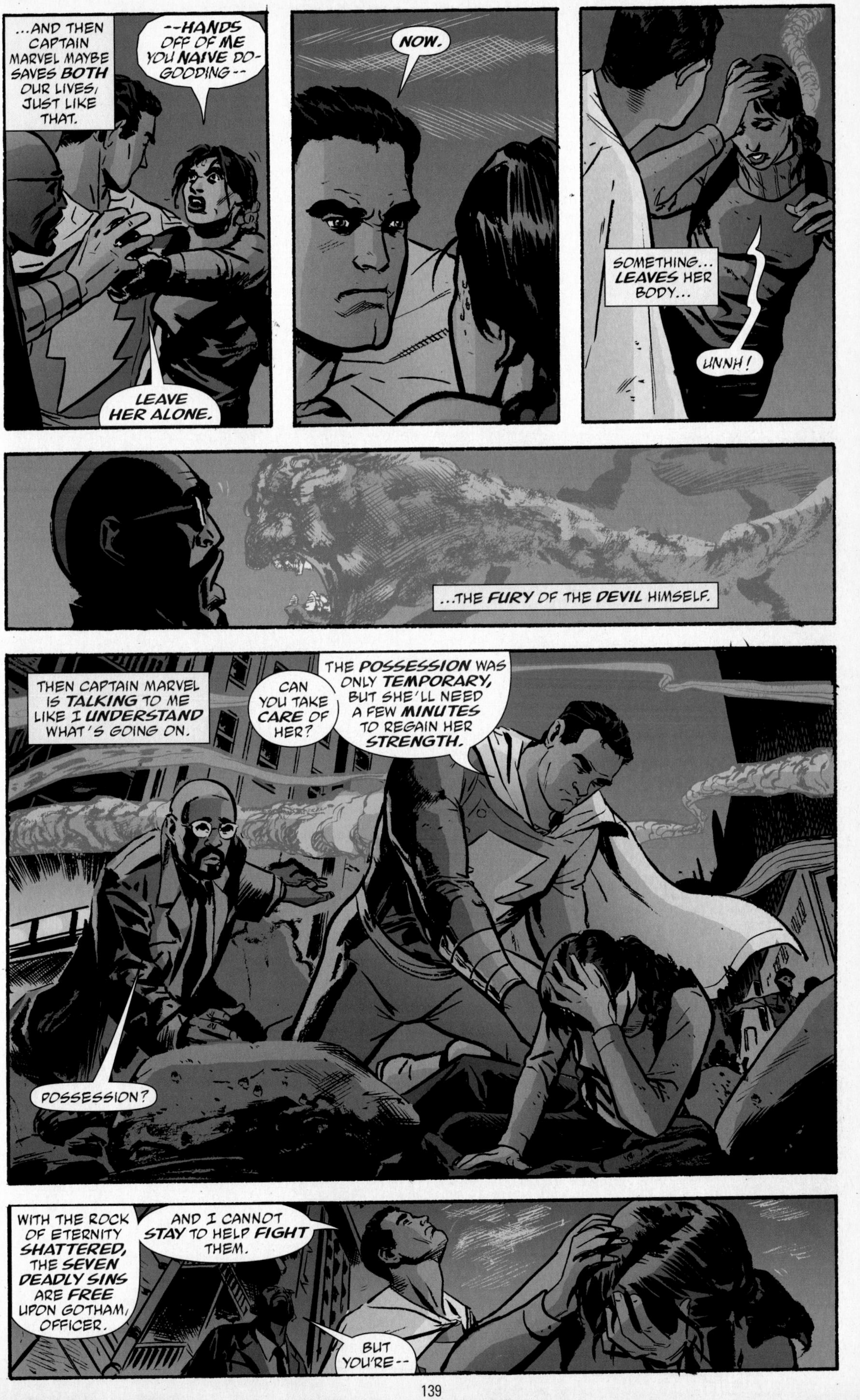
...AND THEN CAPTAIN MARVEL MAYBE SAVES BOTH OUR LIVES, JUST LIKE THAT.
--HANDS OFF OF ME YOU NAIVE DO-GOODING--
LEAVE HER ALONE.
NOW.
SOMETHING... LEAVES HER BODY...
UNNH!
...THE FURY OF THE DEVIL HIMSELF.
THEN CAPTAIN MARVEL IS TALKING TO ME LIKE I UNDERSTAND WHAT'S GOING ON.
CAN YOU TAKE CARE OF HER?
THE POSSESSION WAS ONLY TEMPORARY, BUT SHE'LL NEED A FEW MINUTES TO REGAIN HER STRENGTH.
POSSESSION?
WITH THE ROCK OF ETERNITY SHATTERED, THE SEVEN DEADLY SINS ARE FREE UPON GOTHAM, OFFICER.
AND I CANNOT STAY TO HELP FIGHT THEM.
BUT YOU'RE--

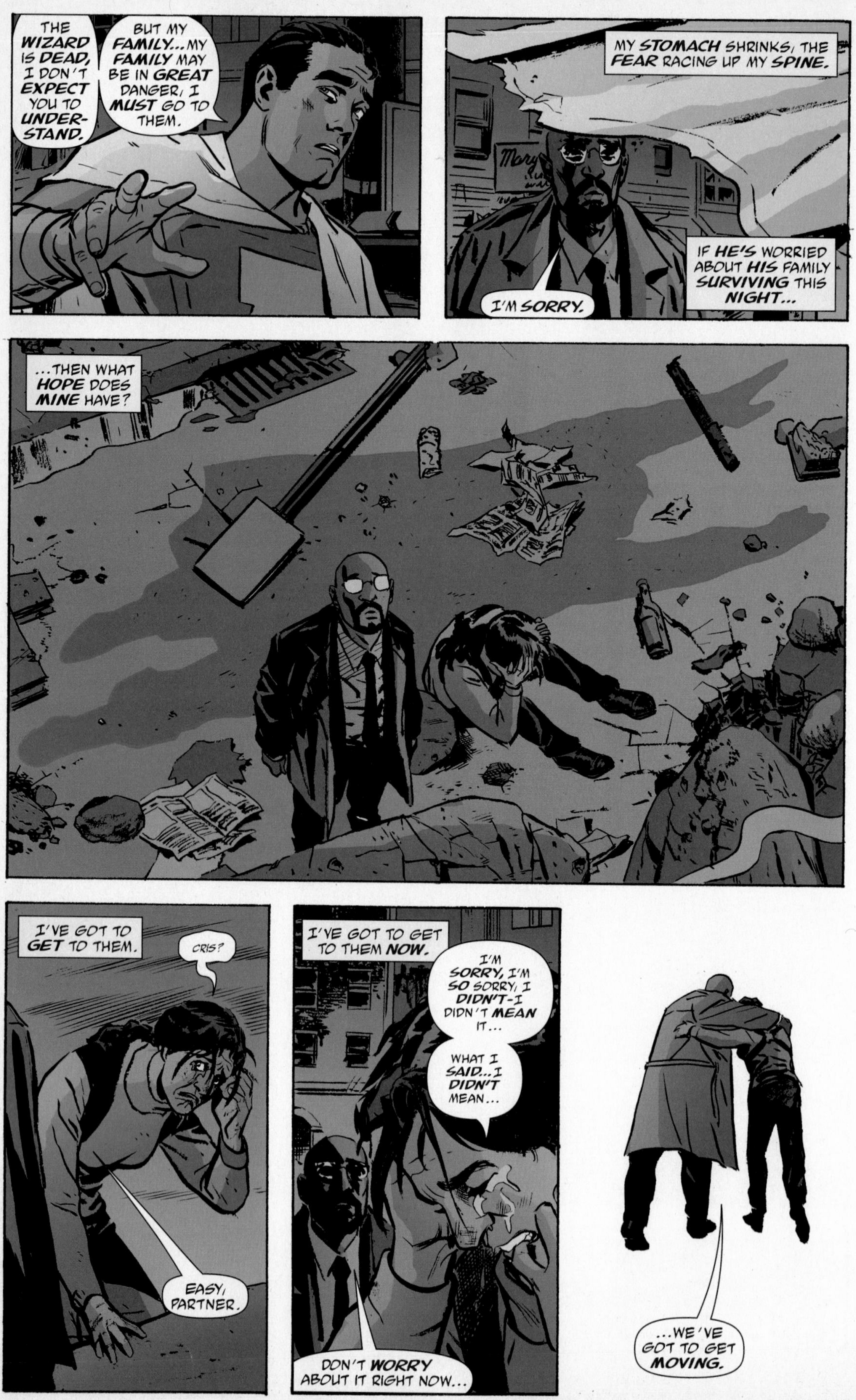
THE WIZARD IS DEAD, I DON'T EXPECT YOU TO UNDERSTAND.
BUT MY FAMILY... MY FAMILY MAY BE IN GREAT DANGER, I MUST GO TO THEM.
MY STOMACH SHRINKS, THE FEAR RACING UP MY SPINE.
I'M SORRY.
IF HE'S WORRIED ABOUT HIS FAMILY SURVIVING THIS NIGHT...
...THEN WHAT HOPE DOES MINE HAVE?
I'VE GOT TO GET TO THEM.
CRIS?
EASY, PARTNER.
I'VE GOT TO GET TO THEM NOW.
I'M SORRY, I'M SO SORRY, I DIDN'T-I DIDN'T MEAN IT...
WHAT I SAID...I DIDN'T MEAN...
DON'T WORRY ABOUT IT RIGHT NOW...
...WE'VE GOT TO GET MOVING.

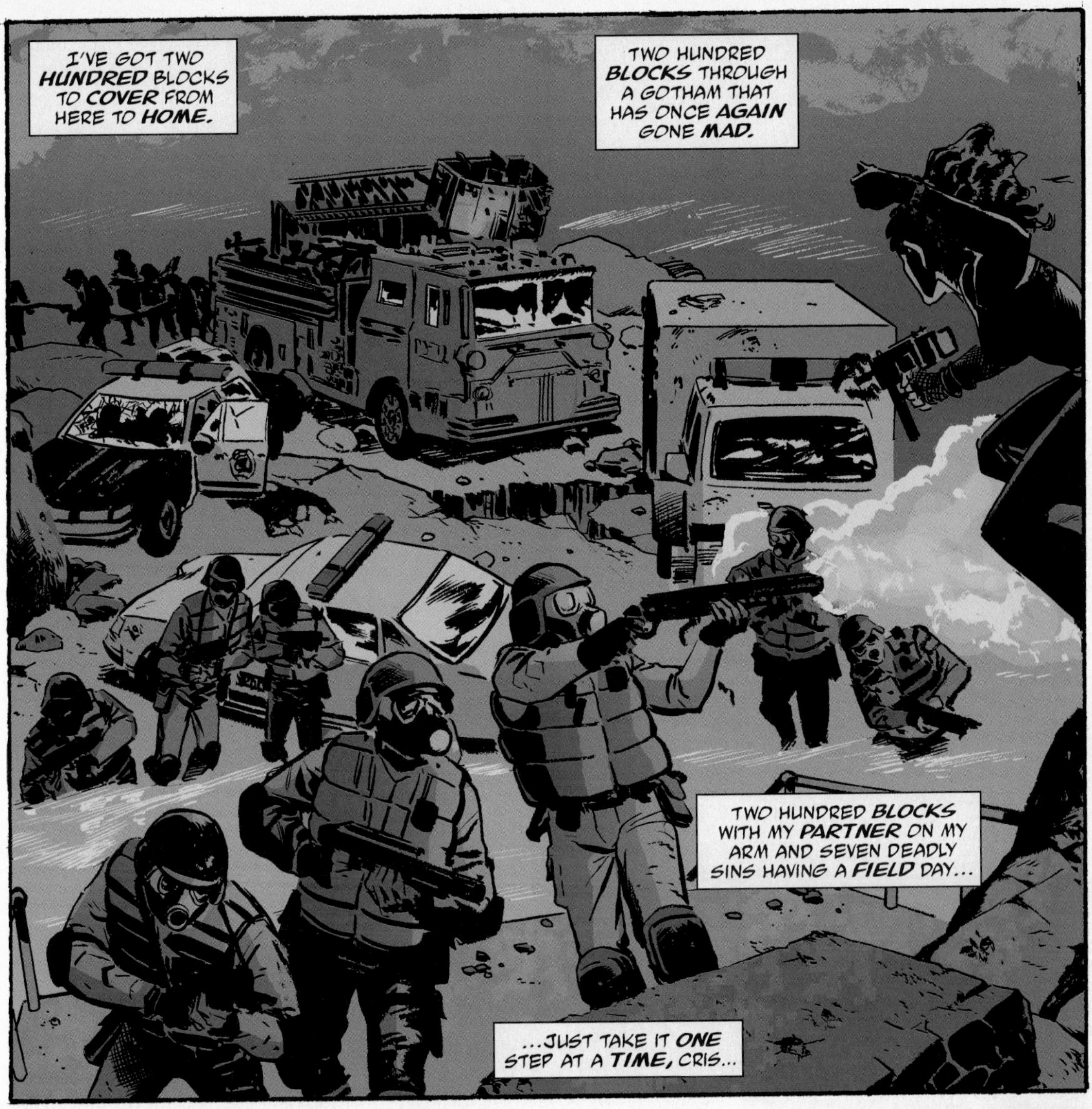
I'VE GOT TWO HUNDRED BLOCKS TO COVER FROM HERE TO HOME.
TWO HUNDRED BLOCKS THROUGH A GOTHAM THAT HAS ONCE AGAIN GONE MAD.
TWO HUNDRED BLOCKS WITH MY PARTNER ON MY ARM AND SEVEN DEADLY SINS HAVING A FIELD DAY...
...JUST TAKE IT ONE STEP AT A TIME, CRIS...

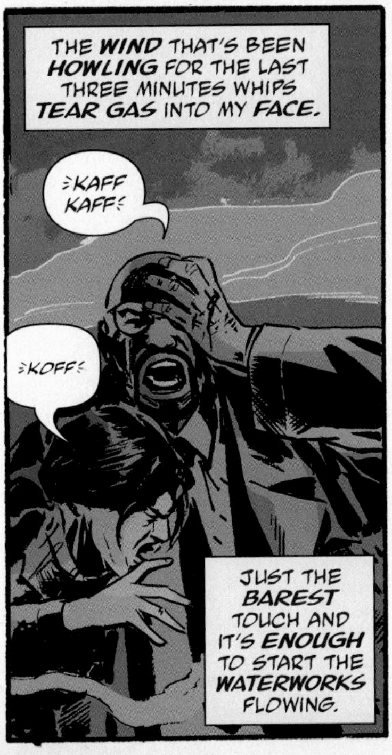
THE WIND THAT'S BEEN HOWLING FOR THE LAST THREE MINUTES WHIPS TEAR GAS INTO MY FACE.
KAFF KAFF
KOFF
JUST THE BAREST TOUCH AND IT'S ENOUGH TO START THE WATERWORKS FLOWING.

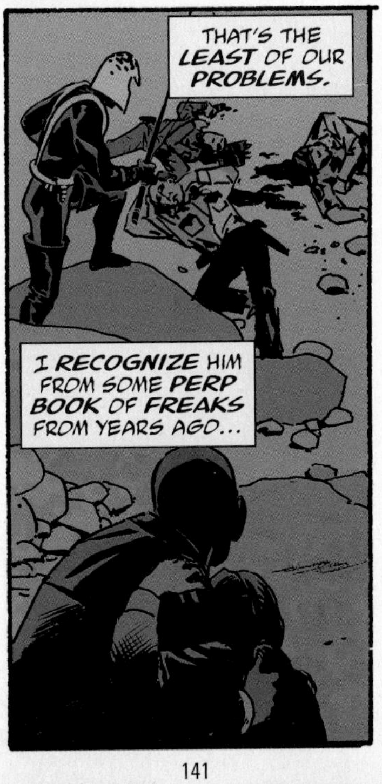
THAT'S THE LEAST OF OUR PROBLEMS.
I RECOGNIZE HIM FROM SOME PERP BOOK OF FREAKS FROM YEARS AGO...

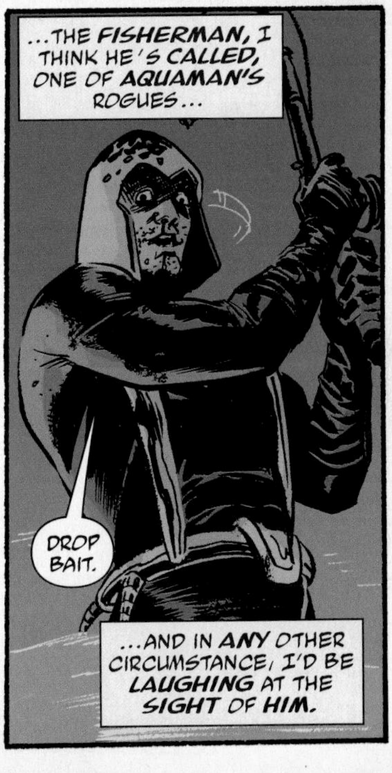
...THE FISHERMAN, I THINK HE'S CALLED, ONE OF AQUAMAN'S ROGUES...
DROP BAIT.
...AND IN ANY OTHER CIRCUMSTANCE, I'D BE LAUGHING AT THE SIGHT OF HIM.

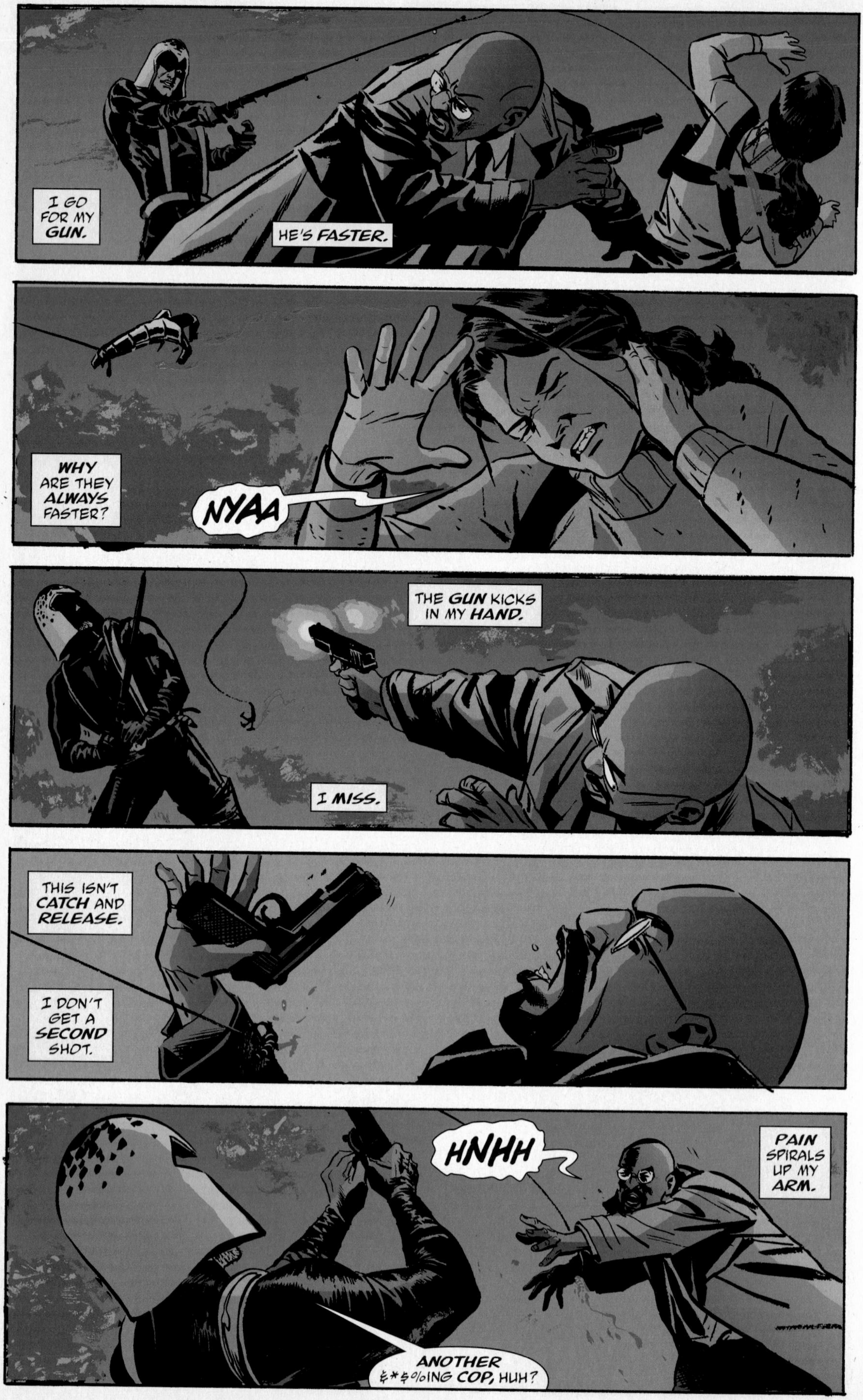

I GO FOR MY GUN.
HE'S FASTER.
WHY ARE THEY ALWAYS FASTER?
NYAA
THE GUN KICKS IN MY HAND.
I MISS.
THIS ISN'T CATCH AND RELEASE.
I DON'T GET A SECOND SHOT.
HNHH
PAIN SPIRALS UP MY ARM.
ANOTHER ¢*$%ING COP, HUH?

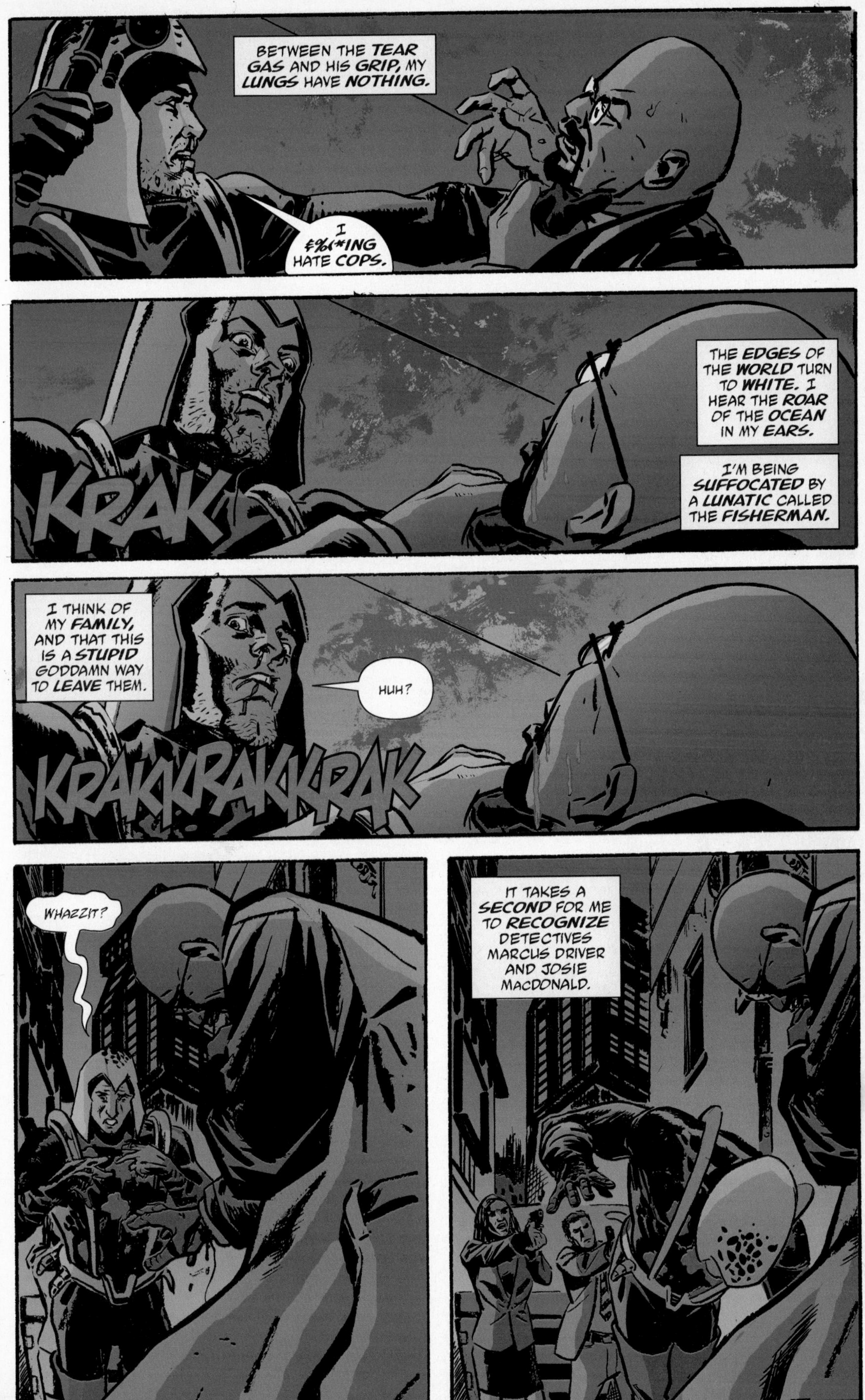
BETWEEN THE TEAR GAS AND HIS GRIP, MY LUNGS HAVE NOTHING.
I £%(*ING HATE COPS.
THE EDGES OF THE WORLD TURN TO WHITE. I HEAR THE ROAR OF THE OCEAN IN MY EARS.
I'M BEING SUFFOCATED BY A LUNATIC CALLED THE FISHERMAN.
KRAK
I THINK OF MY FAMILY, AND THAT THIS IS A STUPID GODDAMN WAY TO LEAVE THEM.
HUH?
KRAKKRAKKRAK
WHAZZIT?
IT TAKES A SECOND FOR ME TO RECOGNIZE DETECTIVES MARCUS DRIVER AND JOSIE MACDONALD.

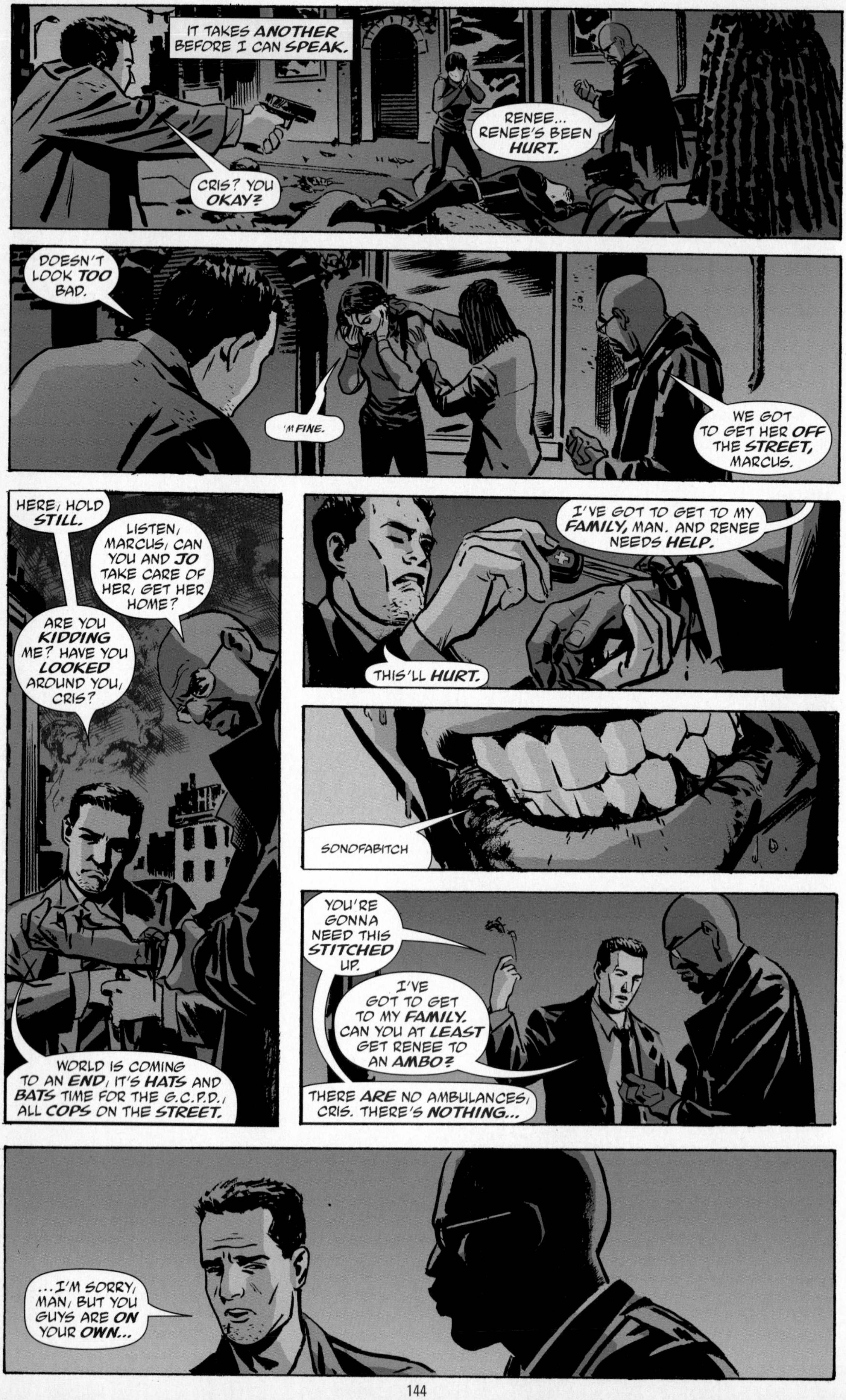
IT TAKES ANOTHER BEFORE I CAN SPEAK.
CRIS? YOU OKAY?
RENEE... RENEE'S BEEN HURT.
DOESN'T LOOK TOO BAD.
'M FINE.
WE GOT TO GET HER OFF THE STREET, MARCUS.
HERE, HOLD STILL.
LISTEN, MARCUS, CAN YOU AND JO TAKE CARE OF HER, GET HER HOME?
ARE YOU KIDDING ME? HAVE YOU LOOKED AROUND YOU, CRIS?
WORLD IS COMING TO AN END, IT'S HATS AND BATS TIME FOR THE G.C.P.D., ALL COPS ON THE STREET.
I'VE GOT TO GET TO MY FAMILY, MAN. AND RENEE NEEDS HELP.
THIS'LL HURT.
SONOFABITCH
YOU'RE GONNA NEED THIS STITCHED UP.
I'VE GOT TO GET TO MY FAMILY. CAN YOU AT LEAST GET RENEE TO AN AMBO?
THERE ARE NO AMBULANCES, CRIS. THERE'S NOTHING...
...I'M SORRY, MAN, BUT YOU GUYS ARE ON YOUR OWN...

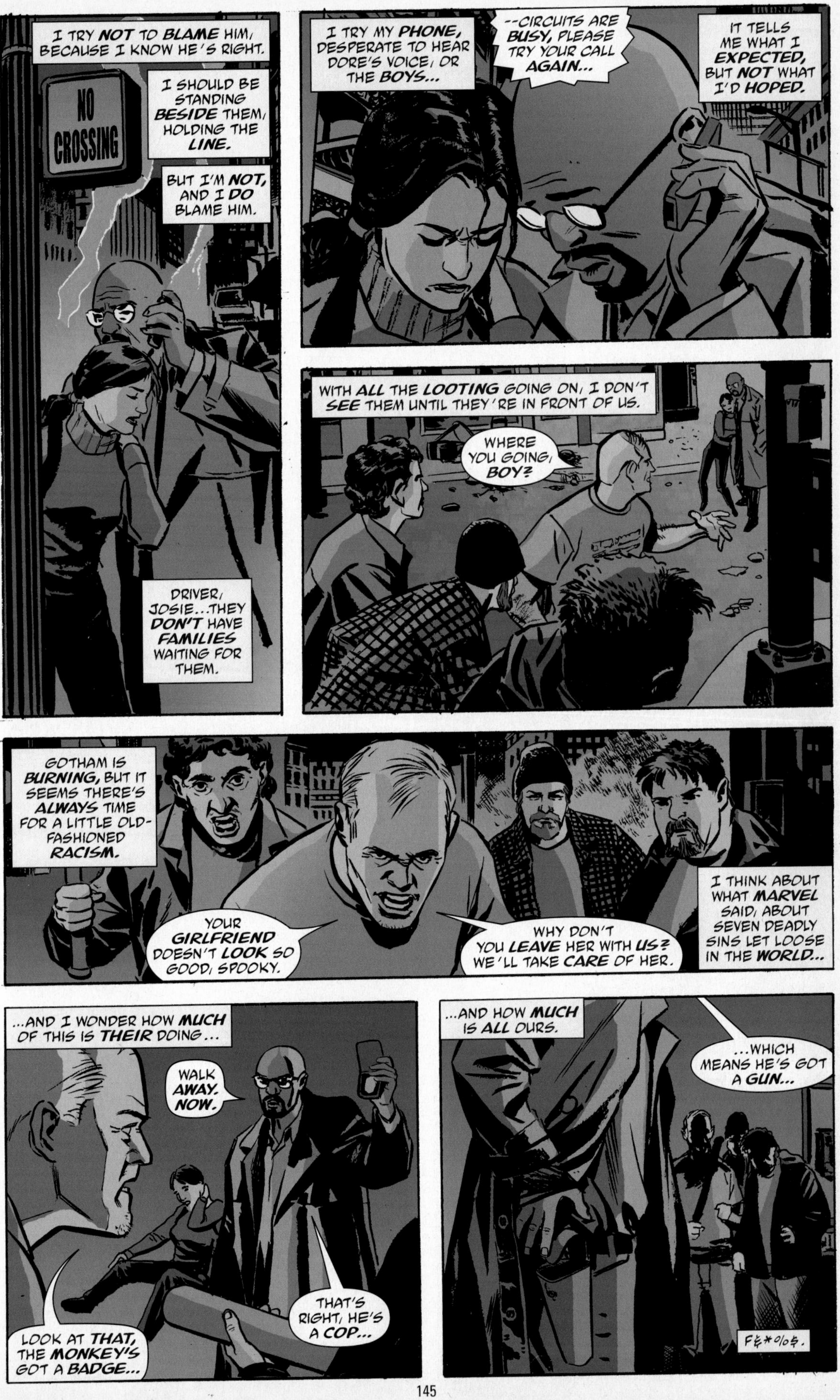
I TRY NOT TO BLAME HIM, BECAUSE I KNOW HE'S RIGHT.
NO CROSSING
I SHOULD BE STANDING BESIDE THEM, HOLDING THE LINE.
BUT I'M NOT, AND I DO BLAME HIM.
DRIVER, JOSIE...THEY DON'T HAVE FAMILIES WAITING FOR THEM.
I TRY MY PHONE, DESPERATE TO HEAR DORE'S VOICE, OR THE BOYS...
--CIRCUITS ARE BUSY, PLEASE TRY YOUR CALL AGAIN...
IT TELLS ME WHAT I EXPECTED, BUT NOT WHAT I'D HOPED.
WITH ALL THE LOOTING GOING ON, I DON'T SEE THEM UNTIL THEY'RE IN FRONT OF US.
WHERE YOU GOING, BOY?
GOTHAM IS BURNING, BUT IT SEEMS THERE'S ALWAYS TIME FOR A LITTLE OLD-FASHIONED RACISM.
YOUR GIRLFRIEND DOESN'T LOOK SO GOOD, SPOOKY.
WHY DON'T YOU LEAVE HER WITH US? WE'LL TAKE CARE OF HER.
I THINK ABOUT WHAT MARVEL SAID, ABOUT SEVEN DEADLY SINS LET LOOSE IN THE WORLD...
...AND I WONDER HOW MUCH OF THIS IS THEIR DOING...
WALK AWAY. NOW.
LOOK AT THAT, THE MONKEY'S GOT A BADGE...
THAT'S RIGHT, HE'S A COP...
...AND HOW MUCH IS ALL OURS.
...WHICH MEANS HE'S GOT A GUN...
F&*%$.

...TOO...

NOT SO **TOUGH** WITHOUT **HEAT**...

I DON'T WANT TO **DIE** LIKE THIS.

...ARE YOU, BOY?

I HAVE TO GET **HOME**.

AAHGGG!!

BLAMM

CRIS.

HELP ME **UP**.

HNN NHHNN HNH!

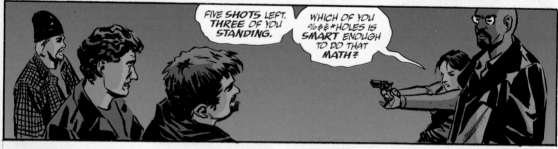

FIVE SHOTS LEFT. **THREE** OF YOU STANDING.

WHICH OF YOU %/¢&#*HOLES IS **SMART** ENOUGH TO DO THAT **MATH?**

YEAH, THAT'S WHAT I THOUGHT.

I'M GETTING YOU **HOME**, RENEE.

NO...

xenon

...THERE...

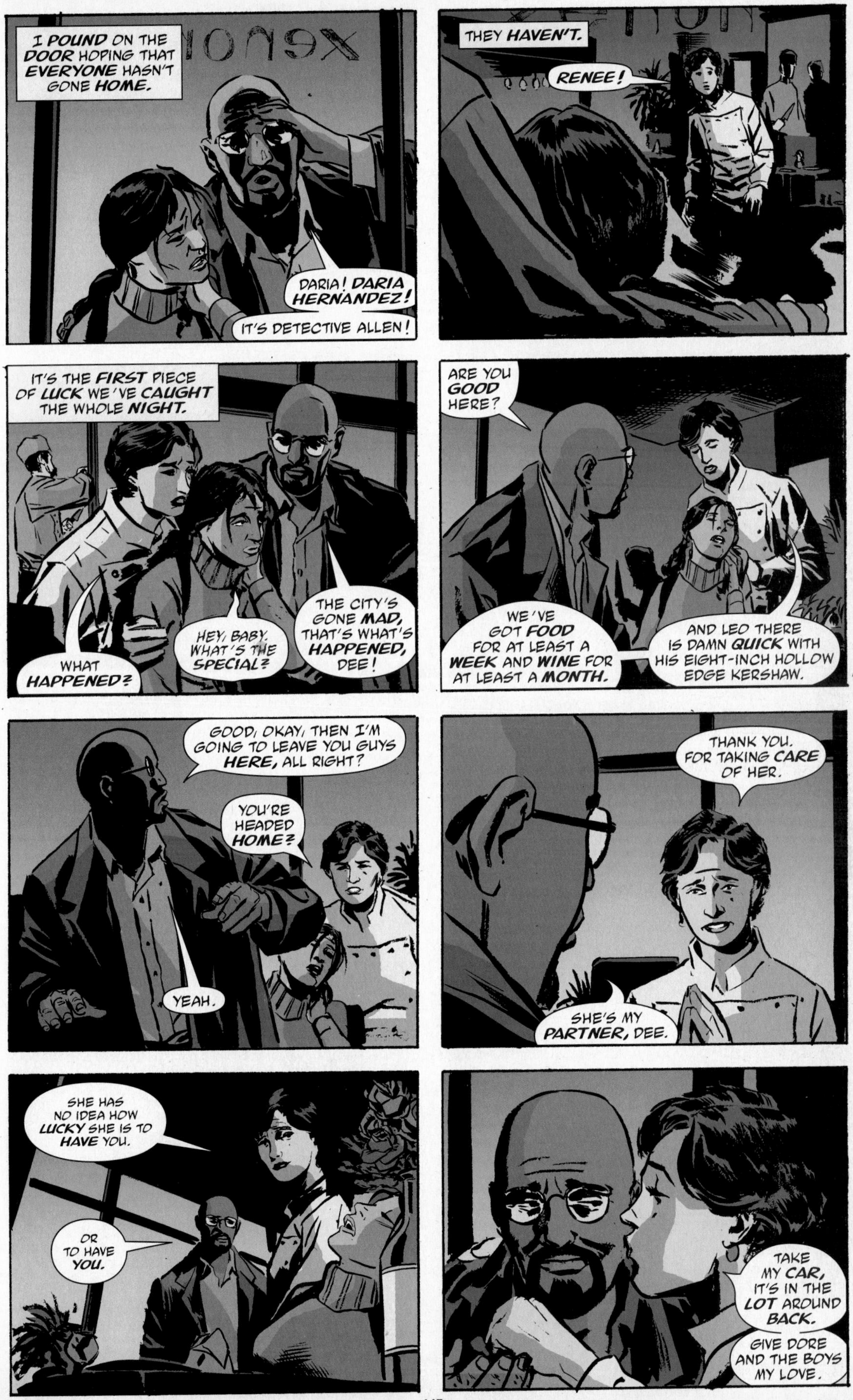

I POUND ON THE DOOR HOPING THAT EVERYONE HASN'T GONE HOME.
DARIA! DARIA HERNANDEZ!
IT'S DETECTIVE ALLEN!
THEY HAVEN'T.
RENEE!
IT'S THE FIRST PIECE OF LUCK WE'VE CAUGHT THE WHOLE NIGHT.
WHAT HAPPENED?
HEY, BABY. WHAT'S THE SPECIAL?
THE CITY'S GONE MAD, THAT'S WHAT'S HAPPENED, DEE!
ARE YOU GOOD HERE?
WE'VE GOT FOOD FOR AT LEAST A WEEK AND WINE FOR AT LEAST A MONTH.
AND LEO THERE IS DAMN QUICK WITH HIS EIGHT-INCH HOLLOW EDGE KERSHAW.
GOOD, OKAY, THEN I'M GOING TO LEAVE YOU GUYS HERE, ALL RIGHT?
YOU'RE HEADED HOME?
YEAH.
THANK YOU. FOR TAKING CARE OF HER.
SHE'S MY PARTNER, DEE.
SHE HAS NO IDEA HOW LUCKY SHE IS TO HAVE YOU.
OR TO HAVE YOU.
TAKE MY CAR, IT'S IN THE LOT AROUND BACK.
GIVE DORE AND THE BOYS MY LOVE.

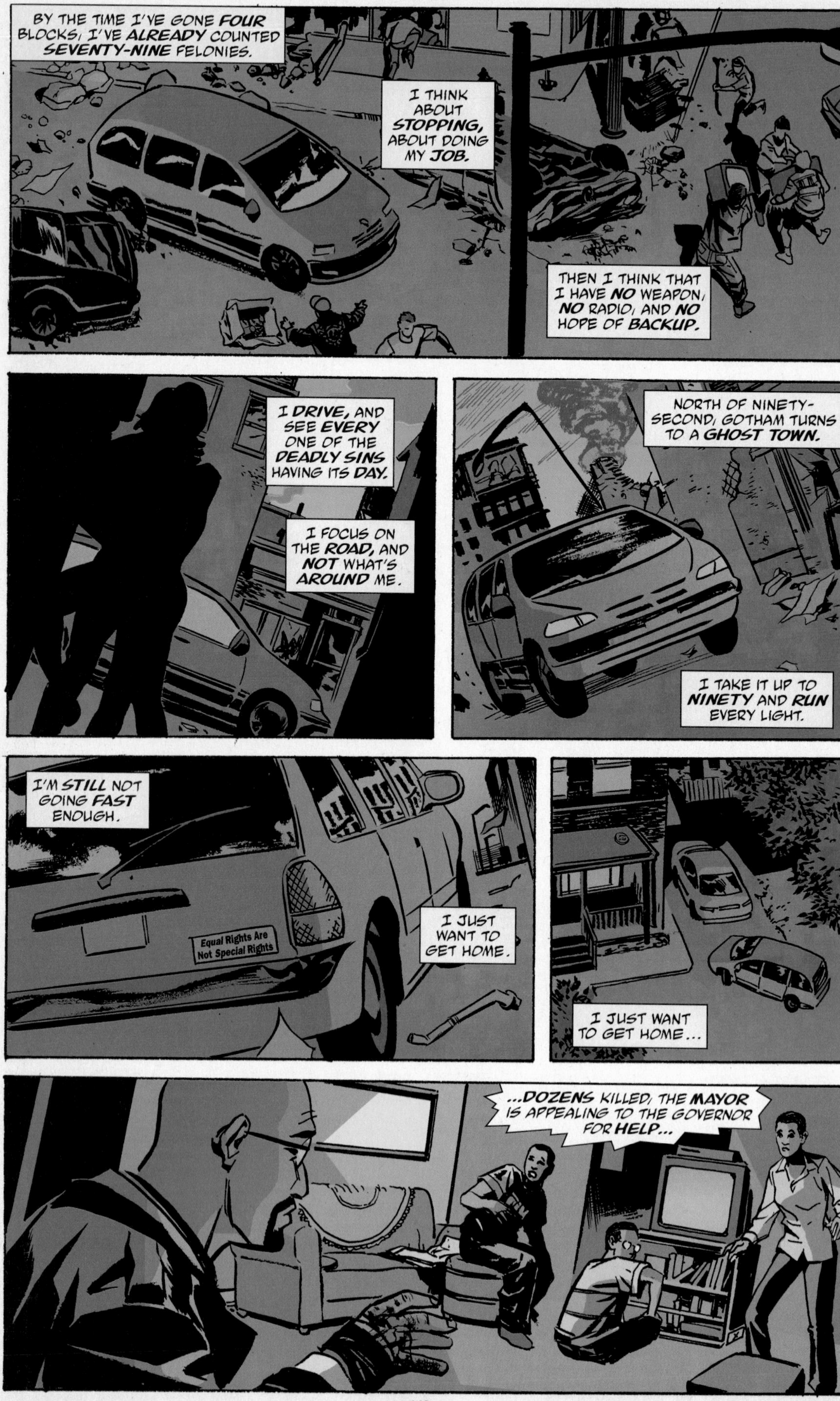
BY THE TIME I'VE GONE FOUR BLOCKS, I'VE ALREADY COUNTED SEVENTY-NINE FELONIES.
I THINK ABOUT STOPPING, ABOUT DOING MY JOB.
THEN I THINK THAT I HAVE NO WEAPON, NO RADIO, AND NO HOPE OF BACKUP.
I DRIVE, AND SEE EVERY ONE OF THE DEADLY SINS HAVING ITS DAY.
I FOCUS ON THE ROAD, AND NOT WHAT'S AROUND ME.
NORTH OF NINETY-SECOND, GOTHAM TURNS TO A GHOST TOWN.
I TAKE IT UP TO NINETY AND RUN EVERY LIGHT.
I'M STILL NOT GOING FAST ENOUGH.
Equal Rights Are Not Special Rights
I JUST WANT TO GET HOME.
I JUST WANT TO GET HOME...
...DOZENS KILLED, THE MAYOR IS APPEALING TO THE GOVERNOR FOR HELP...

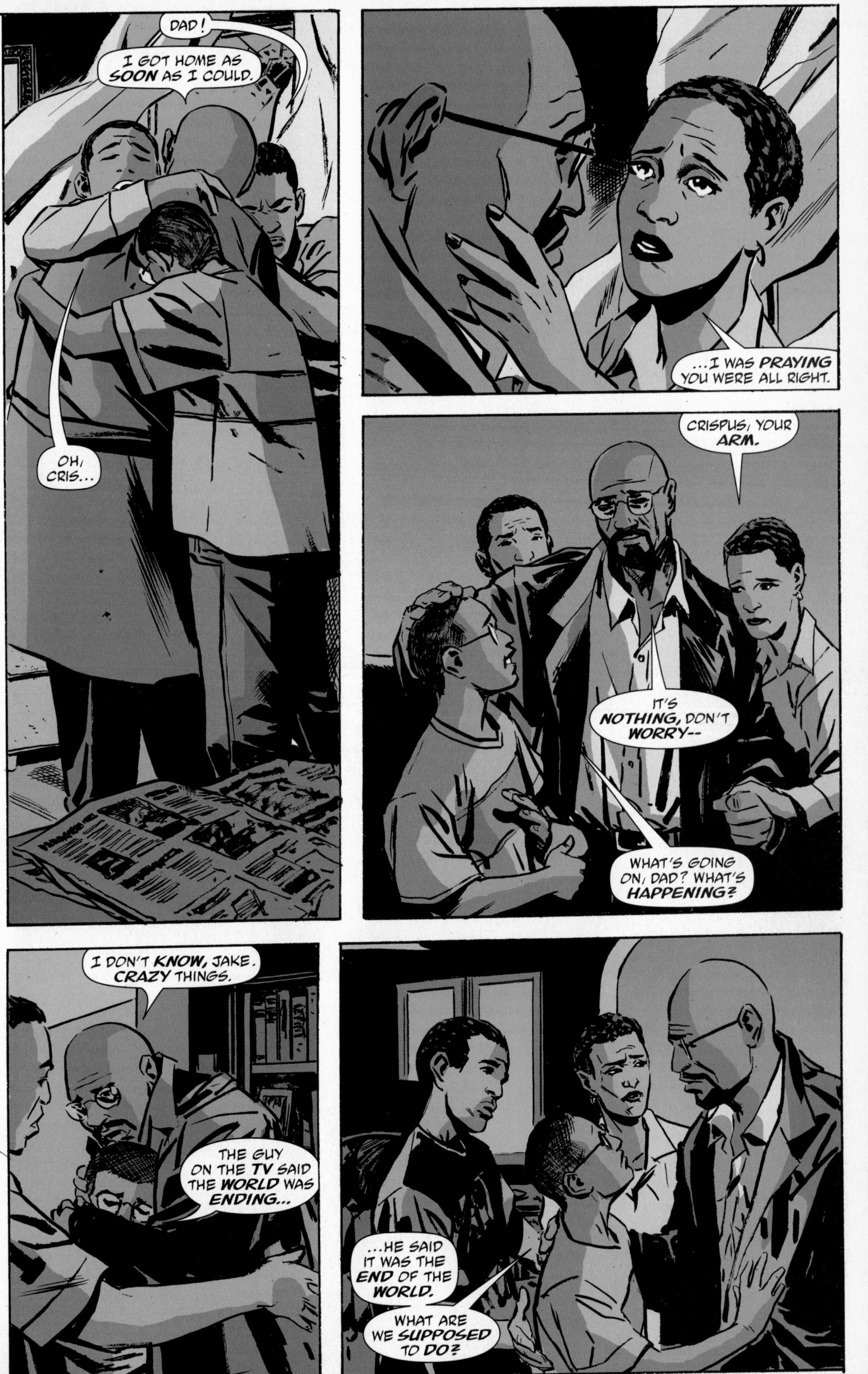
DAD!
I GOT HOME AS SOON AS I COULD.
OH, CRIS...
...I WAS PRAYING YOU WERE ALL RIGHT.
CRISPUS, YOUR ARM.
IT'S NOTHING, DON'T WORRY--
WHAT'S GOING ON, DAD? WHAT'S HAPPENING?
I DON'T KNOW, JAKE. CRAZY THINGS.
THE GUY ON THE TV SAID THE WORLD WAS ENDING...
...HE SAID IT WAS THE END OF THE WORLD.
WHAT ARE WE SUPPOSED TO DO?

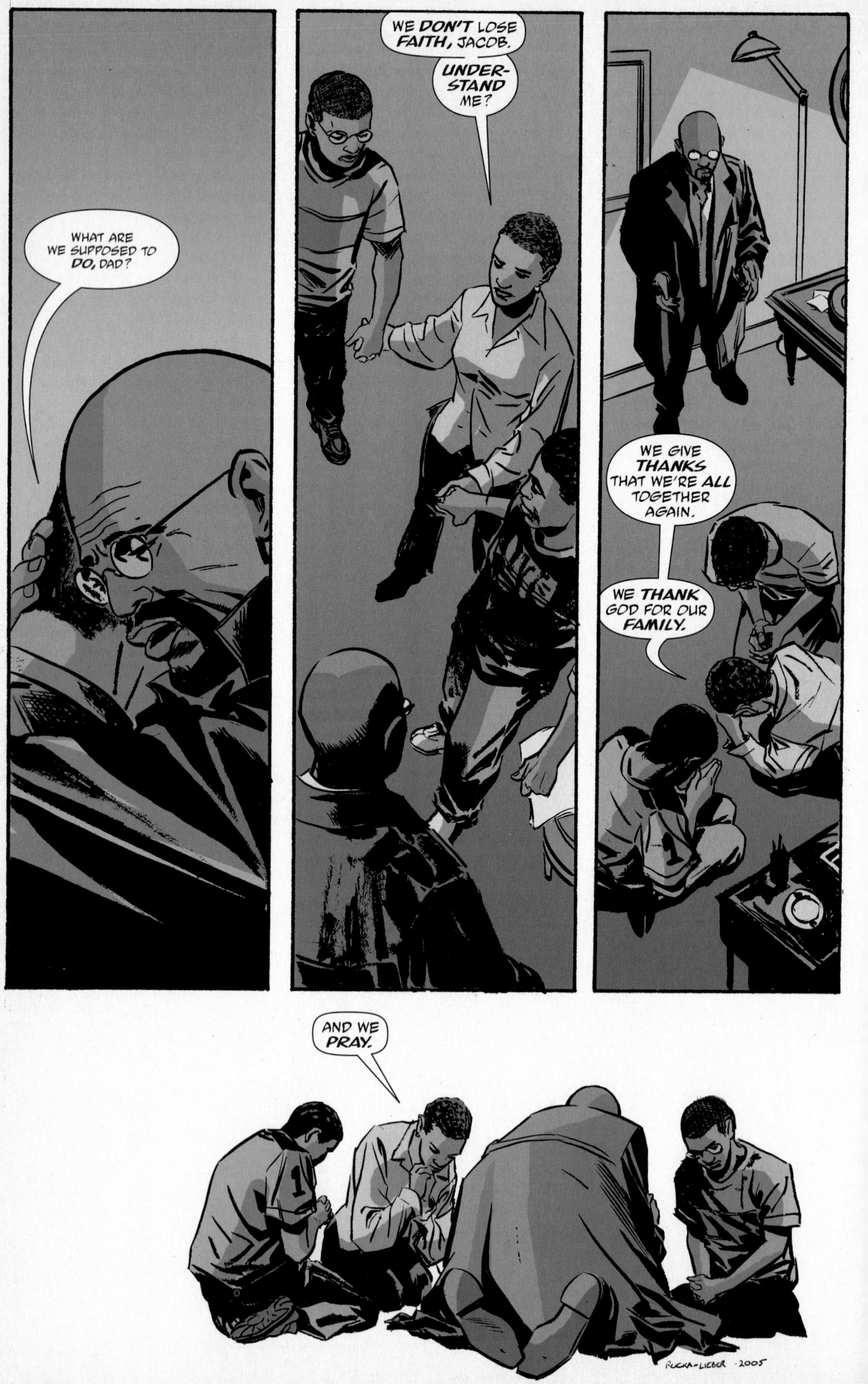
WHAT ARE WE SUPPOSED TO DO, DAD?
WE DON'T LOSE FAITH, JACOB.
UNDER-STAND ME?
WE GIVE THANKS THAT WE'RE ALL TOGETHER AGAIN.
WE THANK GOD FOR OUR FAMILY.
AND WE PRAY.
RUCKA-LIEBER -2005

THE END

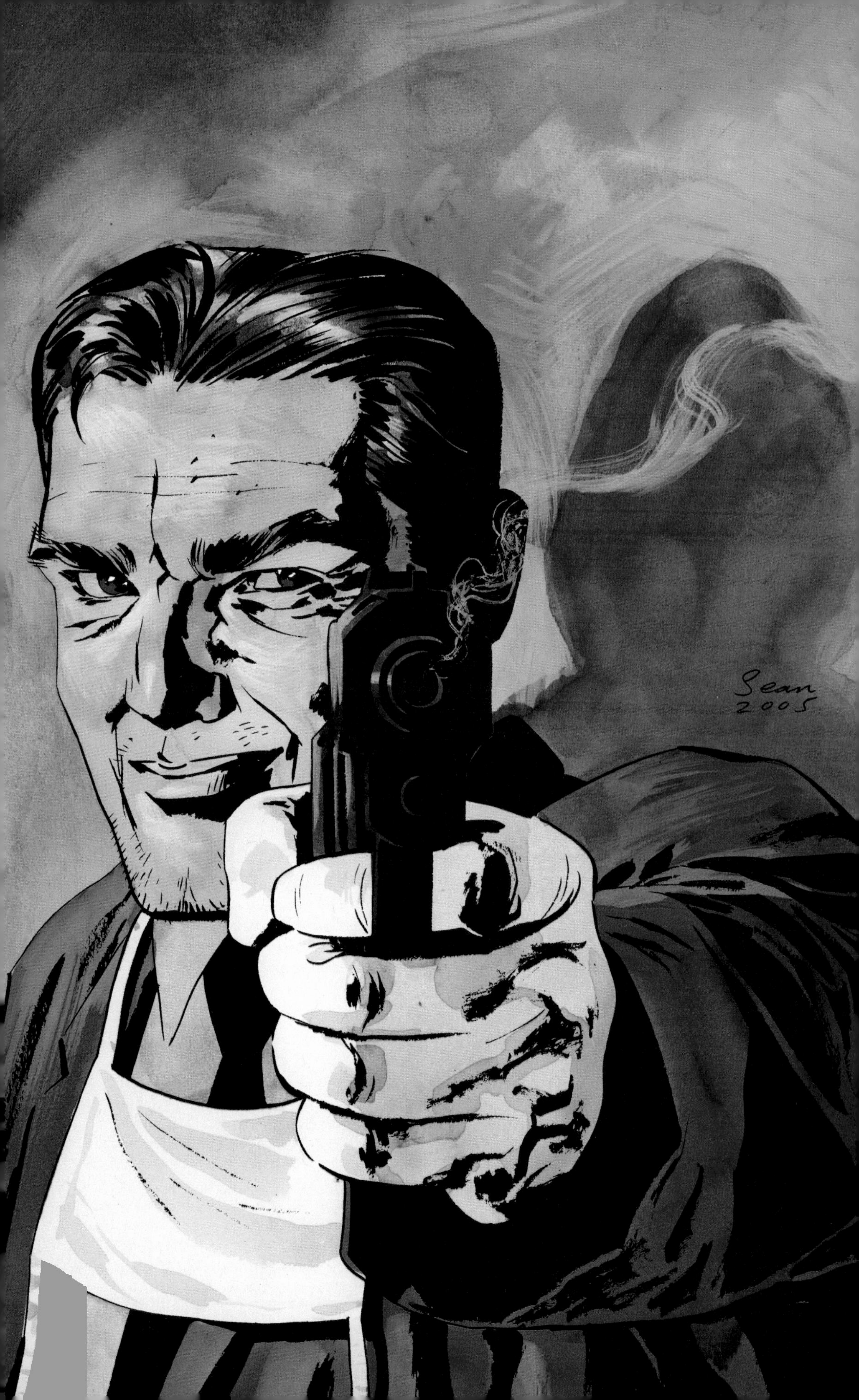
Sean
2005

CORRIGAN II

Written by
GREG RUCKA
Art by
KANO & STEFANO GAUDIANO
Colors by
LEE LOUGHRIDGE
Letters by
CLEM ROBINS

In a Police Department with a well earned reputation for being one of the most corrupt, Crime Scene Technician Jim Corrigan has mastered the art of payoffs, extortion and exploitation. While investigating Corrigan, Inspector Manuel "Manny" Esperanza of the Internal Affairs Division learned of a scheme to frame M.C.U. Detective Crispus Allen. Manny informed Allen's partner, Renee Montoya, of the plot. Montoya used excessive force to get the information she needed from Corrigan, which cleared Allen, but her actions spared Corrigan from further investigation into his illicit affairs. He is essentially untouchable. Allen knew nothing of Montoya's actions or their repercussions, until now...

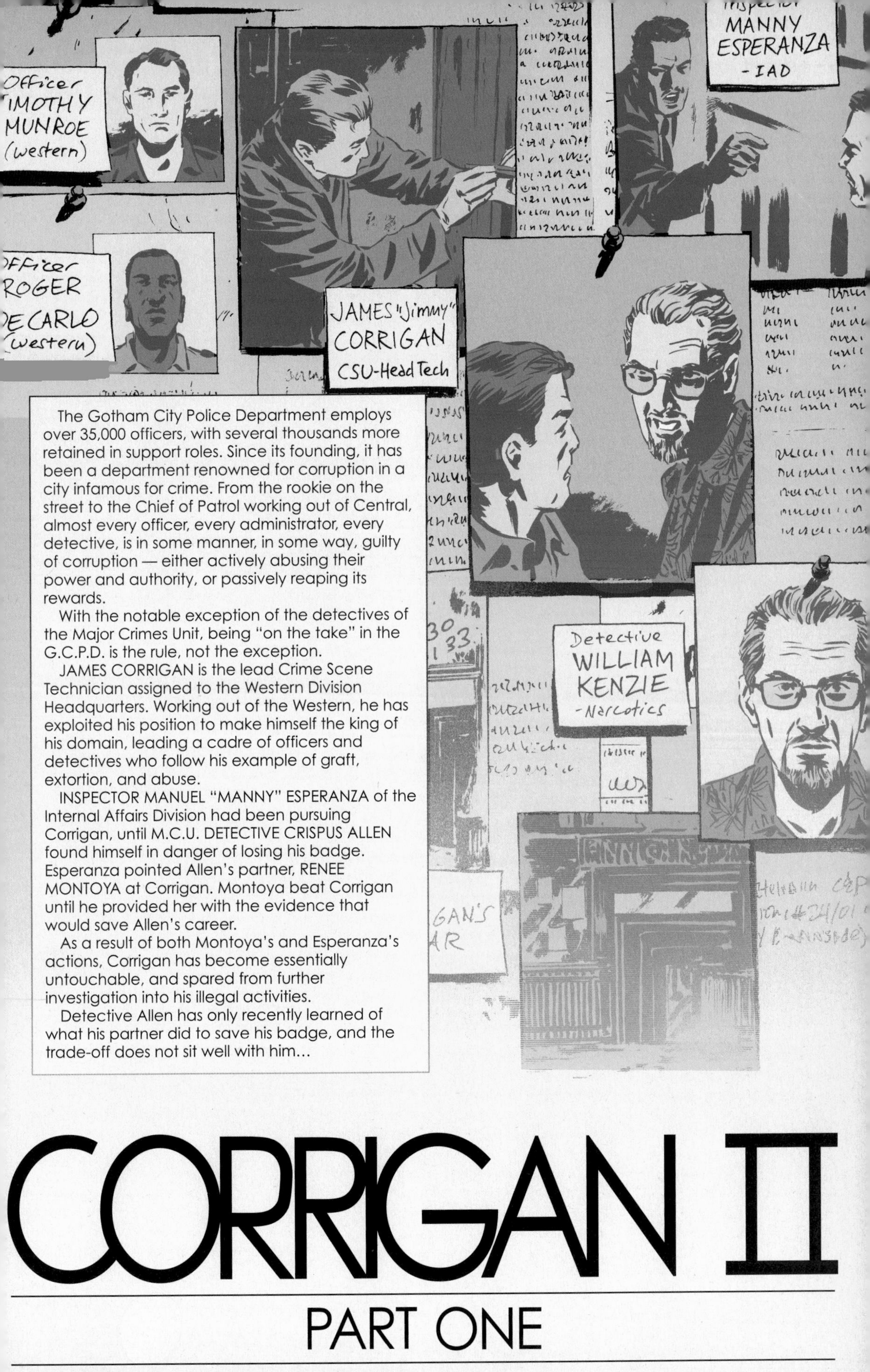
Officer
IMOTHY
MUNROE
(western)
MANNY
ESPERANZA
-IAD
FFicer
ROGER
E CARLO
(western)
JAMES "Jimmy"
CORRIGAN
CSU-Head Tech
Detective
WILLIAM
KENZIE
-Narcotics

The Gotham City Police Department employs over 35,000 officers, with several thousands more retained in support roles. Since its founding, it has been a department renowned for corruption in a city infamous for crime. From the rookie on the street to the Chief of Patrol working out of Central, almost every officer, every administrator, every detective, is in some manner, in some way, guilty of corruption — either actively abusing their power and authority, or passively reaping its rewards.

With the notable exception of the detectives of the Major Crimes Unit, being "on the take" in the G.C.P.D. is the rule, not the exception.

JAMES CORRIGAN is the lead Crime Scene Technician assigned to the Western Division Headquarters. Working out of the Western, he has exploited his position to make himself the king of his domain, leading a cadre of officers and detectives who follow his example of graft, extortion, and abuse.

INSPECTOR MANUEL "MANNY" ESPERANZA of the Internal Affairs Division had been pursuing Corrigan, until M.C.U. DETECTIVE CRISPUS ALLEN found himself in danger of losing his badge. Esperanza pointed Allen's partner, RENEE MONTOYA at Corrigan. Montoya beat Corrigan until he provided her with the evidence that would save Allen's career.

As a result of both Montoya's and Esperanza's actions, Corrigan has become essentially untouchable, and spared from further investigation into his illegal activities.

Detective Allen has only recently learned of what his partner did to save his badge, and the trade-off does not sit well with him...

CORRIGAN II

PART ONE

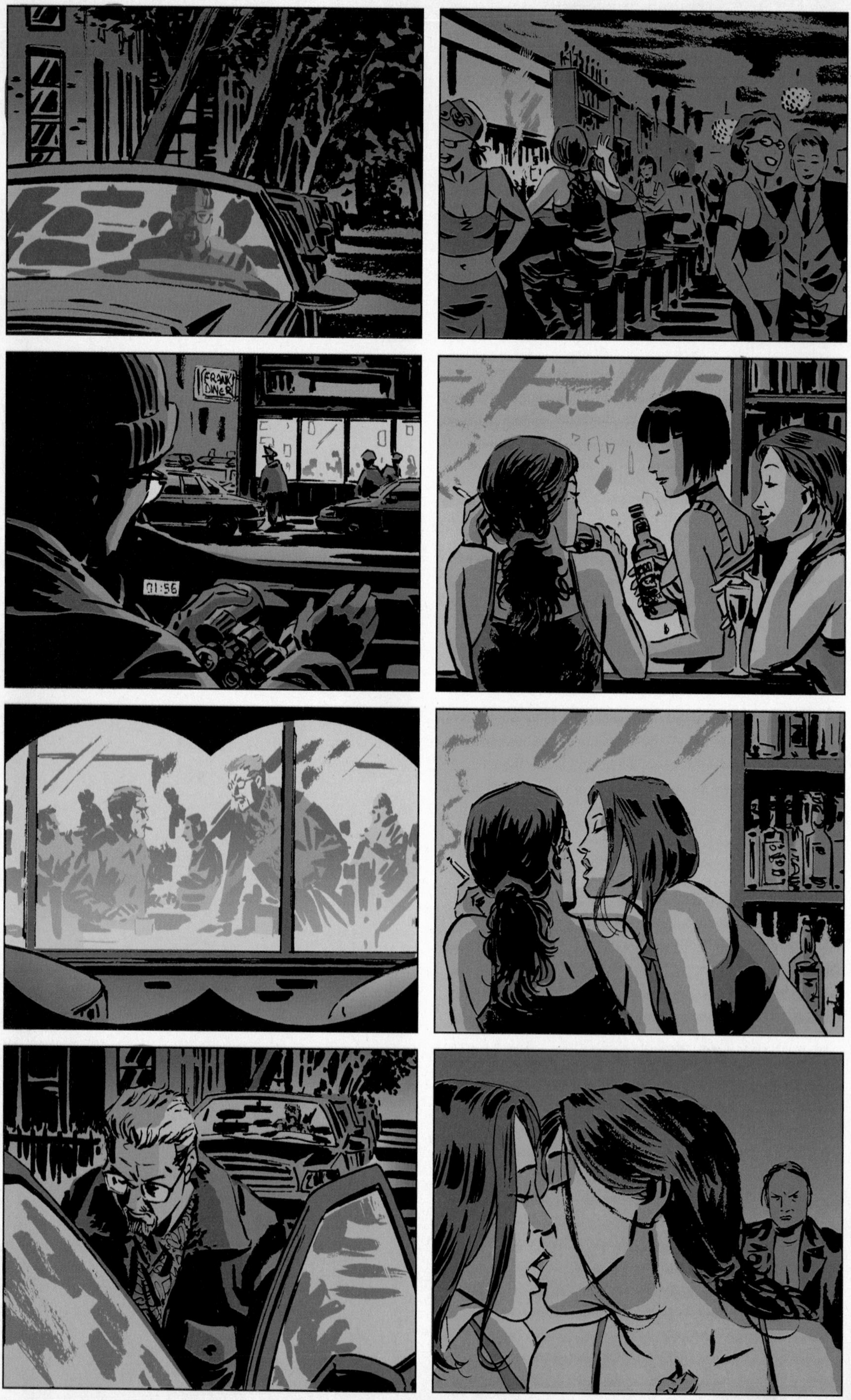
FRANK'S DINER
01:56

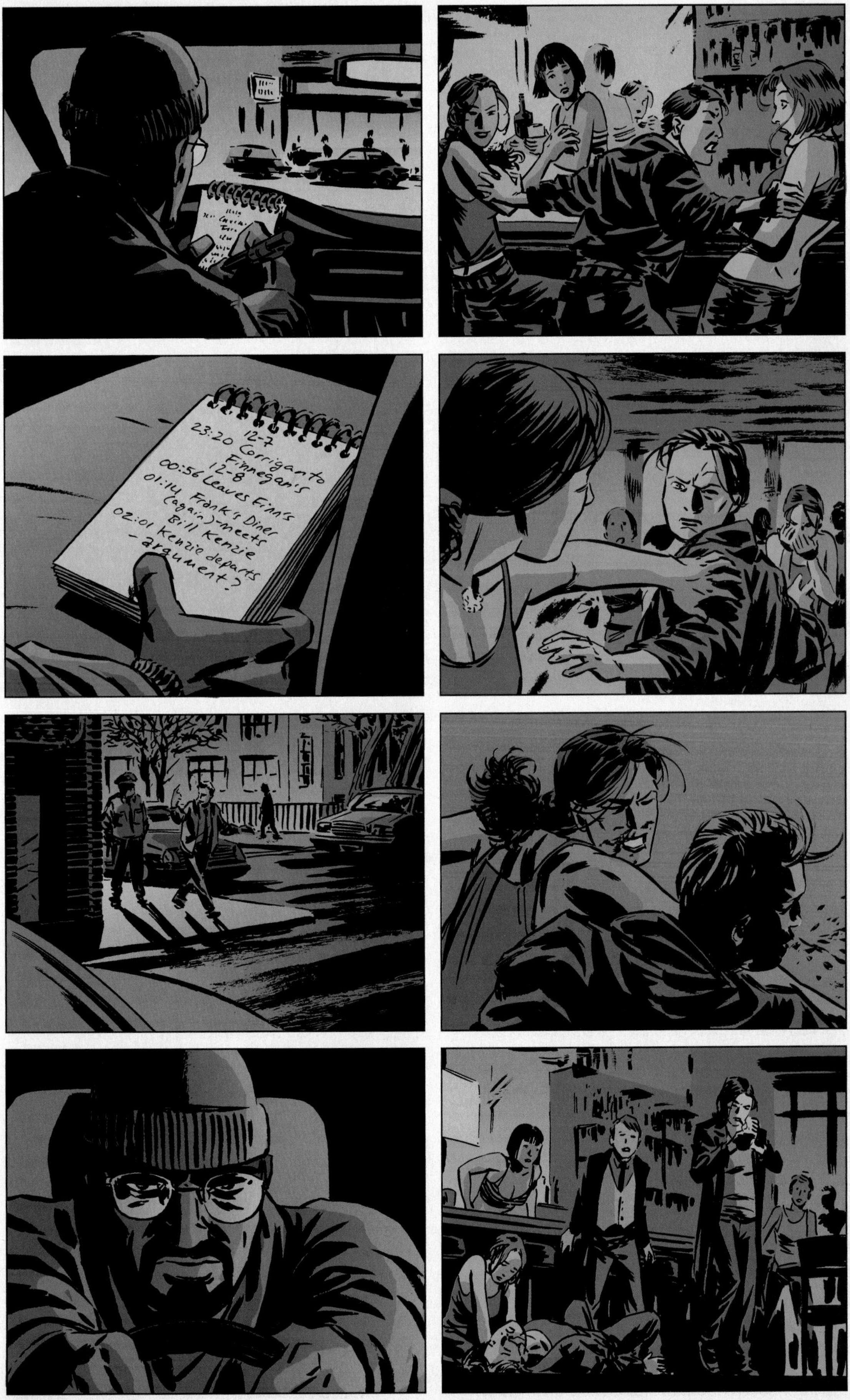
12-7
23:20 Corrigan to
Finnegan's
12-8
00:56 Leaves Finn's
01:14 Frank's Diner
(again)-meets
Bill Kenzie
02:01 Kenzie departs
-argument?

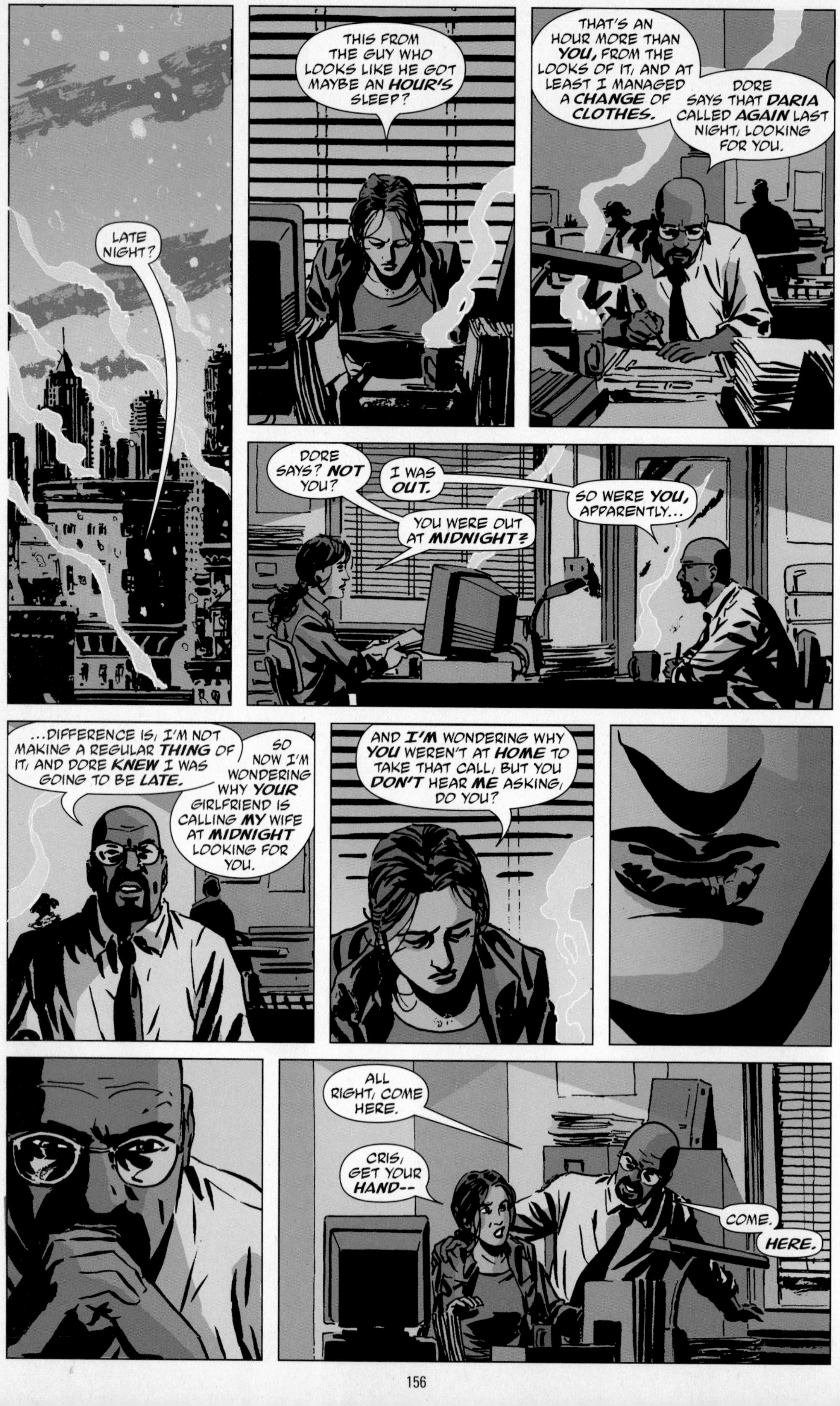
LATE NIGHT?
THIS FROM THE GUY WHO LOOKS LIKE HE GOT MAYBE AN HOUR'S SLEEP?
THAT'S AN HOUR MORE THAN YOU, FROM THE LOOKS OF IT, AND AT LEAST I MANAGED A CHANGE OF CLOTHES.
DORE SAYS THAT DARIA CALLED AGAIN LAST NIGHT, LOOKING FOR YOU.
DORE SAYS? NOT YOU?
I WAS OUT.
SO WERE YOU, APPARENTLY...
YOU WERE OUT AT MIDNIGHT?
...DIFFERENCE IS, I'M NOT MAKING A REGULAR THING OF IT, AND DORE KNEW I WAS GOING TO BE LATE.
SO NOW I'M WONDERING WHY YOUR GIRLFRIEND IS CALLING MY WIFE AT MIDNIGHT LOOKING FOR YOU.
AND I'M WONDERING WHY YOU WEREN'T AT HOME TO TAKE THAT CALL, BUT YOU DON'T HEAR ME ASKING, DO YOU?
ALL RIGHT, COME HERE.
CRIS, GET YOUR HAND--
COME. HERE.

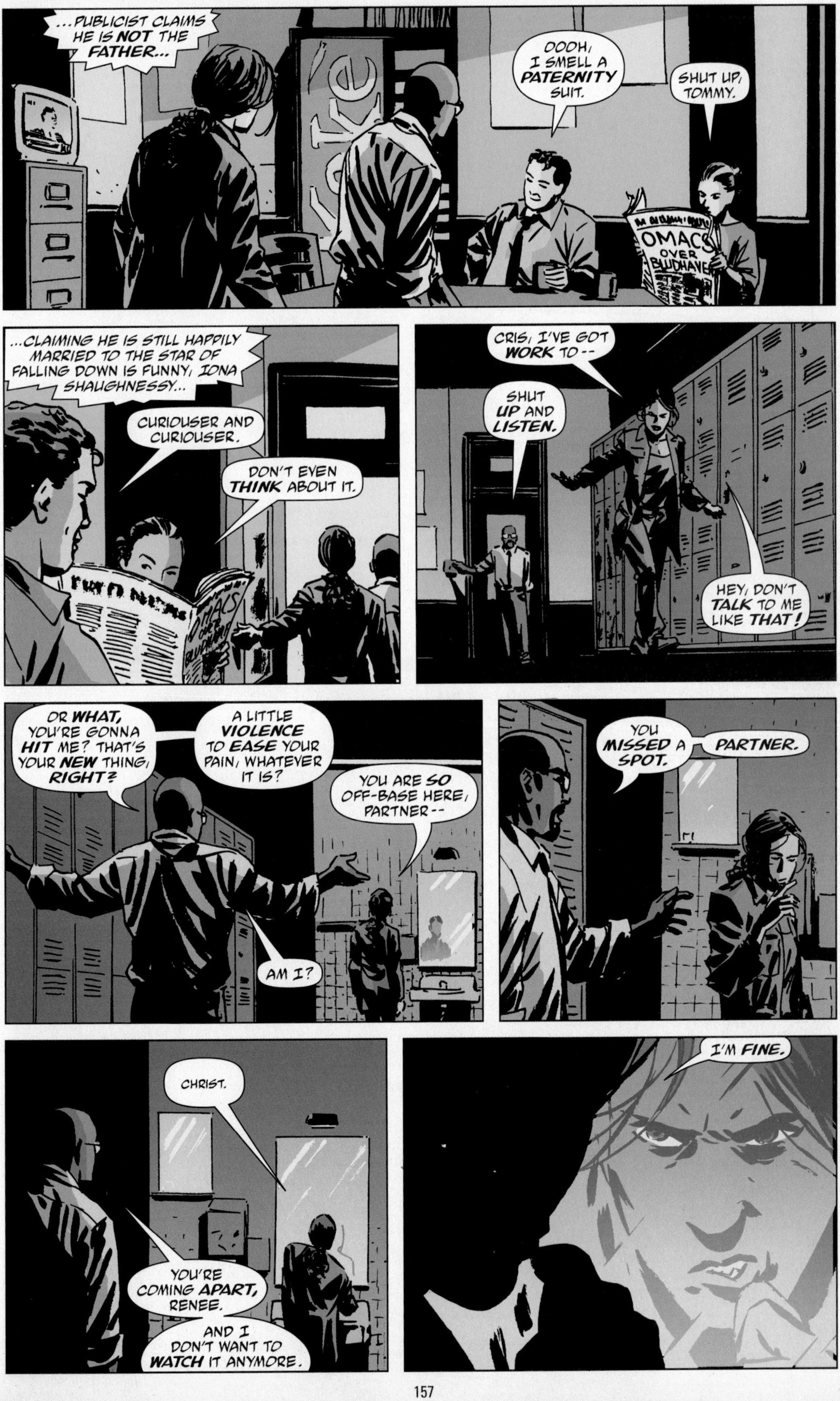

...PUBLICIST CLAIMS HE IS NOT THE FATHER...
OOOH, I SMELL A PATERNITY SUIT.
SHUT UP, TOMMY.
OMACS OVER BLUDHAVEN
...CLAIMING HE IS STILL HAPPILY MARRIED TO THE STAR OF FALLING DOWN IS FUNNY, IONA SHAUGHNESSY...
CURIOUSER AND CURIOUSER.
DON'T EVEN THINK ABOUT IT.
CRIS, I'VE GOT WORK TO --
SHUT UP AND LISTEN.
HEY, DON'T TALK TO ME LIKE THAT!
OR WHAT, YOU'RE GONNA HIT ME? THAT'S YOUR NEW THING, RIGHT?
A LITTLE VIOLENCE TO EASE YOUR PAIN, WHATEVER IT IS?
YOU ARE SO OFF-BASE HERE, PARTNER --
AM I?
YOU MISSED A SPOT.
PARTNER.
CHRIST.
YOU'RE COMING APART, RENEE.
AND I DON'T WANT TO WATCH IT ANYMORE.
I'M FINE.

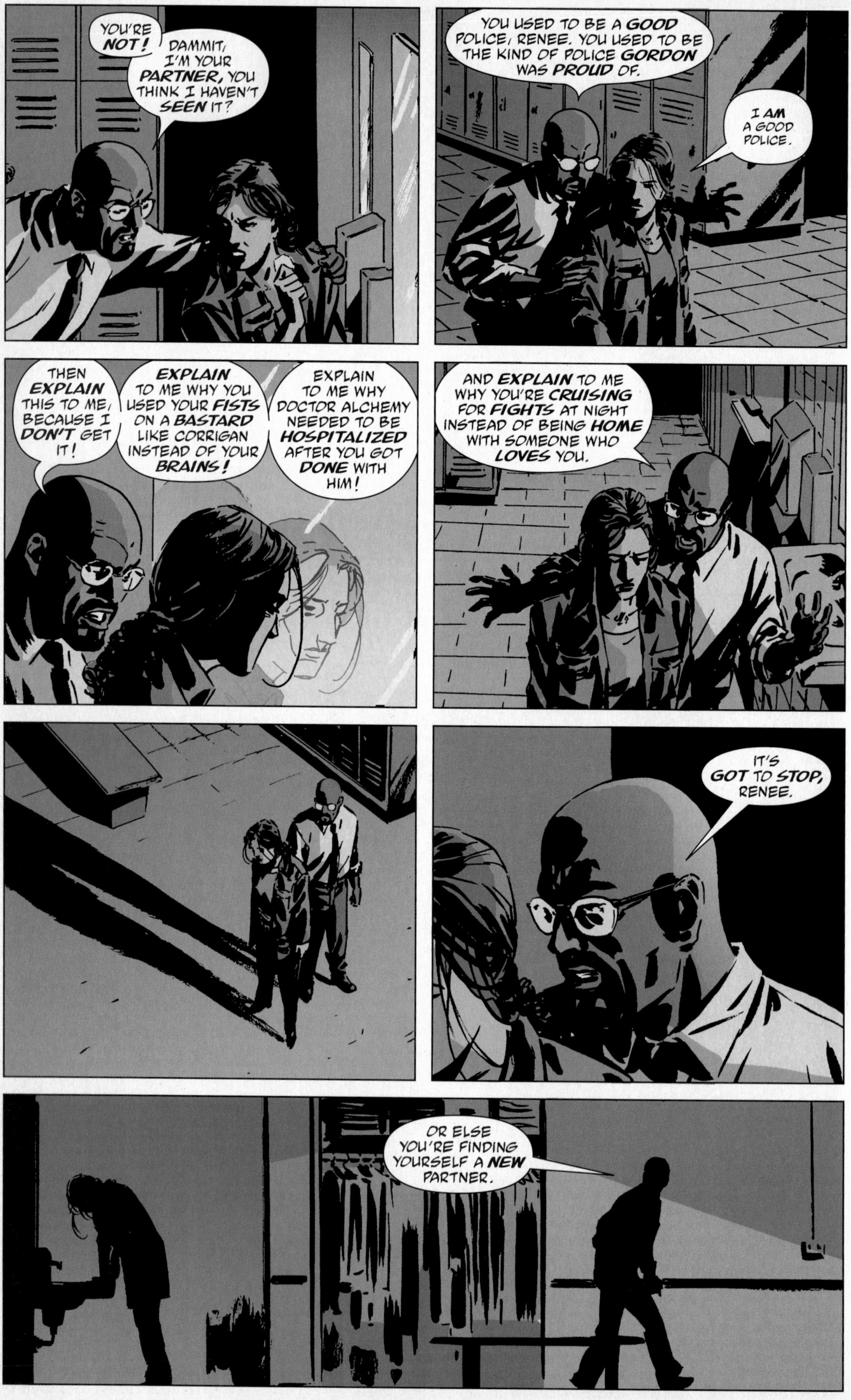

YOU'RE NOT!
DAMMIT, I'M YOUR PARTNER, YOU THINK I HAVEN'T SEEN IT?
YOU USED TO BE A GOOD POLICE, RENEE. YOU USED TO BE THE KIND OF POLICE GORDON WAS PROUD OF.
I AM A GOOD POLICE.
THEN EXPLAIN THIS TO ME, BECAUSE I DON'T GET IT!
EXPLAIN TO ME WHY YOU USED YOUR FISTS ON A BASTARD LIKE CORRIGAN INSTEAD OF YOUR BRAINS!
EXPLAIN TO ME WHY DOCTOR ALCHEMY NEEDED TO BE HOSPITALIZED AFTER YOU GOT DONE WITH HIM!
AND EXPLAIN TO ME WHY YOU'RE CRUISING FOR FIGHTS AT NIGHT INSTEAD OF BEING HOME WITH SOMEONE WHO LOVES YOU.
IT'S GOT TO STOP, RENEE.
OR ELSE YOU'RE FINDING YOURSELF A NEW PARTNER.

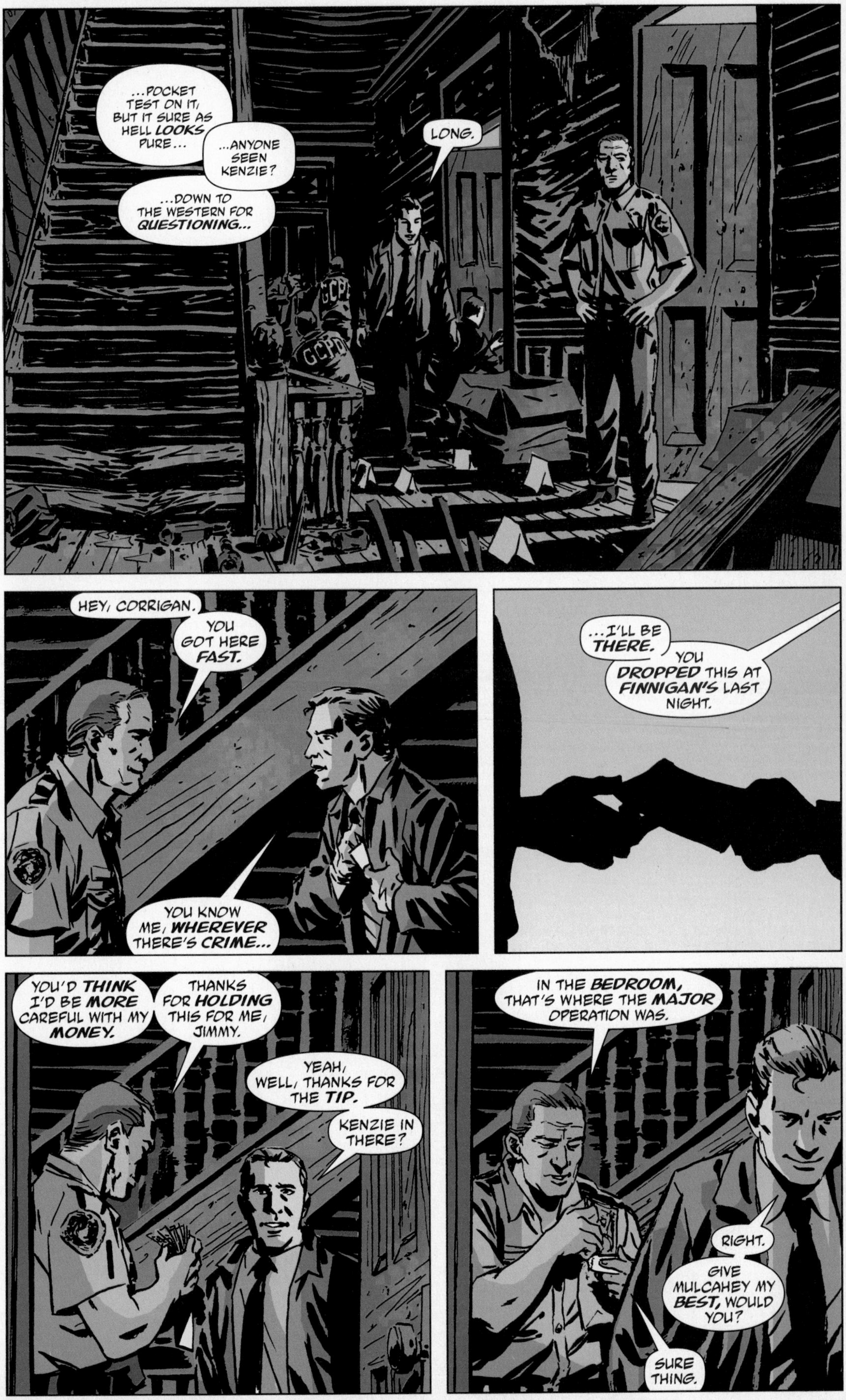
...POCKET TEST ON IT, BUT IT SURE AS HELL LOOKS PURE...
...ANYONE SEEN KENZIE?
...DOWN TO THE WESTERN FOR QUESTIONING...
LONG.
HEY, CORRIGAN.
YOU GOT HERE FAST.
YOU KNOW ME, WHEREVER THERE'S CRIME...
...I'LL BE THERE.
YOU DROPPED THIS AT FINNIGAN'S LAST NIGHT.
YOU'D THINK I'D BE MORE CAREFUL WITH MY MONEY.
THANKS FOR HOLDING THIS FOR ME, JIMMY.
YEAH, WELL, THANKS FOR THE TIP.
KENZIE IN THERE?
IN THE BEDROOM, THAT'S WHERE THE MAJOR OPERATION WAS.
RIGHT.
GIVE MULCAHEY MY BEST, WOULD YOU?
SURE THING.

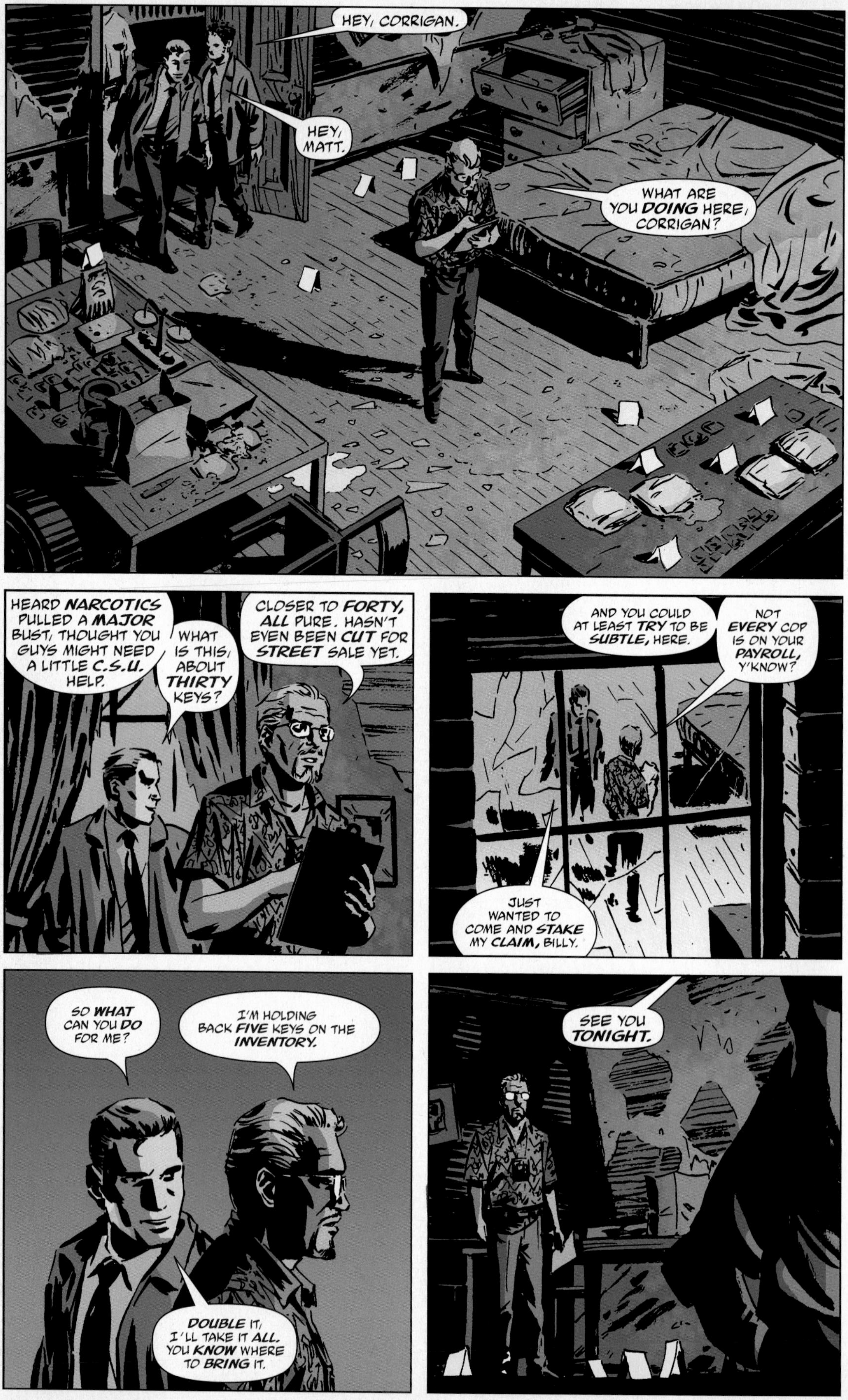
HEY, CORRIGAN.
HEY, MATT.
WHAT ARE YOU DOING HERE, CORRIGAN?
HEARD NARCOTICS PULLED A MAJOR BUST, THOUGHT YOU GUYS MIGHT NEED A LITTLE C.S.U. HELP.
WHAT IS THIS, ABOUT THIRTY KEYS?
CLOSER TO FORTY, ALL PURE. HASN'T EVEN BEEN CUT FOR STREET SALE YET.
AND YOU COULD AT LEAST TRY TO BE SUBTLE, HERE.
NOT EVERY COP IS ON YOUR PAYROLL, Y'KNOW?
JUST WANTED TO COME AND STAKE MY CLAIM, BILLY.
SO WHAT CAN YOU DO FOR ME?
I'M HOLDING BACK FIVE KEYS ON THE INVENTORY.
DOUBLE IT, I'LL TAKE IT ALL. YOU KNOW WHERE TO BRING IT.
SEE YOU TONIGHT.

CRIS.

HMM?

CRIS.

I'M SORRY, OKAY?

YEAH, THERE'S SINCERITY JUST DRIPPING FROM THAT APOLOGY.

CUT ME A LITTLE SLACK, WE'RE IN THE MIDDLE OF THE GODDAMN SQUADROOM!

THAT'S A GOOD EXCUSE. TELL ME ANOTHER.

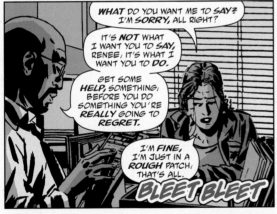

WHAT DO YOU WANT ME TO SAY? I'M SORRY, ALL RIGHT?

IT'S NOT WHAT I WANT YOU TO SAY, RENEE; IT'S WHAT I WANT YOU TO DO.

GET SOME HELP, SOMETHING, BEFORE YOU DO SOMETHING YOU'RE REALLY GOING TO REGRET.

I'M FINE, I'M JUST IN A ROUGH PATCH, THAT'S ALL.

BLEET BLEET

SURE. AND I'M THE SCARECROW.

BLEET

BLEET

M.C.U., ALLEN...

...I CAN DO IT NOW, JUST TELL ME WHERE...

...NO, NOT THERE...

...THAT'LL WORK. GIVE ME TWENTY MINUTES.

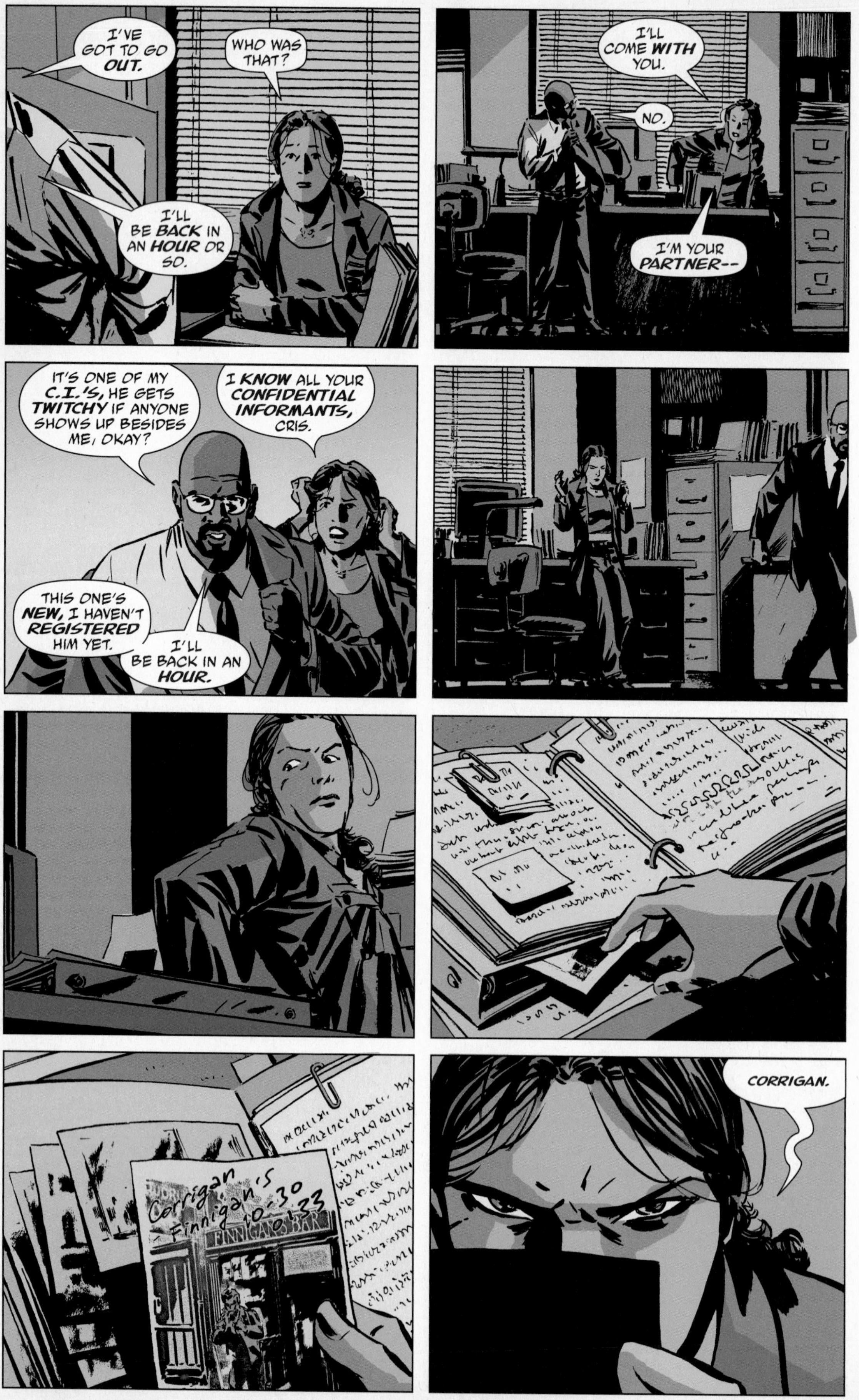
I'VE GOT TO GO OUT.
WHO WAS THAT?
I'LL BE BACK IN AN HOUR OR SO.
I'LL COME WITH YOU.
NO.
I'M YOUR PARTNER--
IT'S ONE OF MY C.I.'S, HE GETS TWITCHY IF ANYONE SHOWS UP BESIDES ME, OKAY?
I KNOW ALL YOUR CONFIDENTIAL INFORMANTS, CRIS.
THIS ONE'S NEW, I HAVEN'T REGISTERED HIM YET.
I'LL BE BACK IN AN HOUR.
Corrigan
Finnigan's
10-30
10-33
FINNIGAN'S BAR
CORRIGAN.

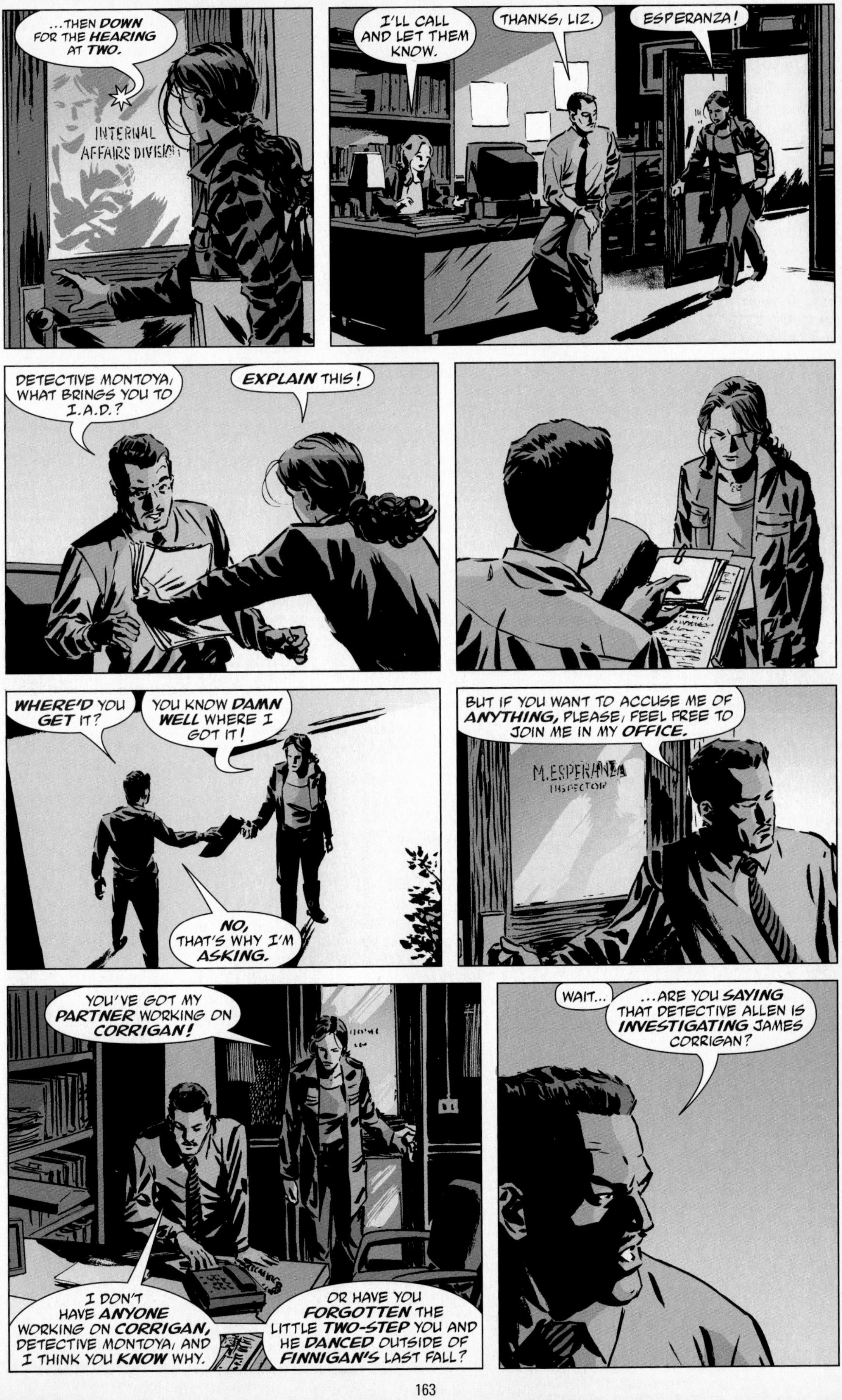
...THEN DOWN FOR THE HEARING AT TWO.
INTERNAL AFFAIRS DIVISION
I'LL CALL AND LET THEM KNOW.
THANKS, LIZ.
ESPERANZA!
DETECTIVE MONTOYA, WHAT BRINGS YOU TO I.A.D.?
EXPLAIN THIS!
WHERE'D YOU GET IT?
YOU KNOW DAMN WELL WHERE I GOT IT!
NO, THAT'S WHY I'M ASKING.
BUT IF YOU WANT TO ACCUSE ME OF ANYTHING, PLEASE, FEEL FREE TO JOIN ME IN MY OFFICE.
M. ESPERANZA
INSPECTOR
YOU'VE GOT MY PARTNER WORKING ON CORRIGAN!
I DON'T HAVE ANYONE WORKING ON CORRIGAN, DETECTIVE MONTOYA, AND I THINK YOU KNOW WHY.
OR HAVE YOU FORGOTTEN THE LITTLE TWO-STEP YOU AND HE DANCED OUTSIDE OF FINNIGAN'S LAST FALL?
WAIT...
...ARE YOU SAYING THAT DETECTIVE ALLEN IS INVESTIGATING JAMES CORRIGAN?

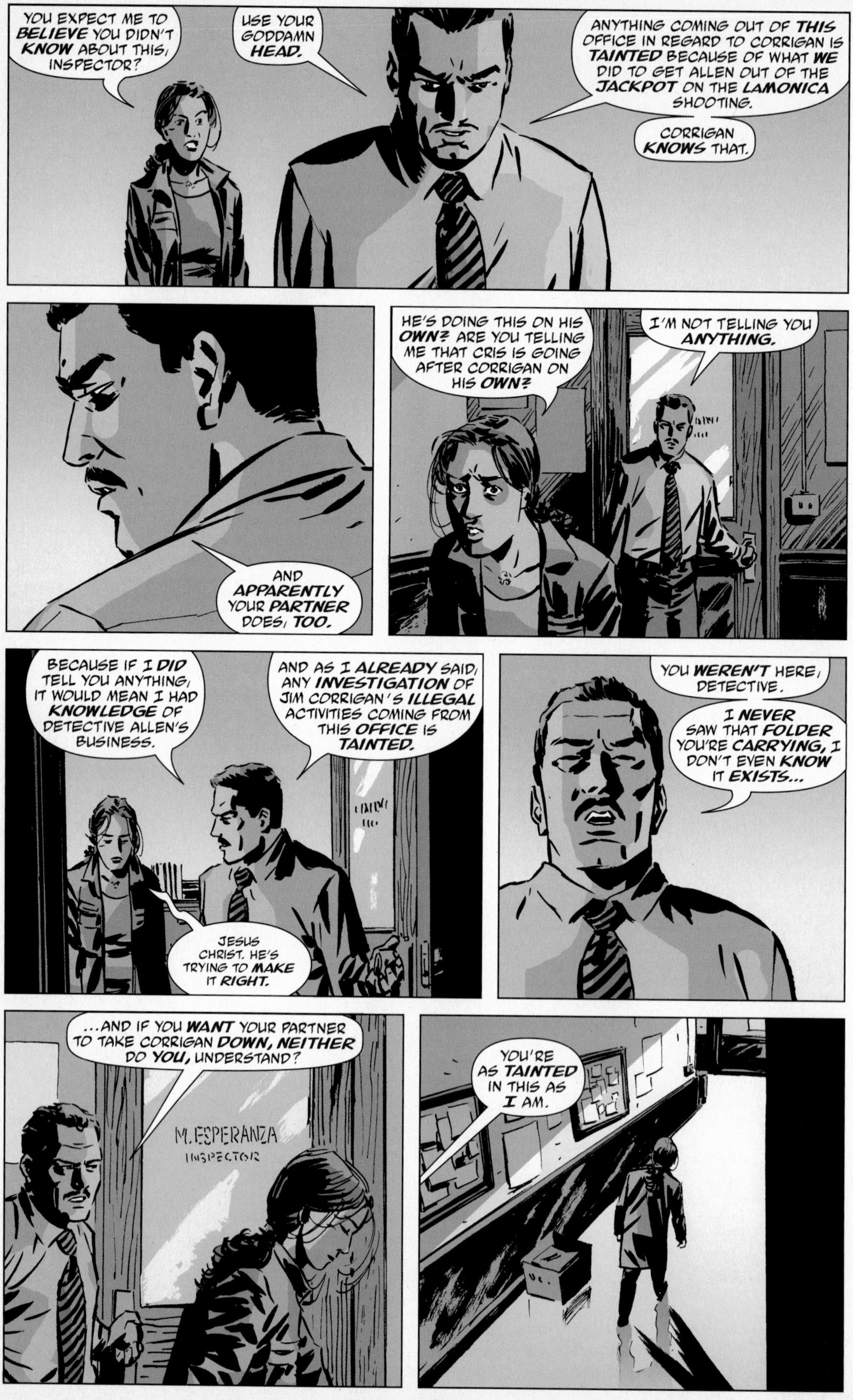
YOU EXPECT ME TO BELIEVE YOU DIDN'T KNOW ABOUT THIS, INSPECTOR?
USE YOUR GODDAMN HEAD.
ANYTHING COMING OUT OF THIS OFFICE IN REGARD TO CORRIGAN IS TAINTED BECAUSE OF WHAT WE DID TO GET ALLEN OUT OF THE JACKPOT ON THE LAMONICA SHOOTING.
CORRIGAN KNOWS THAT.
AND APPARENTLY YOUR PARTNER DOES, TOO.
HE'S DOING THIS ON HIS OWN? ARE YOU TELLING ME THAT CRIS IS GOING AFTER CORRIGAN ON HIS OWN?
I'M NOT TELLING YOU ANYTHING.
BECAUSE IF I DID TELL YOU ANYTHING, IT WOULD MEAN I HAD KNOWLEDGE OF DETECTIVE ALLEN'S BUSINESS.
AND AS I ALREADY SAID, ANY INVESTIGATION OF JIM CORRIGAN'S ILLEGAL ACTIVITIES COMING FROM THIS OFFICE IS TAINTED.
JESUS CHRIST. HE'S TRYING TO MAKE IT RIGHT.
YOU WEREN'T HERE, DETECTIVE.
I NEVER SAW THAT FOLDER YOU'RE CARRYING, I DON'T EVEN KNOW IT EXISTS...
...AND IF YOU WANT YOUR PARTNER TO TAKE CORRIGAN DOWN, NEITHER DO YOU, UNDERSTAND?
M. ESPERANZA
INSPECTOR
YOU'RE AS TAINTED IN THIS AS I AM.

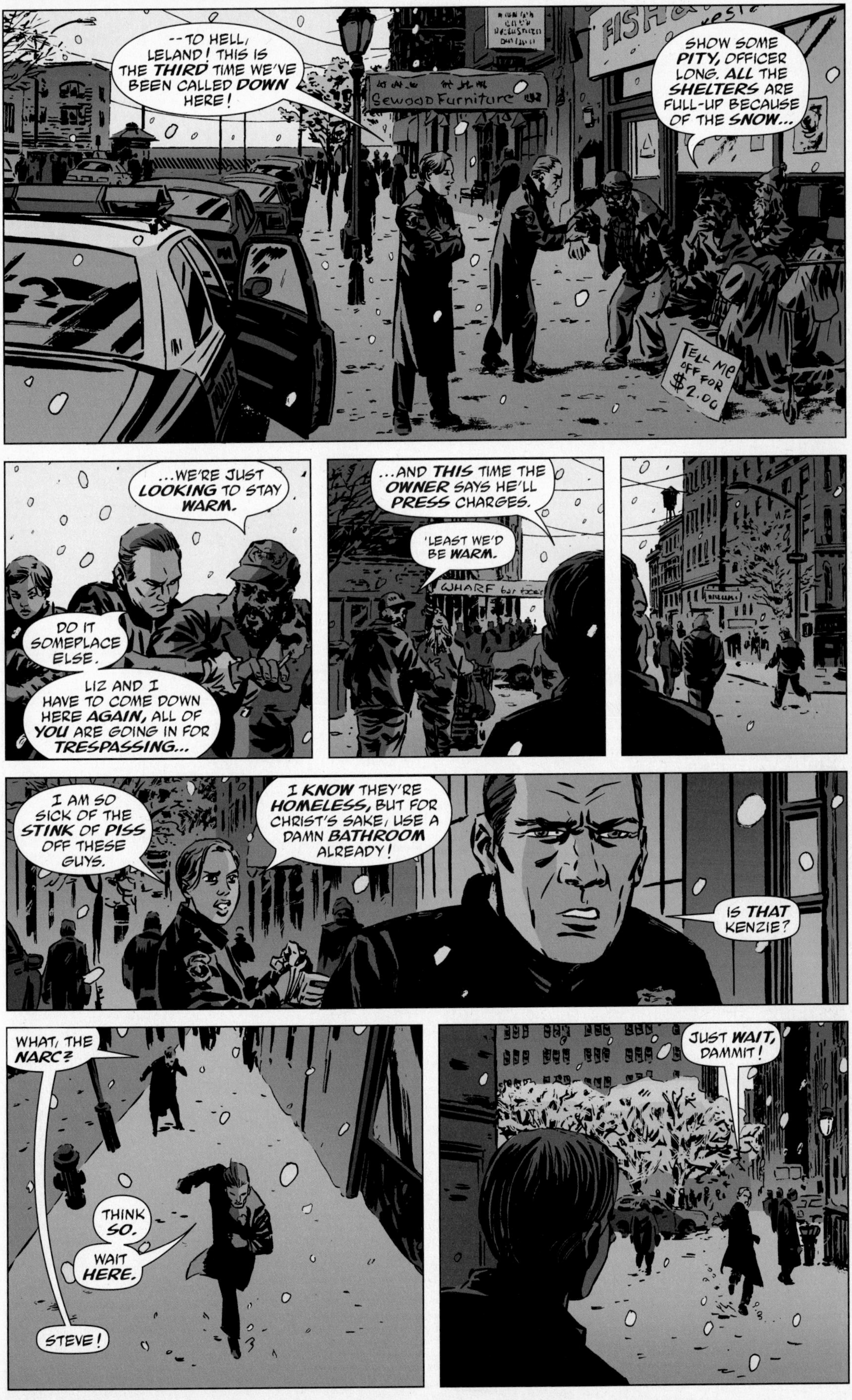
--TO HELL, LELAND! THIS IS THE THIRD TIME WE'VE BEEN CALLED DOWN HERE!
SHOW SOME PITY, OFFICER LONG. ALL THE SHELTERS ARE FULL-UP BECAUSE OF THE SNOW...
Sewood Furniture
FISH
TELL ME OFF FOR $2.00
...WE'RE JUST LOOKING TO STAY WARM.
DO IT SOMEPLACE ELSE.
LIZ AND I HAVE TO COME DOWN HERE AGAIN, ALL OF YOU ARE GOING IN FOR TRESPASSING...
...AND THIS TIME THE OWNER SAYS HE'LL PRESS CHARGES.
'LEAST WE'D BE WARM.
WHARF
I AM SO SICK OF THE STINK OF PISS OFF THESE GUYS.
I KNOW THEY'RE HOMELESS, BUT FOR CHRIST'S SAKE, USE A DAMN BATHROOM ALREADY!
IS THAT KENZIE?
WHAT, THE NARC?
THINK SO.
WAIT HERE.
STEVE!
JUST WAIT, DAMMIT!

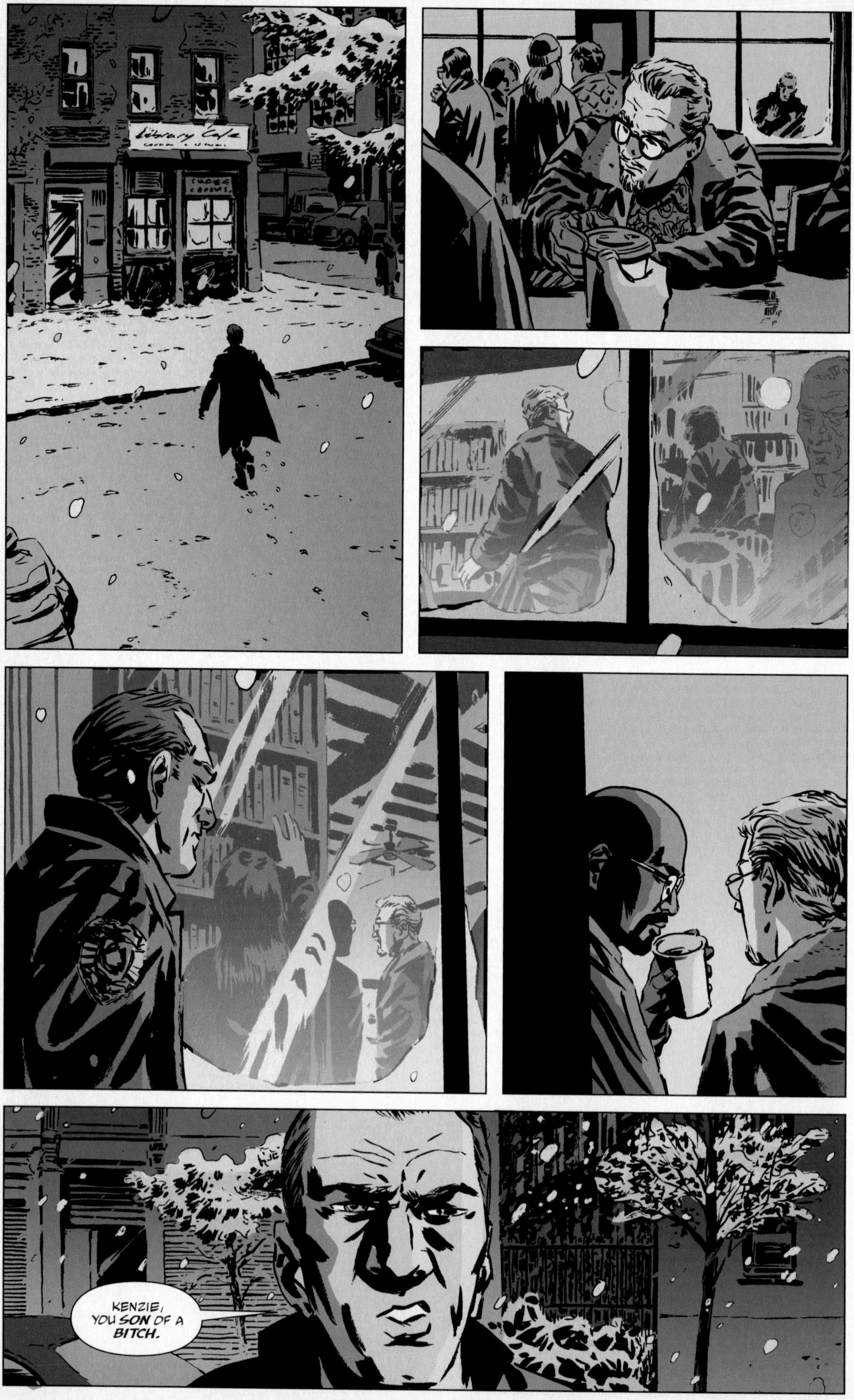
Library Cafe
KENZIE, YOU SON OF A BITCH.

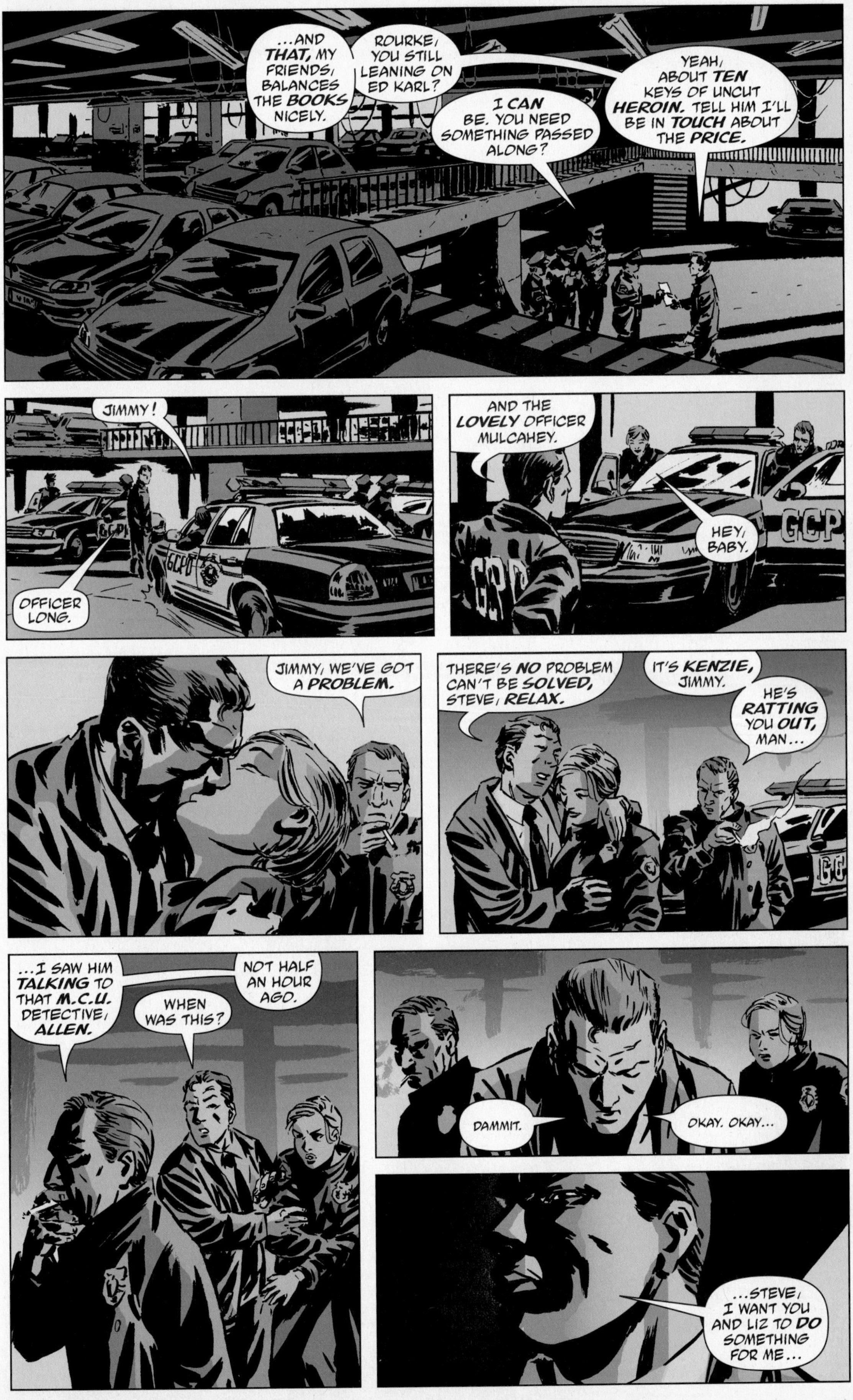
...AND THAT, MY FRIENDS, BALANCES THE BOOKS NICELY.
ROURKE, YOU STILL LEANING ON ED KARL?
I CAN BE. YOU NEED SOMETHING PASSED ALONG?
YEAH, ABOUT TEN KEYS OF UNCUT HEROIN. TELL HIM I'LL BE IN TOUCH ABOUT THE PRICE.
JIMMY!
OFFICER LONG.
AND THE LOVELY OFFICER MULCAHEY.
HEY, BABY.
JIMMY, WE'VE GOT A PROBLEM.
THERE'S NO PROBLEM CAN'T BE SOLVED, STEVE, RELAX.
IT'S KENZIE, JIMMY.
HE'S RATTING YOU OUT, MAN...
...I SAW HIM TALKING TO THAT M.C.U. DETECTIVE, ALLEN.
WHEN WAS THIS?
NOT HALF AN HOUR AGO.
DAMMIT.
OKAY. OKAY...
...STEVE, I WANT YOU AND LIZ TO DO SOMETHING FOR ME...

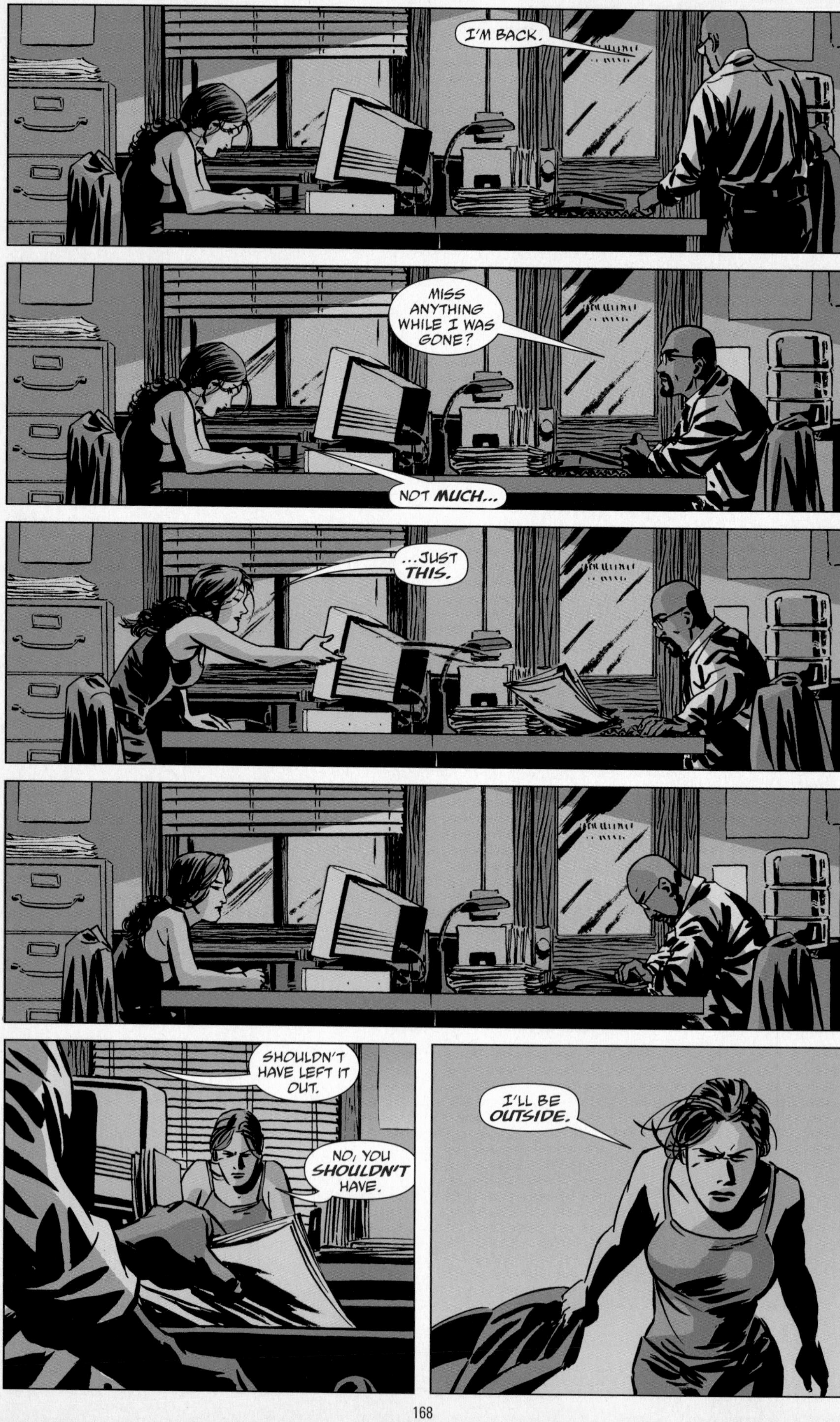
I'M BACK.
MISS ANYTHING WHILE I WAS GONE?
NOT MUCH...
...JUST THIS.
SHOULDN'T HAVE LEFT IT OUT.
NO, YOU SHOULDN'T HAVE.
I'LL BE OUTSIDE.

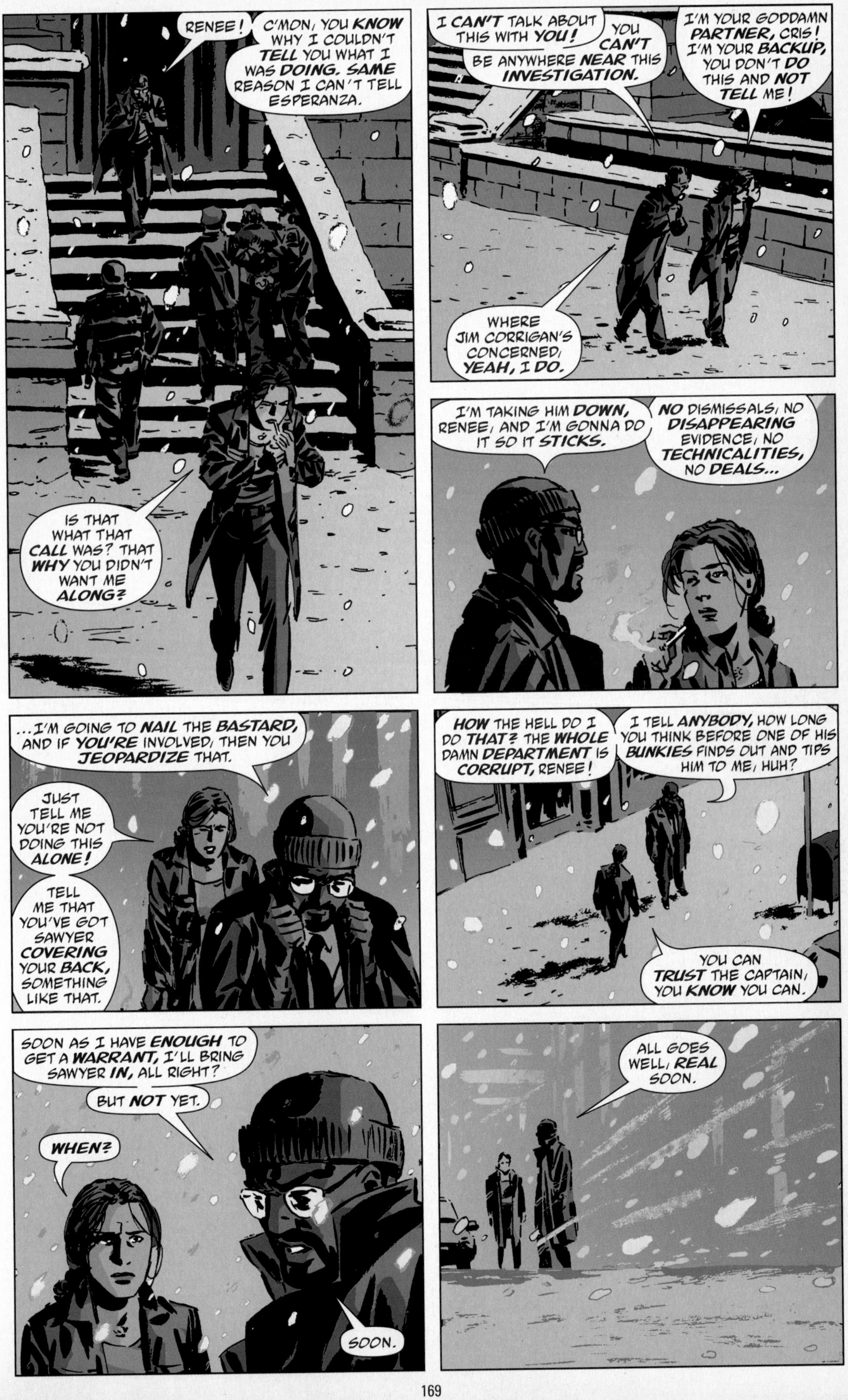

RENEE!
C'MON, YOU KNOW WHY I COULDN'T TELL YOU WHAT I WAS DOING. SAME REASON I CAN'T TELL ESPERANZA.
IS THAT WHAT THAT CALL WAS? THAT WHY YOU DIDN'T WANT ME ALONG?
I CAN'T TALK ABOUT THIS WITH YOU!
YOU CAN'T BE ANYWHERE NEAR THIS INVESTIGATION.
I'M YOUR GODDAMN PARTNER, CRIS! I'M YOUR BACKUP, YOU DON'T DO THIS AND NOT TELL ME!
WHERE JIM CORRIGAN'S CONCERNED, YEAH, I DO.
I'M TAKING HIM DOWN, RENEE, AND I'M GONNA DO IT SO IT STICKS.
NO DISMISSALS, NO DISAPPEARING EVIDENCE, NO TECHNICALITIES, NO DEALS...
...I'M GOING TO NAIL THE BASTARD, AND IF YOU'RE INVOLVED, THEN YOU JEOPARDIZE THAT.
JUST TELL ME YOU'RE NOT DOING THIS ALONE!
TELL ME THAT YOU'VE GOT SAWYER COVERING YOUR BACK, SOMETHING LIKE THAT.
HOW THE HELL DO I DO THAT? THE WHOLE DAMN DEPARTMENT IS CORRUPT, RENEE!
I TELL ANYBODY, HOW LONG YOU THINK BEFORE ONE OF HIS BUNKIES FINDS OUT AND TIPS HIM TO ME, HUH?
YOU CAN TRUST THE CAPTAIN, YOU KNOW YOU CAN.
SOON AS I HAVE ENOUGH TO GET A WARRANT, I'LL BRING SAWYER IN, ALL RIGHT?
BUT NOT YET.
WHEN?
SOON.
ALL GOES WELL, REAL SOON.

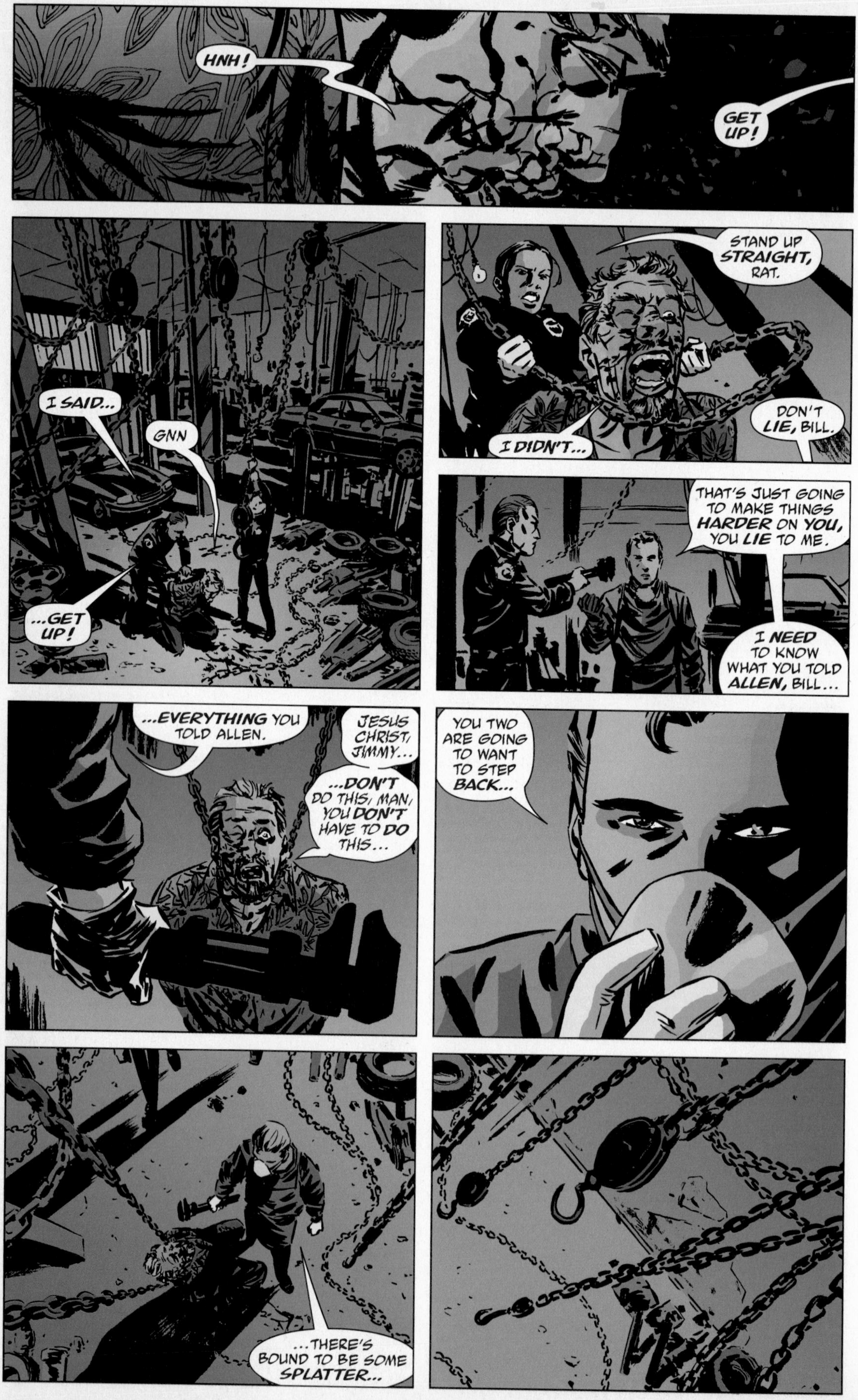
HNH!
GET UP!
I SAID...
GNN
...GET UP!
STAND UP STRAIGHT, RAT.
I DIDN'T...
DON'T LIE, BILL.
THAT'S JUST GOING TO MAKE THINGS HARDER ON YOU, YOU LIE TO ME.
I NEED TO KNOW WHAT YOU TOLD ALLEN, BILL...
...EVERYTHING YOU TOLD ALLEN.
JESUS CHRIST, JIMMY...
...DON'T DO THIS, MAN, YOU DON'T HAVE TO DO THIS...
YOU TWO ARE GOING TO WANT TO STEP BACK...
...THERE'S BOUND TO BE SOME SPLATTER...

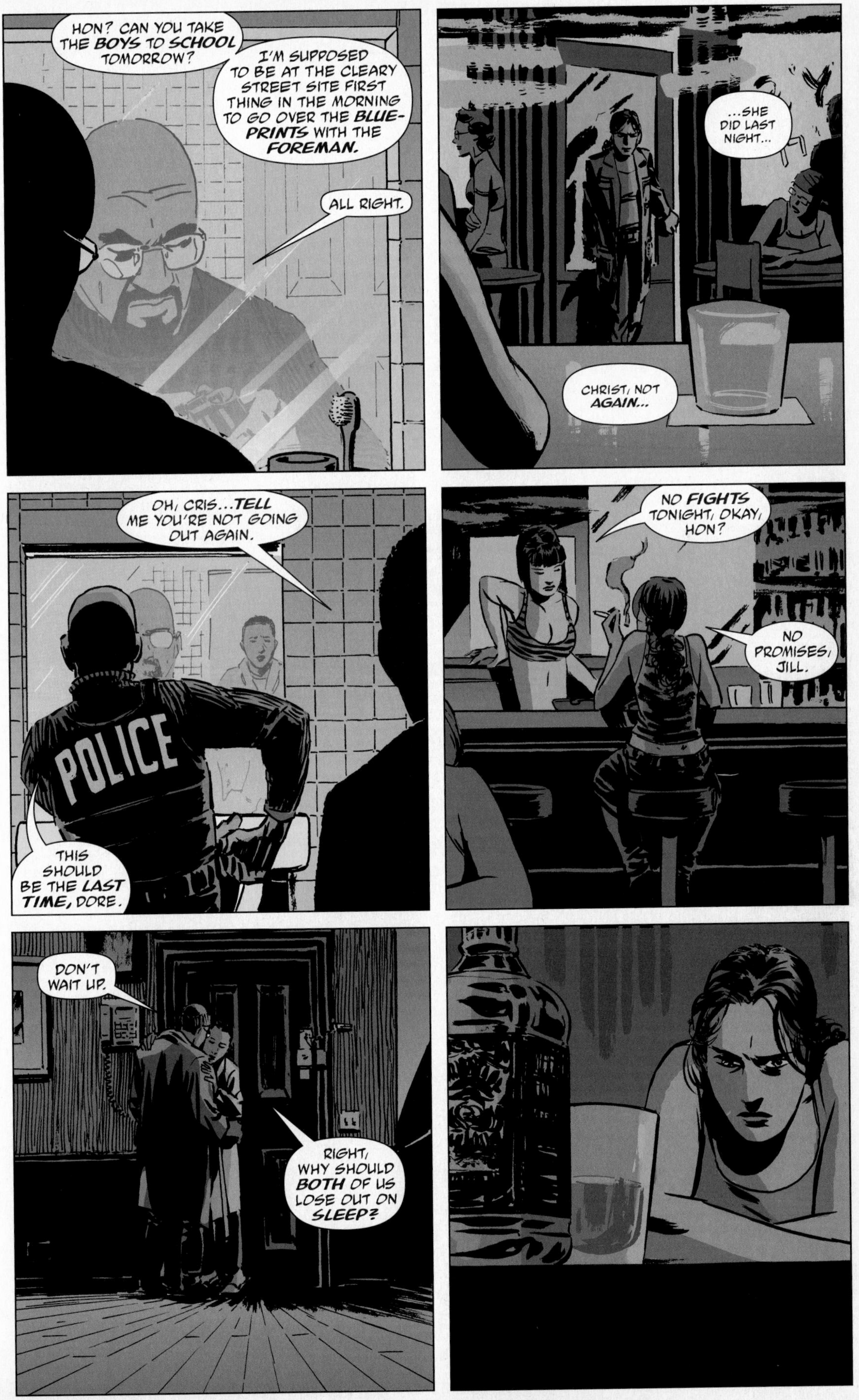
HON? CAN YOU TAKE THE BOYS TO SCHOOL TOMORROW?
I'M SUPPOSED TO BE AT THE CLEARY STREET SITE FIRST THING IN THE MORNING TO GO OVER THE BLUE-PRINTS WITH THE FOREMAN.
ALL RIGHT.
...SHE DID LAST NIGHT...
CHRIST, NOT AGAIN...
OH, CRIS...TELL ME YOU'RE NOT GOING OUT AGAIN.
POLICE
THIS SHOULD BE THE LAST TIME, DORE.
NO FIGHTS TONIGHT, OKAY, HON?
NO PROMISES, JILL.
DON'T WAIT UP.
RIGHT, WHY SHOULD BOTH OF US LOSE OUT ON SLEEP?

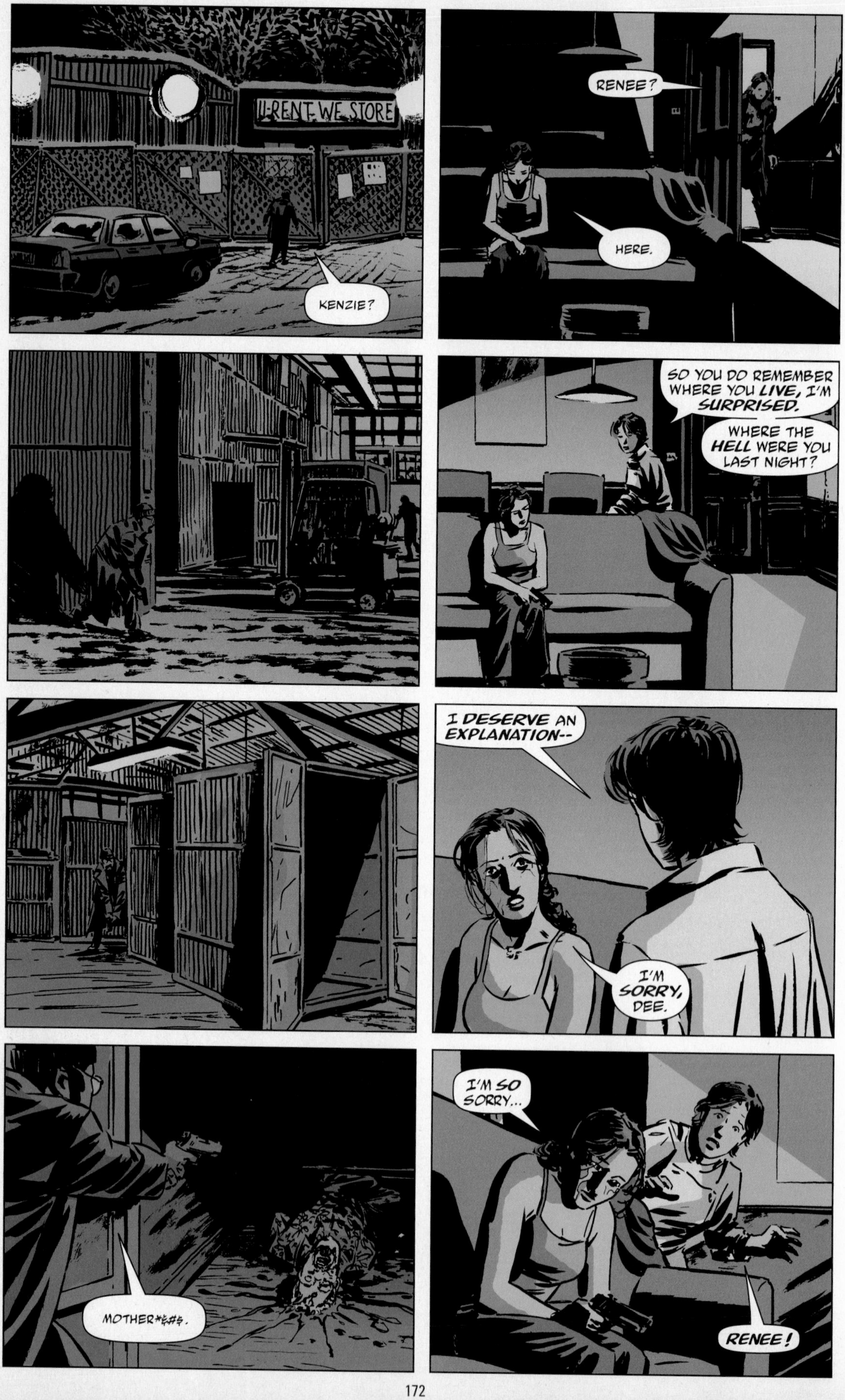
U-RENT-WE STORE
KENZIE?
RENEE?
HERE.
SO YOU DO REMEMBER WHERE YOU LIVE, I'M SURPRISED.
WHERE THE HELL WERE YOU LAST NIGHT?
I DESERVE AN EXPLANATION--
I'M SORRY, DEE.
MOTHER*&#$.
I'M SO SORRY...
RENEE!

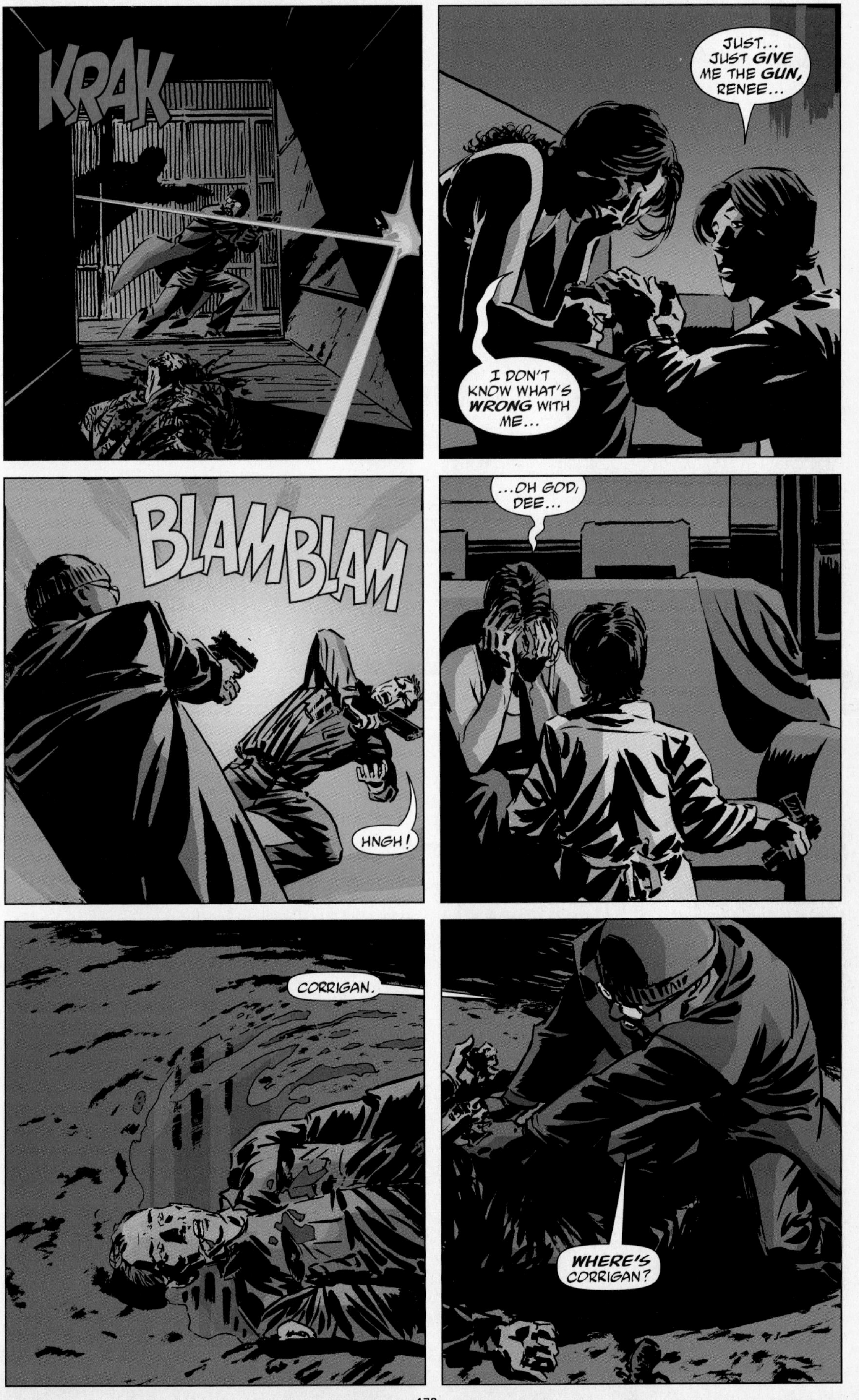
KRAK
JUST... JUST GIVE ME THE GUN, RENEE...
I DON'T KNOW WHAT'S WRONG WITH ME...
BLAMBLAM
HNGH!
...OH GOD, DEE...
CORRIGAN.
WHERE'S CORRIGAN?

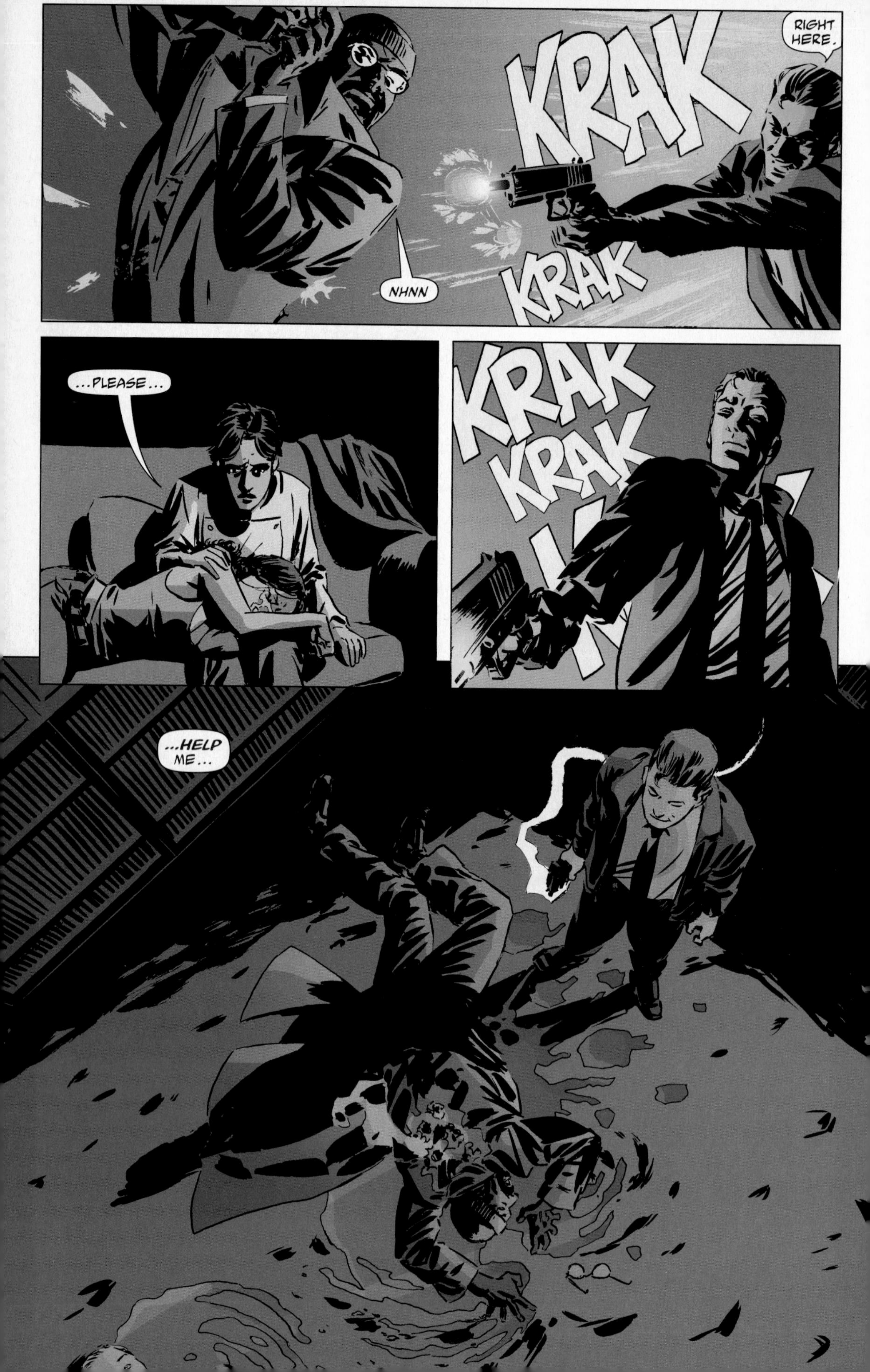
RIGHT HERE.
KRAK
KRAK
NHNN
...PLEASE...
KRAK
KRAK
...HELP ME...

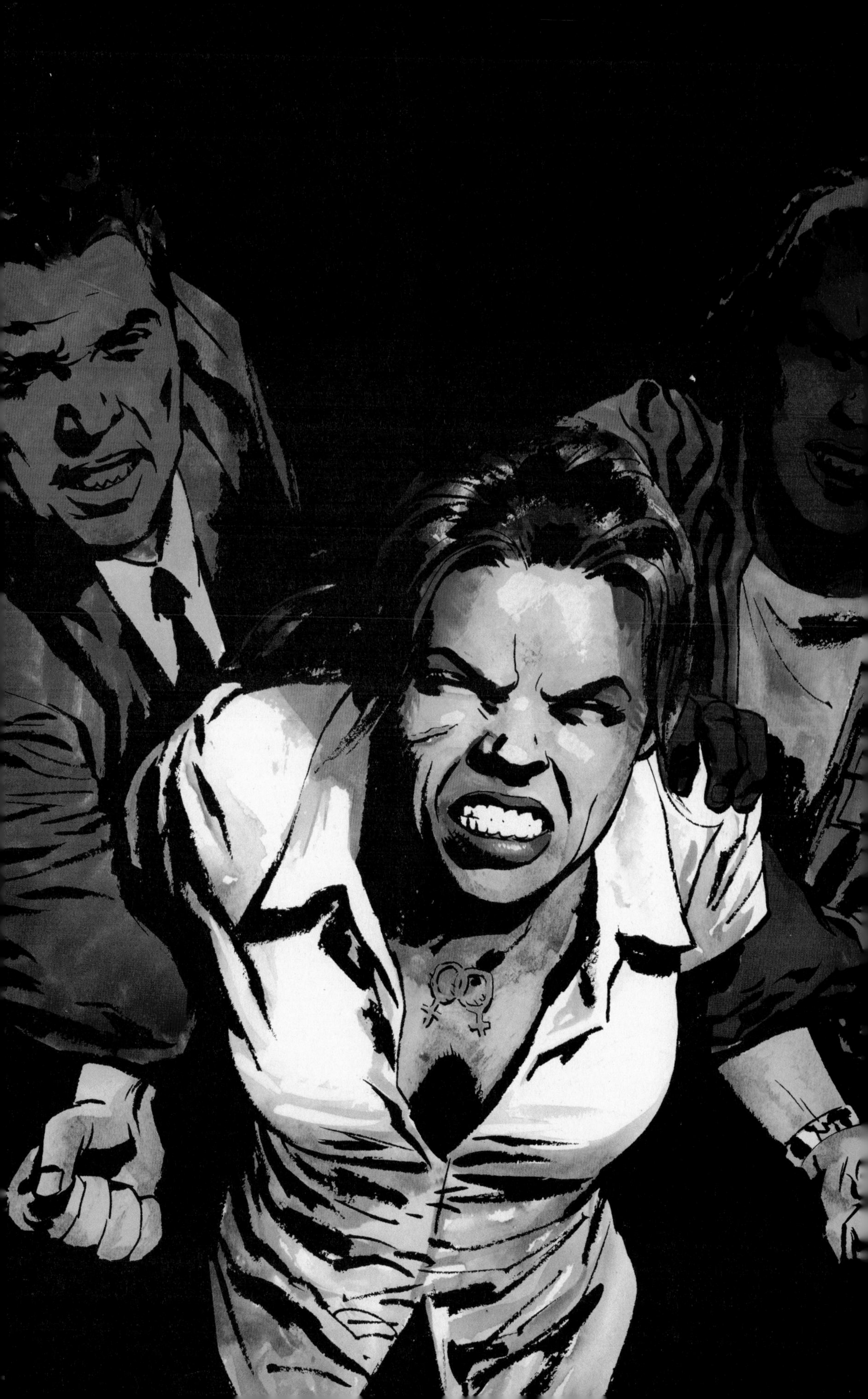

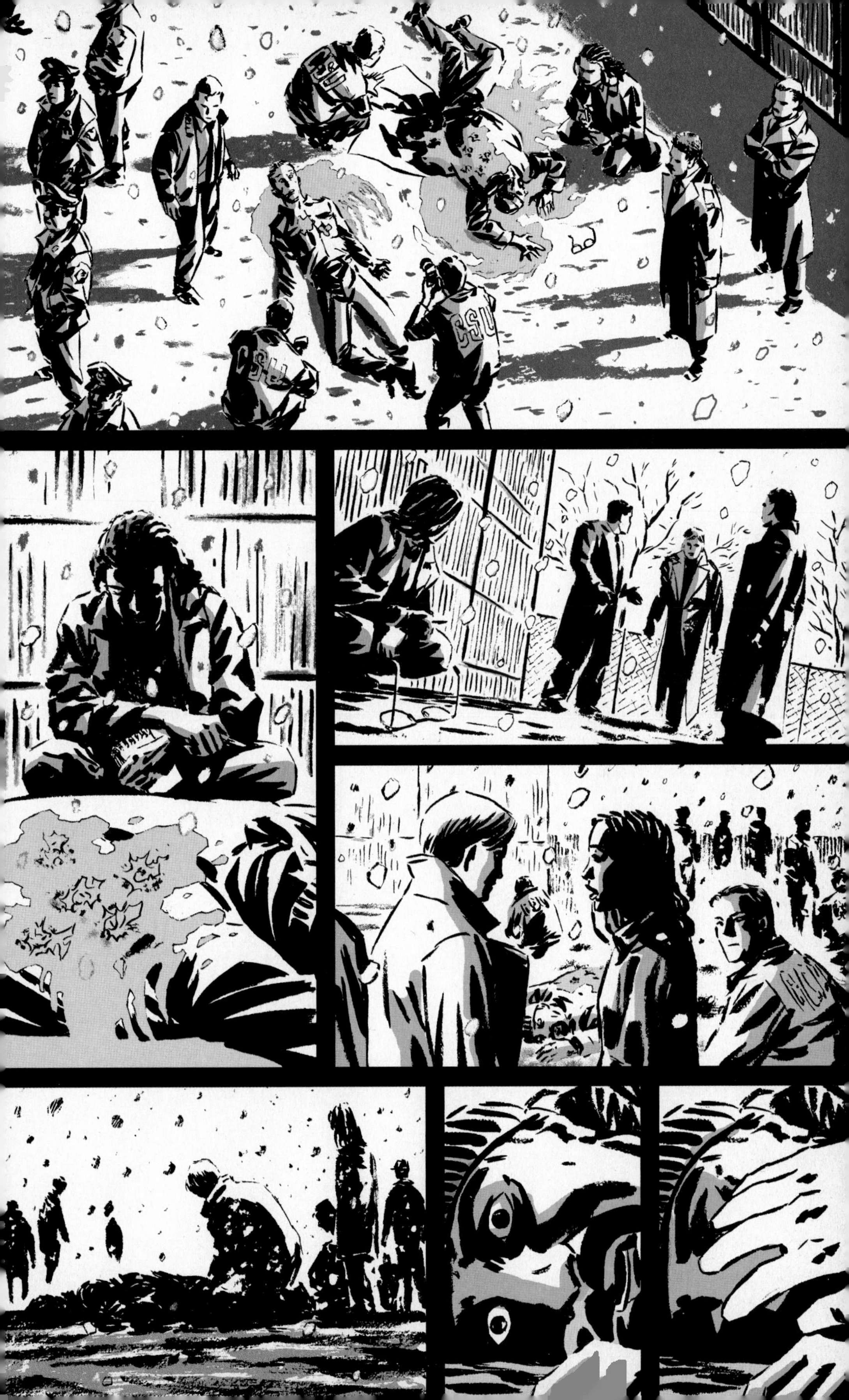
CSU

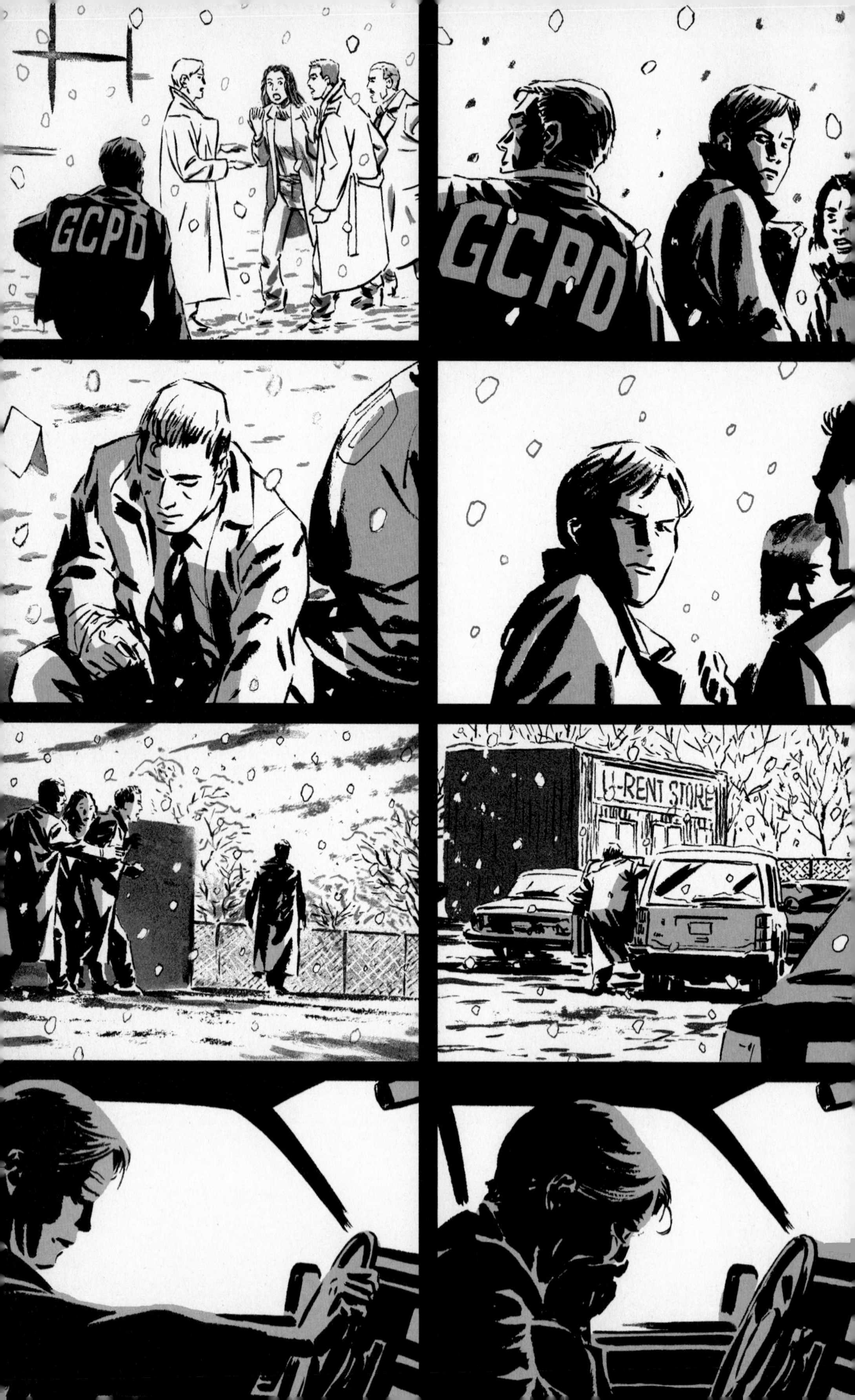
GCPD
GCPD
U-RENT STORE

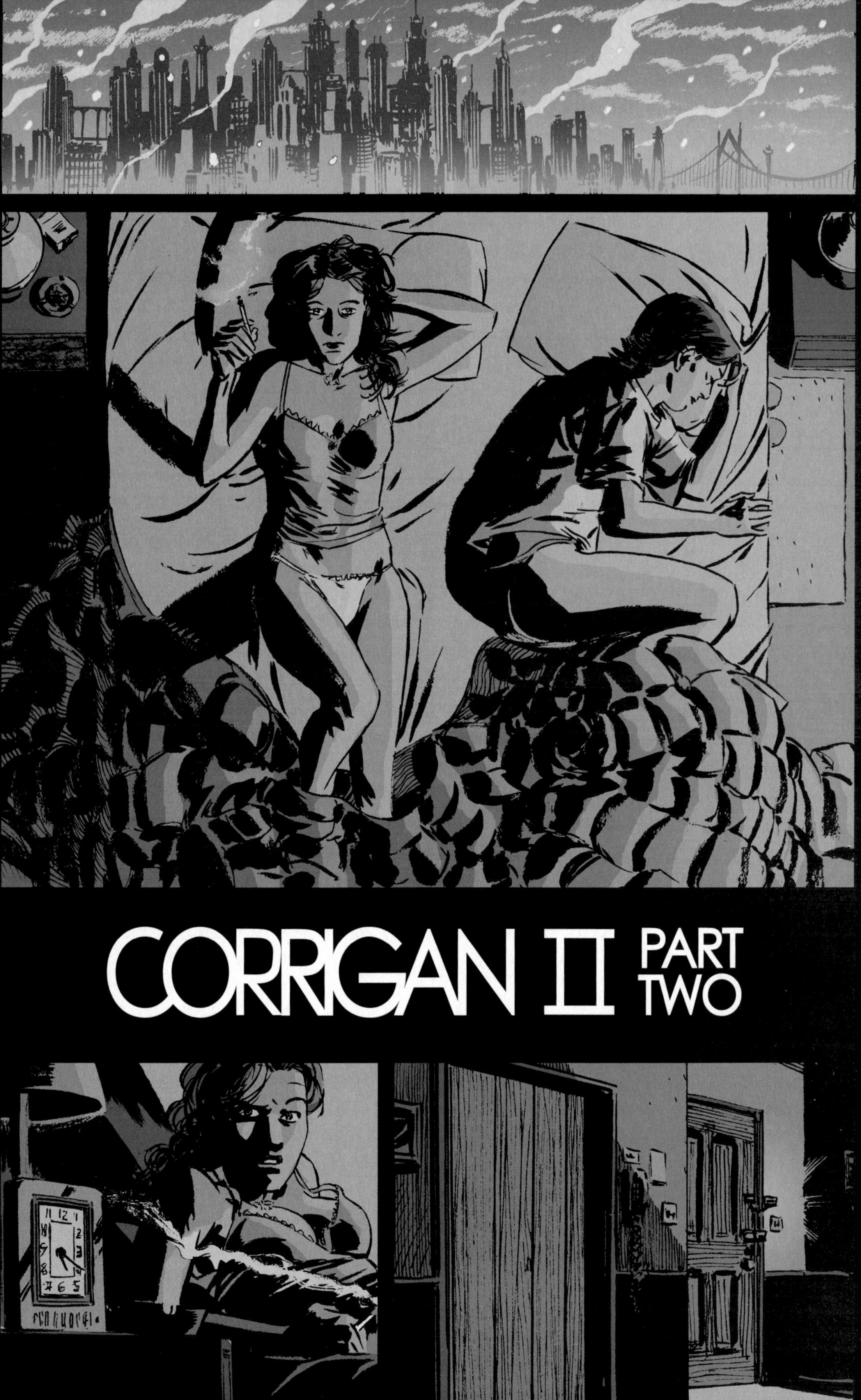
CORRIGAN II PART TWO

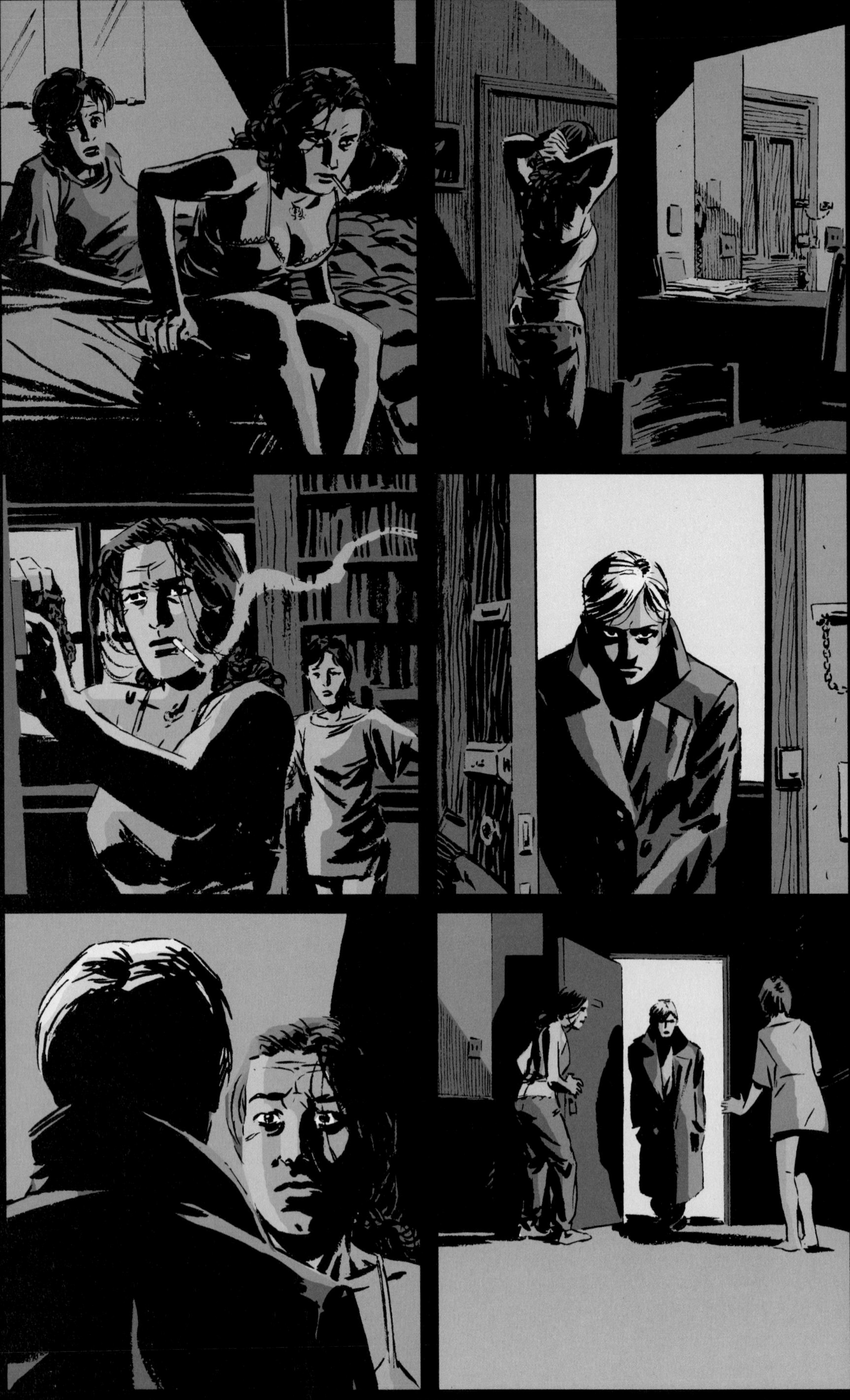

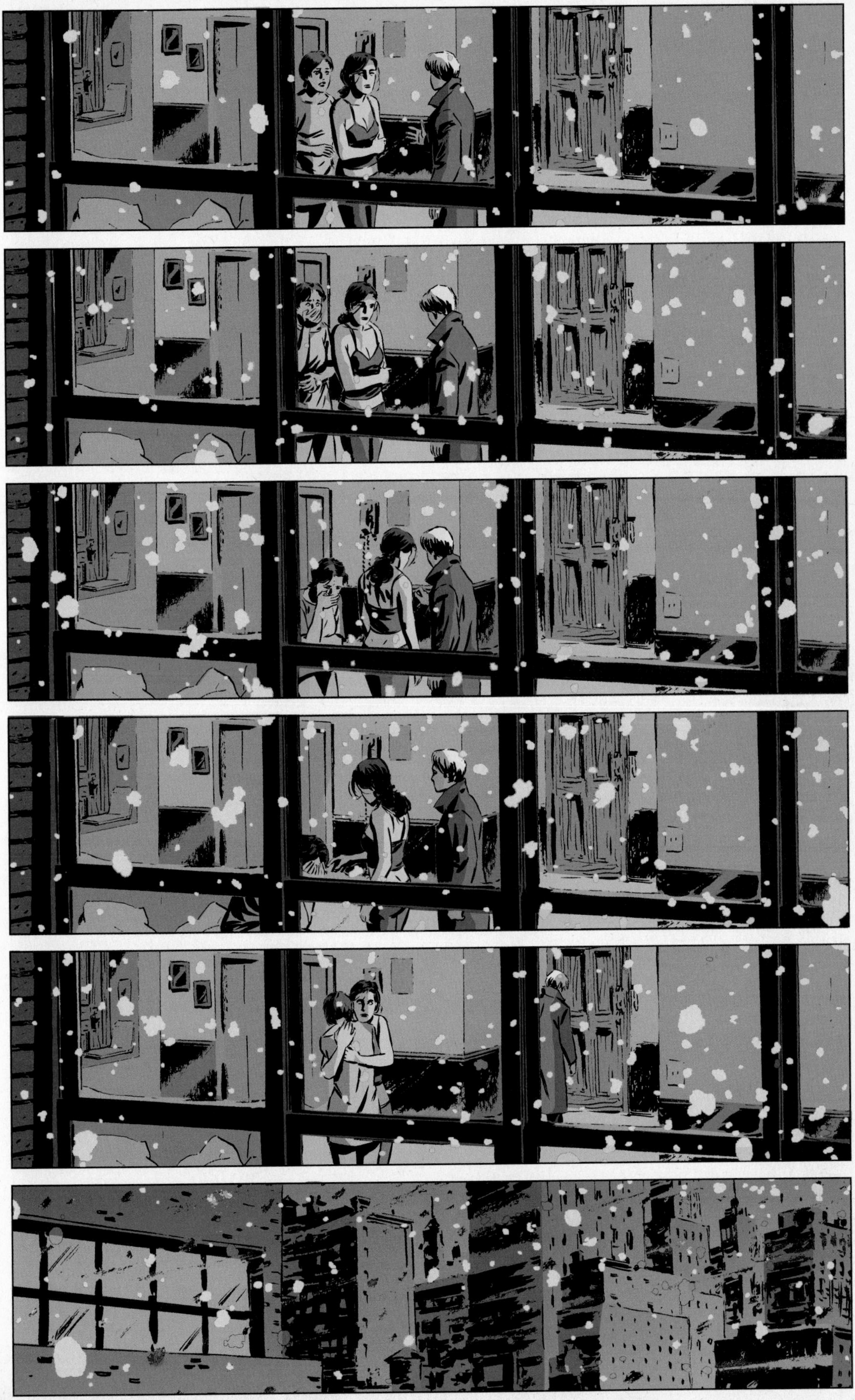

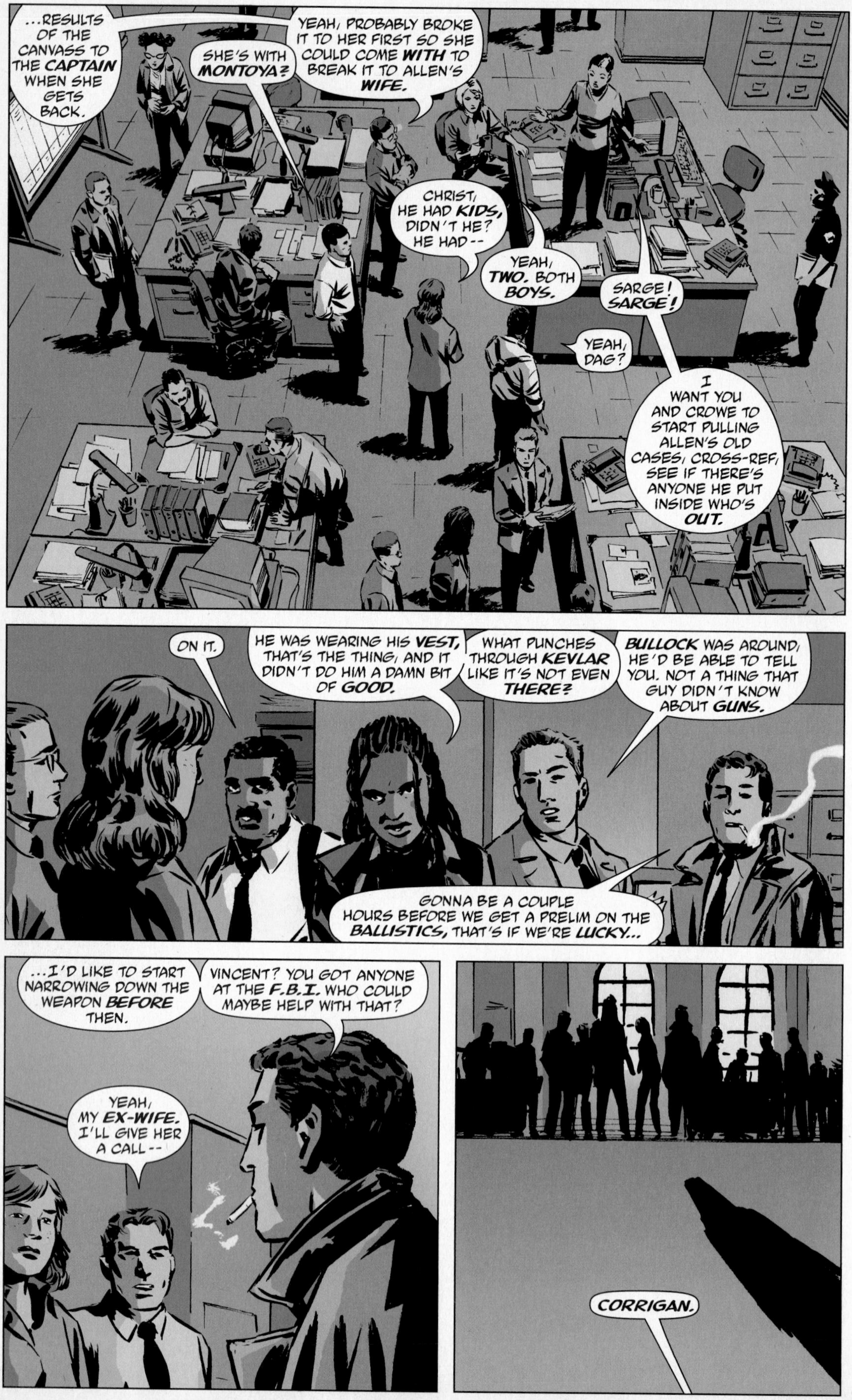
...RESULTS OF THE CANVASS TO THE CAPTAIN WHEN SHE GETS BACK.
SHE'S WITH MONTOYA?
YEAH, PROBABLY BROKE IT TO HER FIRST SO SHE COULD COME WITH TO BREAK IT TO ALLEN'S WIFE.
CHRIST, HE HAD KIDS, DIDN'T HE? HE HAD--
YEAH, TWO. BOTH BOYS.
SARGE! SARGE!
YEAH, DAG?
I WANT YOU AND CROWE TO START PULLING ALLEN'S OLD CASES, CROSS-REF, SEE IF THERE'S ANYONE HE PUT INSIDE WHO'S OUT.
ON IT.
HE WAS WEARING HIS VEST, THAT'S THE THING, AND IT DIDN'T DO HIM A DAMN BIT OF GOOD.
WHAT PUNCHES THROUGH KEVLAR LIKE IT'S NOT EVEN THERE?
BULLOCK WAS AROUND, HE'D BE ABLE TO TELL YOU. NOT A THING THAT GUY DIDN'T KNOW ABOUT GUNS.
GONNA BE A COUPLE HOURS BEFORE WE GET A PRELIM ON THE BALLISTICS, THAT'S IF WE'RE LUCKY...
...I'D LIKE TO START NARROWING DOWN THE WEAPON BEFORE THEN.
VINCENT? YOU GOT ANYONE AT THE F.B.I. WHO COULD MAYBE HELP WITH THAT?
YEAH, MY EX-WIFE. I'LL GIVE HER A CALL--
CORRIGAN.

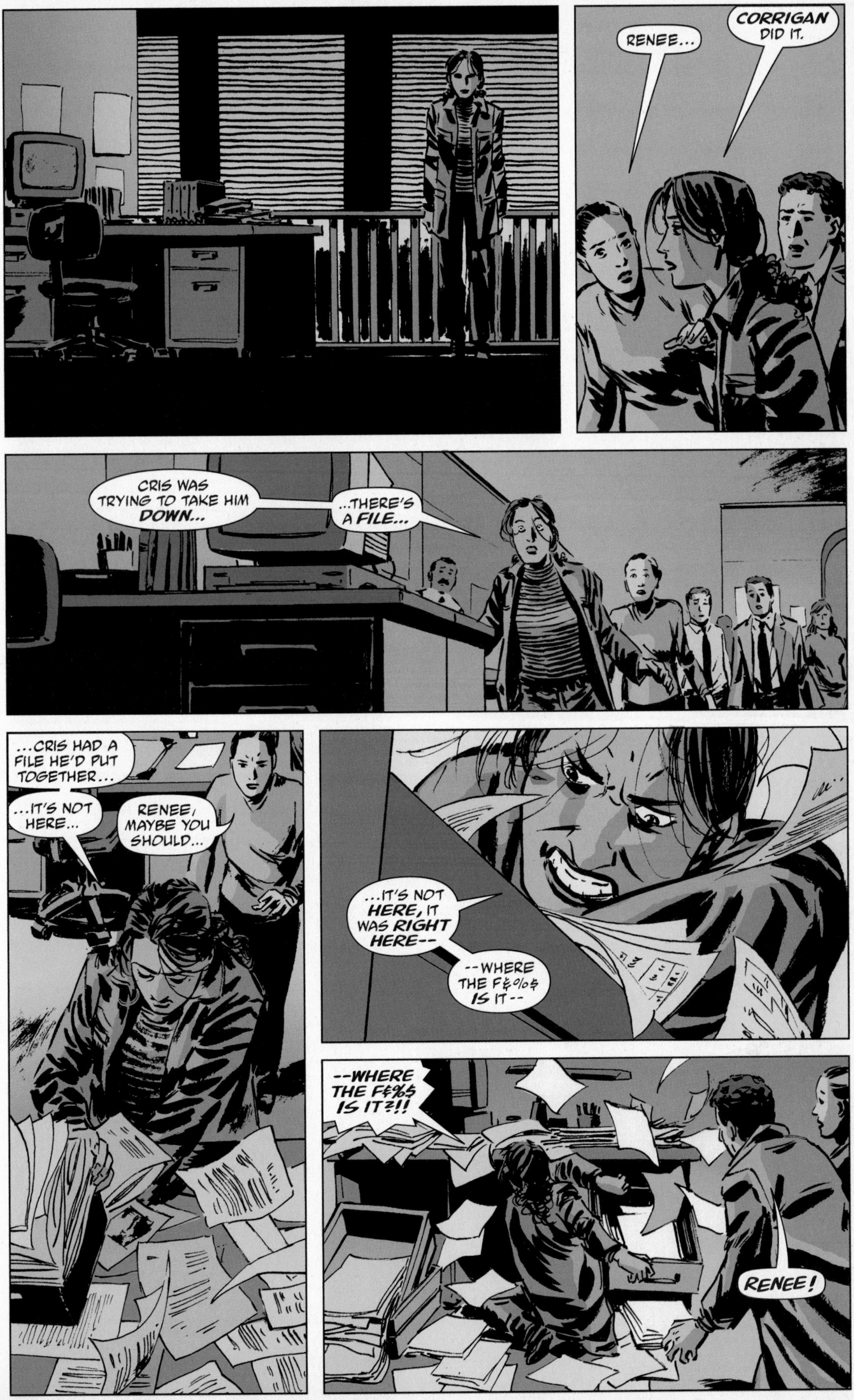
RENEE...
CORRIGAN DID IT.
CRIS WAS TRYING TO TAKE HIM DOWN...
...THERE'S A FILE...
...CRIS HAD A FILE HE'D PUT TOGETHER...
...IT'S NOT HERE...
RENEE, MAYBE YOU SHOULD...
...IT'S NOT HERE, IT WAS RIGHT HERE--
--WHERE THE F&%$ IS IT--
--WHERE THE F&%$ IS IT?!!
RENEE!

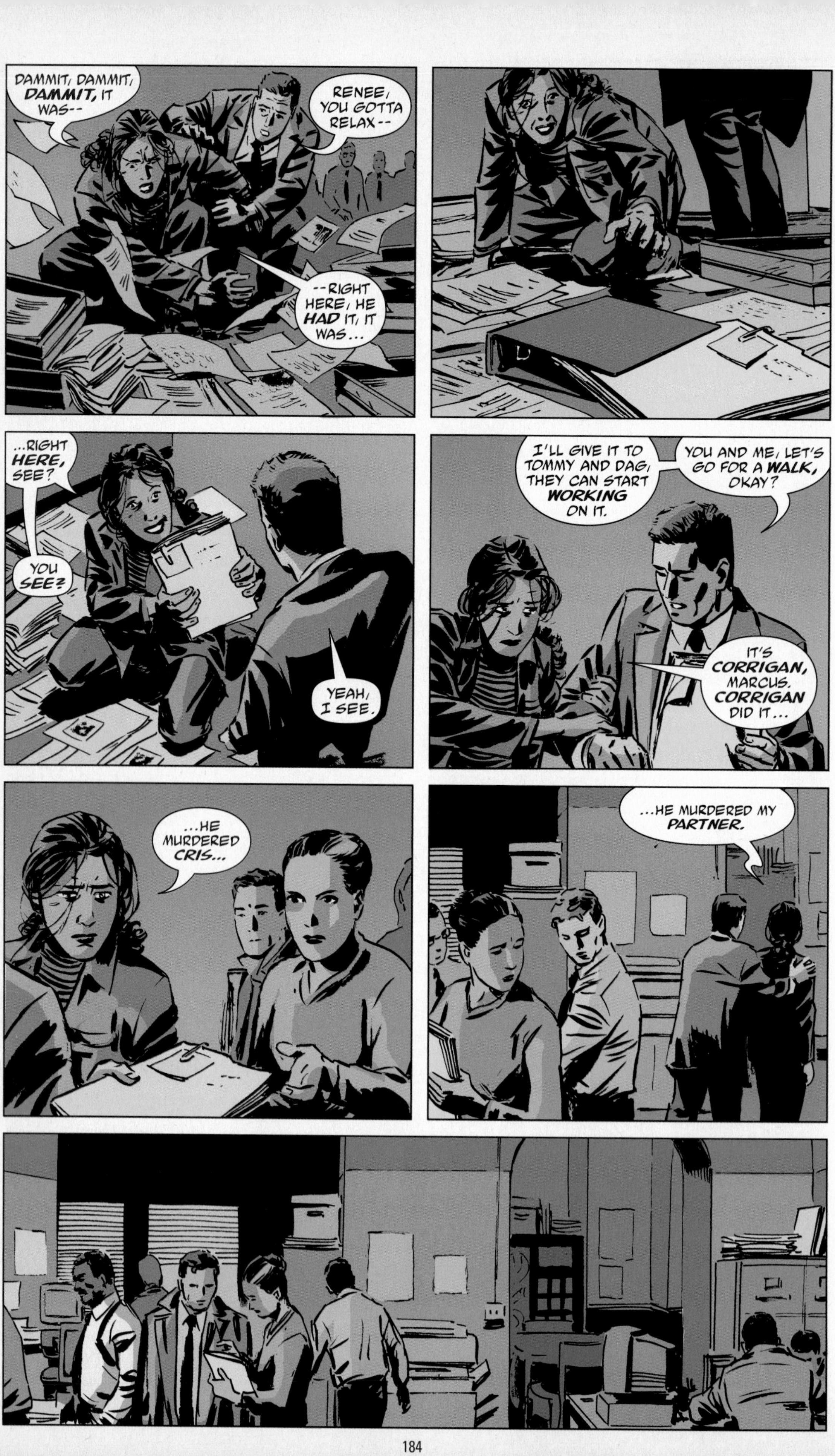
DAMMIT, DAMMIT, DAMMIT, IT WAS--
RENEE, YOU GOTTA RELAX--
--RIGHT HERE, HE HAD IT, IT WAS...
...RIGHT HERE, SEE?
YOU SEE?
YEAH, I SEE.
I'LL GIVE IT TO TOMMY AND DAG, THEY CAN START WORKING ON IT.
YOU AND ME, LET'S GO FOR A WALK, OKAY?
IT'S CORRIGAN, MARCUS. CORRIGAN DID IT...
...HE MURDERED CRIS...
...HE MURDERED MY PARTNER.

WHY DON'T YOU SIT DOWN?

NO...

...NO, I NEED TO GET *OUT* THERE, I NEED TO *HELP*...

JUST TAKE A COUPLE MINUTES, *OKAY,* RENEE?

CATCH YOUR *BREATH.*

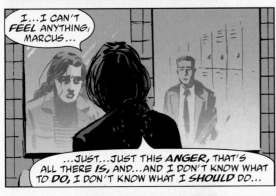

I...I CAN'T *FEEL* ANYTHING, MARCUS...

...JUST...JUST THIS *ANGER,* THAT'S ALL THERE *IS,* AND...AND I DON'T KNOW WHAT TO *DO,* I DON'T KNOW WHAT I *SHOULD* DO...

...IT'S LIKE... IT'S LIKE...

...LIKE EVERYTHING'S WRAPPED IN *GRAY WOOL.*

LIKE YOU'RE *WATCHING* YOURSELF, BUT YOU'RE NOT IN *CONTROL.*

LIKE EVERYTHING YOU *FEEL,* EVERYTHING YOU *HEAR* IS COMING FROM FAR *AWAY.*

I KNOW. IT'S HOW I FELT AFTER *FREEZE* KILLED CHARLIE.

WHEN DOES IT *END?*

WHEN IT'S *OVER.*

185

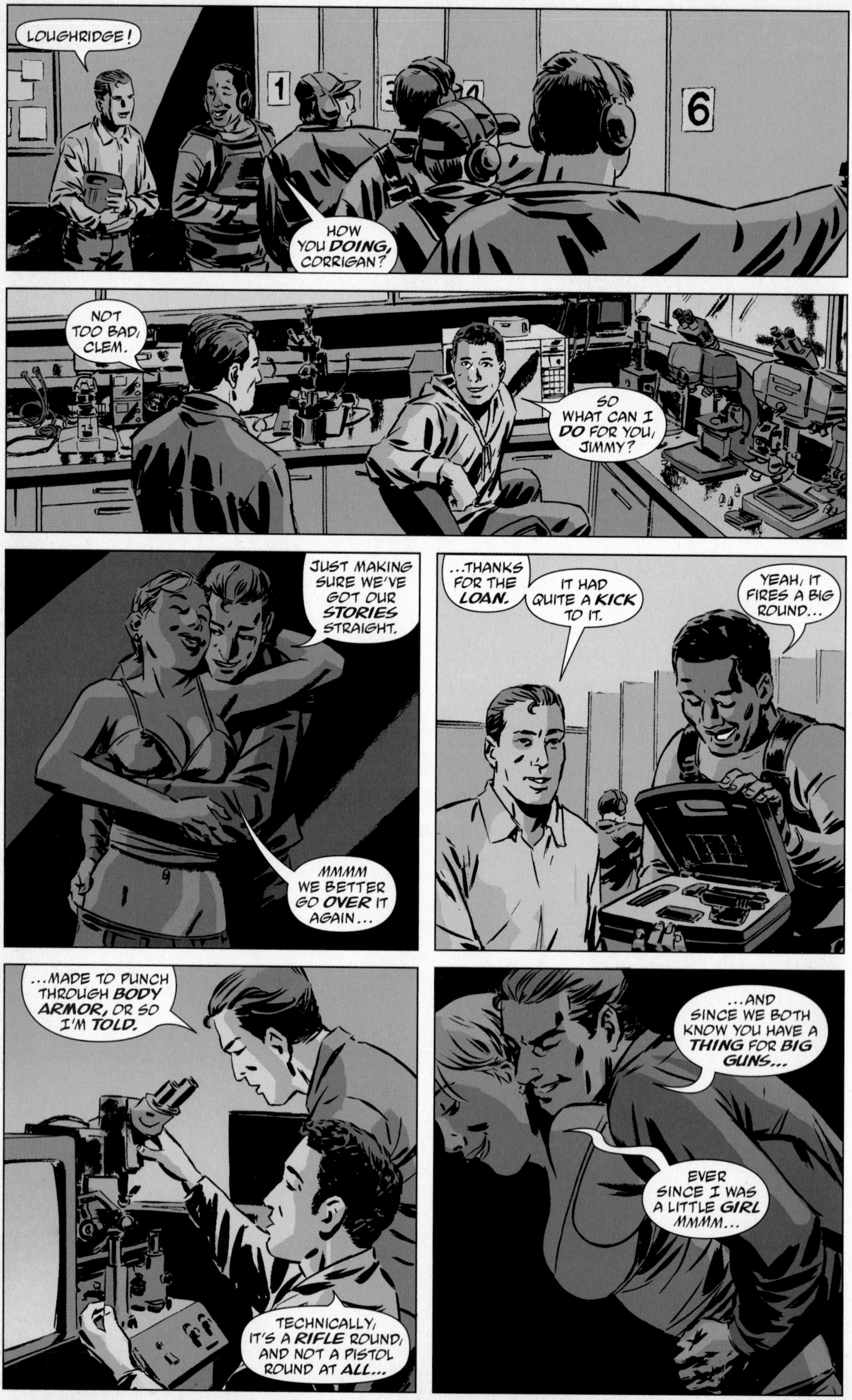
LOUGHRIDGE!
HOW YOU DOING, CORRIGAN?
6
NOT TOO BAD, CLEM.
SO WHAT CAN I DO FOR YOU, JIMMY?
JUST MAKING SURE WE'VE GOT OUR STORIES STRAIGHT.
MMMM WE BETTER GO OVER IT AGAIN...
...THANKS FOR THE LOAN.
IT HAD QUITE A KICK TO IT.
YEAH, IT FIRES A BIG ROUND...
...MADE TO PUNCH THROUGH BODY ARMOR, OR SO I'M TOLD.
TECHNICALLY, IT'S A RIFLE ROUND, AND NOT A PISTOL ROUND AT ALL...
...AND SINCE WE BOTH KNOW YOU HAVE A THING FOR BIG GUNS...
EVER SINCE I WAS A LITTLE GIRL MMMM...

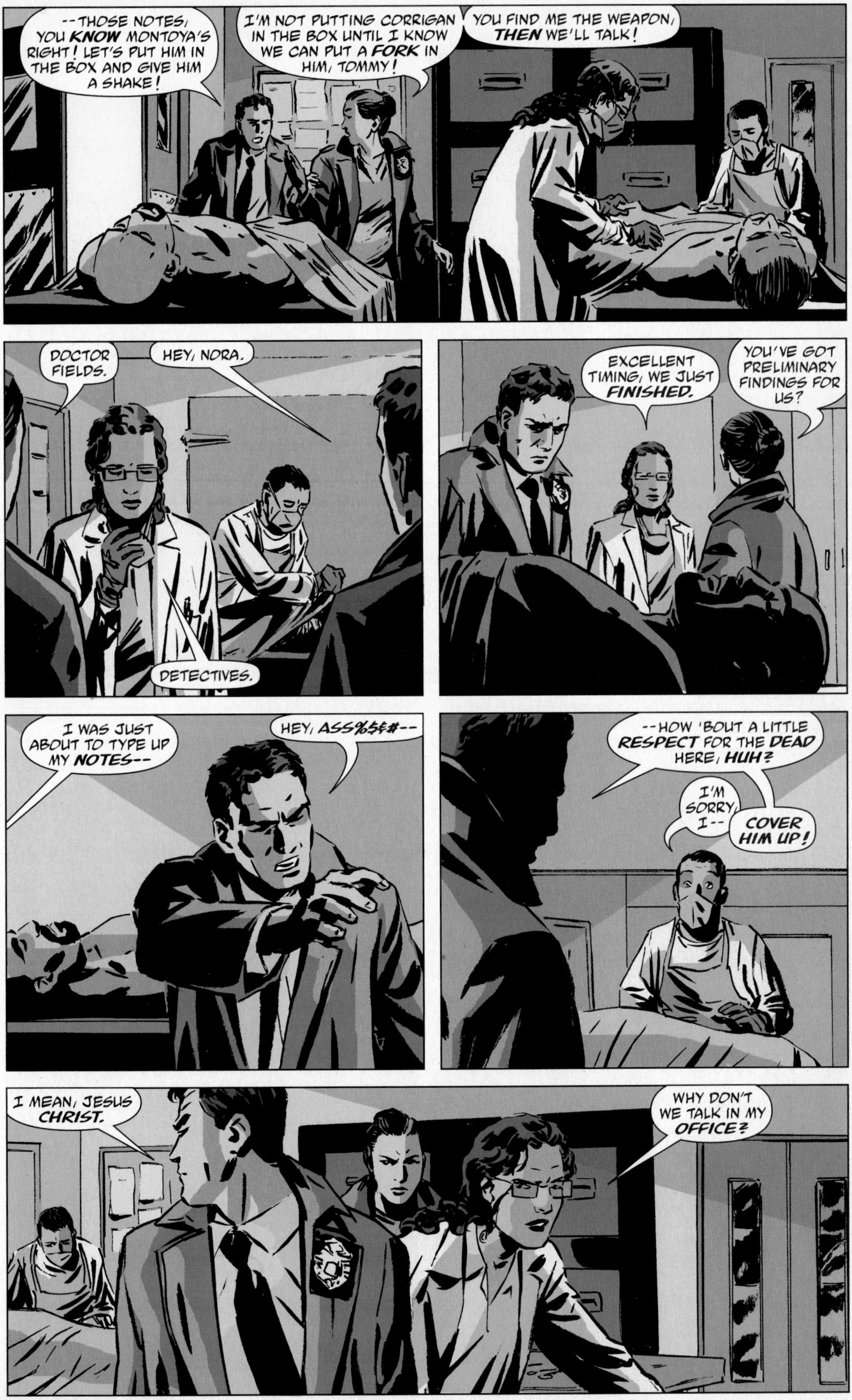
--THOSE NOTES, YOU **KNOW** MONTOYA'S RIGHT! LET'S PUT HIM IN THE BOX AND GIVE HIM A SHAKE!
I'M NOT PUTTING CORRIGAN IN THE BOX UNTIL I KNOW WE CAN PUT A **FORK** IN HIM, TOMMY!
YOU FIND ME THE WEAPON, **THEN** WE'LL TALK!
DOCTOR FIELDS.
HEY, NORA.
DETECTIVES.
EXCELLENT TIMING, WE JUST **FINISHED.**
YOU'VE GOT PRELIMINARY FINDINGS FOR US?
I WAS JUST ABOUT TO TYPE UP MY **NOTES--**
HEY, **ASS%$£#--**
--HOW 'BOUT A LITTLE **RESPECT** FOR THE **DEAD** HERE, **HUH?**
I'M SORRY, I--
COVER HIM UP!
I MEAN, JESUS **CHRIST.**
WHY DON'T WE TALK IN MY **OFFICE?**

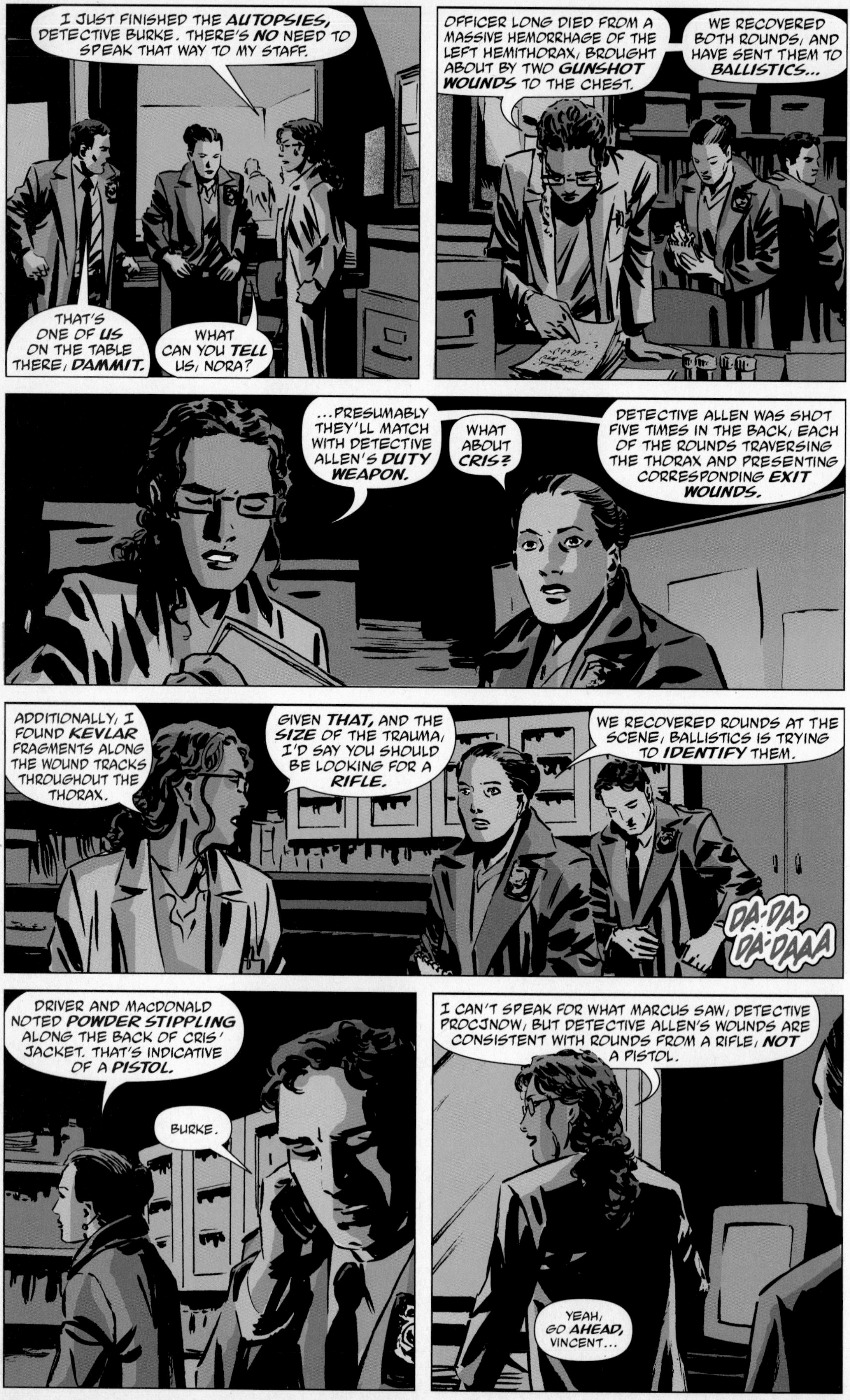
I JUST FINISHED THE AUTOPSIES, DETECTIVE BURKE. THERE'S NO NEED TO SPEAK THAT WAY TO MY STAFF.
THAT'S ONE OF US ON THE TABLE THERE, DAMMIT.
WHAT CAN YOU TELL US, NORA?
OFFICER LONG DIED FROM A MASSIVE HEMORRHAGE OF THE LEFT HEMITHORAX, BROUGHT ABOUT BY TWO GUNSHOT WOUNDS TO THE CHEST.
WE RECOVERED BOTH ROUNDS, AND HAVE SENT THEM TO BALLISTICS...
...PRESUMABLY THEY'LL MATCH WITH DETECTIVE ALLEN'S DUTY WEAPON.
WHAT ABOUT CRIS?
DETECTIVE ALLEN WAS SHOT FIVE TIMES IN THE BACK, EACH OF THE ROUNDS TRAVERSING THE THORAX AND PRESENTING CORRESPONDING EXIT WOUNDS.
ADDITIONALLY, I FOUND KEVLAR FRAGMENTS ALONG THE WOUND TRACKS THROUGHOUT THE THORAX.
GIVEN THAT, AND THE SIZE OF THE TRAUMA, I'D SAY YOU SHOULD BE LOOKING FOR A RIFLE.
WE RECOVERED ROUNDS AT THE SCENE, BALLISTICS IS TRYING TO IDENTIFY THEM.
DA-DA-DA-DAAA
DRIVER AND MACDONALD NOTED POWDER STIPPLING ALONG THE BACK OF CRIS' JACKET. THAT'S INDICATIVE OF A PISTOL.
BURKE.
I CAN'T SPEAK FOR WHAT MARCUS SAW, DETECTIVE PROCJNOW, BUT DETECTIVE ALLEN'S WOUNDS ARE CONSISTENT WITH ROUNDS FROM A RIFLE, NOT A PISTOL.
YEAH, GO AHEAD, VINCENT...

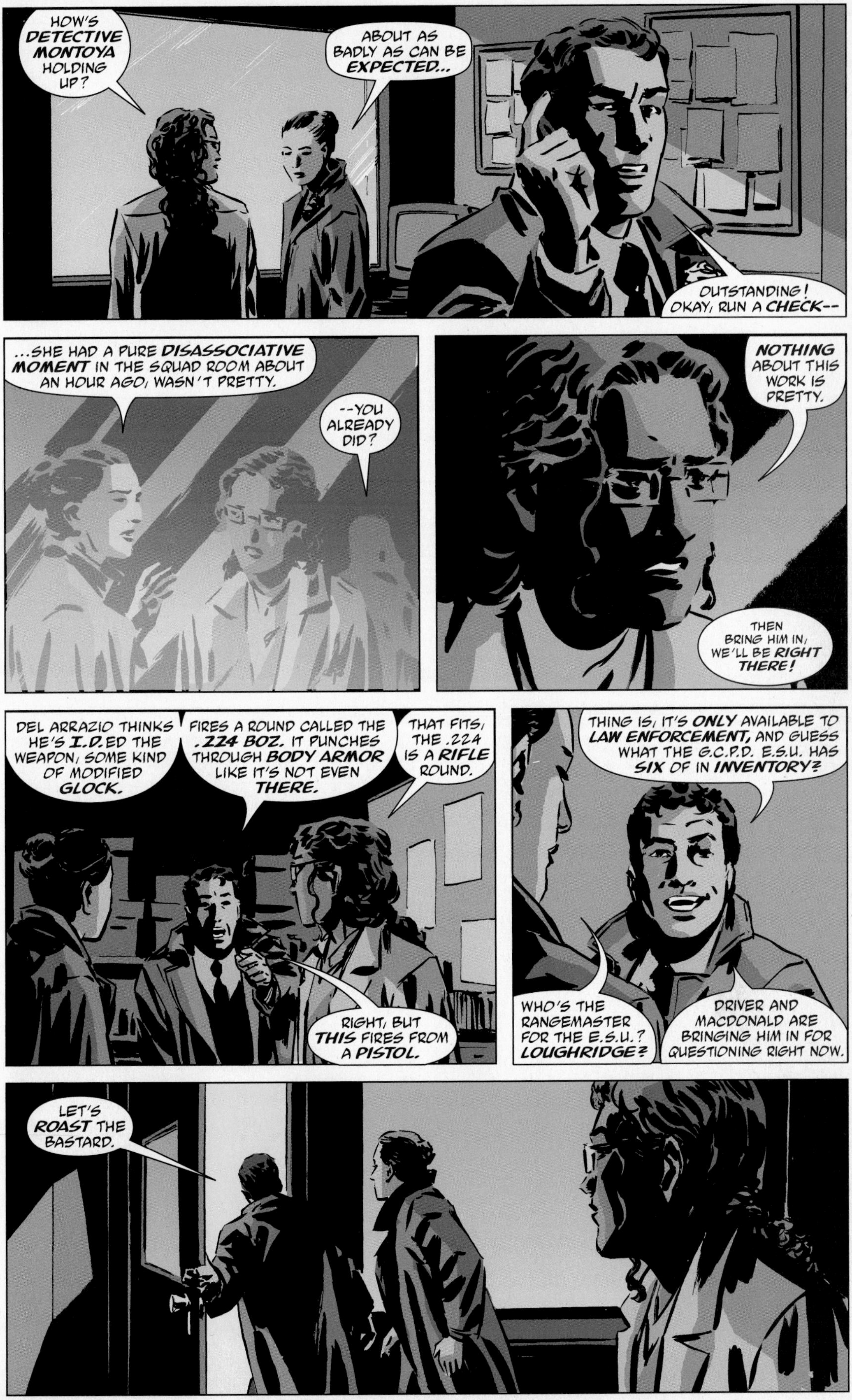
HOW'S DETECTIVE MONTOYA HOLDING UP?
ABOUT AS BADLY AS CAN BE EXPECTED...
OUTSTANDING! OKAY, RUN A CHECK--
...SHE HAD A PURE DISASSOCIATIVE MOMENT IN THE SQUAD ROOM ABOUT AN HOUR AGO, WASN'T PRETTY.
--YOU ALREADY DID?
NOTHING ABOUT THIS WORK IS PRETTY.
THEN BRING HIM IN, WE'LL BE RIGHT THERE!
DEL ARRAZIO THINKS HE'S I.D.ED THE WEAPON, SOME KIND OF MODIFIED GLOCK.
FIRES A ROUND CALLED THE .224 BOZ. IT PUNCHES THROUGH BODY ARMOR LIKE IT'S NOT EVEN THERE.
THAT FITS, THE .224 IS A RIFLE ROUND.
RIGHT, BUT THIS FIRES FROM A PISTOL.
THING IS, IT'S ONLY AVAILABLE TO LAW ENFORCEMENT, AND GUESS WHAT THE G.C.P.D. E.S.U. HAS SIX OF IN INVENTORY?
WHO'S THE RANGEMASTER FOR THE E.S.U.? LOUGHRIDGE?
DRIVER AND MACDONALD ARE BRINGING HIM IN FOR QUESTIONING RIGHT NOW.
LET'S ROAST THE BASTARD.

--WHY WE COULDN'T DO THIS DOWN AT THE RANGE.

YOU BRING ME IN *HERE*, YOU'RE MAKING ME FEEL LIKE I'VE DONE SOMETHING *WRONG*, GUYS.

HAVE YOU DONE SOMETHING *WRONG*, SERGEANT LOUGHRIDGE?

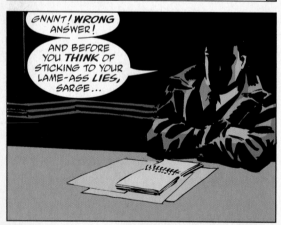

DON'T PLAY ME LIKE THAT, DRIVER. I'M ON THE *JOB*, JUST LIKE *YOU* GUYS.

YOU GOT A *QUESTION* FOR ME, JUST *ASK* IT.

HOW MANY *G-TWO-TWO-FOUR* SEMI-AUTOS YOU GOT IN E.S.U. INVENTORY, SARGE?

SIX, *ALL* OF THEM *ACCOUNTED* FOR.

YOU SIGN ANY OF THEM *OUT* IN THE LAST DAY OR SO?

NO.

GNNNT! *WRONG* ANSWER!

AND BEFORE YOU *THINK* OF STICKING TO YOUR LAME-ASS *LIES*, SARGE...

...ALLOW ME TO INFORM YOU THAT WE THINK ONE OF YOUR TWO-TWO-FOURS WAS USED IN A *CAPITAL CRIME.*

WHICH MAKES YOU AN *ACCESSORY*, AND FIRST IN LINE FOR THE *ELECTRIC CHAIR.*

CARE TO TRY *AGAIN?*

CALM DOWN, MAN!

I SAID I DIDN'T *SIGN* ANY OF THEM *OUT...*

...BUT *MAYBE* I LET SOMEONE *BORROW* ONE AS A *FAVOR...*

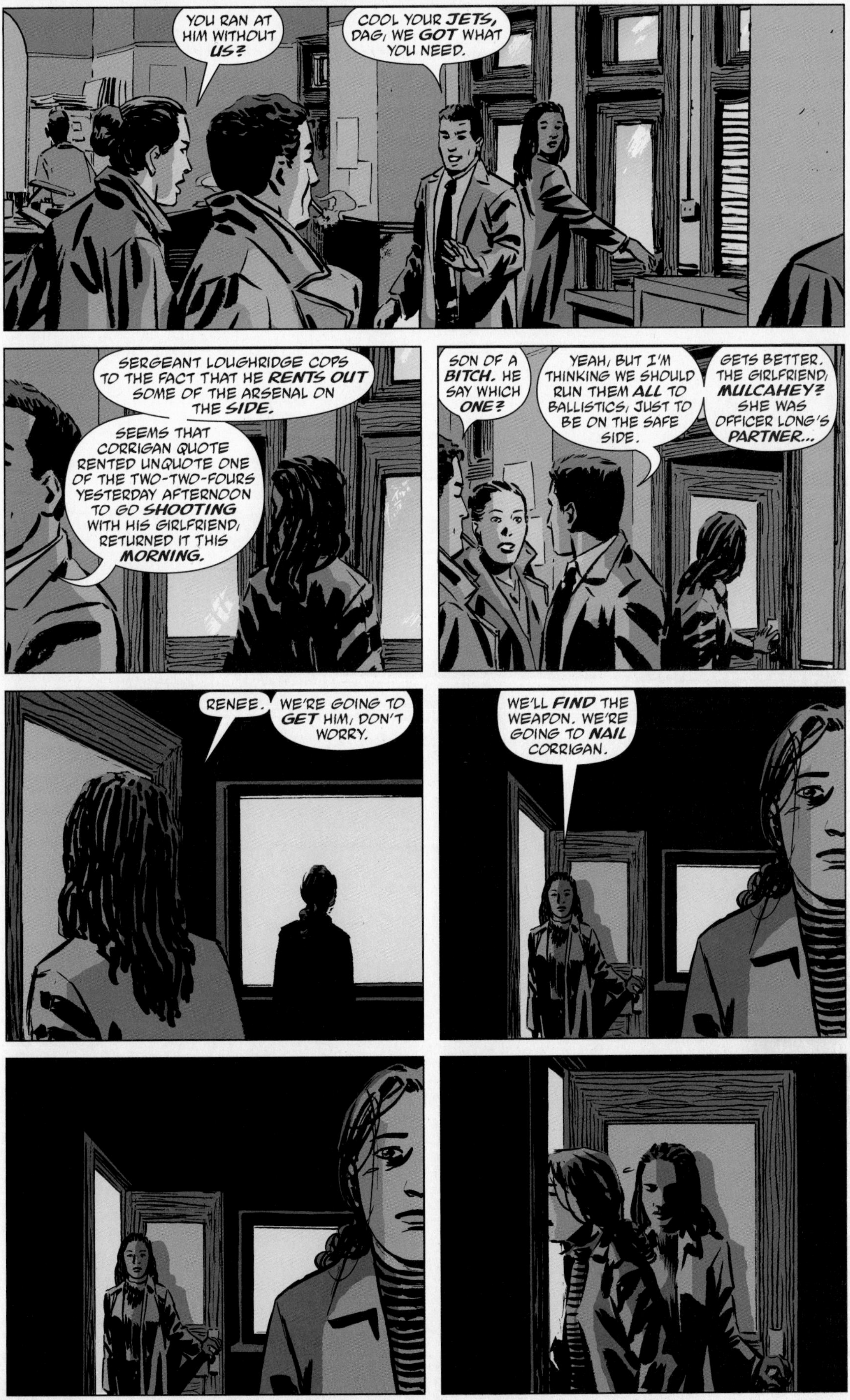
YOU RAN AT HIM WITHOUT US?
COOL YOUR JETS, DAG, WE GOT WHAT YOU NEED.
SERGEANT LOUGHRIDGE COPS TO THE FACT THAT HE RENTS OUT SOME OF THE ARSENAL ON THE SIDE.
SEEMS THAT CORRIGAN QUOTE RENTED UNQUOTE ONE OF THE TWO-TWO-FOURS YESTERDAY AFTERNOON TO GO SHOOTING WITH HIS GIRLFRIEND, RETURNED IT THIS MORNING.
SON OF A BITCH. HE SAY WHICH ONE?
YEAH, BUT I'M THINKING WE SHOULD RUN THEM ALL TO BALLISTICS, JUST TO BE ON THE SAFE SIDE.
GETS BETTER. THE GIRLFRIEND, MULCAHEY? SHE WAS OFFICER LONG'S PARTNER...
RENEE.
WE'RE GOING TO GET HIM, DON'T WORRY.
WE'LL FIND THE WEAPON. WE'RE GOING TO NAIL CORRIGAN.

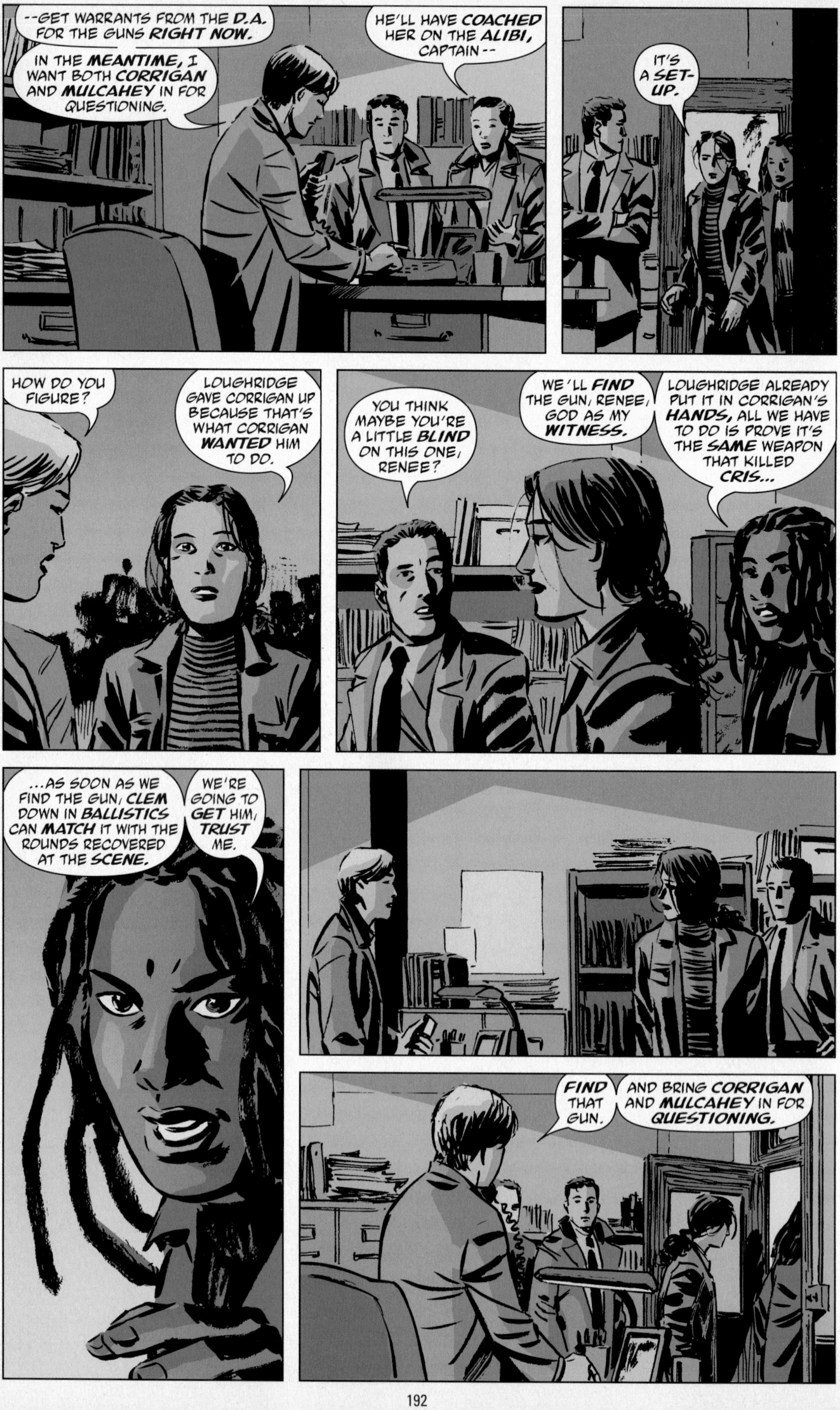
--GET WARRANTS FROM THE D.A. FOR THE GUNS RIGHT NOW.
IN THE MEANTIME, I WANT BOTH CORRIGAN AND MULCAHEY IN FOR QUESTIONING.
HE'LL HAVE COACHED HER ON THE ALIBI, CAPTAIN--
IT'S A SET-UP.
HOW DO YOU FIGURE?
LOUGHRIDGE GAVE CORRIGAN UP BECAUSE THAT'S WHAT CORRIGAN WANTED HIM TO DO.
YOU THINK MAYBE YOU'RE A LITTLE BLIND ON THIS ONE, RENEE?
WE'LL FIND THE GUN, RENEE, GOD AS MY WITNESS.
LOUGHRIDGE ALREADY PUT IT IN CORRIGAN'S HANDS, ALL WE HAVE TO DO IS PROVE IT'S THE SAME WEAPON THAT KILLED CRIS...
...AS SOON AS WE FIND THE GUN, CLEM DOWN IN BALLISTICS CAN MATCH IT WITH THE ROUNDS RECOVERED AT THE SCENE.
WE'RE GOING TO GET HIM, TRUST ME.
FIND THAT GUN.
AND BRING CORRIGAN AND MULCAHEY IN FOR QUESTIONING.

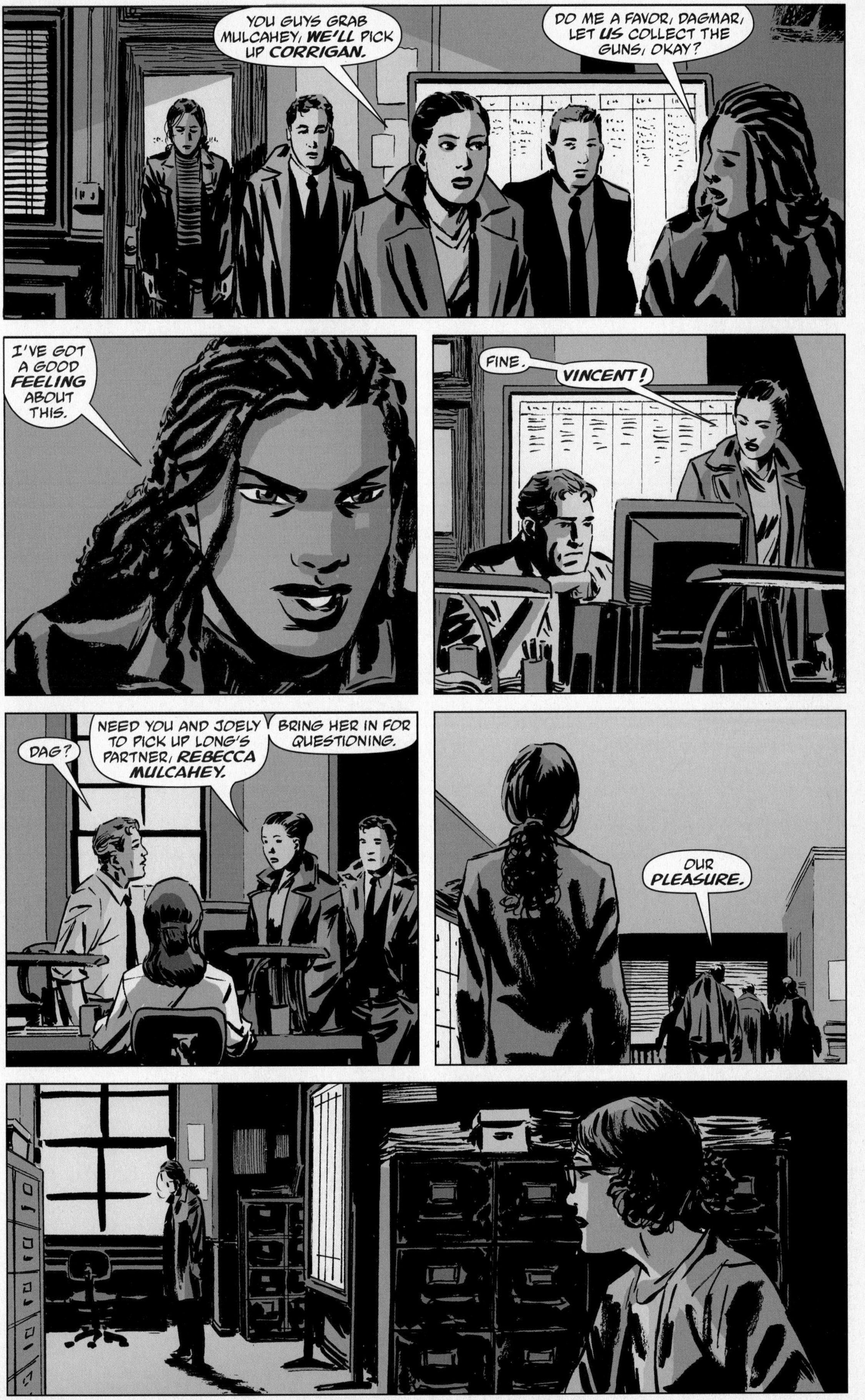

YOU GUYS GRAB MULCAHEY, WE'LL PICK UP CORRIGAN.
DO ME A FAVOR, DAGMAR, LET US COLLECT THE GUNS, OKAY?
I'VE GOT A GOOD FEELING ABOUT THIS.
FINE.
VINCENT!
DAG?
NEED YOU AND JOELY TO PICK UP LONG'S PARTNER, REBECCA MULCAHEY.
BRING HER IN FOR QUESTIONING.
OUR PLEASURE.

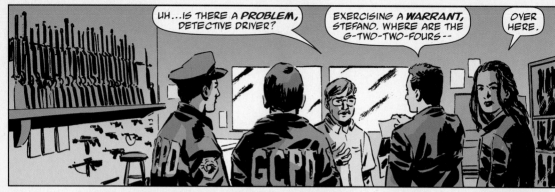

UH...IS THERE A *PROBLEM*, DETECTIVE DRIVER?

EXERCISING A *WARRANT*, STEFANO. WHERE ARE THE G-TWO-TWO-FOURS--

OVER HERE.

ALL *RIGHT*, I'M *COMING*, DAMMIT --

BZZZT BZZZT

JIMMY.

YEAH, I *KNOW*.

COME TO *MOMMA*.

--STOP LEANING ON THE *BUZZER*...

OFFICER MULCAHEY?

I'M DETECTIVE BARTLETT, THIS IS SERGEANT DEL ARRAZIO. WE WERE HOPING YOU'D *ACCOMPANY* US BACK TO *CENTRAL*...

...TO HELP US ANSWER A FEW *QUESTIONS*. YOU DON'T MIND COMING WITH US, *DO* YOU, JIMMY?

IT'D BE MY *PLEASURE*, DETECTIVE BURKE...

...ANYTHING TO *HELP*...

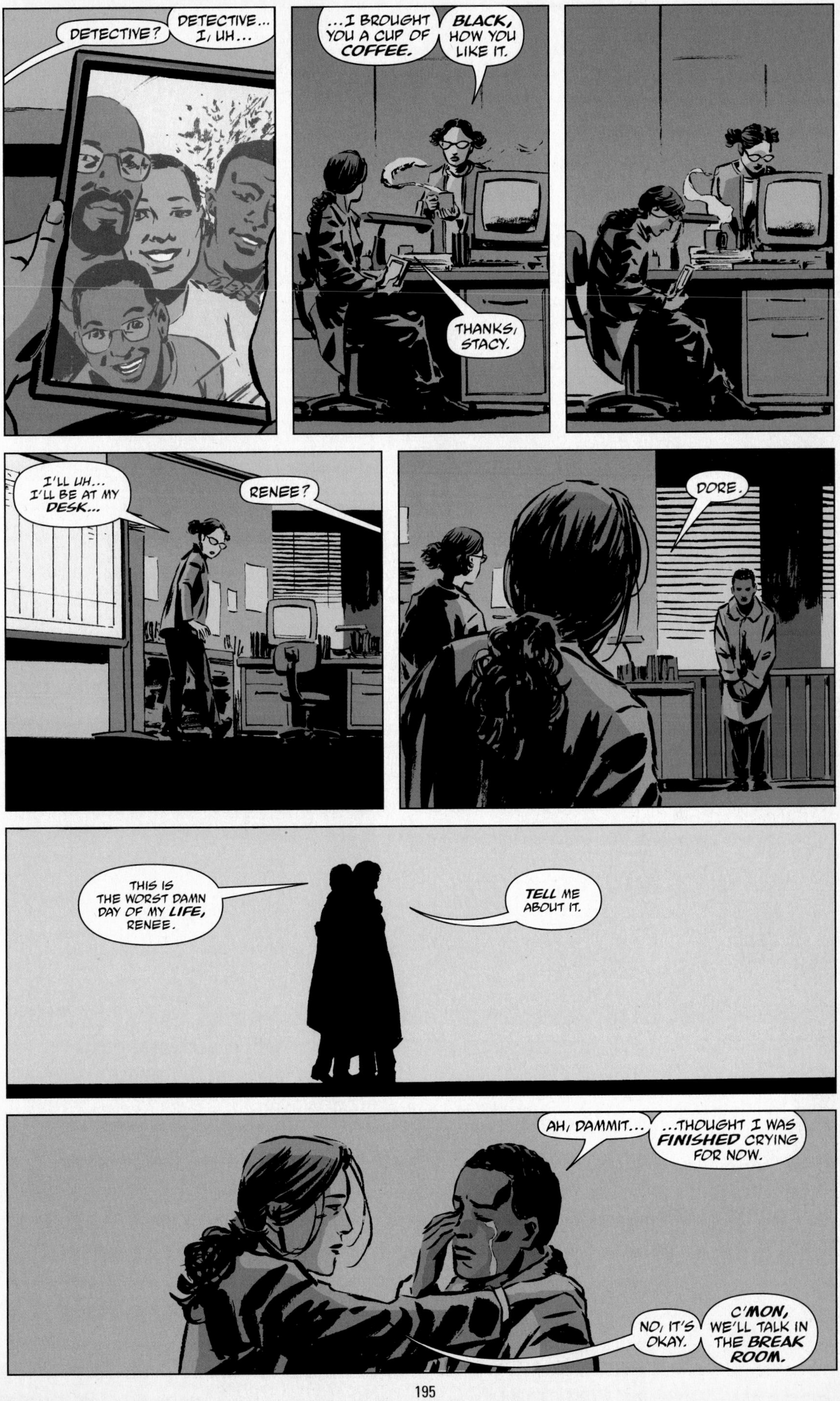
DETECTIVE?
DETECTIVE... I, UH...
...I BROUGHT YOU A CUP OF COFFEE.
BLACK, HOW YOU LIKE IT.
THANKS, STACY.
I'LL UH... I'LL BE AT MY DESK...
RENEE?
DORE.
THIS IS THE WORST DAMN DAY OF MY LIFE, RENEE.
TELL ME ABOUT IT.
AH, DAMMIT...
...THOUGHT I WAS FINISHED CRYING FOR NOW.
C'MON, WE'LL TALK IN THE BREAK ROOM.
NO, IT'S OKAY.

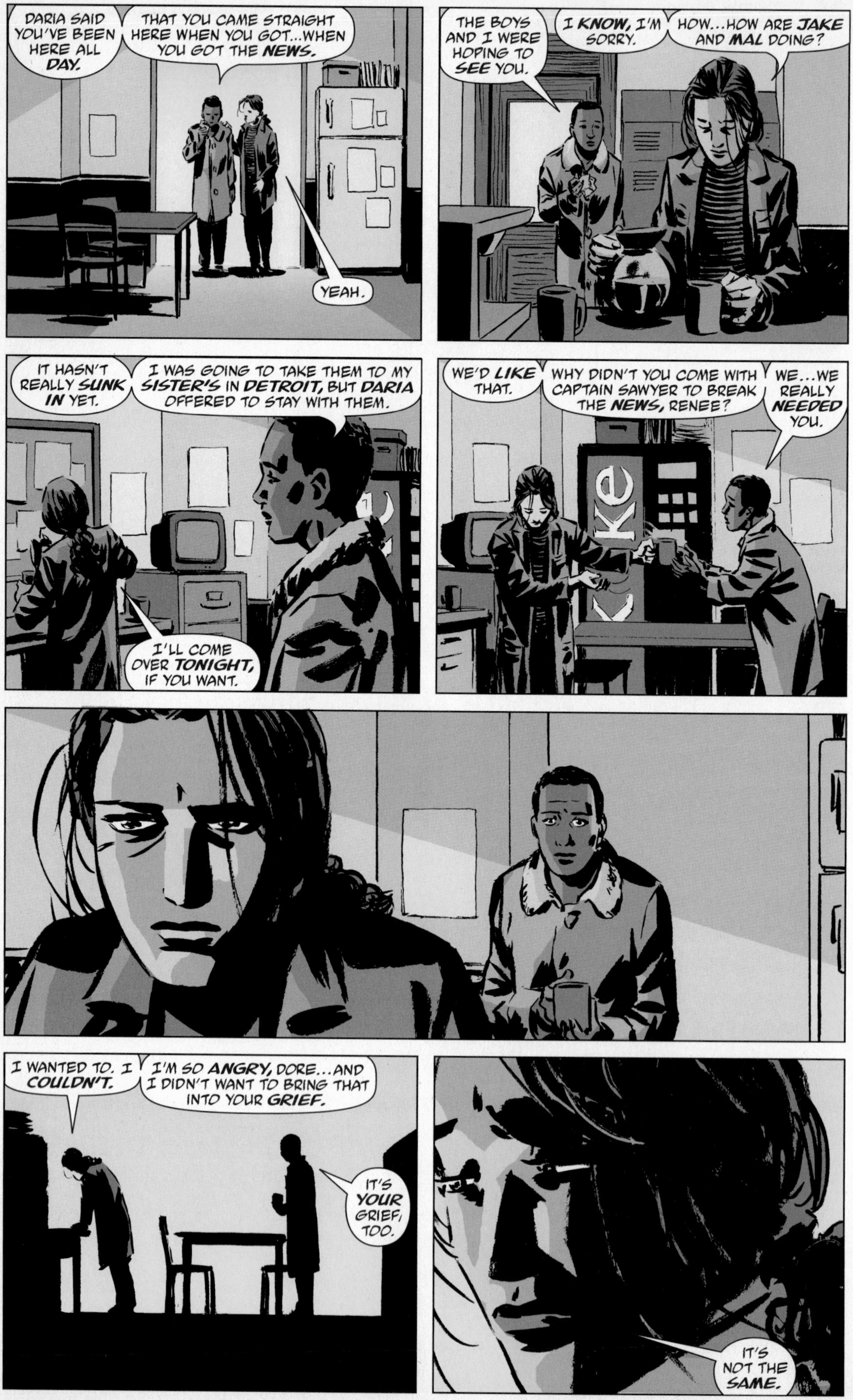
DARIA SAID YOU'VE BEEN HERE ALL DAY.
THAT YOU CAME STRAIGHT HERE WHEN YOU GOT...WHEN YOU GOT THE NEWS.
YEAH.
THE BOYS AND I WERE HOPING TO SEE YOU.
I KNOW, I'M SORRY.
HOW...HOW ARE JAKE AND MAL DOING?
IT HASN'T REALLY SUNK IN YET.
I WAS GOING TO TAKE THEM TO MY SISTER'S IN DETROIT, BUT DARIA OFFERED TO STAY WITH THEM.
I'LL COME OVER TONIGHT, IF YOU WANT.
WE'D LIKE THAT.
WHY DIDN'T YOU COME WITH CAPTAIN SAWYER TO BREAK THE NEWS, RENEE?
WE...WE REALLY NEEDED YOU.
I WANTED TO. I COULDN'T.
I'M SO ANGRY, DORE...AND I DIDN'T WANT TO BRING THAT INTO YOUR GRIEF.
IT'S YOUR GRIEF, TOO.
IT'S NOT THE SAME.

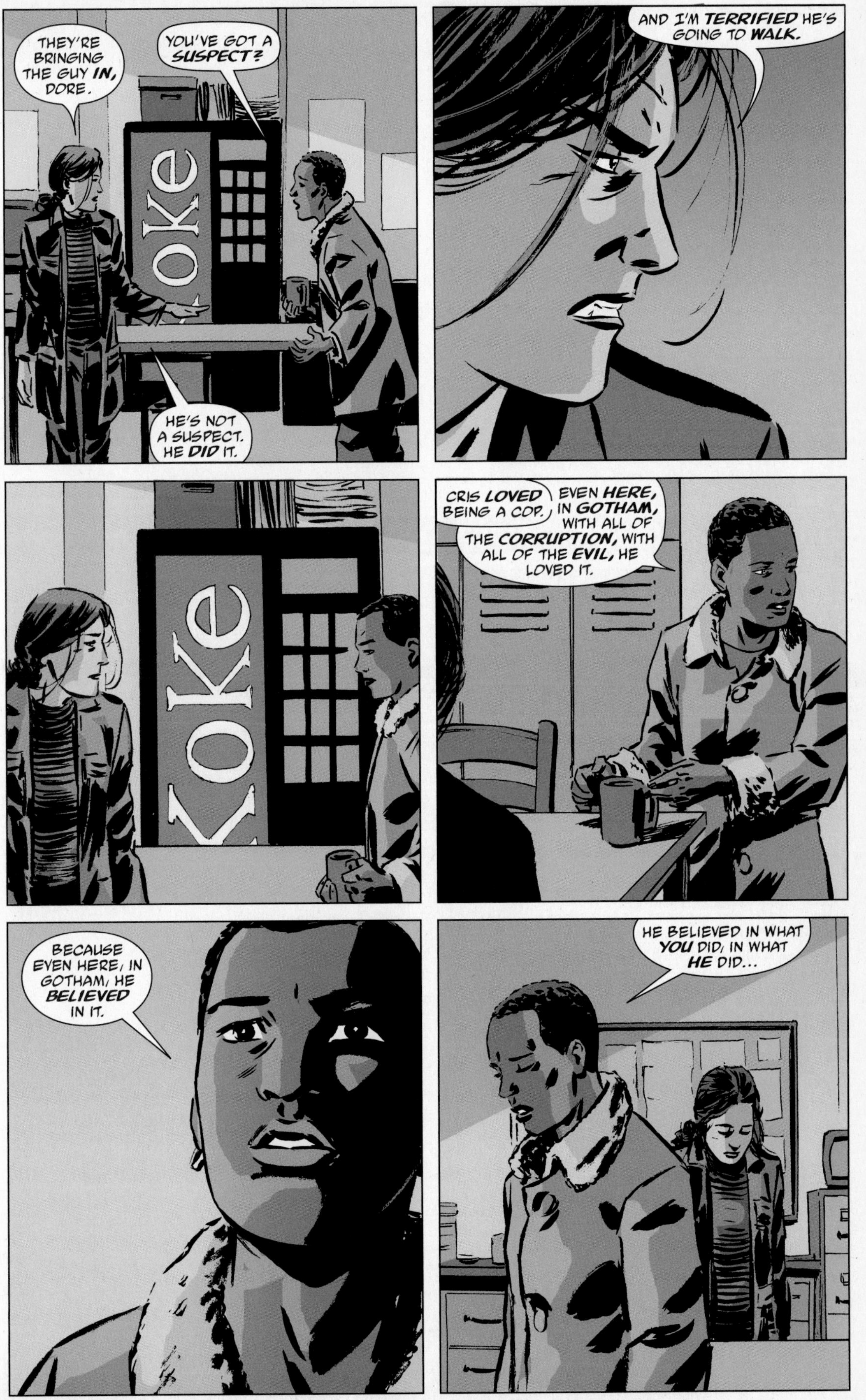
THEY'RE BRINGING THE GUY IN, DORE.
YOU'VE GOT A SUSPECT?
HE'S NOT A SUSPECT. HE DID IT.
AND I'M TERRIFIED HE'S GOING TO WALK.
CRIS LOVED BEING A COP.
EVEN HERE, IN GOTHAM, WITH ALL OF THE CORRUPTION, WITH ALL OF THE EVIL, HE LOVED IT.
BECAUSE EVEN HERE, IN GOTHAM, HE BELIEVED IN IT.
HE BELIEVED IN WHAT YOU DID, IN WHAT HE DID...

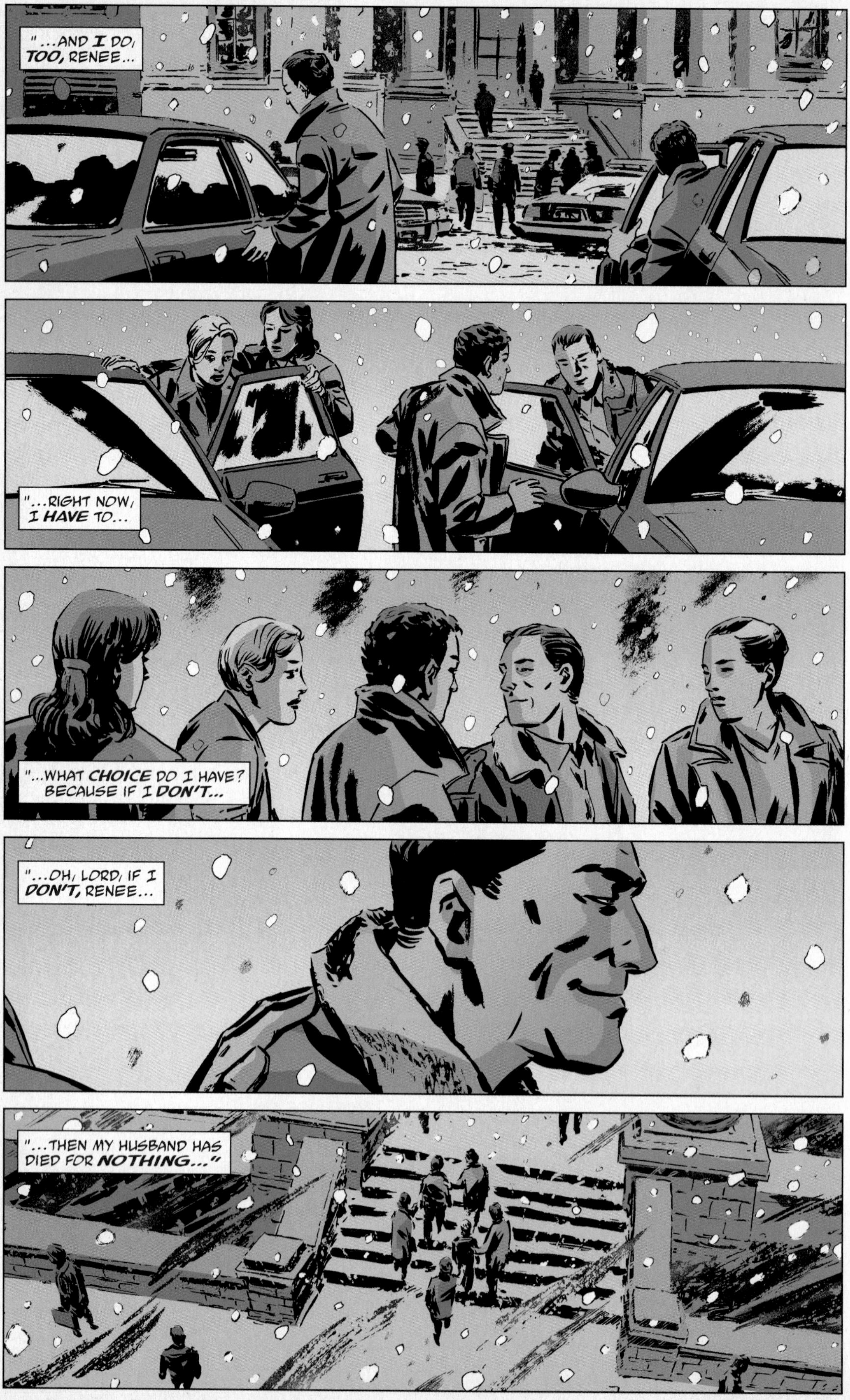
"...AND I DO, TOO, RENEE...
"...RIGHT NOW, I HAVE TO...
"...WHAT CHOICE DO I HAVE? BECAUSE IF I DON'T...
"...OH, LORD, IF I DON'T, RENEE...
"...THEN MY HUSBAND HAS DIED FOR NOTHING..."

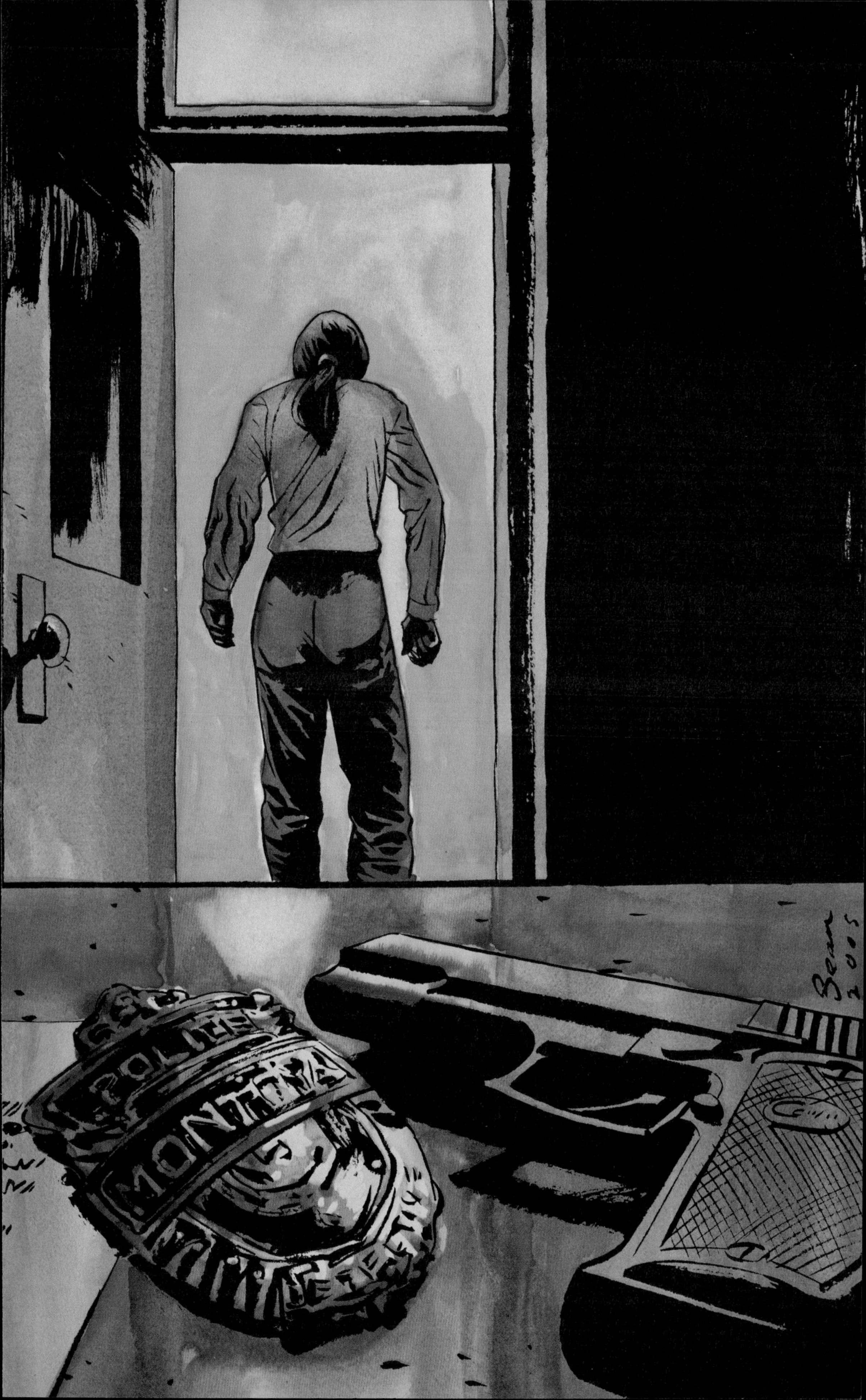
POLICE

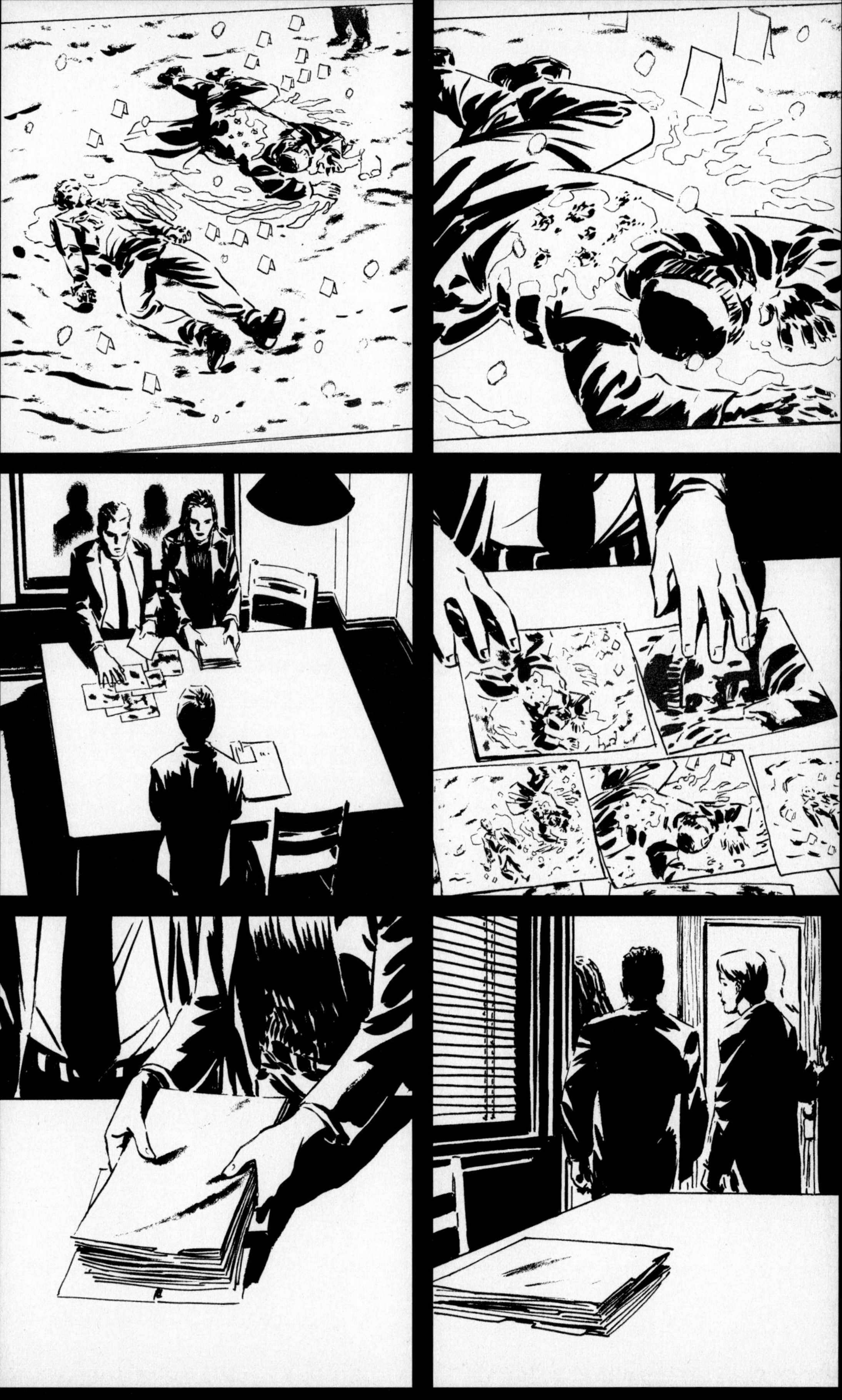

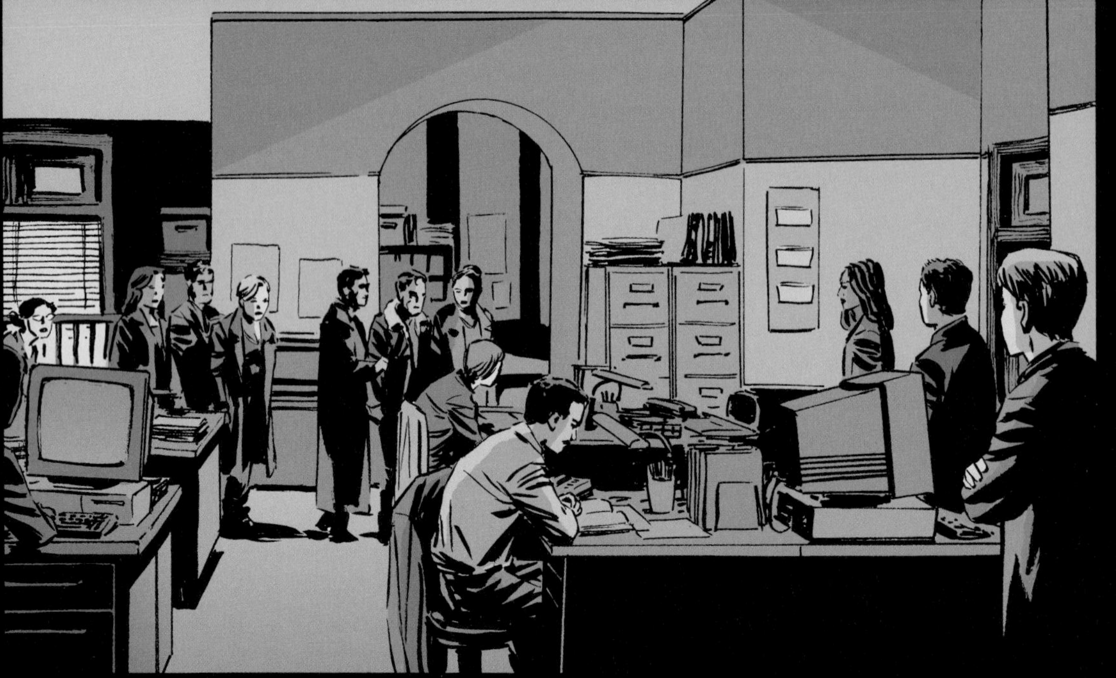

CORRIGAN II

PART THREE

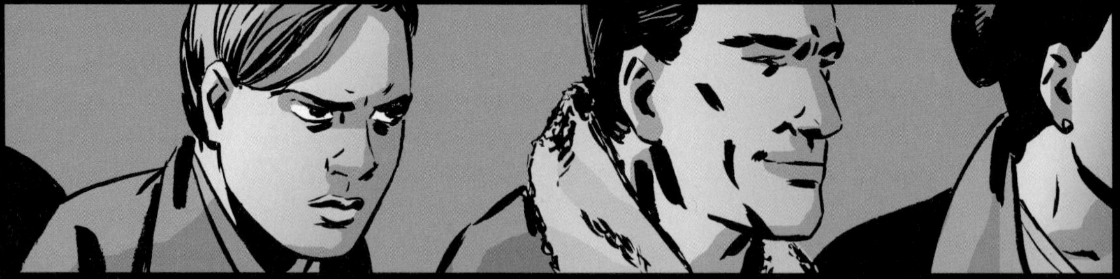

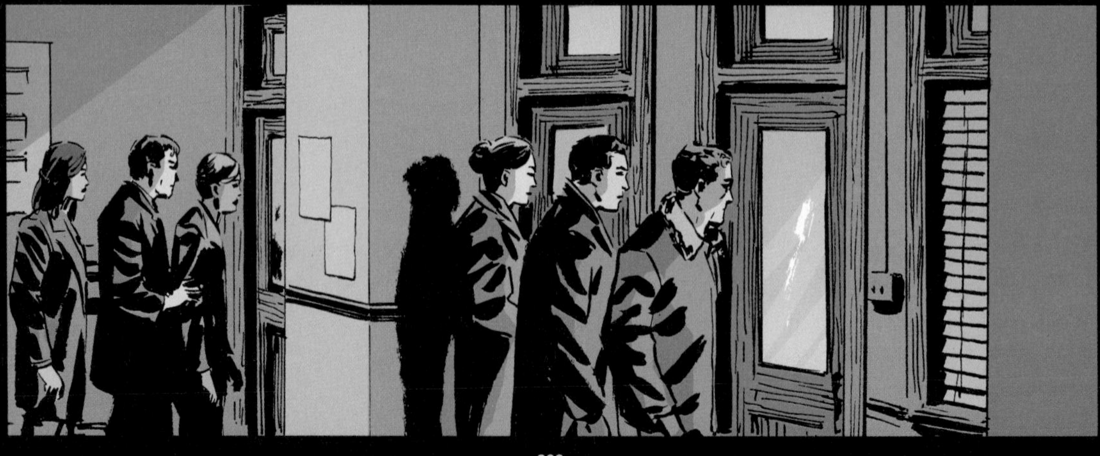

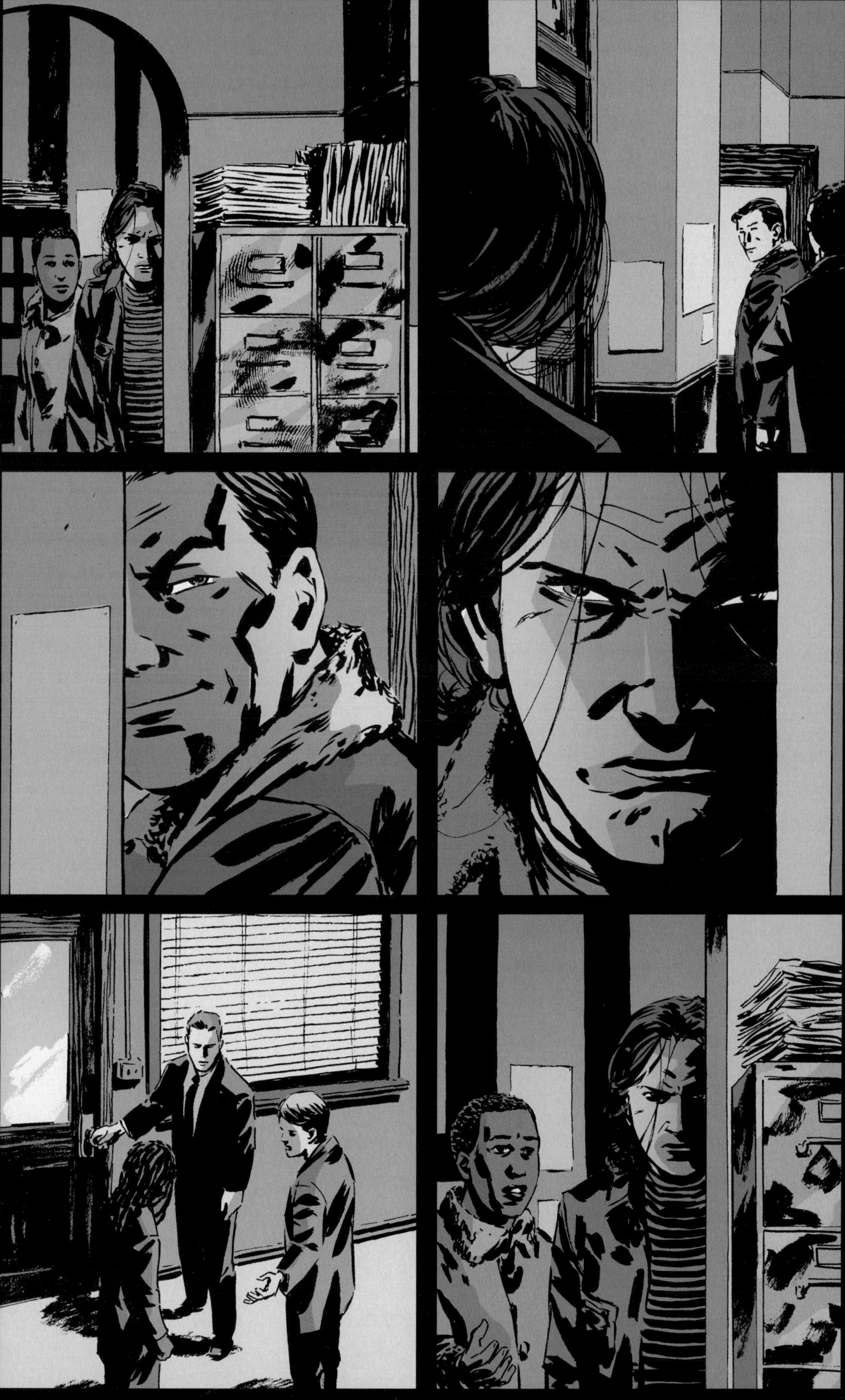

SORRY TO HEAR ABOUT YOUR PARTNER.

YEAH. YEAH, IT PRETTY MUCH *SUCKS.*

YOU AND LONG HAD BEEN *PARTNERED* FOR, WHAT, THREE YEARS?

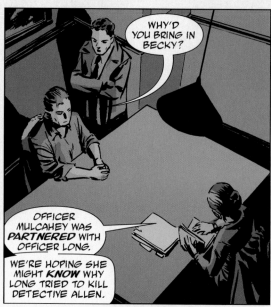

WHY'D YOU BRING IN BECKY?

OFFICER MULCAHEY WAS *PARTNERED* WITH OFFICER LONG.

WE'RE HOPING SHE MIGHT *KNOW* WHY LONG TRIED TO KILL DETECTIVE ALLEN.

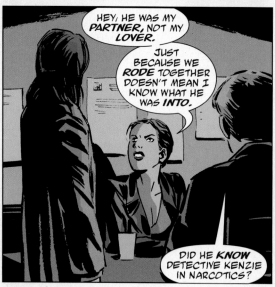

HEY, HE WAS MY *PARTNER,* NOT MY *LOVER.*

JUST BECAUSE WE *RODE* TOGETHER DOESN'T MEAN I KNOW WHAT HE WAS *INTO.*

DID HE *KNOW* DETECTIVE KENZIE IN NARCOTICS?

YOU THINK LONG KILLED KENZIE, THEN TRIED TO KILL ALLEN?

DON'T YOU?

C'MON, DETECTIVE PROCJNOW, MY JOB IS TO *COLLECT* THE EVIDENCE, *NOT* TO *INTERPRET* IT.

NO, I WAS OUT WITH *JIMMY,* AS I'M SURE YOU ALREADY *KNOW,* DETECTIVE DEL ARRAZIO.

DOING WHAT?

WE WENT *SHOOTING.*

NO, NOT AT THE RANGE, WE WENT OUT TO BRENTWOOD.

TO THE WOODS.

DID ANYONE *SEE* YOU?

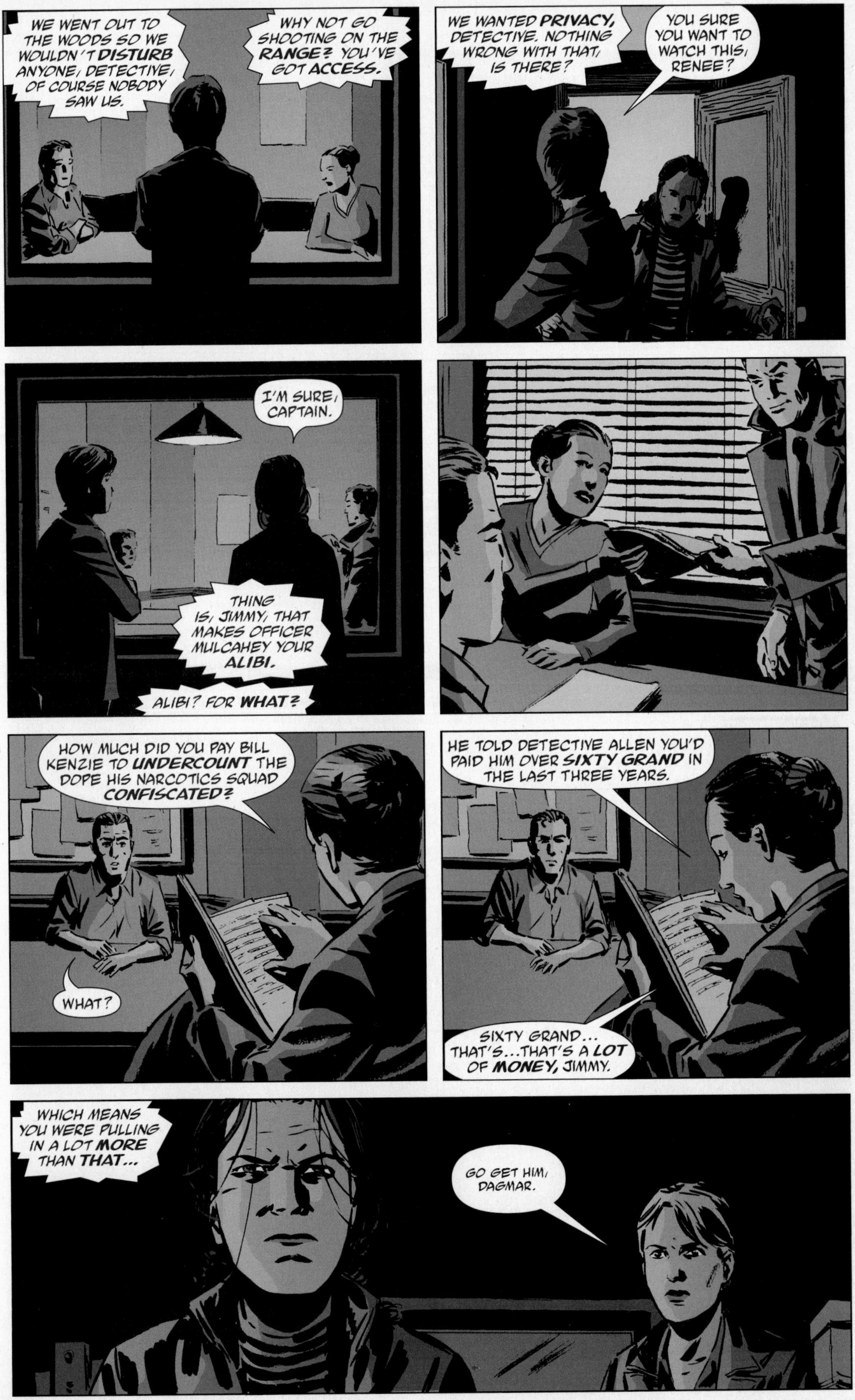
WE WENT OUT TO THE WOODS SO WE WOULDN'T **DISTURB** ANYONE, DETECTIVE, OF COURSE NOBODY SAW US.
WHY NOT GO SHOOTING ON THE **RANGE?** YOU'VE GOT **ACCESS.**
WE WANTED **PRIVACY,** DETECTIVE. NOTHING WRONG WITH THAT, IS THERE?
YOU SURE YOU WANT TO WATCH THIS, RENEE?
I'M SURE, CAPTAIN.
THING IS, JIMMY, THAT MAKES OFFICER MULCAHEY YOUR **ALIBI.**
ALIBI? FOR **WHAT?**
HOW MUCH DID YOU PAY BILL KENZIE TO **UNDERCOUNT** THE DOPE HIS NARCOTICS SQUAD **CONFISCATED?**
WHAT?
HE TOLD DETECTIVE ALLEN YOU'D PAID HIM OVER **SIXTY GRAND** IN THE LAST THREE YEARS.
SIXTY GRAND... THAT'S...THAT'S A **LOT** OF **MONEY,** JIMMY.
WHICH MEANS YOU WERE PULLING IN A LOT **MORE** THAN **THAT...**
GO GET HIM, DAGMAR.

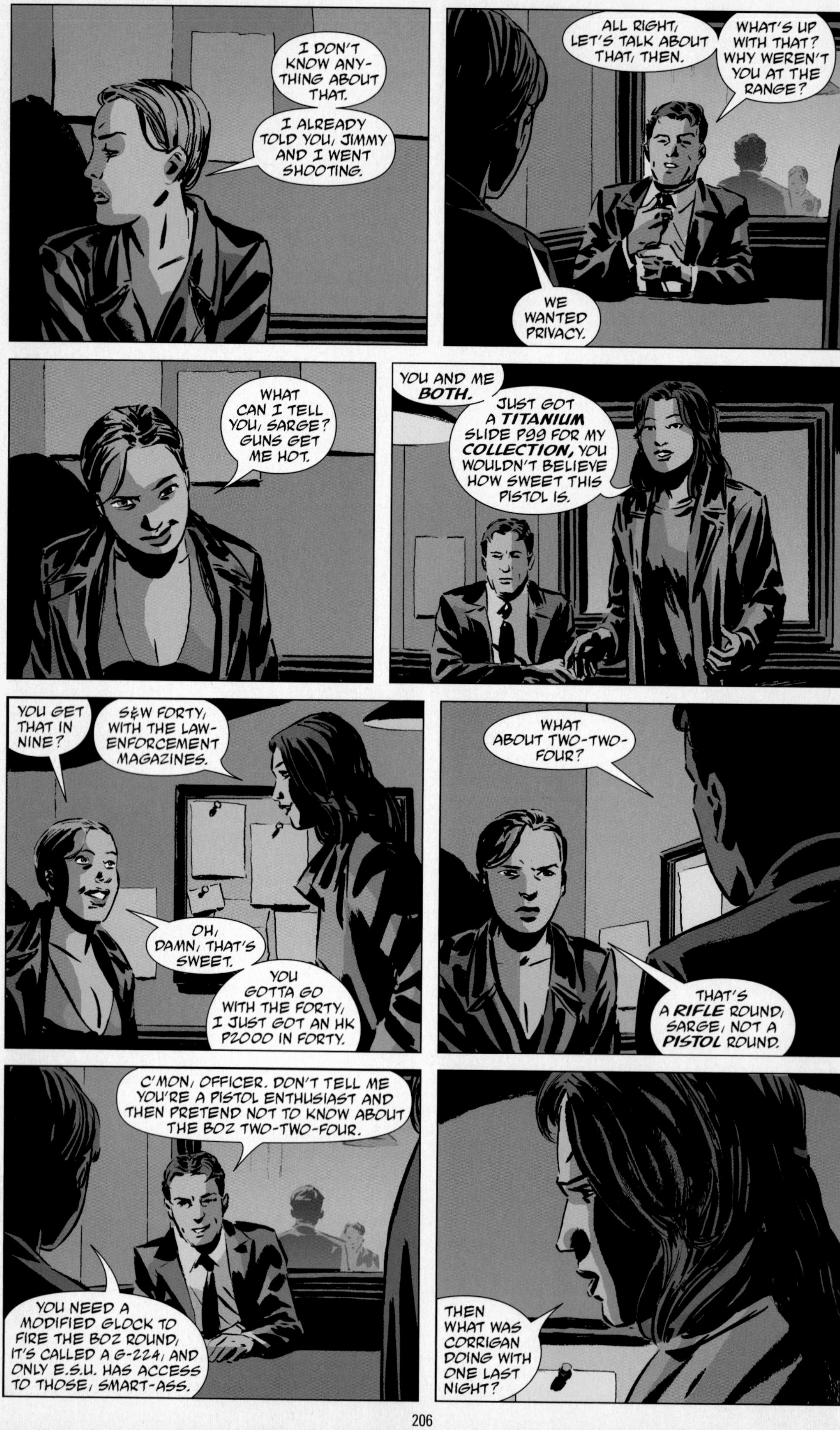

I DON'T KNOW ANYTHING ABOUT THAT.
I ALREADY TOLD YOU, JIMMY AND I WENT SHOOTING.
ALL RIGHT, LET'S TALK ABOUT THAT, THEN.
WHAT'S UP WITH THAT? WHY WEREN'T YOU AT THE RANGE?
WE WANTED PRIVACY.
WHAT CAN I TELL YOU, SARGE? GUNS GET ME HOT.
YOU AND ME BOTH.
JUST GOT A TITANIUM SLIDE P99 FOR MY COLLECTION, YOU WOULDN'T BELIEVE HOW SWEET THIS PISTOL IS.
YOU GET THAT IN NINE?
S&W FORTY, WITH THE LAW-ENFORCEMENT MAGAZINES.
OH, DAMN, THAT'S SWEET.
YOU GOTTA GO WITH THE FORTY, I JUST GOT AN HK P2000 IN FORTY.
WHAT ABOUT TWO-TWO-FOUR?
THAT'S A RIFLE ROUND, SARGE, NOT A PISTOL ROUND.
C'MON, OFFICER. DON'T TELL ME YOU'RE A PISTOL ENTHUSIAST AND THEN PRETEND NOT TO KNOW ABOUT THE BOZ TWO-TWO-FOUR.
YOU NEED A MODIFIED GLOCK TO FIRE THE BOZ ROUND, IT'S CALLED A G-224, AND ONLY E.S.U. HAS ACCESS TO THOSE, SMART-ASS.
THEN WHAT WAS CORRIGAN DOING WITH ONE LAST NIGHT?

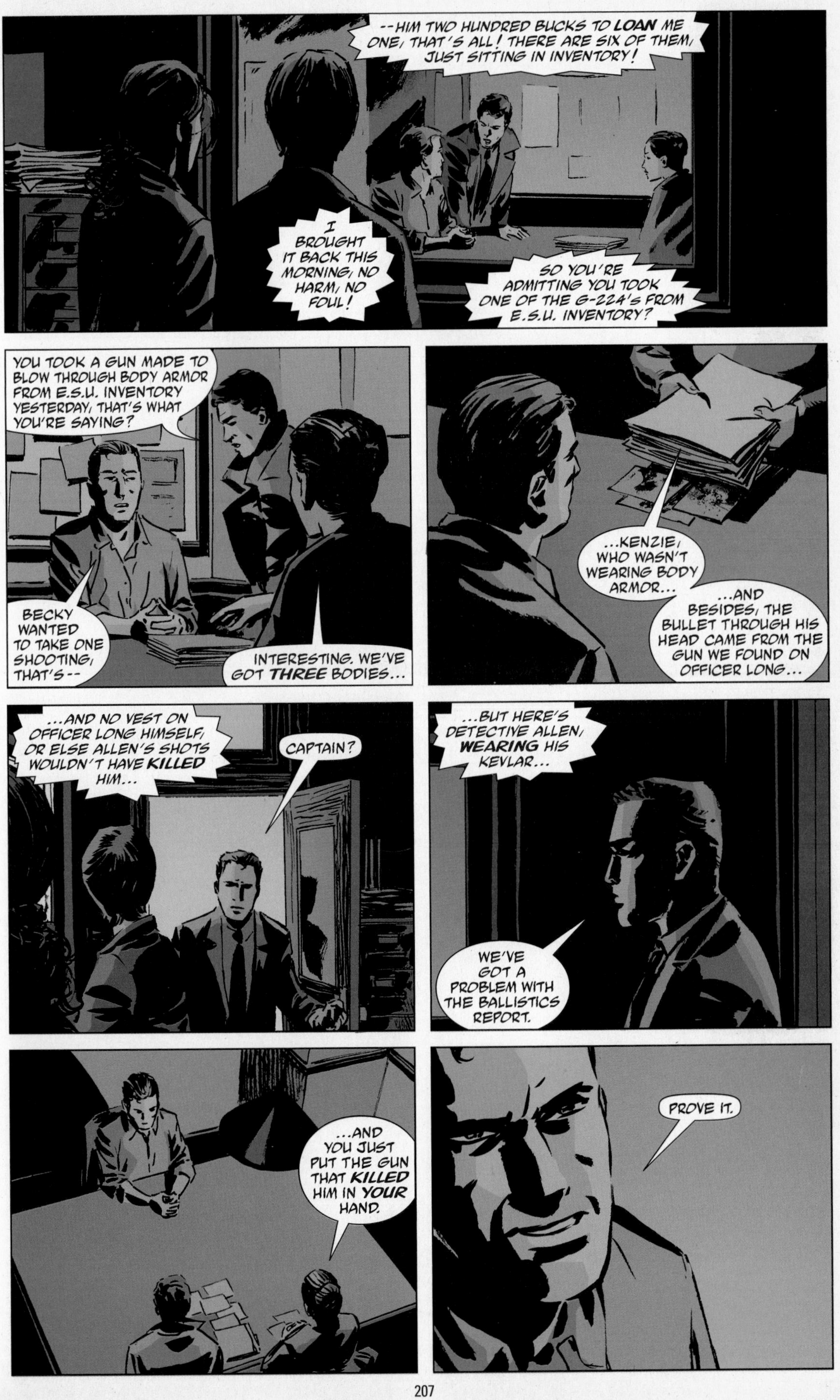
--HIM TWO HUNDRED BUCKS TO LOAN ME ONE, THAT'S ALL! THERE ARE SIX OF THEM, JUST SITTING IN INVENTORY!
I BROUGHT IT BACK THIS MORNING, NO HARM, NO FOUL!
SO YOU'RE ADMITTING YOU TOOK ONE OF THE G-224'S FROM E.S.U. INVENTORY?
YOU TOOK A GUN MADE TO BLOW THROUGH BODY ARMOR FROM E.S.U. INVENTORY YESTERDAY, THAT'S WHAT YOU'RE SAYING?
BECKY WANTED TO TAKE ONE SHOOTING, THAT'S--
INTERESTING. WE'VE GOT THREE BODIES...
...KENZIE, WHO WASN'T WEARING BODY ARMOR...
...AND BESIDES, THE BULLET THROUGH HIS HEAD CAME FROM THE GUN WE FOUND ON OFFICER LONG...
...AND NO VEST ON OFFICER LONG HIMSELF, OR ELSE ALLEN'S SHOTS WOULDN'T HAVE KILLED HIM...
CAPTAIN?
...BUT HERE'S DETECTIVE ALLEN, WEARING HIS KEVLAR...
WE'VE GOT A PROBLEM WITH THE BALLISTICS REPORT.
...AND YOU JUST PUT THE GUN THAT KILLED HIM IN YOUR HAND.
PROVE IT.

WHAT THE HELL'S HAPPENED?

ROBINS &$#*ED US, THAT'S WHAT &*%$ING HAPPENED!

EXPLAIN.

WE BROUGHT ALL SIX OF THE G-224s IN FOR TESTING, *INCLUDING* THE MURDER WEAPON, SWEAR TO GOD.

ROBINS SAYS *NONE* OF THE GUNS MATCH, HE SAYS THE ROUNDS THAT KILLED CRIS CAME FROM A &*%#ING *RIFLE*...

...A BUSHMASTER .223, LIKE THE *BELTWAY SNIPERS* USED, AND *NOT* FROM A G-224.

SON OF A BITCH.

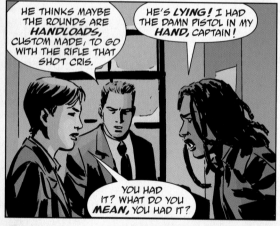

HE THINKS MAYBE THE ROUNDS ARE *HANDLOADS*, CUSTOM MADE, TO GO WITH THE RIFLE THAT SHOT CRIS.

HE'S *LYING!* I HAD THE DAMN PISTOL IN MY *HAND*, CAPTAIN!

YOU HAD IT? WHAT DO YOU *MEAN*, YOU HAD IT?

I JUST...I *KNOW* HE'S LYING, CAPTAIN.

CORRIGAN BOUGHT HIM OFF, *SOMETHING*, HE'S *LYING*.

SO WE CAN PUT THE GUN IN CORRIGAN'S HAND, BUT WE *CAN'T* PROVE IT'S THE WEAPON THAT KILLED *CRIS*.

SON OF A BITCH...

...HE *PLAYED* US...

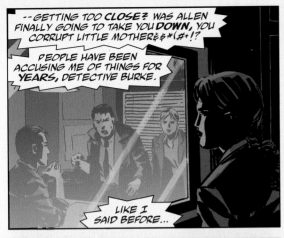

--GETTING TOO **CLOSE**? WAS ALLEN FINALLY GOING TO TAKE YOU **DOWN**, YOU CORRUPT LITTLE MOTHER&&*(#+!?

PEOPLE HAVE BEEN ACCUSING ME OF THINGS FOR **YEARS**, DETECTIVE BURKE.

LIKE I SAID BEFORE...

...**PROVE** IT.

DETECTIVES.

A MOMENT, PLEASE.

GET OUT OF HERE.

I'M SORRY?

YOU HEARD ME.

YOU KNOW WHERE TO FIND ME IF YOU WANT TO TRY AGAIN.

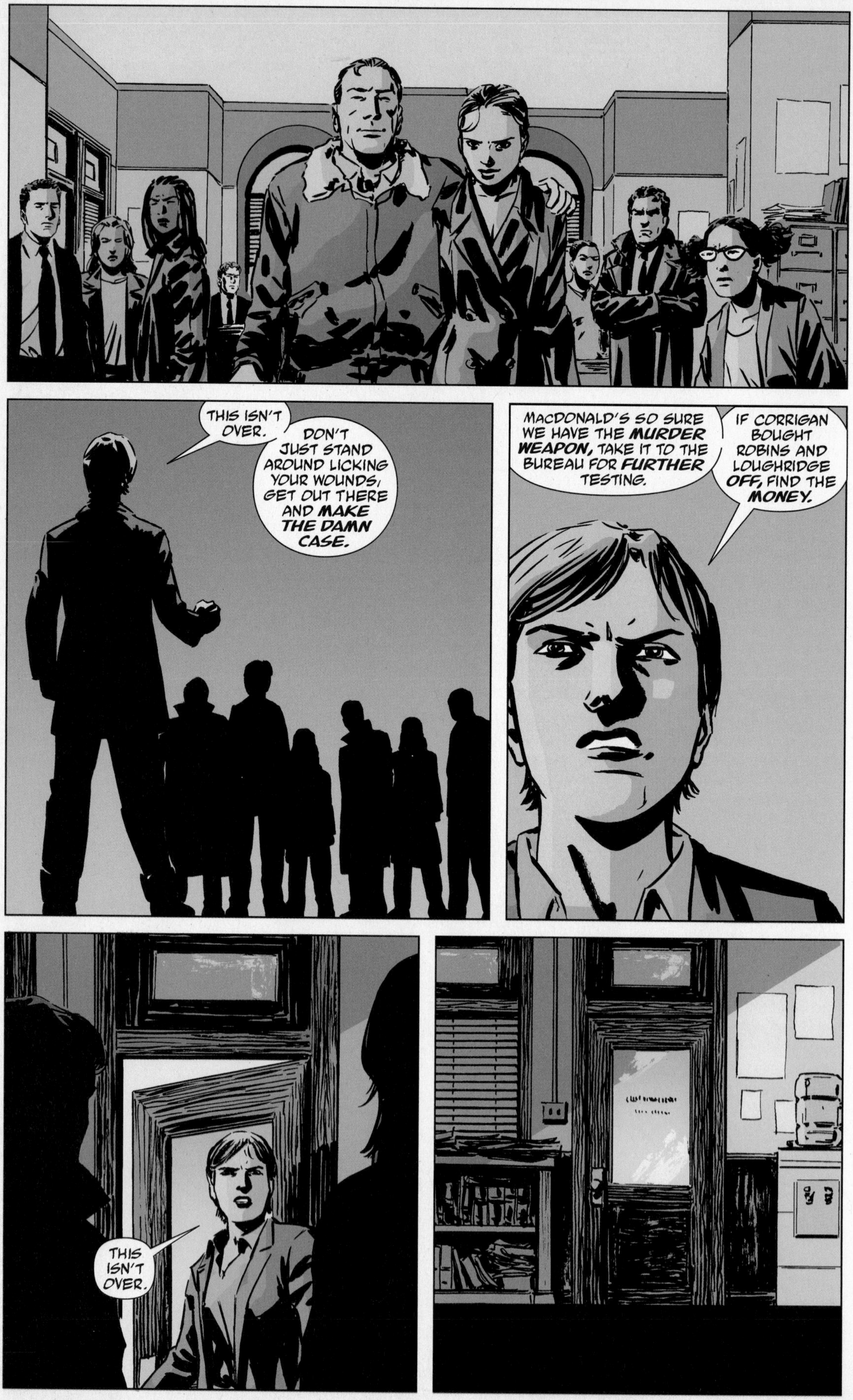
THIS ISN'T OVER.
DON'T JUST STAND AROUND LICKING YOUR WOUNDS, GET OUT THERE AND MAKE THE DAMN CASE.
MACDONALD'S SO SURE WE HAVE THE MURDER WEAPON, TAKE IT TO THE BUREAU FOR FURTHER TESTING.
IF CORRIGAN BOUGHT ROBINS AND LOUGHRIDGE OFF, FIND THE MONEY.
THIS ISN'T OVER.

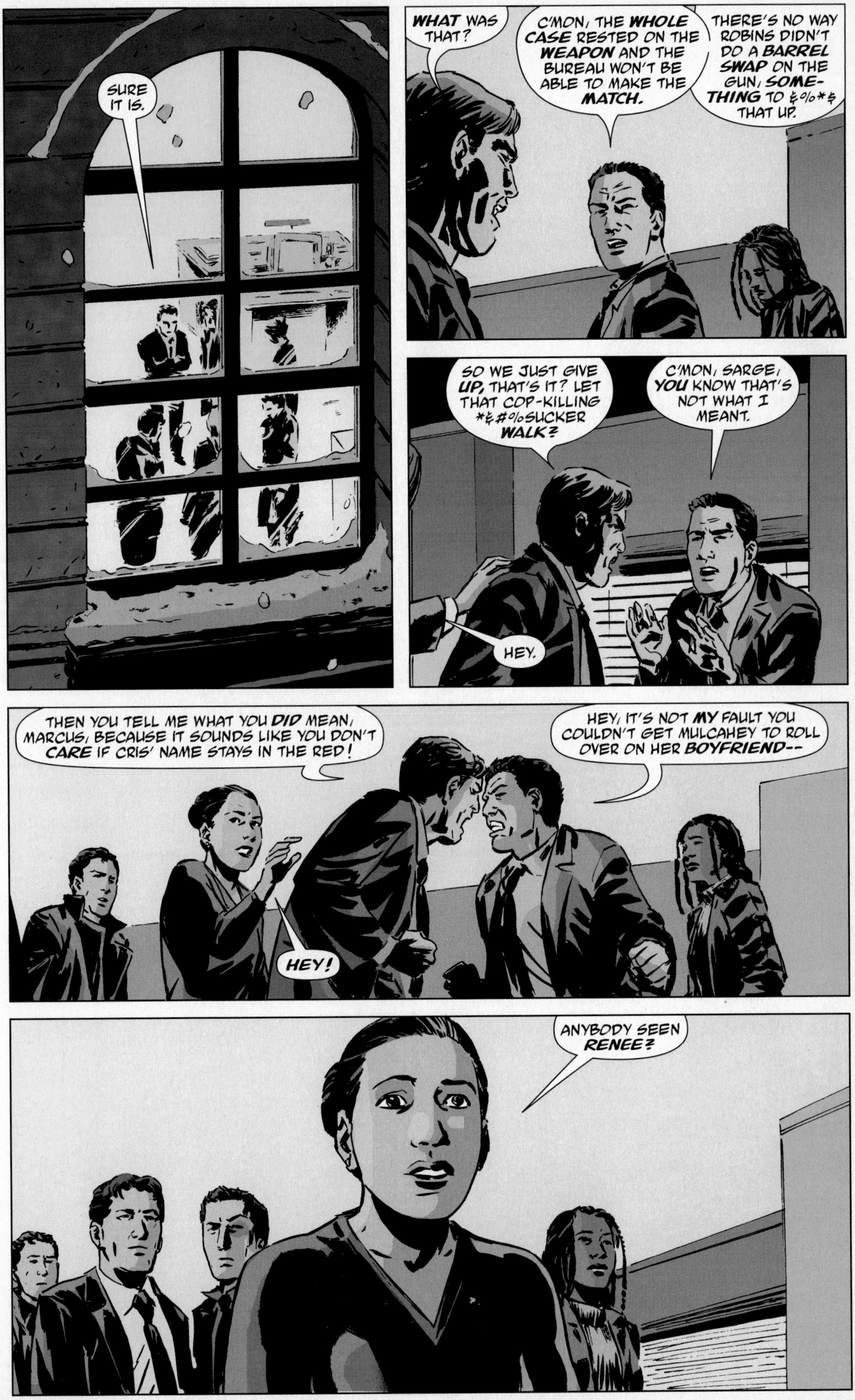
SURE IT IS.
WHAT WAS THAT?
C'MON, THE WHOLE CASE RESTED ON THE WEAPON AND THE BUREAU WON'T BE ABLE TO MAKE THE MATCH.
THERE'S NO WAY ROBINS DIDN'T DO A BARREL SWAP ON THE GUN, SOMETHING TO &%*$ THAT UP.
SO WE JUST GIVE UP, THAT'S IT? LET THAT COP-KILLING *&#%SUCKER WALK?
C'MON, SARGE, YOU KNOW THAT'S NOT WHAT I MEANT.
HEY.
THEN YOU TELL ME WHAT YOU DID MEAN, MARCUS, BECAUSE IT SOUNDS LIKE YOU DON'T CARE IF CRIS' NAME STAYS IN THE RED!
HEY, IT'S NOT MY FAULT YOU COULDN'T GET MULCAHEY TO ROLL OVER ON HER BOYFRIEND--
HEY!
ANYBODY SEEN RENEE?

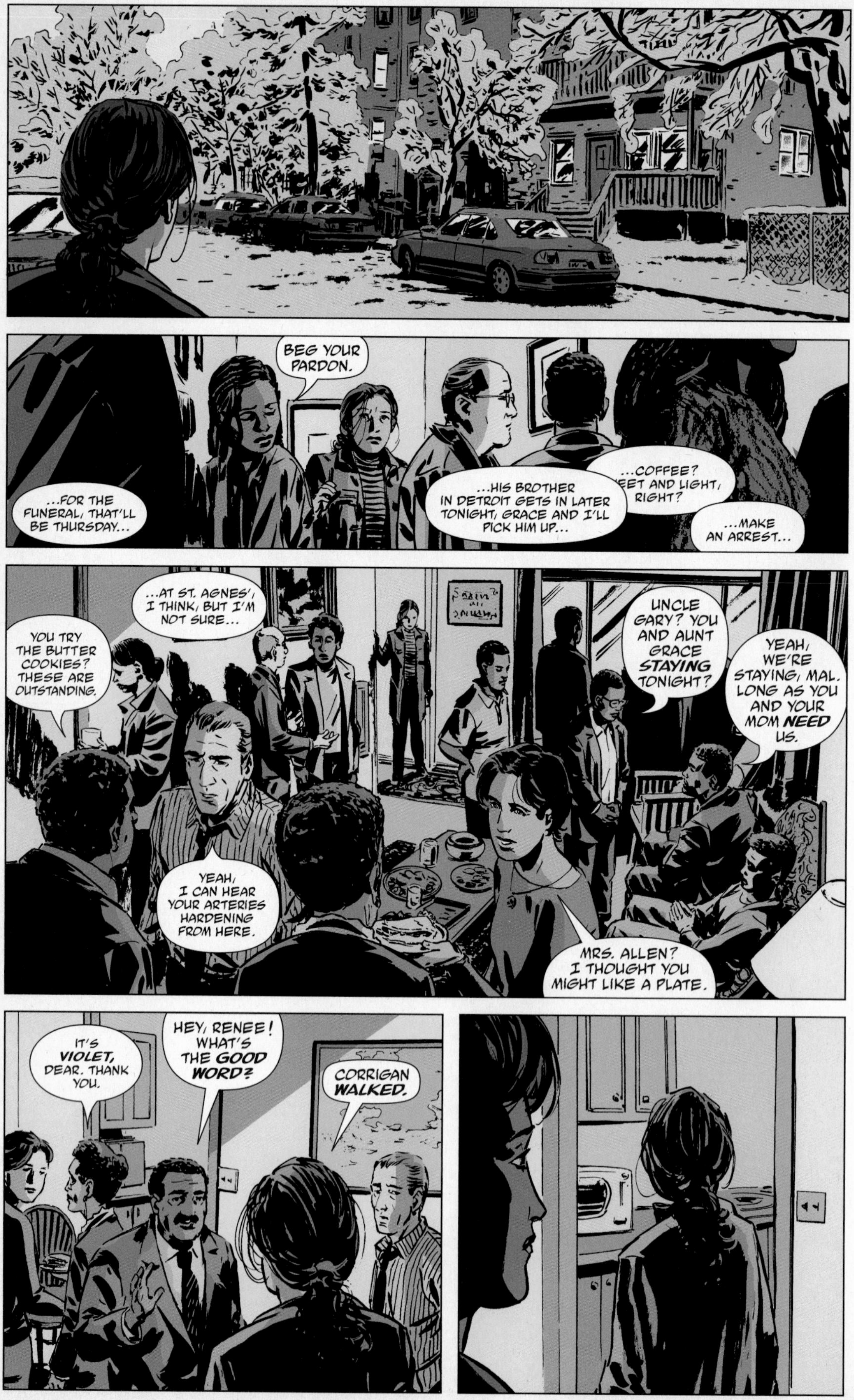
BEG YOUR PARDON.
...FOR THE FUNERAL, THAT'LL BE THURSDAY...
...HIS BROTHER IN DETROIT GETS IN LATER TONIGHT, GRACE AND I'LL PICK HIM UP...
...COFFEE? SWEET AND LIGHT, RIGHT?
...MAKE AN ARREST...
YOU TRY THE BUTTER COOKIES? THESE ARE OUTSTANDING.
...AT ST. AGNES', I THINK, BUT I'M NOT SURE...
UNCLE GARY? YOU AND AUNT GRACE STAYING TONIGHT?
YEAH, WE'RE STAYING, MAL. LONG AS YOU AND YOUR MOM NEED US.
YEAH, I CAN HEAR YOUR ARTERIES HARDENING FROM HERE.
MRS. ALLEN? I THOUGHT YOU MIGHT LIKE A PLATE.
IT'S VIOLET, DEAR. THANK YOU.
HEY, RENEE! WHAT'S THE GOOD WORD?
CORRIGAN WALKED.

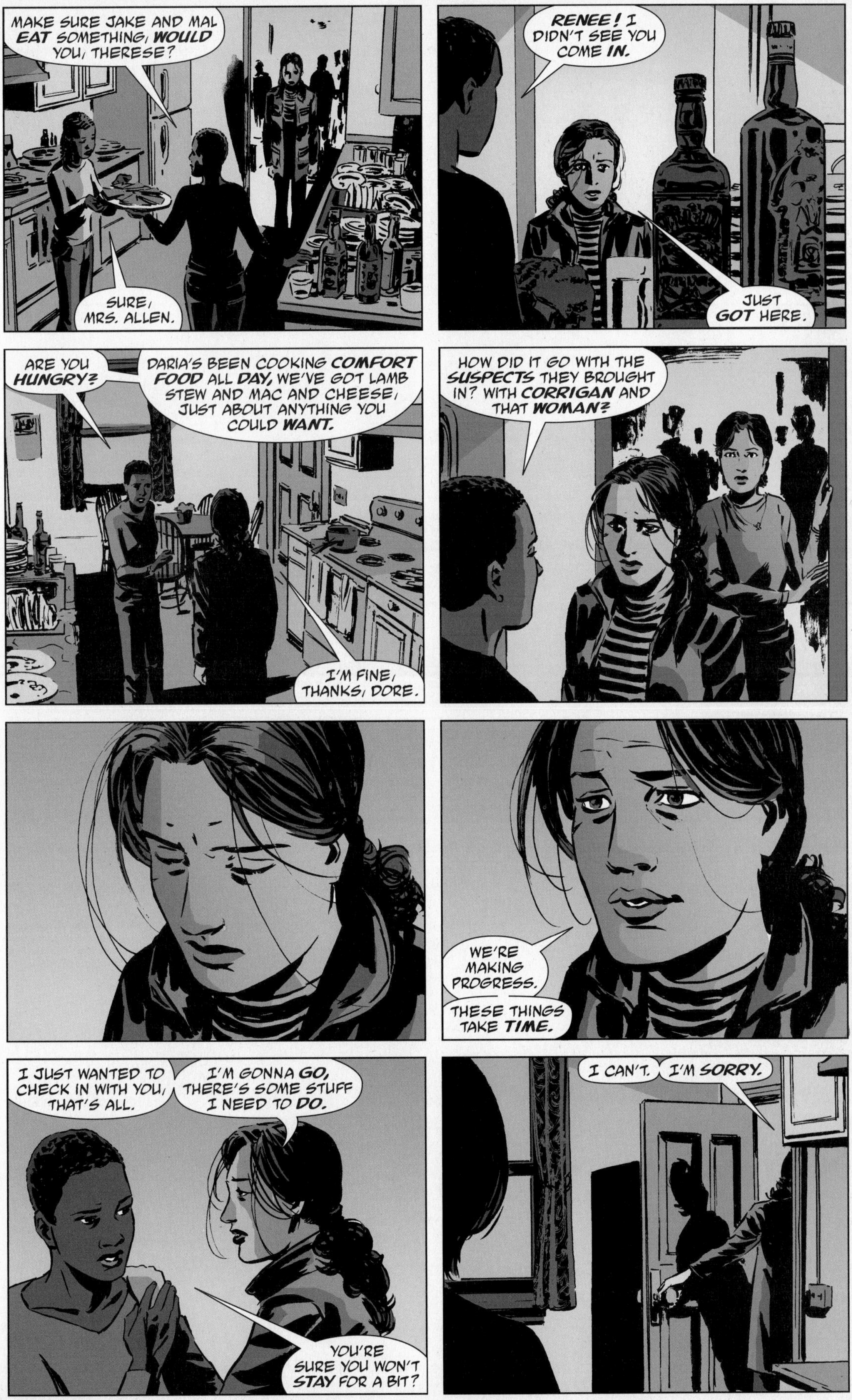
MAKE SURE JAKE AND MAL EAT SOMETHING, WOULD YOU, THERESE?
SURE, MRS. ALLEN.
RENEE! I DIDN'T SEE YOU COME IN.
JUST GOT HERE.
ARE YOU HUNGRY?
DARIA'S BEEN COOKING COMFORT FOOD ALL DAY, WE'VE GOT LAMB STEW AND MAC AND CHEESE, JUST ABOUT ANYTHING YOU COULD WANT.
I'M FINE, THANKS, DORE.
HOW DID IT GO WITH THE SUSPECTS THEY BROUGHT IN? WITH CORRIGAN AND THAT WOMAN?
WE'RE MAKING PROGRESS.
THESE THINGS TAKE TIME.
I JUST WANTED TO CHECK IN WITH YOU, THAT'S ALL.
I'M GONNA GO, THERE'S SOME STUFF I NEED TO DO.
YOU'RE SURE YOU WON'T STAY FOR A BIT?
I CAN'T.
I'M SORRY.

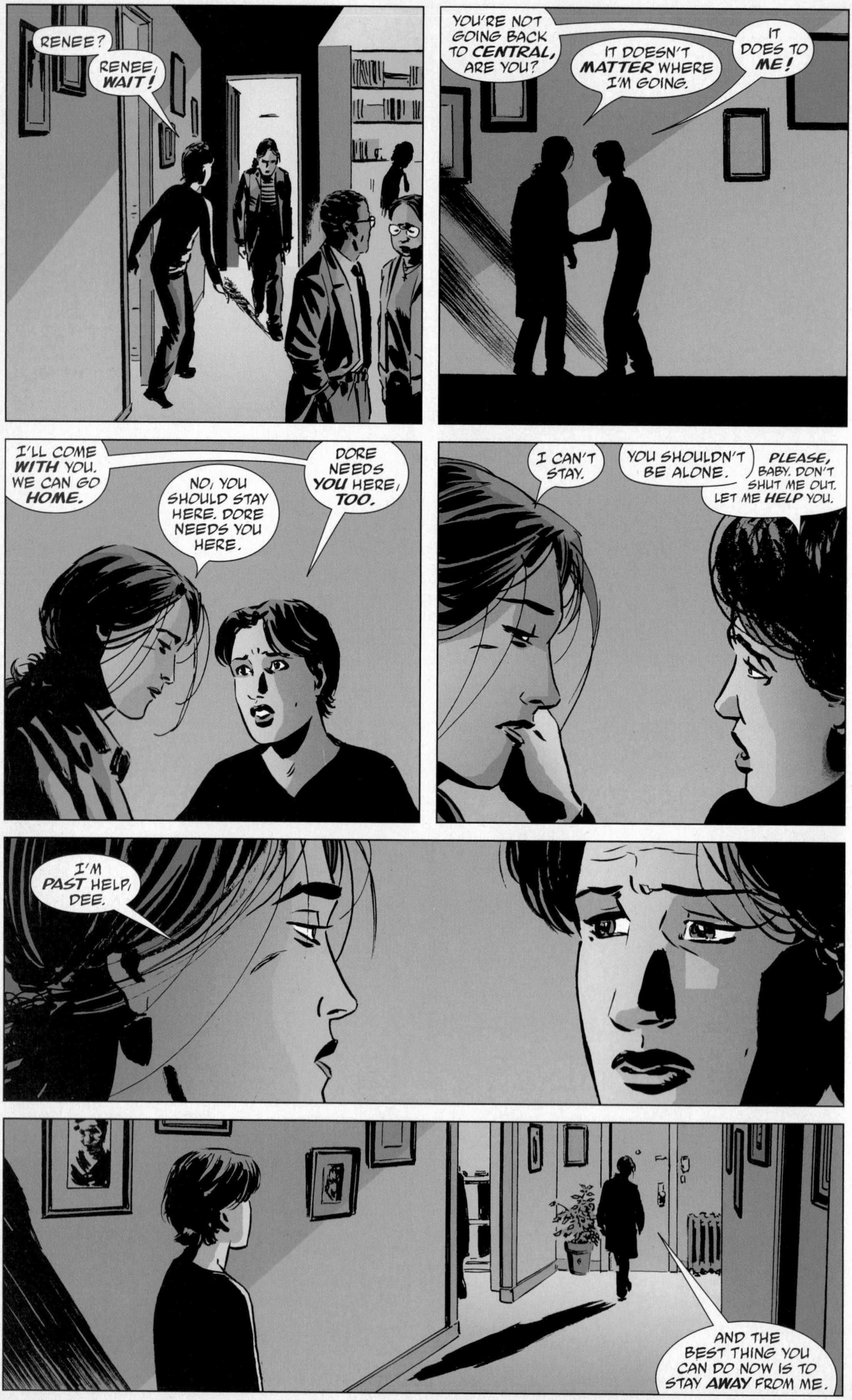
RENEE?
RENEE, WAIT!
YOU'RE NOT GOING BACK TO CENTRAL, ARE YOU?
IT DOESN'T MATTER WHERE I'M GOING.
IT DOES TO ME!
I'LL COME WITH YOU. WE CAN GO HOME.
NO, YOU SHOULD STAY HERE. DORE NEEDS YOU HERE.
DORE NEEDS YOU HERE, TOO.
I CAN'T STAY.
YOU SHOULDN'T BE ALONE.
PLEASE, BABY. DON'T SHUT ME OUT. LET ME HELP YOU.
I'M PAST HELP, DEE.
AND THE BEST THING YOU CAN DO NOW IS TO STAY AWAY FROM ME.

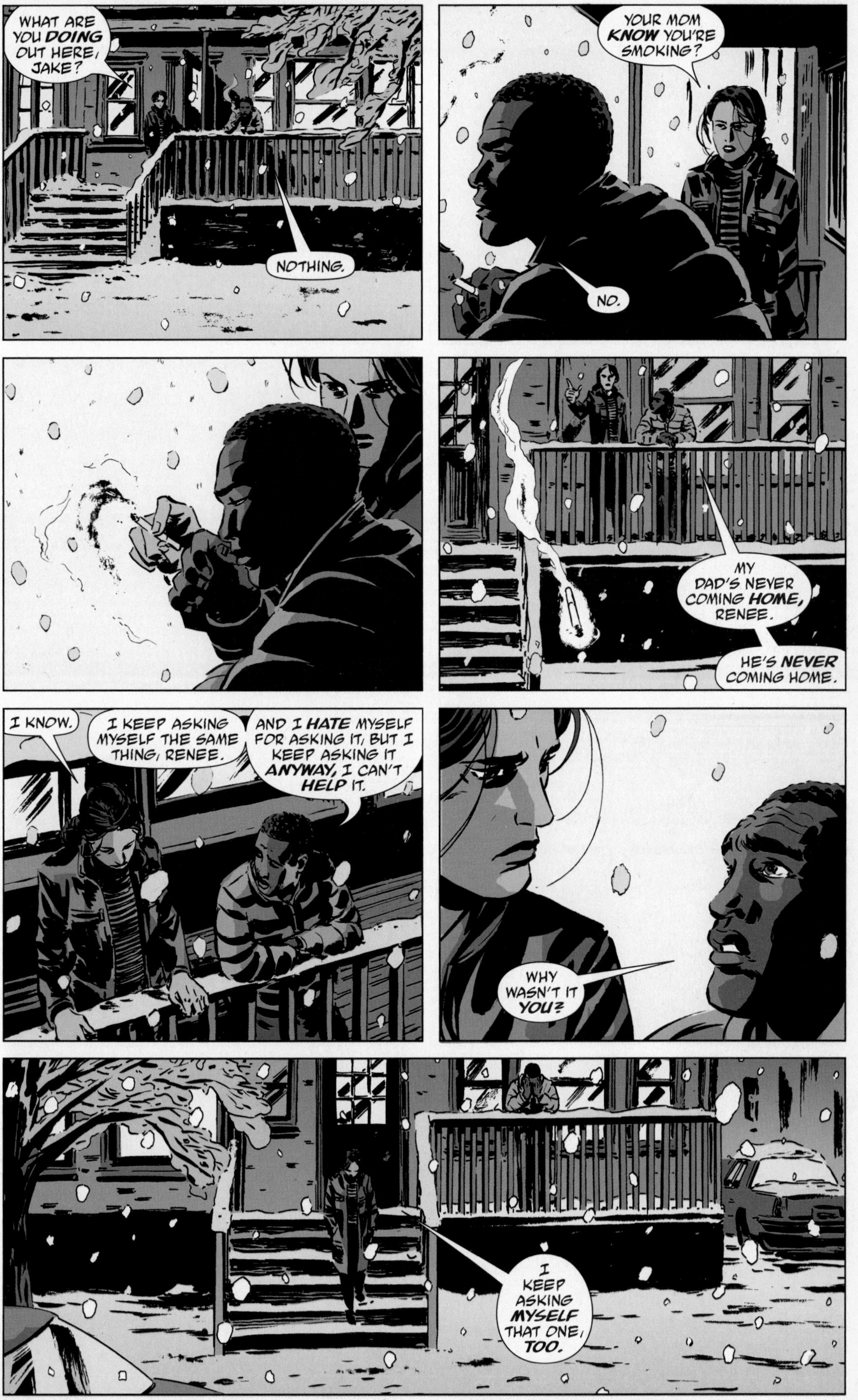
WHAT ARE YOU DOING OUT HERE, JAKE?
NOTHING.
YOUR MOM KNOW YOU'RE SMOKING?
NO.
MY DAD'S NEVER COMING HOME, RENEE.
HE'S NEVER COMING HOME.
I KNOW.
I KEEP ASKING MYSELF THE SAME THING, RENEE.
AND I HATE MYSELF FOR ASKING IT, BUT I KEEP ASKING IT ANYWAY, I CAN'T HELP IT.
WHY WASN'T IT YOU?
I KEEP ASKING MYSELF THAT ONE, TOO.

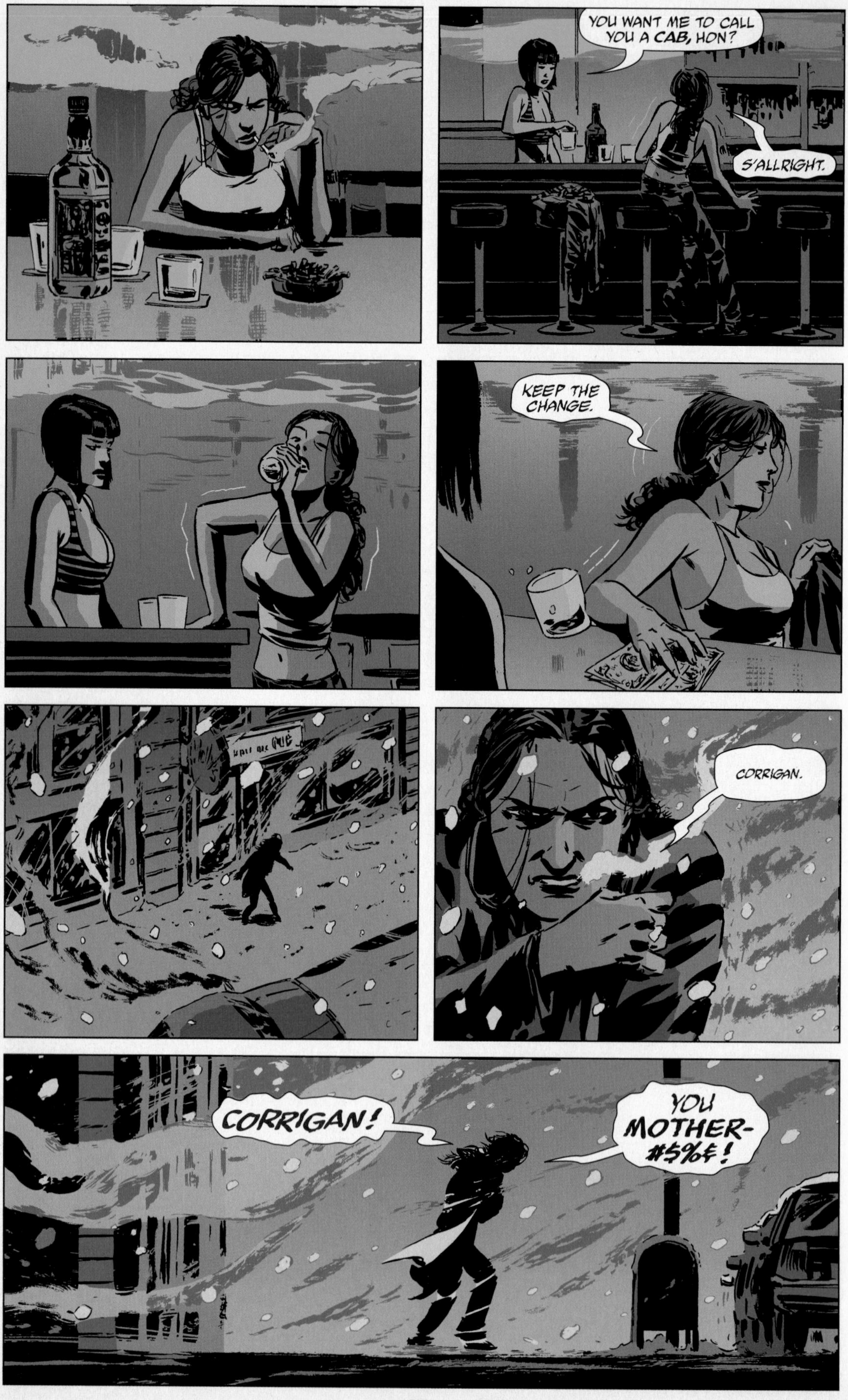
YOU WANT ME TO CALL YOU A CAB, HON?
S'ALLRIGHT.
KEEP THE CHANGE.
CORRIGAN.
CORRIGAN!
YOU MOTHER-#$%&!

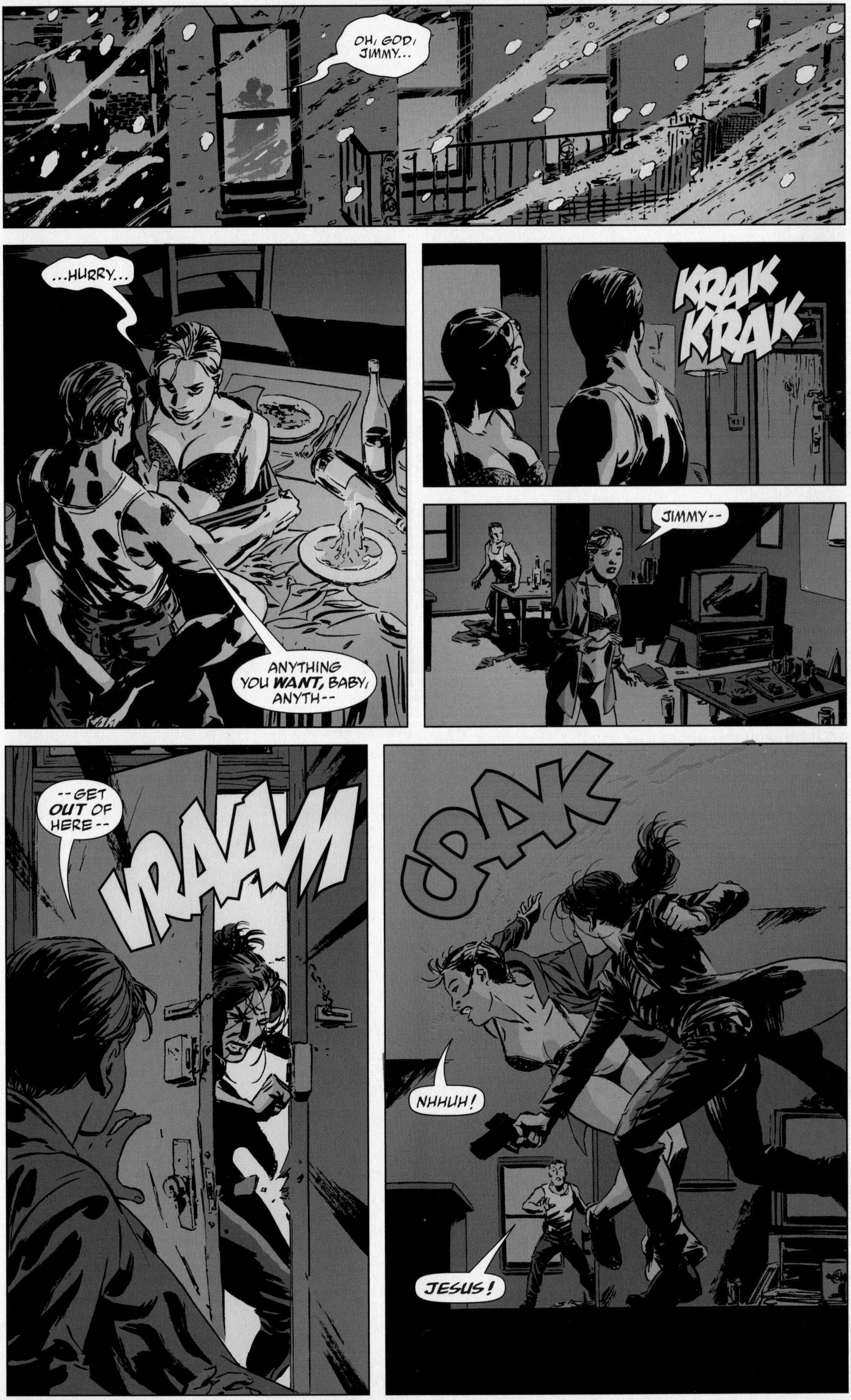

OH, GOD, JIMMY...
...HURRY...
ANYTHING YOU WANT, BABY, ANYTH--
KRAK KRAK
JIMMY--
--GET OUT OF HERE--
VRAAM
CRAK
NHHUH!
JESUS!

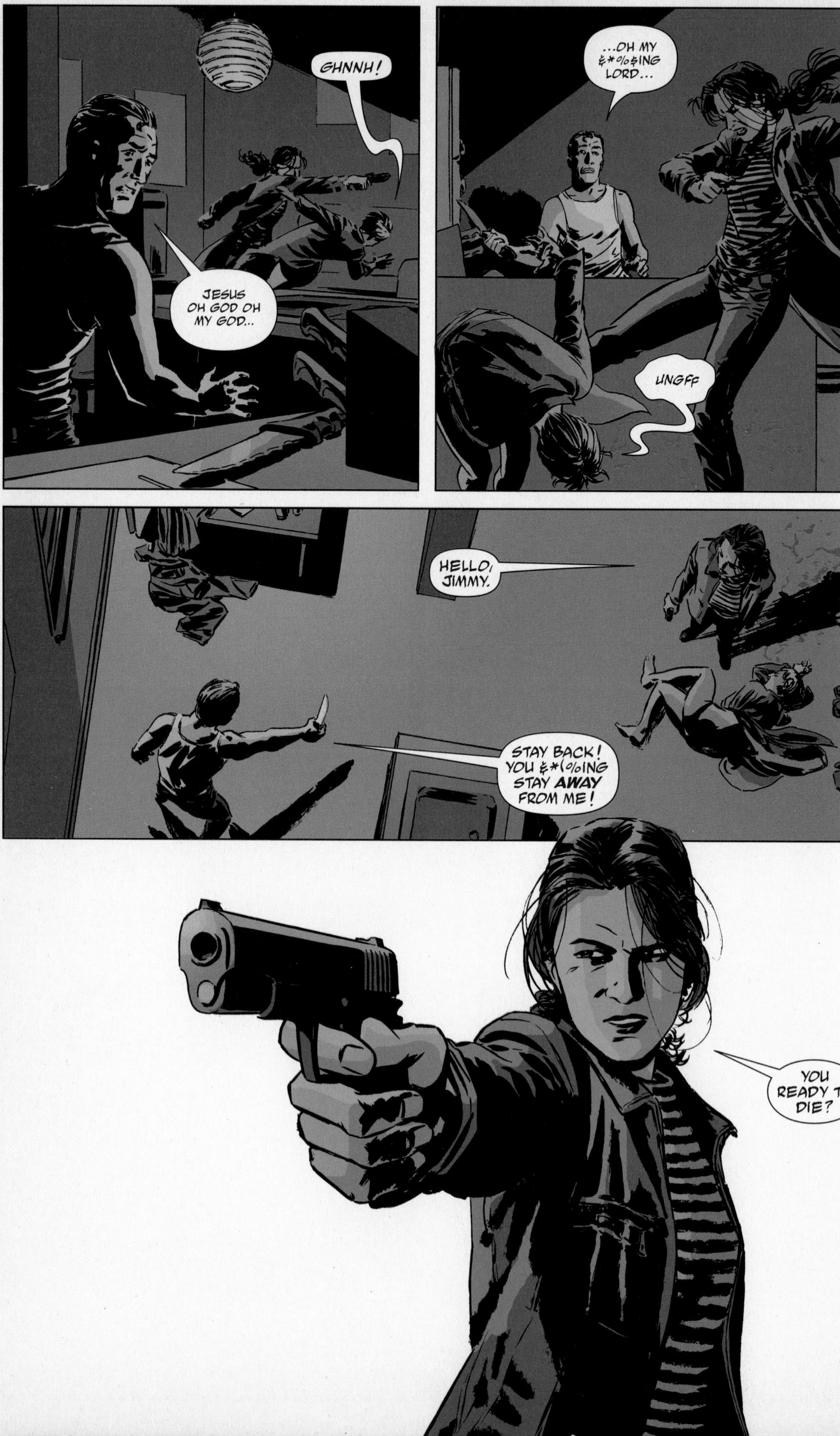
GHNNH!
JESUS OH GOD OH MY GOD...
...OH MY &*%$ING LORD...
UNGFF
HELLO, JIMMY.
STAY BACK! YOU &*(%ING STAY AWAY FROM ME!
YOU READY TO DIE?

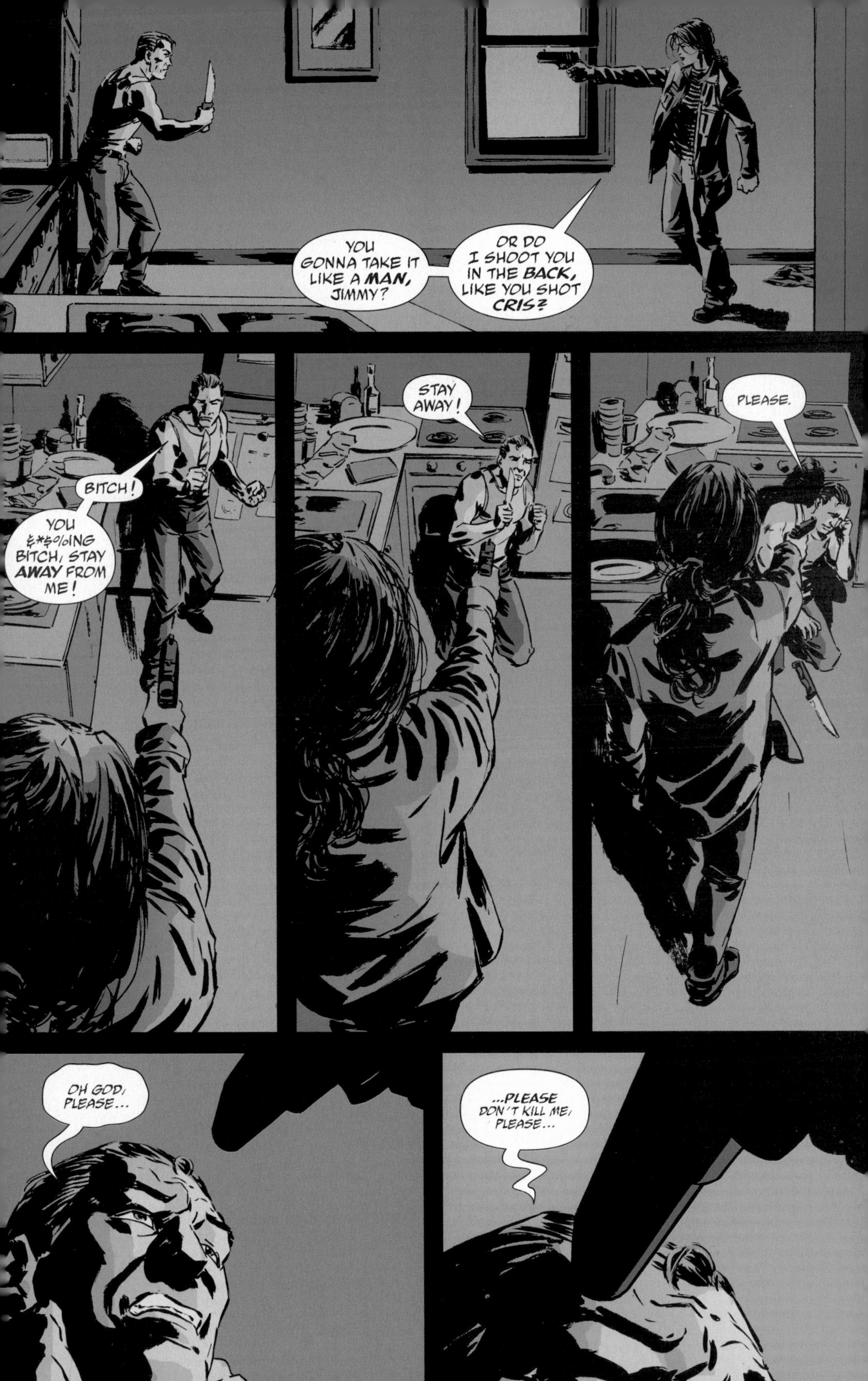
YOU GONNA TAKE IT LIKE A MAN, JIMMY?
OR DO I SHOOT YOU IN THE BACK, LIKE YOU SHOT CRIS?
BITCH!
YOU &*$%ING BITCH, STAY AWAY FROM ME!
STAY AWAY!
PLEASE.
OH GOD, PLEASE...
...PLEASE DON'T KILL ME, PLEASE...

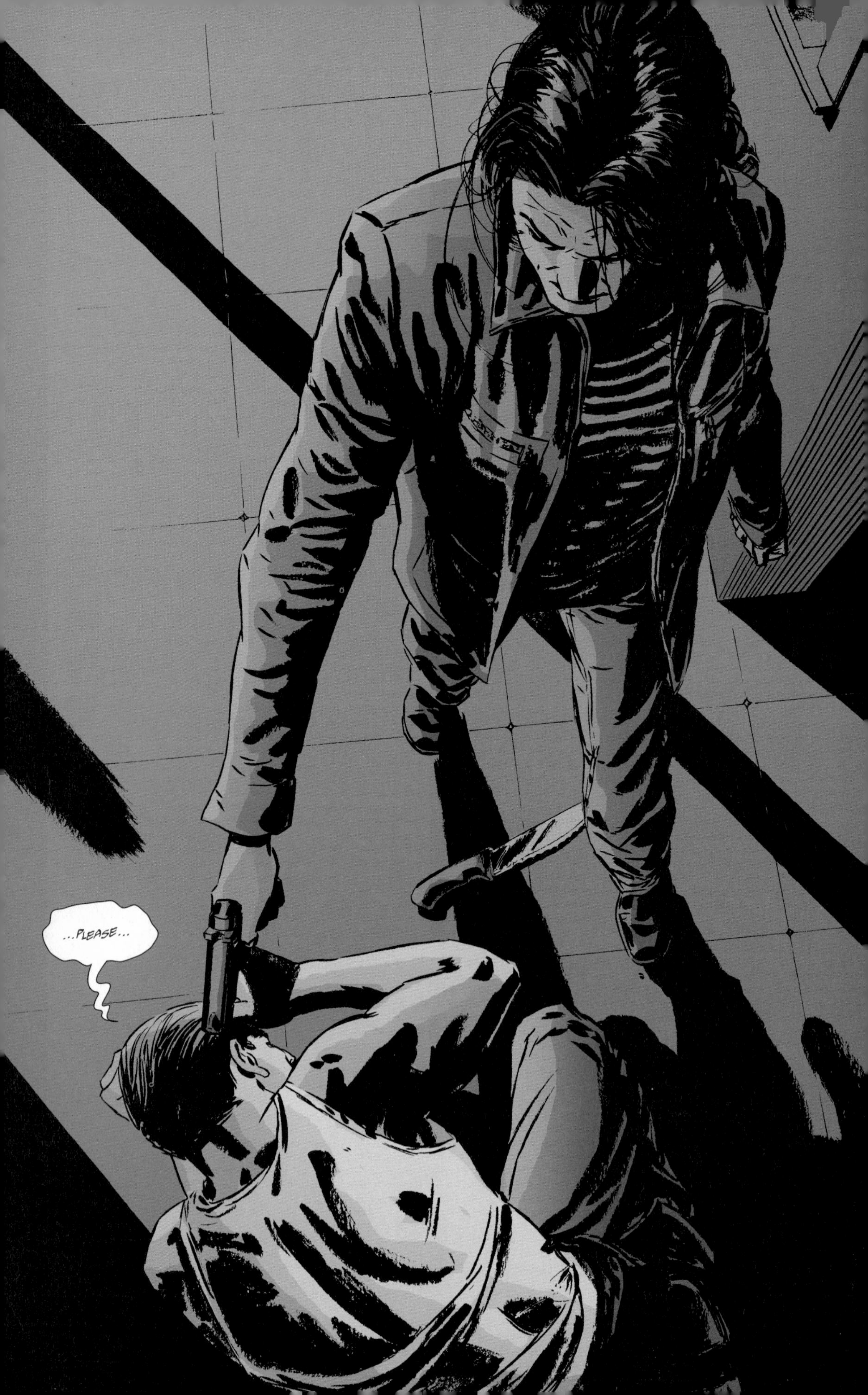
...PLEASE...

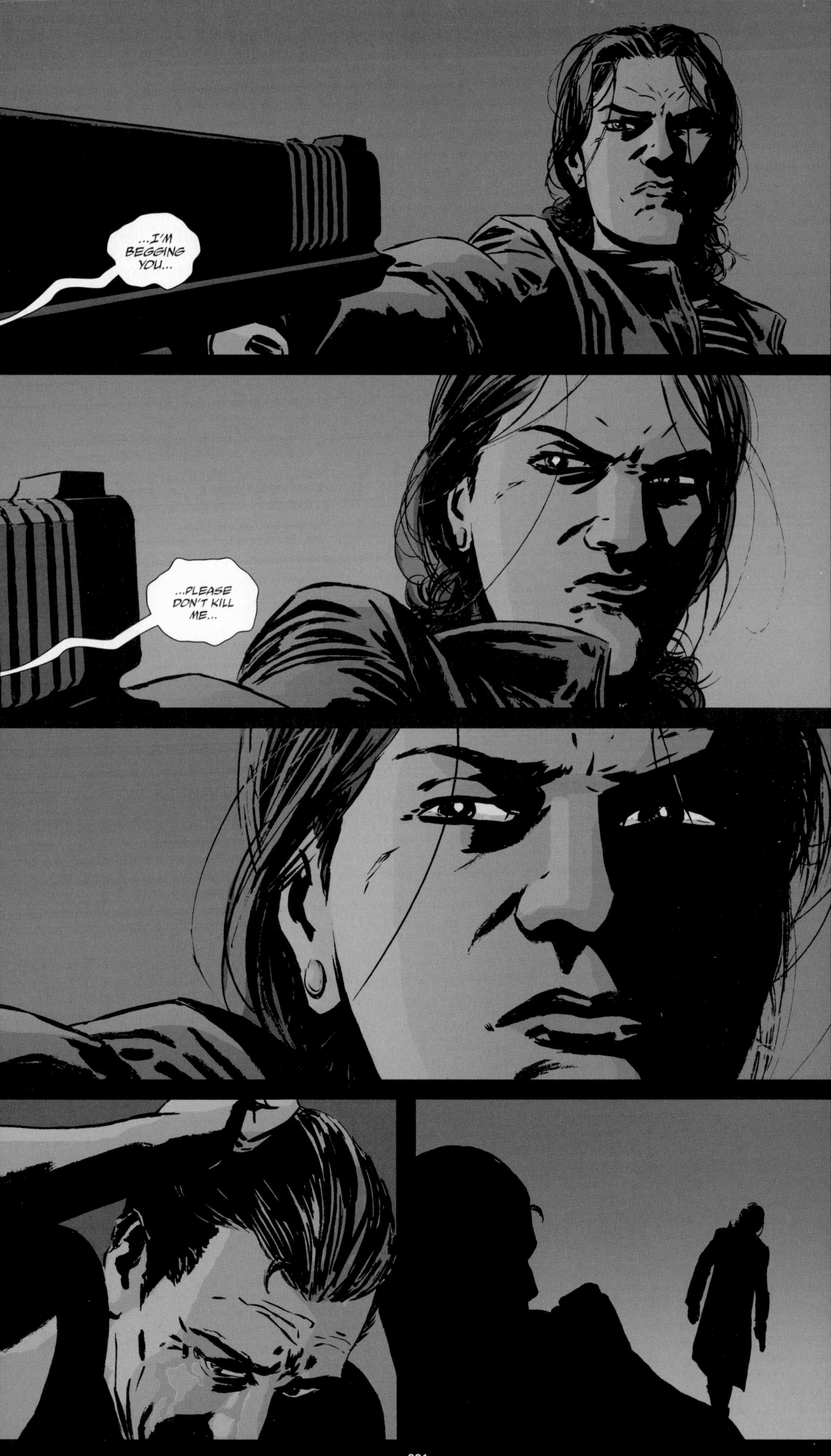
...I'M BEGGING YOU...
...PLEASE DON'T KILL ME...

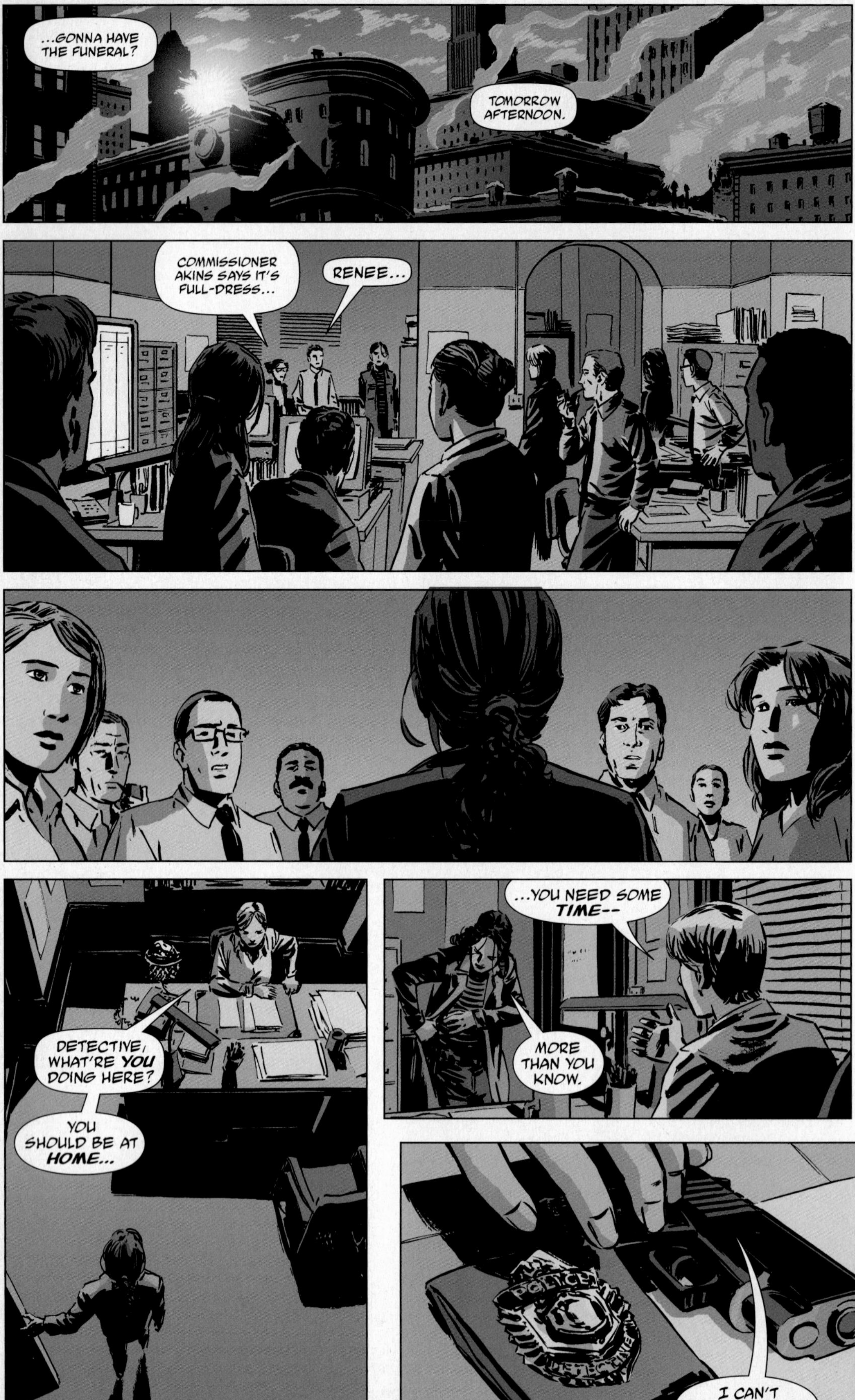
...GONNA HAVE THE FUNERAL?
TOMORROW AFTERNOON.
COMMISSIONER AKINS SAYS IT'S FULL-DRESS...
RENEE...
DETECTIVE, WHAT'RE YOU DOING HERE?
YOU SHOULD BE AT HOME...
...YOU NEED SOME TIME--
MORE THAN YOU KNOW.
POLICE
DETECTIVE
I CAN'T DO IT ANYMORE, CAPTAIN.

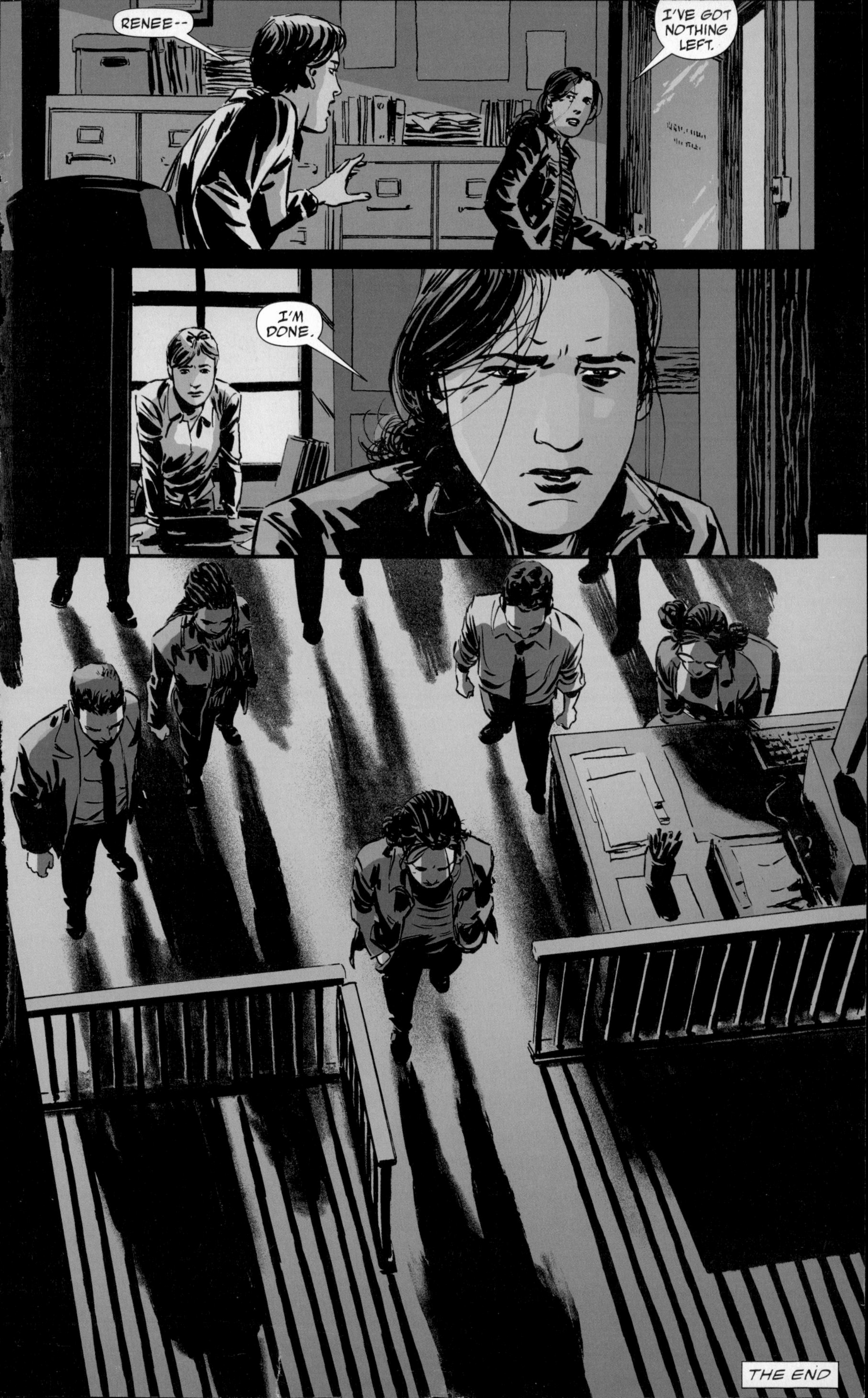
RENEE--
I'VE GOT NOTHING LEFT.
I'M DONE.
THE END

GREG RUCKA

is the author of several novels, including *Finder, Keeper, Smoker, Shooting at Midnight, Critical Space,* and *Patriot Acts* (all of which feature the bodyguard character Atticus Kodiak), plus *Private Wars* and *A Gentleman's Game* (featuring the *Queen & Country* character Tara Chace), *A Fistful of Rain* and more.

In comics, he has written some of the most well known characters in the world, on titles such as ACTION COMICS, DETECTIVE COMICS, BATMAN, WONDER WOMAN, *Wolverine,* and *Elektra.* Other work includes titles such as 52 (with Geoff Johns, Grant Morrison and Mark Waid), GOTHAM CENTRAL and *Daredevil* (with Ed Brubaker), CHECKMATE, and FINAL CRISIS: REVELATIONS. His BATWOMAN: ELEGY book (with J.H. Williams III) has made it to numerous "Best of" lists of 2010, including *Publishers Weekly.*

His creator-owned comics include the award-winning *Queen & Country* and *Whiteout* (which became a major motion picture starring Kate Beckinsale).

ED BRUBAKER

is a one-time cartoonist whose early work in comics includes *Pajama Chronicles, Purgatory USA,* and *Lowlife.* He soon began predominantly writing comics, garnering attention for stories such as the Eisner Award-nominated "An Accidental Death," *The Fall,* and SCENE OF THE CRIME.

Brubaker began alternating his writing projects between DC's mainstream comics line, their mature-readers imprint Vertigo, and their WildStorm imprint. Some projects included BATMAN, DEADENDERS, SANDMAN PRESENTS: DEAD BOY DETECTIVES, CATWOMAN, SLEEPER, THE AUTHORITY, and GOTHAM CENTRAL (with Greg Rucka).

He has also written for Marvel Comics, including *Secret Avengers* and *Captain America* for their superhero line, and *Criminal* and *Incognito* for their Icon imprint.

KANO

is a Spanish comic book artist who broke into the comics industry in 1998 as the artist on Virtex for Oktomica Comics. He soon moved on to work for DC Comics, where he had a lengthy run on ACTION COMICS starring Superman. He also illustrated stories in the series H-E-R-O and GOTHAM CENTRAL. For Marvel, he has worked on titles such as *The Immortal Iron Fist, Beta Ray Bill: Godhunter* and *Marvel Zombies 5.*

STEFANO GAUDIANO

was born in Milan, Italy, and moved to the U.S. in the early '80s. Soon after, Gaudiano became a comic-book artist and published the Eisner Award-nominated limited series *Kafka* (with Steven T. Seagle) while still in college. His art has since been featured in *Dark Horse Presents,* SANDMAN MYSTERY THEATRE, CATWOMAN, BATMAN: FAMILY, *Daredevil, The Pulse, Captain Marvel,* and many more books.

STEVE LIEBER

is best known for his work on Oni Press' *Whiteout* (which became a major motion picture) and its Eisner Award-winning sequel *Whiteout: Melt.* He has also illustrated runs on DC's DETECTIVE COMICS and HAWKMAN, as well as *Conan the Usurper, Grendel Tales: The Devil's Apprentice, Civil War: Frontline, Thunderbolts: Desperate Measures,* and much more. Lieber is also the co-author (with Nat Gertler) of *The Complete Idiot's Guide to Creating a Graphic Novel.*